Central America in the New Millennium

CEDLA Latin America Studies (CLAS)
Series Editor: Michiel Baud

CEDLA
Centrum voor Studie en Documentatie van Latijns Amerika
Centro de Estudios y Documentación Latinoamericanos
Centro de Estudos e Documentação Latino-Americanos
Centre for Latin American Research and Documentation

CEDLA conducts and coordinates social science research, offers university courses, and has a specialized library for the study of the region. The Centre also publishes monographs and a journal on Latin America.

Keizersgracht 395-397
1016 EK Amsterdam
The Netherlands / Países Bajos
www.cedla.uva.nl
[For information on previous volumes published in this series, please contact CEDLA at the above address.]

Volume 102
Central America in the New Millennium: Living Transition and Reimagining Democracy
Edited by Jennifer L. Burrell and Ellen Moodie

Central America in the New Millenium

Living Transition and Reimagining Democracy

Edited by

Jennifer L. Burrell
and
Ellen Moodie

Berghahn Books
NEW YORK • OXFORD

Published in 2013 by
Berghahn Books
www.berghahnbooks.com

English-language edition

Library of Congress Cataloging-in-Publication Data

Central America in the new millennium : living transition and reimagining democracy / edited by Jennifer L. Burrell and Ellen Moodie.
p. cm. — (CEDLA Latin America studies (CLAS) ; v. 102)
Includes bibliographical references and index.
ISBN 978-0-85745-752-3 (hardback : alk. paper) —
ISBN 978-0-85745-753-0 (ebk.)
1. Central America—Politics and government—21st century.
2. Democratization—Central America. 3. Democracy—Central America.
4. Central America—Economic policy. 5. Central America—Social policy.
I. Burrell, Jennifer L. II. Moodie, Ellen.
JL1416.C455 2012
320.9728—dc23

2012012564

British Library Cataloguing in Publication Data

A catalogue record for this book is available from the British Library

Printed in the United States on acid-free paper

ISBN 978-0-85745-752-3 (hardback)
ISBN 978-0-85745-753-0 (e-book)

Contents

Part II: Indigeneity, Race and Human Rights in the (Post) Multicultural Moment

Part III: Dominant, Residual, and Emergent Economic Strategies

Part IV: A Place on the Map: Surviving on Pasts, Presents, and Futures

Figures, Maps, and Tables

Figures

Tables

Acknowledgments

This book began as a conversation over mojitos in a hotel bar in San Juan, Puerto Rico, in March 2006, when we, Jennifer L. Burrell and Ellen Moodie, began talking about how "we never talk to each other." We meant that anthropologists working in Central American nations did not seem to mix it up much at the Latin American Studies Association (LASA) meetings: Guatemalanists maneuver within their network, Salvadoranists seem to debate mainly among themselves, etc. So we decided to do something about it. First, we proposed an invited session for the next LASA meeting, in Montreal (2007): Jennifer Bickham Mendez and Rosario Montoya joined us, along with discussant Marc Edelman. Then we organized a Wenner-Gren International Workshop in Albany, New York. There, most of the authors in this book gathered. Everyone at the event contributed to a series of truly invigorating conversations, in which Jennifer Bickham Mendez worked magic in her role as discussant. (Bob Carmack, Jason Cross, Marc Edelman, Liza Grandia, Staffan Lövfing, and Brandt Peterson could not participate in this publication, but their engagement with the work still echoes in the final versions of the chapters.) After more than five years, we have talked and talked and continue talking. We hope we have facilitated many other conversations among diverse Central Americanists: whether between those in the isthmus and those in the who live north or south, or among those who work in Costa Rica rainforests and those who study Guatemalan indigenous craft practices.

As with any long-term project, we have many people and institutions to thank. First, we are grateful to our funders, including the Wenner-Gren Foundation, the Department of Anthropology and the Center for Latin American and Caribbean Studies (CLACS) of the University of Illinois at Urbana-Champaign, and the Department of Anthropology, College of Arts and Sciences and Institute for Mesoamerican Studies at University at Albany-SUNY. We would not have been able to gather so many people on several brilliant September days in upstate New York without them. Steve Leigh and Andrew Orta, heads of the Illinois Department of Anthropology, were both very supportive, as was Nils Jacobsen of CLACS. Marilyn Masson, then director of the Institute for Mesoamerican Studies and Aaron Broadwell, chair of the University at Albany Anthropology Department provided crucial and wide-ranging assistance. We also thank our wonderful research assistants, Ilona Flores, who helped hold us together at the beginning, and Katie O'Brien, who saved us with the last details of the manuscript at the end. The administration staff at both U of I and UAlbany were also key, to bringing this volume to fruition, especially Julia Spitz, Dan White, Linda Lamouret Goodwin and Jaime Moore. In addition, we thank Gabriela Torres, Mo Hume and the CEDLA Board for helpful comments, as well as Luis Vivanco and Ciska Raventós for close readings and engagement.

Finally, Ellen would like to thank her writing group—Ericka Beckman, Anna Stenport, and Yasemin Yildiz—for comments on the introduction, and Jennifer Burrell in particular for her patience and tolerance, as well as wise counsel. Jennifer would like to thank Alex Dupuy and Lila Jenova Dupuy for forbearance and sustenance, and, of course, Ellen Moodie, for collegiality, inspiration, and a truly generative collaboration.

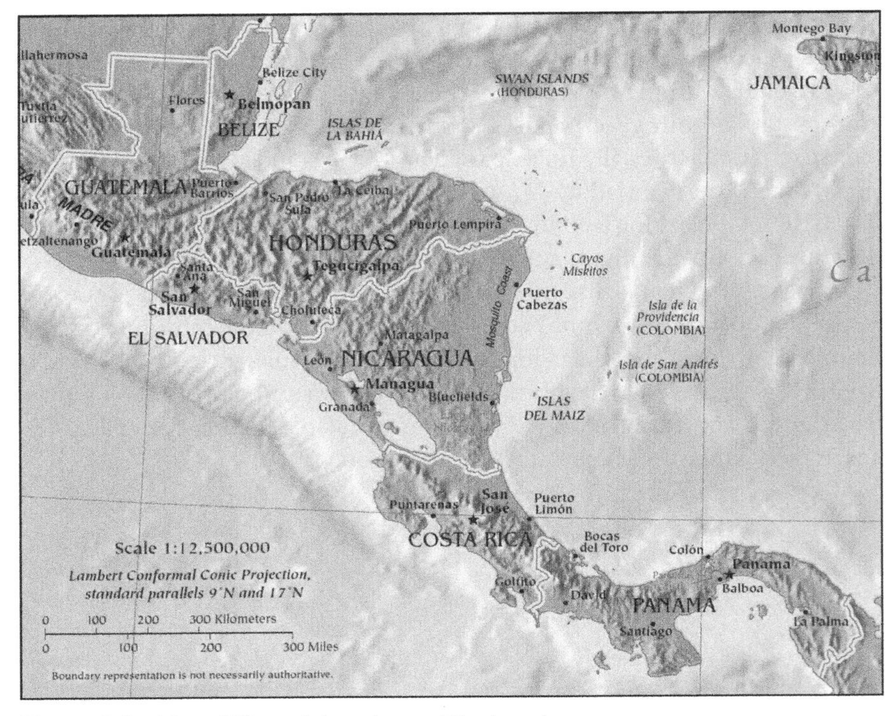

Figure 0.1. Map of Central America, public domain

Introduction

Ethnographic Visions of Millennial Central America

*Jennifer L. Burrell and Ellen Moodie**

It used to be that the isthmus between Mexico and Colombia was a place to watch. Some thirty years ago, Nicaragua, El Salvador, and Guatemala regularly burst onto world headlines. Central America had become a space of urgent geopolitical consequence, much as Vietnam had formed a significant historical node more than a decade earlier, or as Afghanistan and Iraq became a critical global focus more than a decade later. Central American voices resisting what Salvadoran poet Claribel Alegría (1988) called the "crude realities" that inundate the region were part of the internationally mass-mediated everyday. In this book we return to that site of 1980s world attention. Though long ago elbowed off the global center stage (ceremoniously so, with handshakes, peace accords, and internationally certified elections), Central Americans continue their struggles.

The (re-)marginalization of Central America may seem, to some, to be a return to a proper order of things. The cinched waist between North and South was thrust into political prominence in a last gasp of that bloated twentieth-century paroxysm of paranoia, the Cold War, in its particular North American form. By the early 1990s, history had "ended" (Fukuyama 1992). The Berlin Wall had fallen, the Soviet Union had disintegrated, and "freedom" was spreading across the globe as liberal-democratic leaders replaced despots and dictatorships from Poland to Chile. That is the triumphal story repeated worldwide. But, as we revisit the seemingly now-dormant volcanic terrain, we suggest another way of understanding Central America's political "disappearance." In this introduction we propose that in order to uphold a new, post-Cold War world order, these spaces *had to* be disappeared, much like the *desaparacidos* (disappeared political opponents) during wartime. We argue that Central America's effective erasure from geopolitical significance was the inevitable structural outcome of capitalist processes, especially in an era of neoliberal democratization.

* The order of our names is alphabetical, reflecting equal weight in the editing of this book and the writing of this introduction.

Of course "Central America" and Central Americans are often hiding in plain sight: absent presences, as Susan Coutin (2007) describes undocumented migrants in the liminal spaces between the United States and El Salvador. Indeed, economic and political reorganization of the late twentieth and early twenty-first centuries has rendered some aspects of the region hyper-visible, reframing and revisualizing the same spaces on the world map once charted by the gold-seeking brothers Gonzalo and Pedro de Alvarado (among other Spanish conquerors) and the Tlaxaltecan soldiers who accompanied them back in the 1520s. Now these countries are sites of indigeneity and multiculturalism, and of eco-tourism and fair-trade coffee cooperatives—as well as of bands of delinquent gangs, narco-traffickers, assassins for hire, and "illegal aliens" menacing citizens in the North. These visions, usually drained of the revolutionary fervor and political spectacle that once characterized the region, appear through specific processes, practices, and techniques of contemporary forms of globalization and democratization. This book takes readers to these emergent Central American spaces, offering ethnographic glimpses of a range of ways of being in the new millennium.

Democracy, Security, Multiculturalism, and Neoliberalism

Most of the chapters in this book emerged from a Wenner-Gren International Workshop in 2008. The anthropologists and sociologists who wrote them emphasize particular formations and specific local responses to four open, interrelated themes: democracy, security, multiculturalism and neoliberalism. We consider each to be a primary keyword, in Raymond Williams's (1976) sense. Williams's project, similarly conducted at a moment during which the world appeared to be on the brink of something "new," explored how certain keywords take on new meaning in relation to politics and societal values. Democracy, for example, as we discuss below, has taken on a different resonance in the post-Cold War, "free" market moment, so much so that some scholars label today's dominant version "market democracy." In this volume Ciska Raventós demonstrates how Costa Rican activists contested the twinning of the terms as they used democratic procedures to challenge the inevitability of free-market orthodoxy in their movement against the Dominican Republic-Central America-United States Free Trade Agreement (CAFTA-DR). This agreement served to eliminate trade tariffs on U.S. goods exported to the area, to open local markets for U.S. investment in the region, and, ostensibly, to eliminate corruption through the promotion of transparency, among other provisions. Meant to function like the North American Free Trade Agreement (NAFTA), which established a free trade zone between Canada, Mexico, and the United States, it encountered widespread opposition when it was put up to votes across the region.

Or consider security: the ethnographic accounts in this volume suggest a dual sense of security, pertaining both to violence and freedom from violence as well as to the ability to achieve or maintain livelihoods and necessities such as food, housing, employment, and education—what the United Nations refers to in part as "human security." Jennifer Burrell's chapter on the formation of community-based security committees to combat so-called gangs of young men who returned from the North shows how the regional preoccupation with security has multiple meanings for the Mam Maya of northwestern Guatemala as they cross transnational borders. As they do, they move in and out of entitlement to rights: from protectors of local security in Guatemala to security risks themselves in the United States.

Multiculturalism, too, takes on layered meanings in Central America in the new millennium: while the concept would seem to be liberatory, embracing racial and ethnic identifications once banished under processes of *mestizaje,* Charles Hale (2005, 2006b) and others challenge such simplistic assessments. They see "neoliberal multiculturalism" as an "emergent regime of governance that shapes, delimits, and produces cultural difference rather than suppresses it" (Hale 2005, 13), arguing that, carefully managed by the state, the recognition of difference can encourage ethnic and racial "others" to join the forward march of neoliberalism rather than to challenge it. In his chapter Mark Anderson describes the struggle of the Garifuna in Honduras to benefit from their multicultural difference (and their "happy character," as a former president put it), so valued in tourism promotion of the new neoliberal era. In her chapter Claudia Dary Fuentes scrutinizes another facet of multiculturalism: the difficulty of acknowledging the ongoing existence of racism in Guatemala as the postwar nation struggles to impose a (limited) vision of inclusion.

Neoliberalism is a keyword and political economic paradigm so common now that it has almost lost its specificity. Originally promulgated as a set of economic reforms based in the democratic potential of the free market—the liberation of individual entrepreneurial freedoms and skills (Harvey 2005, 2)—the ideology has become firmly embedded in contemporary cultural logics, institutions, and political practice. Its earliest iterations in the region were promoted through the World Bank and the International Monetary Fund and realized in everyday life through the deprivation and suffering promoted by structural adjustment policies. Specific policies and practices included deregulation, the privatization of publicly held companies, a reduction in public expenditures and the withdrawal of the state from social provision, the opening of markets, and courting foreign investment in order to repay loans. In the 1990s, a categorical shift from open market economic policies to the substitution of market for state and society occurred, in what John Gledhill (2004) has referred to as a movement from neoliberalism to neoliberalization. With this, Gledhill (2004, 340) indexes the ever-deepening ideology of capitalism that has come to embrace the production of social life itself, commoditizing "the most intimate of human relations and the production of identity and personhood."

Neoliberalism always forms the backdrop, and often becomes a central theme, in this collection's chapters. Culture, economic choices, and livelihood strategies, as well as security and violence and democratic processes, have all come to be neoliberalized in very specific ways. Luis Vivanco's chapter, on environmental governance and the audit practices employed in green certification processes in Costa Rica, shows how power shifts from states to non-state actors in the state's shadows (Trouillot 2001). The alliances among agrarian groups in the aftermath of the Honduran coup, addressed by Jefferson C. Boyer and Wilfredo Cardona Peñalva in their chapter, show another mode of operating outside the state—one that encourages transnational organizing through a particularly neoliberal gaze, as these relationships are mobilized to encourage the development of markets. Exploring these interconnections, in this book we seek to further recast the region not as an area of the world engulfed in violence and chaos or their aftermath, but as one where the logic of neoliberalism can be traced through processes that shape contemporary geopolitics.

Each of the chapters in this book locates social processes within post-Cold War transitions. The chapters show that these changes are enmeshed as much in economic life as they are in political life. The social processes examined are as entrenched in history as they are indicators of the future. They are also ongoing, challenging any assumption that political and economic projects are completed or achieved. What is elided from so many postwar narratives of Central America are the difficulties of democratization in the post-Cold War world of the 1990s and the post-September 11 universe of the 2000s, encompassed by free-trade mandates of neoliberal globalization and preoccupations with "security." These processes of neoliberal democratization have reoriented the geopolitical map, producing new, regionally specific notions and practices of democracy, and reconfiguring relationships between multiculturally recast citizens and the state. Moreover, we know that the flows, coherencies and inconsistencies of this area have been moving beyond the isthmus as Central American wage-labor migrants, documented and undocumented, fleeing multiple insecurities and seeking new security, have crossed multiple borders.

Central America on the World Stage

Geopolitical history locates "Central America" in five countries: Guatemala, El Salvador, Honduras, Nicaragua, and Costa Rica.[1] The isthmus emerged forcefully as a place that mattered on the contemporary world stage in 1979, when the Sandinista National Liberation Front (FSLN) overthrew the dictator Anastasio Somoza in Nicaragua, an occurrence the Guatemalan historian Edelberto Torres-Rivas (1993, 124) cites as a "transcendental, historical rupture in the framework of the Central American crisis." Soon after, the Salvadoran rebels, the Farabundo Martí National Liberation Front (FMLN), inspired by their neighbors, united five guerrilla groups and launched an offensive in the capital, San Salvador. Though that effort failed, the civil war that followed lasted a dozen years more. Guatemalan resistance, too, by then twenty-two years old, intensified at that moment. The revolutionary movements and counterinsurgent violence in the three small, impoverished countries mobilized international military firepower and also seized world imagination in a way that is perhaps difficult to comprehend today. For example, the British punk-rock band The Clash named a best-selling album *Sandinista!* and Cuban Nueva Trova balladist Silvio Rodríguez released "*Canción urgente para Nicaragua*" ("Urgent Song for Nicaragua") in 1980, just a year after the Nicaraguan revolutionaries took power. Anglo-Indian novelist Salman Rushdie (1987) visited the country and wrote a short book about the new socialist hope. The North American poet Adrienne Rich (1986, 220), developing her theory of the "politics of location," described seeing President Ronald Reagan on television in the mid-1980s: "Tonight as I turned a switch searching for 'the news,' that shinily animated silicone mask was on television again, telling the citizens of my country we are menaced by Communism from El Salvador, ... that the suffering peasants of Latin America must be stopped just as Hitler had to be stopped." United States-based writer Joan Didion (1983) and film director Oliver Stone (2001) imagined their separate *Salvadors,* a postmodern reportorial novella and a frenetic Hollywood film, respectively.

This unglamorous, hardscrabble, hungry strip of anger and hope inspired Hollywood: It was former actor Reagan, after all, who became obsessed with El Salvador and Nicaragua falling to Communists. The Oscar-nominated film *El Norte* (Nava 1983) by Gregory Nava chronicles the journey to the United States of Guatemalan siblings fleeing a genocidal attack on their Maya village. Nava's 1995 film *My Family/Mi Familia* (Nava 1995) tells the story of a Mexican-American family in East Los Angeles, in which a Salvadoran character "Isabel" appears in the 1980s period of the plot; rescued by a nun, she is an always already tragic figure who must die. A "Central American" in the North was usually synonymous with a refugee, a victim, someone fleeing *something,* often something savage and unspeakable. That something, Central America, was both conspicuous and clandestine.

Central America took a prominent place on the U.S. political stage, becoming the focus of rancorous Congressional debates. The Iran-Contra Affair uncovered in 1986 combined hypervisibility and invisibility: U.S. government officials had secretly channeled the profits from illegal arms sales to Iran to finance the Contras, the Nicaraguan counterinsurgent force, revealing Washington's investment in Central American politics. Reagan called the Contras (along with the Afghan mujahedeen) the "moral equivalent of our founding fathers." His successor George H.W. Bush made his own stance in the region, invading nearby Panama in 1989.[2] There, military forces arrested dictator General Manuel Noriega on drug trafficking charges.[3]

While undermining Nicaraguan and Panamanian leaders, the United States supported Salvadoran, Honduran, and Guatemalan militaries throughout the 1980s. Not all governments followed suit: Spain terminated diplomatic relations with Guatemala after the burning of the Spanish Embassy in January 1980. Police had fired upon Mayans occupying the ambassador's office to protest violence against their communities. Thirty-seven people were burned alive in that incident, a fraction of the tens of thousands of highland Indians who would be killed or disappeared during General Efrain Rios Montt's counterinsurgency campaign, and of the 200,000 who perished in the thirty-six year armed conflict. Spain called the incident a violation of "the most elementary norms of international law." One dramatic European response to the atrocities was to award the Guatemalan indigenous activist Rigoberta Menchú Tum the Nobel Peace Prize in Oslo in 1992, the second Central American so honored in five years. Costa Rican President Óscar Arias Sánchez had won the prize for his work for peace in the region in 1987 (though the wars abated only in the last gasps of the Cold War). Especially throughout North America and Europe, but also in other parts of the world, solidarity with the people of Central America became a point of passionate organizing within local communities, churches, and civic groups. Many contributors to this volume first connected to the people and politics of the region during this time.

These solidarity groups often arose after hearing a Central American—a Salvadoran labor organizer, a Honduran human-rights activist, a Mayan refugee—speak out personally against terror and oppression. Whether political exiles or peasants, factory workers or market women, hundreds of thousands of Central Americans fled their native countries starting in the late 1970s.[4] Some landed asylum status in Edmonton or Stockholm; many dwelt in undocumented marginality in Los Angeles, Houston, and New York; others found refuge closer by, in Honduras, Belize, Costa Rica, or Mexico. Few migrants talked publicly of politics, though the revolutionary forces had offices in Europe and North America. Often they worked silently, caring for children in Long Island mansions, separating chicken parts in North Carolina poultry processing plants, or pruning roses in Santa Monica gardens. But their presence in new sites testified to fear, violence, and poverty, as well as organized resistance, at home—and indexed the deeply entrenched globality of the crisis.

While Central Americans entered global popular culture and public discourse, politically motivated scholars worked to deepen understanding of the isthmus and historicize the crisis. They often sought to uncover agency and action rather than the passivity and victimhood common in mass-mediated images of Central Americans. Indeed, the 1970s–1980s revolutionary movements and counterinsurgency wars in El Salvador, Guatemala, and Nicaragua produced a spate of studies on peasant revolutions, and then, later, investigations into the effects of war and violence as well as on the struggles of marginalized populations. Anthropologists Carol A. Smith, Jefferson C. Boyer, and Martin Diskin produced a two-part series on "Central America since 1979" in the *Annual Review of Anthropology* (1987; 1988), declaring the urgency of overcoming a "thin and shallow" research base after "the triumph of one and the threat of two other revolutionary movements in the region." The British political historian James Dunkerley (1988) turned from work on the 1954 Bolivian revolution to delve into Central American politics. He joined other social scientists in asking why, if imperialism, repression, and poverty explained the regional conflict, did only Nicaraguans, Salvadorans, and Guatemalans launch broad resistance, and not (apparently) Hondurans and Costa Ricans? By the time his *Power in the Isthmus* came out, Dunkerley (1988, xi) testified to the public presence of Central America on the global stage, declaring:

> It is now possible to buy a review of Honduran politics, a study of Coca Cola workers in Guatemala or a survey of the peasantry of northern El Salvador in inexpensive paperback editions. This would have been inconceivable before 1979, when the Nicaraguan revolution ended decades of autocratic rule, challenged U.S. hegemony in the Americas and drove the isthmus into international headlines. ... Central America has become established as a prominent and permanent fixture in U.S. foreign policy as well as an issue of some consequence to domestic political life.

Triumph of Peace and Democracy?

Central America did not, as we know, remain so much of a "permanent fixture in U.S. foreign policy," although it continues to figure in economic policy. The typical narrative of what happened next recites the triumph of peace and democratization. Images flash up to confirm the story: the elections in Nicaragua in 1990, which the FSLN lost and then peacefully passed power to an opposition coalition; the United Nations-brokered peace accords first in El Salvador in 1992 and then in Guatemala in 1996. Signatures, handshakes. End of history. By the final scene of the film *The Juror* (1996), the Mafia-fleeing protagonist played by Demi Moore heads south of the border into the seemingly timeless ethnicized embrace of the pan-indigenous Central Americans, who exemplify a mysterious and noble past as well as a utopian multicultural future in their handwoven Mayan *traje* (clothing) and colorful ceremonies. Central Americans had returned to their bit-part roles, and Central America had reverted to its liminal position, in popular representation: "an unknown, nebulous zone," as Ana Patricia Rodriguez describes Maryland college classroom encounters with Central America and its literature. For her students, "Central America as a whole lies suspended somewhere between amorphous masses on the north and south and the east and west. As if it were an island, Central America appears without physical, geographic, and historical ties to the rest of the Western hemisphere and the world" (Rodriguez 2009, 2).

As a site of political struggle, it seems Central America has largely been erased from global imagination. Students and activists once compelled by Rigoberta Menchú's *testimonio* story of survival and resistance (Burgos Debray 1984) now organize for other causes: Rwanda and the Balkans, Palestine and Darfur, Haiti and Tibet; more recently, Arab Spring protestors in Tunis and Cairo. Current scholarship often reflects, wonderingly, on the fleeting nature of attention to Central America—once "the most important place in the world for the United States," in the words of former U.S. Ambassador to the United Nations, Jeane Kirkpatrick (LeFeber 1983, 1). As John A. Booth, Christine J. Wade, and Thomas W. Walker (2005, 3) ask, "Had the region in the early 2000s resumed its prior status of placid geopolitical backwater of the United States, or had it merely slipped from the sight of the media?"

So many of us who remain committed to understanding Central America have asked ourselves: Is such erasure an inevitable feature of a fast-paced media world? Is it a sign of compassion fatigue, in which people can only endure so many sad stories? Or does it involve "the neoliberalization of compassion," in which we all engage in a familial globality with no action or sentiment needed other than imagining ourselves as part of a community that cares (Fadlalla 2008)? (Or is it that people really only want certain kinds of clearly delineated sad stories, and when the plot gets too complicated they turn away?)

This departure of Central America from prominent geopolitical interest, and the disappearance of Central Americans as usually sympathetic (if often passive) figures in the public sphere of the United States and Europe and other parts of the wealthy North, is, we argue, not just an unavoidable aspect of contemporary global relations and limited news holes. It may be that there is a narrow "slot," whether savage or not (Trouillot 1991), for places peripheral to the global centers.[5] But we argue that the fact that Central America has faded from the geopolitical map is not an unfortunate but inevitable byproduct of a certain dominant way of seeing the world. It is precisely the goal of such a worldview.

Thus, despite dominant academic and popular rhetoric of interrelatedness, of globalization, of post-state realities (and of an acephalous multitude rising up [Hardt and Negri 2004]), this cut-up way of seeing still defines most global imaginaries. The world is still separated into bits and cases and situations. Geopolitical strategies demand that "places" such as the countries of Central America be talked about as somehow bounded: still billiard balls, as Eric Wolf (1983) put it more thirty years ago. Wolf was warning his fellow anthropologists to change their approaches to the study of the world, insisting that they attend to the capitalist processes that transcend individual cases ("cultures" and "peoples"). Social scientists today often do consider their research in the context of global interrelations. But the billiard-ball concept continues to be an apt metaphor for the principal apparatus many people employ to imagine geopolitics.

If the world materializes in most people's consciousness in patches and pieces (like the multicolored maps on classroom walls), then some parts can be explained away. This way of seeing is ultimately a practice of fetishization, with powerful effects. In a fragmented world, no one can easily see forces of larger global processes that define and construct them. Indeed, the very name of the "free" trade agreement negotiated to cover Central America offers a clue to this process of disassembly and selective reconstitution: CAFTA-DR, named as if the Caribbean half-island of ten million people, the five Central American countries of forty million, and the United States (with 315 million) were all equal partners in a deal. Yet that name situates once again in the public imagination a *thing*, as Wolf would put it; a thing that can be categorized and put away, or, worse, established as a target.

How can we see the bundles of relationships that Wolf and many others tell us comprise the world? We can, after all, only see individual people and their interactions, in specific places and distinct moments. It is difficult enough to envision global processes, much less see them. As anthropologists, we are committed to understanding the global through examinations of the local and local interconnections. This is the project that we collectively address in *Central America in the New Millennium*. Suggesting that Central America's disappearance was structurally inevitable in the current world order, in this collection, we move beyond historic moments—the guerrilla offensives, the assassinations, the peace agreements, the earthquakes—and examine the regional circumstances and daily lives within frames of democratization and neoliberalism, as they shape lived experiences of transition.

Ethnographic Approaches

Seeing global processes, as ethnographically minded social scientists, means privileging the everyday as a site of authority, and as a place for comprehending the meanings that large-scale processes like security, neoliberalization, democracy, and multiculturalism come to have for individuals, communities, and groups. Ethnography is both method and theory, allowing researchers to embrace the subjective meaning of behavior—not just what people do, or say they do—but how and why their motivations are constructed or shaped. Theoretically, ethnography is empirical and includes in-depth description of everyday life and practices. It provides a basis for challenging positivistic approaches, for decentering topics that otherwise defy qualitative inquiry. The contributors to this volume have spent years investigating movements or changes where they live, or returning again and again to the region, in many cases for decades, to conduct research. An emphasis on ethnography as a way of rendering visible the region thus provides an important counterpoint to "disappearing" tendencies and billiard-ball thinking.

These chapters resist Central America's erasure by insisting on the relevance of the local. Each shows some aspect of how the macro-level political economy sociologist William I. Robinson (2003) describes in *Transnational Conflicts* works on the ground; how it manifests at the micro-level of human experience and in everyday political effects. Each chapter examines what people say and feel about their lives and the choices they make, and how they understand the times they live in. While many of the contributors in the book trace dynamics of power and politics, the struggles of various vulnerable populations—whether middle-class protestors in Costa Rica, urban residents in El Salvador, or poor peasants in rural Honduras—rather than the logic of elites, is the impetus for *Central America in the New Millennium*.

Although the conflicts have formally ended, many international social scientists initially drawn by those struggles continue to work in the region. A number of scholars ethnographically examine the effects of war and violence as well as the struggles of marginalized populations to define their own fates.[6] By bringing diverse Central American sites together in one volume, we expand on this critically important work by accounting for the ways in which these experiences are tied to larger regional transitions. For example, Costa Rica has constructed a national identity outside conflicts and yet by the mid-2000s was in the midst of a crisis of participatory democracy. Honduras might not have been directly affected by the civil wars (though its military received tremendous support from the North). But as the June 2009 coup demonstrated, it has struggled with many of the same social and economic problems erupting elsewhere in the region. Building on theoretical literature addressing post-Cold War democratization, and endeavoring to understand how processes of change reverberate regionally even as disappearing acts take place within larger geopolitical realms, *Central America in the New Millennium* seeks to account for these commonalities in terms of Central American particularity, as well as globally resonating discourses and economic and political processes.

Historical Struggles for Sovereignty and Identity

The five Central American countries have a common history and identity that provides the ground from which to consider issues of free-market orthodoxy and neoliberal democratization. Guatemala, El Salvador, Honduras, Nicaragua, and Costa Rica never reunited after their chaotic post-independence federation fell apart in 1838. Dunkerley (1988, 20) discerns a "tension between unity and diversity" from the earliest days, suggesting that contradictions in social structure that led to the conflicts of the late 1970s had been seeded a century earlier. He dates the problems to the region's liberal revolutions, starting with Guatemala in 1871 and culminating in Nicaragua in 1893. The emergent liberal regimes aimed to access the world market: first with coffee, then, bananas; later, sugar, cotton, and cattle. Mining of gold and silver also played a small role in the isthmus in the nineteenth and early twentieth centuries. (High gold and mineral prices at the turn of the millennium returned transnational mining corporations to the region. Communities have organized against mines, protesting small benefits in relation to risks of environmental contamination and water diversion—sometimes with violent responses.[7])

The oligarchies and elites that arose to control the region's riches at the end of the nineteenth century faced new challenges in the twentieth century. The global Depression and then World War II slowed, but did not significantly change, Central America's integration into the world economy. Despite uprisings and revolutions in the 1930s and 1940s, "nowhere—not even in Guatemala after the agrarian reform of 1952—did the bourgeoisie lose its control over either land or the commanding heights of the economy," Dunkerley (1988, 87) argues (contrasting this trend with the rise of populist regimes elsewhere in Latin America). Rather, the ways the (modernizing) ruling class and dominant bloc wielded power shifted. "This bloc remained dependent upon landed power for its authority and the maintenance of the relations of production," he writes, adding that "in moments of crisis such dependence became very clear and direct" (Dunkerley 1988, 87). In the 1930s and beyond, military men, later with lawyers, administrators, technicians, and professional politicians, directed the state apparatus throughout the isthmus (except in Costa Rica).

Central Americans' struggles for sovereignty and democracy—sometimes violent and loud, sometimes clandestine and surreptitious, sometimes even orderly and open—stretch back across the twentieth century. Street names and movements memorialize martyrs and heroes who resisted some form of totalitarian, military, or imperialist oppression in the name of democracy: among them are Farabundo Martí and Augusto César Sandino in El Salvador and Nicaragua, of course; José Figueres Ferrer in Costa Rica; Jacobo Arbenz in Guatemala; and Ramón Villeda Morales in Honduras. That *struggle* so often dominates politics on the isthmus could be, and often is, seen as a lack, a problem; but, as Ellen Moodie points out in her chapter, following Chantal Mouffe (2005), such contradictions may be inherent in the nature of a democracy (and struggles to attain democracy) in which there is no final certainty. So often Central America is seen as a place of chaos and upheaval. But it is also the site of (sometimes burning) desires for democracy. The chaos and upheaval—the death squads, paramilitaries, assassinations, and other signs of violence—precisely index efforts *for* democracy at a time when widespread repression against the threats of subversion were the common reaction to social movements.

Though in the 1930s Central American governments repressed opposition relatively easily, in the mid 1940s democratic demands forced new strategies by those in power. The Allied victory in World War II—fought, after all, in the name of freedom and democracy—inspired colonized and oppressed people across the world. The concept of democracy at that moment carried a different resonance. By the time the United Nations was founded in 1945, democracy was broadly seen as entailing both human freedom and social equality. Historian Greg Grandin (2004, 4), working with Guatemalans who struggled against the "daily traps of humiliation and savagery" of an exclusionary, exploitative society, argues that in the mid twentieth century, many Central Americans shared "a commonsensical understanding of democracy not as a procedural constitutionalism but as the felt experience of individual sovereignty and social solidarity."

In 1944, Guatemalans deposed dictator Jorge Ubico in the October Revolution. That same year in El Salvador, a coalition of urban workers and professionals rose up to overthrow the president, General Maximiliano Hernández Martínez. There the Salvadoran military quickly retook power. Activists in El Salvador and throughout Central America could only watch from a distance the decade-long rise of a broad, participative democracy during Guatemala's "Ten Years of Spring." But in 1954, President Jacobo Arbenz, whose land reform had antagonized the powerful United Fruit Company, was overthrown in a CIA-backed coup (see Smith and Adams 2011). As the Salvadoran military had done a decade earlier, the new government suppressed all opposition and clamped down on dissent. Costa Ricans, too, rose up during the 1940s; in 1948, José Figueres Ferrer led an uprising when Rafael Angel Calderón

Guardia (president from 1940 to 1944) refused to relinquish power after losing a presidential election. Following a 44-day civil war in which 2,000 died, the government drafted a constitution granting universal suffrage, embracing women and blacks as full citizens—and abolishing the military.

The 1959 Cuban revolution changed everything—both for Latin Americans yearning to shake off what they saw as the yoke of U.S. imperialism, and for North Americans who saw the spread of Communism as a threat to freedom. Clandestine movements and determined remnants of the Communist Party throughout Central America took heart. New revolutionaries were born, many compelled by collectivist and utopian visions that countered the market-oriented liberalism in statist economies. In 1961, a group of Nicaraguan intellectuals formed the FSLN. They spent nearly two decades planning a popular revolution and insurrection that would lead to the overthrow of their dictator Anastasio Somoza in 1979. The Guatemalan insurgency re-emerged at that time as well. In April 1961, students and members of the outlawed Communist party marched in Guatemala City's streets to protest their government's participation in training Cuban exile mercenaries for the Bay of Pigs invasion. Three protestors were killed when the military opened fire. In El Salvador, some Communist Party members who had long resisted armed insurrection (a legacy of President Hernández Martínez's 1932 massacre of 10,000 indigenous and ladino [non-Indian] peasants after a Communist-led uprising [see Gould and Lauria-Santiago 2008]) began to rethink strategies that deferred revolution. They formed new revolutionary groups to challenge the state (see Lindo-Fuentes et al. 2007). As a result, by the 1980s, Central America became a place where something exciting and vital was occurring. Previously separate sectors united in struggle, and new political alliances formed between urban workers and rural peasants, radicalized Christianity and socialism, and indigenous actors (Grandin 2010, 31).

The movements produced more than political strategy. As Leigh Binford points out in his chapter in this volume, they profoundly changed people's lives. He cites Grandin's concept of "insurgent individuality," developed in his study of events leading up to the 1978 Panzós massacre in Guatemala. Grandin (2004, 181) argues, "Rather than eliminating the boundaries between self and society, collective action distilled for many a more potent understanding of themselves as politically consequent individuals ... [C]ollective actions laid bare the social foundations of the self." Binford proposes a "post-insurgent individuality" among former FMLN combatants and their supporters in the department of Morazán in El Salvador.

While political ideas of democracy were growing and sometimes radicalizing among activist Latin Americans in the 1960s and 1970s, the concept was being deployed in rather different ways within powerful global institutions of the Cold War. Democracy there functioned as the antithesis to an ominous gray image of Soviet Communism. It stood for individualism, property rights, and free-market economics. Promoting this perspective became an urgent task for the United States after Fidel Castro's rise threatened its hegemony in its own "backyard." The John F. Kennedy administration launched the Alliance for Progress in Latin America in 1961, linking "political freedom" with capitalist economic planning, development, and foreign investments. It tolerated some welfare-state features, such as limited agrarian reform, nationalized resources like oil, and social security systems offering limited health care and pensions. Moderate political parties such as the Christian Democrats did grow in strength in most Central American countries. So did peasant and labor movements, as well as paramilitary networks and other forms of surveillance activity aiming to root out subversion, imagined and actual.

Inevitable Revolutions?

One book that circulated widely in the 1980s insisted the revolutionary conflicts that followed the repression and protest of the previous decade were "inevitable." The first edition of Walter LaFeber's (1983) *Inevitable Revolutions: The United States in Central America* illustrates its cover with a photograph of a Sandinista guerrilla brandishing a rocket launcher. The book starts with Reagan warning an April 1983 joint session of the U.S. Congress that "no area of the world was more vital for North American security" (LaFeber 1983, 5). But if people in the North had any sense of these crucial sites at that moment, it was likely of a place of disorder and horror. Perhaps they recalled the 1979 on-camera murder of ABC-TV newsman Bill Stewart by Nicaraguan National Guardsmen. Maybe they heard about the murders of the four North American churchwomen by the Salvadoran National Guard, and the death-squad assassination of Archbishop Óscar Arnulfo Romero (in 1980). From Guatemala, they might have read about the 1980 fire bombing of the Spanish embassy (see above).

Even those Northerners paying attention to Central American atrocities—and struggles for justice—did not likely hear much about what was happening in Honduras, over the 1980s becoming "an unsinkable aircraft carrier" (in the words of the president of Honduras' Christian Democratic Party) (Moreno 1994, 36). By mid-decade it was receiving millions of dollars and hosting bases for the anti-Sandinista Contra force. Buoyed by such bounty, the government conducted its own campaign against subversives, its infamous Battalion 316 "disappearing" some 130 people and repressing nascent resistance among youth (Moreno 1994, 30; Pine 2008, 52–53). One possible reason Honduras did not follow its three neighbors into armed struggle was that its military exercised comparative restraint in repression, killing only about a thousand people in the 1980s and 1990s (Booth et al. 2005, 147–48). It also, like Costa Rica, undertook political and economic reforms.

Still, less than a quarter-century later, younger readers may be baffled as to why the United States was obsessed with the skinny strip of volcanic, earthquake-prone land full of poor peasants (themselves ever erupting). Sure, there is stunning biodiversity between Mexico and Colombia—strange butterflies and exotic ferns. Those environmental riches may gird profitable ecotourism, as Binford and Vivanco (this volume) demonstrate. But this hardly seems enough, even with the potential of future pharmaceutical patents, to have justified such emotional and financial investment into the region by ideologues (right and left) during the 1980s. The reaction seems to be disproportionate today. The adjacent Panama Canal was important, of course, but for the most part did not figure into the debates.

The statistics cited in LeFeber (1983), showing egregious social and economic inequities in the five countries, could perhaps, when added to a long history of military oppression, begin to explain the revolutionary passion among some of the people in Central America at that historical moment (except that many of the numbers remain egregious in this non-revolutionary era). Illiteracy ranged between 50 and 70 percent, except in Costa Rica (10 percent); per capita income, between $640 in Honduras to $1,520 in Costa Rica. All five countries survived as agro-export economies, relying on unstable monocrop commodity exports of coffee and bananas, as well as some cotton, sugar, and timber. But again: in the post-9/11 era of strategic wars on "terror" aimed at the oil-drenched Middle East, U.S. ire over uprisings in "banana republics" hardly seems warranted. The excesses in 1980s North American responses to guerrilla movements in the isthmus—the over-the-top rhetoric by Reagan, Assistant Secretary of State Elliot Abrams, and U.S. Ambassador to the United Nations Jeane Kirkpatrick; the voluminous white papers circulated on the problems in the region; the enormous fortified embassy built in tiny El Salvador; the training of Central American military officers in torture and counterinsurgency at the School of the Americas—suggest something more than practical strategizing for geopolitical and economic advantage. They testify to a possessive, manic investment in a place declared "our" territory, "our backyard," since the Monroe Doctrine. They also reveal a fanatic resolve to overcome the humiliation of Vietnam.

Robinson's (2003) more functionalist explanation for Northern attention to the isthmus offers some logical cover for the North American intervention. He points out that the transitions promoted toward the end of the Cold War were not just toward representative electoral politics; they were also shifts to free-market orthodoxy, seen most vividly with the switch from non-capitalist to capitalist systems in the former Soviet bloc but also evident in economic transformations throughout the Global South. These processes comprise two components of an encompassing historical rearticulation into the global financial system. Robinson contends that what was happening throughout Central America at this time was something much more than post-conflict or post-authoritarian transition. Rather, he writes, the historical moment reflected "a prolonged period of change in the social structure ... reciprocal to and in dialectical interplay with changes at the level of the global system" (Robinson 2003, 57). (Robinson downplays any "democratic" aspect of the post-Cold War changes in governance; he prefers the word "polyarchy" to describe the political systems in most of Central America.)

Here is where Costa Rica's experience is instructive. Costa Rica, the "Switzerland of Central America," abolished its army in 1948 and boasted a stable, democratic social welfare state. Recent approaches to this history point to the crucial importance of the 1940s to this status, when the coup that put Figueres into power left social reforms that had already been initiated in place. The ongoing existence of these reforms provided the political stage for Costa Rica to flourish.

Democracy and Neoliberalism in Central America

In the early 1980s Costa Rica appeared to be the exception to Central American trends. The United States did not have to pour billions into interrupting insurgency *there*. Yet things still fell apart. In what seemed to be "from one day almost to the next," as anthropologist Marc Edelman (1999, 1) writes, "all of a sudden once-comfortable and self-satisfied Costa Ricans beheld rapidly growing numbers of disheveled children singing for coins on buses." In 1981 the country of three million became the first in Latin America to default on its foreign debt obligation. Costa Rica would be considered a "basket case" by 1982, with 100 percent inflation, mounting unemployment, and increasing impoverishment of the population. But a decade later, Costa Rican President Rafael Angel Calderón Fournier would boast to the *New York Times* that "the World Bank, the Inter-American Development Bank, and the International Monetary Fund ... describe [Costa Rica] as a human and economic miracle" (Edelman 1999, 3). The sudden economic change in the country, of course, as Edelman documents, produced many more "losers" than "winners." He suggests that Costa Rica's "success," attributed to neoliberal free-market policies of privatization and breaking down barriers to foreign investment, had much to do with its long history of state-led development before the 1980s. This is something many Costa Ricans recognized as an important aspect of their "unique" situation as they engaged in public or *democracia de la calle* (street democracy) during massive anti-free trade mobilizations between 2005 and 2007, as Raventós shows in her chapter.

The point here is that even "peaceful" Costa Rica, not just genocidal Guatemala, war-torn El Salvador, troubled Honduras, and belligerent Nicaragua, would be radically refashioned for a new capitalist world order.

Since the Cold War ended, democracy-promoting nongovernmental organizations (NGOs) have proliferated globally, joining European and North American efforts at exporting a free-market model of democracy and giving birth to "new forms of political, legal and scientific imperialism" (Guilhot 2005). But in order to understand how democracy operates, as an active, motivating symbol as well as an institutional form, we must examine local meanings and lived experience as they intertwine with these global discourses. In this book, arguments for competing visions of democratic ideology and practice, as well as social justice, emerge in relation to discussions of such topics as indigeneity and politics; human rights; racism; migration; neoliberal and multicultural practices and their interrelationships; and the establishment of different kinds of "value" in relation to regional and global currents. And, of course, visions of democracy become clear in conversations about politics, the past, and the future.

So, in the post-Cold War era, what has this "democracy" meant to Central Americans? To be more specific, what has democracy meant to the forty million Central American citizens in the midst of massive neoliberal restructuring across the region? What has it meant that violence has increased, not decreased, in the post-conflict period? The controversy over the 28 June 2009 coup in Honduras—in which both powerful opponents of ousted President Manuel Zelaya and Zelaya's mass supporters insisted *they* were the democrats—suggests that the term may be emptied of meaning. It is a word bandied about by the far right, the extreme left, and everyone in between. In Guatemala, for example, anthropologist Jennifer Schirmer (1998) has shown us how military officers implicated in genocide claim credit for political liberalization *through* the murders of 75,000 indigenous peasants in 1982: "To achieve democracy, the country first needed to be at peace," one general, once the country's minister of defense, told her. She argues that such leaders, no longer ruling nakedly, gain global legitimacy as they appropriate "the imagery of the rule of law, and the mechanisms and procedures of democracy" (Schirmer 1998, 1, 2). At the same time, political scientist Elisabeth J. Wood (2000, 4) argues that democracy in El Salvador was "forged from below by the sustained insurgency of lower-class actors"; elites agreed to compromise, negotiating peace, because they recognized that popular movements could not be quashed. The left tells a similar story, to a greater or lesser extent, throughout Latin America. As Grandin (2004, xiv) writes, "In country after country, the mass peasant and working class movements that gained ground in the middle of the twentieth century were absolutely indispensable to the advancement of democracy. To the degree that Latin America today may be considered democratic, it was the left, including the Marxist left, that made it so." Perhaps, then, it is not that the term "democracy" has been emptied of meaning, but rather that democracy in Central America means too much. How then, are political lives negotiated in this new climate?

Political Lives, Humanitarianism, and the Negotiation of Futures

Yearning for a better future—something clear from post-World War II development efforts as well as Marxist revolutions (as María Josefina Saldaña-Portillo [2003] demonstrates in her analysis of Sandinista rhetoric)—unites many twentieth-century Cold War subjects and their inheritors. The perceived *loss* of those imagined futures is what many Central Americans lament. As neoliberal logic deepens, a new frontier of political struggle has emerged: the quest for dignified livelihood in the era of Plan Puebla Panama (the multibillion-dollar development plan to unite the nine southern states of Mexico to Central America and Colombia) and CAFTA-DR. If democracy is increasingly market driven, Central Americans have responded with what Henri LeFebvre (1991) has called "the revolution of everyday life."

This revolution has not been televised. It doesn't make for dramatic viewing. At times, it is quiet and plodding, at others, desperate and uncomfortable. On occasion, though, Central America shoves its way onto crowded CNN news screens, as earthquakes topple already flimsily constructed cities, hurricanes and tropical storms sweep shantytowns from precarious perches, sinkholes of unknown depth open in capital cities, and the unrelenting grind of poverty and disease forces people to transnational wage-labor migration at best, and to crime, smuggling, and trafficking at worst. The movie *Sin Nombre* (*Without a Name*) (Fukunaga 2009) hauntingly brings these themes together as its Honduran protagonist negotiates the hazardous journey to the U.S.-Mexican border through Guatemala and then Mexico, where gangs control the train lines that bring frightened yet hopeful migrants to the United States border. In these "economic warzones" (Nordstrom 2007, xviii), the epic crossing is characterized by alternating frissons of fear and excitement. This journey is, after all, a contemporary generational rite of passage for many young Central Americans. Indeed, as the story of Sayra, traveling with her father and uncle to join his family in the United States, and Caspar, escaping from the Mara Salvatrucha gang, shows, it's even possible to fall in love on the treacherous trip. The alienating violence and suffering of *Sin Nombre* is the story so many outside observers now expect from post-revolutionary Central America. Disaster, gangs, poverty, and human rights violations have been the recent historic "slot" of the region (in Trouillot's sense), co-existing with tropes of successful democratic transition. Social scientists have facilitated the continued salience of this slot (with assistance from journalists), usually with the very best of intentions, perpetuating the idea that Central America is a place that is ***put upon,*** by geopolitical and economic machinations, the ongoing violence of politics, the lack of order and security, and of course, by nature herself.

Projects and discourses of human rights, humanitarianism, and development are central to this categorizing project. These languages summon moral and ethical integrity to the re-scripting of governance, reform, democracy building, and ways of being in the world that may inadvertently concretize neoliberal agendas and logics. Commissions of inquiry, postwar human rights workshops, and the preponderance of microfinance schemes are all examples of the deepening thrust of a global agenda that creates new boundaries and meanings for the Global North and South. This global politics of humanity no longer rests on the foundation of international law. Instead, it provides "new promises to generate new legal and political orders, to shape new social realities and relations, to forge new cultural connections and values" (Editorial Collective, Humanity, 2010). These discourses and policies have become the ***modus operandi*** of both right and left, disrupting historical patterns that have framed politics within the region and producing a new breed of political actor. Consider, for example, the newly conservative and fiercely anti-abortion Daniel Ortega at the helm of the current FSLN in Nicaragua. When Hugo Chavez of Venezuela called to congratulate Ortega on his 2006 victory, he apparently chanted, "Long live the Sandinista revolution!" But for many who supported the revolution and its pioneering vision of gender equality, it is difficult to find the vestiges of that historical moment within the current government, as Rosario Montoya describes in her chapter.

The neoliberal production of "victims" defines certain areas of the world as in acute crisis. These areas are subsequently targeted by the new politics of humanity, emergent forms of neoliberal compassion and what Erica Bornstein (2009) calls "regulated philanthropy," highly mediated incursions into the world of poverty alleviation. Or they are subject to journalist Naomi Klein's (2008) "shock doctrine," the rise of free-market policies through the production and exploitation of disaster-shocked people and countries. At stake in the definition of areas of the world, then, is the ability of regions to successfully defy or resist the Sisyphean gifts, in the name of humanitarianism, that bind them to "new economic (dis)orders" (Nordstrom 2007, 261). Indeed, as many Central Americans make clear in this volume, sometimes the "gift" is not worth taking.

The ethnographic studies in this volume provide an alternative glimpse to the struggles that take place within and beyond these mechanisms, showing the agency brought to bear on increasingly complex politico-economic and cultural frameworks that come to animate areas like Central America. Interventions of all kinds, only some of them involving arms, are frequently justified and defined through dichotomies: developed and undeveloped, North and South, rich and poor. By attending to the dialectic nature of these pairings and examining the nature of those just emerging—order and disorder, security and insecurity, sustainable and unsustainable are among the many under interrogation—we show how Central Americans negotiate this contemporary terrain.

Security, Livelihood, and Regional Anxieties

In October 2009, a United Nations report announced, "Central America has become the region with the highest level of non-political crime worldwide" (UNDP 2009). The report noted that crime continues to threaten the region's development as murders soared to 33 per 100,000 inhabitants, a figure three times the global average. The so-called northern triangle of El Salvador, Guatemala, and Honduras is now considered one of the most violent areas of the world. So tormented is the isthmus that a World Bank report (2011) quantified the economic cost of this unrelenting spiral: 8 percent of the gross domestic product of Central American economies is directed toward anti-violence measures.

What does it mean to live in an area so violent? Does such overriding emphasis on crime and violence mask what Loïc Wacquant (2009, 287) suggests are "the new politics and policy of poverty that is a core component in the forging of the neoliberal state"? Citizen concern with violence and security has understandably become paramount. In some countries this includes the breakdown of key institutions, such as police, justice systems, courts, rule of law, and the corresponding rise of vigilantism, lynching, and paramilitarism. Often, older forms of power resurge in new registers. Enrique Desmond Arias and Daniel Goldstein (2010, 20) analyze the prevalence of these forms of violence throughout Latin America, showing that multiple violent actors are now an integral part of civil society, coexisting with organizations that act to expand and deepen democratic functions. These violent pluralities are not aberrations, nor do they signal the erosion of democratic hope. Instead, they are critical mechanisms that bolster the institutions and mechanisms of power fashioned through decades of neoliberal democracy (Arias and Goldstein 2010). Violent groups and individuals often join civil society in the name of security and crime control. Goldstein (2010, 487) clarifies this difficult relation, writing, "'[S]ecurity calls on the power of fear to fill the ruptures that the crises and contradictions of neoliberalism engendered and so functions as a principal tool of state formations and governmentality ... albeit one that is constantly challenged by a range of local actors and state subjects."

This multi-dimensional facet of and preoccupation with "security" is demonstrated in many chapters of this collection, from the "worse-than-the-war" climate that Moodie and Ainhoa Montoya encountered in El Salvador during the two decades after that country's civil war ended, to the shifting meanings and measures experienced by and affecting "securitized" transnational migrants, tracked by Burrell across borders and by Jennifer Bickham Mendez in Williamsburg, Virginia. The rise of *seguridad* (security), mandatory-service committees that have now sprung up in neighborhoods and communities throughout Guatemala and chronicled by Burrell, are arguably now a part of civil society.

Security is not a new preoccupation among scholars of Central America. For most of the past century, the region has been at the center of explorations of historically rooted forms of domination and resistance both locally and globally. From Wolf's "peasant wars" (1999 [1969]) inspired by an earlier post-World War II global order, to Edelman's peasant mobilizations against globalization (1999), livelihood struggles and security concerns, in a broad political economic sense, have been thematic interests in the literature. Community studies and well-developed bodies of work on migration, tourism, and commodities such as coffee and bananas, to one degree or another have taken up debates and questions concerning the interconnections among livelihood struggles and security in ethnographic case studies. This regional tradition shows how security has been a consistent anxiety across time and space in Central America, an ongoing concern evident in the pragmatic considerations of Central American life described in many chapters: those of coffee growers (Tucker and Lyon), the Honduran agrarian movement (Boyer and Cardona Peñalva), Guatemalan vendors (Little) or tourism entrepreneurs (Anderson, Babb, Binford, and Vivanco). Whatever form regional anxieties over security take, the long shadow of the post-September 11 United States security regime has indelibly changed potentials for action, everyday life and livelihood possibilities for millions of Central Americans.

Lives are reordered, recategorized, and shifted through space and time as security increasingly becomes the central organizational and political paradigm of our time, rooted as it is in forms and practices of neoliberal democracy and governing techniques. Considering its multiple meanings over time reveals oft-hidden relationships. Such an examination unveils links between ideas of security and democracy; it points to how the sociopolitical climate created through mandates established in relation to rising crime reinforce ongoing structural violence.

Re-visualizing Contemporary Central America

In the 1983 film *El Norte,* a young Mayan brother and sister, Enrique and Rosa, escape from ethnic and political persecution in Guatemala and make their way to the United States. The threat to them was universally understood: flee or face the barrel of a gun. As the film closes, Rosa, who lies on her deathbed dying of typhus contracted from their brutal border crossing, asks, "In our homeland there's no place for us; they want to kill us. In Mexico, there's only poverty. And in the North, we aren't accepted. When are we going to find a home, maybe only in death?"

More than a quarter century later, *Sin Nombre* constructs a similar premise for the epic of border crossing/s, when Sayra heads north with her father and uncle. The family members' flight from entrenched poverty and ongoing structural violence is less dramatic than that of their filmic predecessors Enrique and Rosa. They are migrating, like hundreds of thousands of others before them, with a dream for a better life. In the almost three decades that separate these films, border crossings have transformed into an almost expected rite of passage, a necessity for many Central Americans and for the farms and factories that employ them in the North. Indeed, the remittances these workers send home gird the economies of much of Central America. These citizens' absences in their homelands manifest in the presence of two-story homes in rural villages and wide air-conditioned malls in the cities (Coutin 2007). Many people from the isthmus have become productive citizens in the North, and their compatriots keep on coming. They continue to confront obstacles. Situations like the 2007 New Bedford, Massachusetts, raid of a factory making military vests—resulting in 361 arrests of (mostly) undocumented Salvadorans and Guatemalans, and as many as 200 children separated from their parents (Abraham 2007, Houston Chronicle 2007)—or the 2008 Postville, Iowa, raid of a kosher slaughterhouse—in which 400 undocumented migrants were similarly arrested (Hsu 2008)—have become the cost of risk, for both workers and employers. The underside of the story, the huge amounts of "empowerment debt" (Elyachar 2005) taken on to finance migration, remain in the shadows, further obscuring what neoliberal democratization has come to mean.[8] This is very much part of the new landscape of Central America, a result of the intensification of a regional process ongoing for the past century.

Particular spaces in the world may be "disappeared" and erased as the inevitable response to quickening capitalist processes under neoliberal democratization. But what incidents like those at Postville and New Bedford make clear is that in a new world geopolitical (dis)order, Central America may be ***desaparacido*** (disappeared) in one way, but in another, it is everywhere. It is in factory floors in free-trade zones in Tecpán, Guatemala, and on the labels of the clothes shipped to Toronto boutiques; it is in coffee plantations in Santa Barbara, Honduras, and the free-trade beans sold in Stockholm cafes; it is in classrooms of schools and universities in San Francisco, California, and behind podiums in the United Nations; and it is in gardens and restaurants on West Hempstead, Long Island.

David Harvey (2010, 215–60) devotes the final chapter of *The Enigma of Capital* to challenging the irrationality of contemporary capitalism and capital flows, asking, "What is to be done? And who is going to do it?" The collective efforts of Central Americans we chronicle in this book—the myriad ways of opposing the reorganization of space, the everyday struggles to make a dignified living, the ongoing debates about what change means—offer a counterweight to rhetoric of neoliberal free market democracy and the geopolitical politics of disenfranchisement and immiseration that it promotes. The sixteen chapters that follow in *Central America in the New Millennium* chronicle the diverse things Central Americans are *doing*, often in obscurity. The book is divided into four parts, each ethnographically tracking imaginations, strategies, and modes of participation. The essays provide ethnographic insight into local worlds and their interaction with hope for change, democracy, and social justice.

Part I, "Imagining Democracy after the Cold War," demonstrates the imbrication of past fantasies of democracy (and hopes for the future) with the realities of present disillusionment in an insecure, neoliberal moment. Rosario Montoya, in "Contradiction and Struggle under the Leftist Phoenix: Rural Nicaragua at the Thirtieth Anniversary of the Revolution," considers what remains of the revolution after President Daniel Ortega's 2006 election. Though she echoes many Nicaraguan critiques of the new-millennial FSLN, she finds other legacies of the 1980s in changes of campesino men and women's subjectivities.

While the rural Nicaraguans Rosario Montoya has come to know intimately over nearly a quarter-century have struggled in the transition from Sandinista socialism to neoliberal democracy, the Salvadorans Ainhoa Montoya lived and worked with in a small city during 2008-2009 were imagining for the first time the real possibility of a leftist elected to power in their country. Ainhoa Montoya argues in "The Violence of Cold War Polarities and the Fostering of Hope: The 2009 Elections in Postwar El Salvador" that the 2009 electoral campaign, which the FMLN's Mauricio Funes eventually won, allowed Salvadorans to engage in wartime conflicts with which many of them had not come to terms. She examines the right-wing Nationalist Republican Alliance (ARENA)'s mobilization of mass media propaganda to enact a politics of fear. Funes prevailed, she argues, because he was able to address the pressing social and economic anxieties that had multiplied during twenty years of neoliberal rule.

Soon after Funes took office in El Salvador, Honduras's leftist president, Manuel "Mel" Zelaya was ousted in the controversial 28 June 2009 military coup in Tegucigalpa. Observers saw the dramatic response of many Hondurans, protesting (or supporting) the coup and the governments that followed, as a new development—the *catrachos* (the common nickname for Hondurans) finally catching up to their more radical isthmusian neighbors. Jefferson Boyer and Wilfredo Cardona Peñalva in their chapter, "Daring to Hope in the Midst of Despair: The Agrarian Question within the Anti-Coup Resistance Movement in Honduras," contextualize activism historically. After the coup, confronting government repression, key leaders and members of peasant and agrarian movements that had long ago split began talking to each other again. The authors discuss hope for new organizing and emergent approaches to sustainable agriculture in the country, as part of a larger movement for food sovereignty.

Like Hondurans, Costa Ricans were not known for their activism in the late twentieth century; and also like Hondurans, Costa Ricans in the new millennium began to show their movement muster. In "My Heart Says NO": Political Experiences of the Struggle against CAFTA-DR in Costa Rica," Ciska Raventós writes of an emergent democratic ethos among *ticos* (the nickname for Costa Ricans) who saw the free trade agreement as further threatening their once envied social welfare system. In order to build an opposition against well-funded corporate and elite supporters of the agreement, ticos throughout the country participated in an unprecedented grassroots mobilization. Although the referendum was ultimately defeated, Raventós finds hope in the legacies of new political subjectivities, modes of political action, and connections between groups.

While Costa Ricans were reinvigorated by a form of democratic activism in the new millennium, a number of Salvadorans in the decade after the war found themselves to be disenchanted by the concept. "It's worse than the war," many of them repeated wonderingly, after the 1992 peace accords did not produce the secure environment or "community of care" many had imagined would be linked to peace and the lauded transition to democracy. Ellen Moodie in her chapter "Democracy, Disenchantment, and the Future in El Salvador" explores some of the concepts of democracy circulating in San Salvador in the two decades after the war ended, focusing on everyday conversation about crime at a moment when the country's murder rate was among the highest in the world. In the end, though, she finds that visions of a different future—hopes for an alternative democracy—can still animate Salvadorans.

Indigeneity, Race, and Human Rights in the (Post) Multicultural Moment

As K'iche anthropologist and journalist Irma Velásquez Nimatuj (2010/11) writes, "Nearly all of Central America has problems with racism." On 15 March 2010, she was asked to vacate her first-class seat on Copa Flight 795 from Panama to Costa Rica for a late-arriving white male passenger in a business suit. She had been holding her seat assignment since she boarded her flight in Guatemala and was dressed in the handwoven clothing that identified her as an indigenous Guatemalan. Upon being refused a conversation with the captain who had ordered her seat change, Velásquez Nimatuj wrote a letter of complaint to the head of Copa, citing the specific human rights conventions violated in this incident (including Convention 169 of the International Labor Organization, the broadest treaty in the United Nations system pertaining to indigenous people). She expressed her outrage at the "the grossest level of ignorance" displayed by airline employees, "who do not know the racial diversity of the population they must serve in Latin America, home to over thirty million indigenous people, not including people of African descent." Moreover, Velásquez Nimatuj noted, Copa (the airline of Panama) routinely uses images of indigenous peoples to promote their destinations while humiliating and discriminating against them in everyday life.

Velásquez Nimatuj's experience illustrates many of the dynamics that coalesce around issues of indigeneity, race, and rights in Central America in the era of neoliberalism and multiculturalism, the focus of the second section of this book. Limited inclusivity and broad-based marginalization and vulnerability continue to define the experiences of many indigenous and Afro-Caribbean Central Americans. In "*Cuando Nos Internacionalizamos:* Human Rights and Other Universals at the United Nations Permanent Forum on Indigenous Issues," Baron Pineda reminds us that human rights have become the main idiom for political claim-making in the contemporary world. Transporting us to the corridors of power at the United Nations, he shows how international forums and networks, even those that are critiqued by participants, constitute a critical element in waging regional battles.

Claudia Dary Fuentes in her chapter "Acknowledging Racism and State Transformation in Postwar Guatemalan Society" provides an inside look into the little-known postwar efforts of the Guatemalan state to acknowledge racism and to prosecute discrimination through legal mechanisms. She traces legislation and recent court cases that demonstrate the ponderous task of challenging deep-seated social, economic, and cultural institutions that are founded upon and sustain racial hierarchies. Dary Fuentes speaks of the courage defendants in discrimination cases must bring to bear, and the resources mustered to relive trauma repeatedly as cases wend their ways to resolution, as demonstrated by Velásquez Nimatuj.

Jennifer Burrell's chapter, "Ephemeral Rights and Securitized Lives: Migration, *Mareros,* and Power in Millennial Guatemala," explores another facet of the Central American's engagement with human rights and its related idiom, security. Tracing these themes in relation to transnational wage-labor migrants, she shows how rights take on an ephemeral quality as border crossing and regional anxieties about *maras* (gangs) shift individuals in and out of claim-making possibilities.

Dominant, Residual, and Emergent Economic Strategies

In November 2008, Queen Elizabeth paid a visit to the London School of Economics and asked how economists had failed to predict the worst financial crisis since the Great Depression of the 1930s. Months later, they responded, blaming the "psychology of denial" for the "failure of the collective imagination of many bright people" (Guardian 2009). More recently, experts have admitted that there is little understanding of the "systemic risks" inherent in free-market capitalism (Harvey 2010, 261). These economists, bankers, development experts, and policy makers have much to learn from the everyday and pragmatic struggles of Central Americans.

Starting Part III of this book, Honduran coffee grower José Maldonado acted against "expert" advice and predominant market logic, expanding his coffee holdings at a time when worldwide prices hit record lows, and profit was many years away. But for him, weathering crisis is normal, one of the variables he figures in to his livelihood calculations. Maldonado also diversified crops. He realized much of his labor needs as a coffee producer depended on his family and he wanted them to have other opportunities. In "Honduras's Smallholder Coffee Farmers, the Coffee Crisis, and Neoliberal Policy: Disjunctures in Knowledge and Conundrums for Development," Catherine Tucker demonstrates how, given cultural and social factors outside the market, it made good sense to hold on to and even expand coffee lands.

The vendors Walter E. Little works with in Antigua Guatemala are well aware of the inherent inequalities contained within free trade agreements and how they serve to sustain enduring class, race, and gender-based differences. In "Maya Handicraft Vendors' CAFTA-DR Discourses: 'Free Trade Is Not for Everyone in Guatemala,'" Catarina, a vendor and Maya textile expert opines, "CAFTA is just an excuse for vendors who don't know how sell." Part of the art and expertise of vending, in her view, is to exercise flexibility and creativity in the face of challenging circumstances, such as the huge drop in tourism in Guatemala in 2002. Catarina's fellow vendors mostly agree with this assessment, concluding, "Free trade is not for everyone."

The coffee cooperative members and eco-tourism small business owners that Sarah Lyon and Luis Vivanco have worked with are exceptionally astute in measuring the positive aspects and the pitfalls of certification programs and niche markets, and their imposition of a one-size-fits-all model onto disparate circumstances. While fair trade has brought many benefits to certified small farmers in Central America, Lyon in her chapter "'Here the Campesino Is Dead': Can Central America's Smallholders Be Saved?" shows how fair-trade agreements are not and cannot be the final solution for smallholders across the region, as advocated in existing market-based poverty solutions. In his exploration of the transnational sustainable tourism certification movement in Costa Rica, "Certifying Sustainable Tourism in Costa Rica: Environmental Governance and Accountability in a Transitional Era," Vivanco focuses on the lived experiences of the transition from an interventionist welfare state to a neoliberal "shadow state" of market-based processes and pseudo-regulation devoid of the transparency once so prized nationally—the very things that the Costa Rican CAFTA-NO protestors found so objectionable. Because small business owners are often unable to afford the requirements demanded for formal eco-certification, they find themselves with ever-diminishing access to a domain they helped to establish.

In the cradle of North American democracy, Williamsburg, Virginia, we see some of the results of deepening dispossession in relationship to another economic strategy: wage-labor migration to the Nuevo South, a relatively new receiving destination that poses challenges to social integration. In "Central America Comes to the 'Cradle of Democracy': Immigration and Neoliberalization in Williamsburg, Virginia," Jennifer Bickham Mendez's poignant account of migrant struggles to create lives for themselves against a backdrop of institutionalized and officially sanctioned marginalization and "disappearance" in the United States suggests the question: How sustainable is the current global economic system upon which so many depend?

A Place on the Map: Surviving on Pasts, Presents, and Futures

Central America in the New Millennium not only explores a "new" (and expanded) Central America, existing in the political, economic, and multicultural flux of the present, but also examines the very act of *representing* that Central America. Many of the authors writing in this volume, largely based outside the region (with the exceptions of Cardona Peñalva, Dary Fuentes, and Raventós), first glimpsed Central America as tourists of one form or another. Most of us hasten to explain that we traveled south in solidarity with a struggle, or in order to support a group of people, even as we imagined "studying" (with or among) Central Americans. Leigh Binford, for example, already a committed political economist with longstanding research in Oaxaca, Mexico, first visited El Salvador when he participated in a solidarity delegation during the civil war of the 1980s. He served as an election observer in the first post-Peace Accords vote in 1994 in the former guerrilla stronghold of northern Morazán before publishing his monograph (1996) on the El Mozote massacre that occurred there.

A few days after returning from his first trip to the region in a decade, Binford presented at our 2008 Wenner-Gren workshop the paper that became his chapter in Part IV, "Migration, Tourism, and Post-Insurgent Individuality in Northern Morazán, El Salvador." He had learned that many projects borne in the hope of the immediate postwar moment had floundered in the wake of the zone's integration into the postwar neoliberal reality. However, perhaps ironically, development failures in part contributed to the reappearance of the "natural" environment that, along with historical sites, today draws national and international visitors. He hopefully suggests that members of the NGO PRODETUR, founded by former guerrillas, exhibit a kind of "post-insurgent individuality" resisting the worst abuses of capitalism though some forms of collective action.

Like Salvadorans, Nicaraguans have had a bit of a global "image problem": their country is often seen as a place of danger, which can limit mass tourist appeal. Florence Babb has spent the past decade examining tourism practices in post-conflict and post-revolutionary sites. In her chapter "Intimate Encounters: Sex and Power in Nicaraguan Tourism" she focuses on a country she has returned to over and over for more than twenty years. Following Binford, Babb reflects on the paradoxical nature of tourism efforts; in Nicaragua's case it is the irony of the fact that the Sandinistas, who in 1979 banned the use of sexualized images of women in the media, now employ sexualized images of women to attract international visitors. Sex work and romance tourism are just a part of what she has observed in neoliberal Nicaragua, but they get at some of the most vexing problems that often accompany tourism, particularly in the Global South.

Babb points to Nicaragua's use of sex, as in "tanned beauties," in selling itself as a global attraction. In "Notes on Tourism, Ethnicity, and the Politics of Cultural Value in Honduras," Mark Anderson writes of how race has become the key for Honduran tourism publicity. Marginalized politically, the ethnic/indigenous/Afro-Honduran Garifuna communities located on the Atlantic Coast have become the center of state and tourism industry efforts to draw international travelers. The Garifuna themselves are frustrated by their failure to realize the value of their own culture in the context of tourism (whether they object to their objectification or hope to cash in on it). Anderson argues that the inability of Garifuna to profit from their culture should lead us to examine the cultural and economic appropriation found within tourism, an industry that masks its own forms of cultural exploitation under the guise of cultural promotion and recognition. As we listen to debates among Garifuna, we recognize a self-awareness present in so many chapters in this book, whether Rosario Montoya's Nicaraguan campesinos struggling to hold on to hope, Binford's post-insurgent individuals faithful to collectivist visions, Little's politically engaged vendors resisting their marginality in the global market, or Tucker's strategic smallholders considering much more than immediate returns on their crop.

Notes

1. These five countries were briefly united as the United Provinces of Central America after independence from Spain (1823–1838).
2. Though Panama, carved out of Colombia after a 1903 U.S.-backed revolt, is not considered part of the political entity Central America, its strategic location folded it into political discussions of the crisis at that moment.
3. As former CIA director, Bush knew Noriega well; the general had long been on the CIA payroll for helping to sabotage the left in Nicaragua and El Salvador.
4. One estimate is that 250,000 people died in Central American wars between 1974 and 1996 and over a million were internally displaced (García 2006). Exact numbers of migrants are difficult to determine as many arrived without documents and stayed in the United States, but in the 1980s, somewhere around two million refugees left Central America for Mexico, Canada, and the United States.
5. The concept "savage slot" describes the function anthropology once filled—and often still does. Michel-Rolph Trouillot's (1991) argument is that while anthropologists did not invent the "savage" they helped place non-Western peoples and cultures in it.
6. An incomplete list of relevant monographs by these scholars includes Anderson (2009); Babb (2001); Binford (1996); Burrell (2013); Coutin (2007); DeLugan (2012); Fischer (2001); Fischer and Hendrickson (2002); Fischer and Benson (2009); Goldín (2009); Grandia (2012); Hale (2006b); Hayden (2003); Lancaster (1992); Little (2004); Lyon (2011); Mendez (2005); Menjívar (2000; 2011); R. Montoya (2012), Moodie (2010); Nelson (1999; 2009); Offit (2008); O'Neill (2009); Pine (2008); Reichman (2011); Sanford (2004); Silber (2010); Smith-Nonini (2010); Todd (2011); Warren (1998); Wolseth (2011); Zilberg (2011). These volumes each address difficulties of post-conflict legacies in late-twentieth-century Central America, but largely from the vantage point of one nation: themes include memory of violence, racism and genocide, gender relations, and working-class family life.
7. Canada's Pacific Rim Mining Company applied for permits for the El Dorado Mine in Cabanas, El Salvador; Goldcorp Inc., another Canadian concern, has mining projects in Guatemala and Honduras. Controversies have followed both companies' efforts. Some anti-mining activists have been killed. See http://www.oxfamamerica.org/newsandpublications/press_releases/central-american-mining-could-undermine-economic-well-being.
8. Diane and Jan Rus (2008) and David Stoll (2010) offer important correctives for Guatemala and Chiapas, Mexico.

Part I

Imagining Democracy after the Cold War

1 Contradiction and Struggle under the Leftist Phoenix

Rural Nicaragua at the Thirtieth Anniversary of the Revolution

Rosario Montoya

After sixteen years of neoliberal rule, in January 2007 Daniel Ortega, head of the Sandinista Front for National Liberation (FSLN), took power as president of Nicaragua. Ortega's return to office, vowing to enact the "second phase of the [Sandinista] revolution," challenged Nicaragua's disappearance from the global media as a site of struggle in the aftermath of the Sandinista Revolution (1979–1990). It also complicated images of the country peddled over the previous decade by Nicaraguan governments and the tourism industry as a modern liberal democracy, free of its atavistic revolutionary past, offering opportunities for investment, surf and adventure, and a good time amidst "tanned beauties" (Babb, this volume).

While Ortega's reappearance on the national political stage troubled these anodyne images of Nicaraguan politics and society, it hardly represented a revival of the revolution. For behind Ortega's decrying of "savage capitalism" and his calls for "revolution" and "socialism," he hid a political agenda that combined neoliberal principles with an increasingly anti-democratic populism. To find what survives of the revolution today, I argue, we should look not at the FSLN government. Rather, we should examine the political subjectivity and agency of subordinate groups who fought to make the revolution and, despite years of disillusionment and setbacks, continue their struggle to become subjects of their history.

Since the 1990 electoral defeat, when the FSLN declared it would "govern from below," the Sandinista party underwent several changes that transformed it from a revolutionary organization with close ties to its base to a more conventional populist party. This meant an increasing centralization and personalization of leadership in Ortega's figure (Kampwirth 2010); a readiness to make corrupt pacts with FSLN enemies (Dye 2004); openness to the growth of a Sandinista entrepreneurial sector with capitalist interests indistinct from those of the right wing;[1] and the adoption of reactionary gender politics.[2] In the process, a good part of the party's intellectuals left to form the Movement for Sandinista Renovation (MRS); the feminist movement, a set of historic supporters many of whose leaders had emerged from FSLN ranks, also left.

Figure 1.1. Billboard on the road to Masaya advertises Ortega's project for "citizen power" by claiming that "To Keep Your Promise to the People is to Keep Your Promise to God."

Ortega's popular power base (40 percent of the population), however, supported him unconditionally, helping him return to power in 2007. Yet a year into Ortega's presidency, the Sandinistas' initial enthusiasm had turned to ambivalence toward, and even disillusionment with, the performance of Ortega's administration (although not with Ortega himself). This was the case among campesinos from El Tule, a village in the southwestern department of Rivas, where I have carried out research for the past twenty years. For them, as for rural dwellers more generally, a primary reason for disillusionment was the insecurity of tenure of lands they received in the 1980s through the Sandinista Agrarian Reform (SAR).

The Problem of Property

"The problem of property," as it had come to be referred to in Nicaragua, began as soon as neoliberals took over the reins of government. During the 1980s, the Sandinista government had distributed roughly 19 percent of the country's arable land, 14 percent in the form of cooperative property, to landless and land-poor campesinos (Rocha 2010, 30). A preference for collective property kept with the Sandinista government's belief that cooperative production would put an end to what it regarded as the egoistic competitivity of (individualist) capitalist social relations while fostering the socialist spirit. The neoliberals, however, prized and supported individual property. So neoliberal policies began pushing cooperativized campesinos such as those in El Tule to sell. These policies included the withdrawal of credit and technical support for the rural sector and the enactment of commercial policies hostile to small-scale production. The effects of these policies were compounded by an insecurity of tenure stemming from a political environment that favored large-scale producers, including turning a blind eye to former landowner threats of eviction and coercion.

Campesinos' insecurity of tenure lay in the fact that many—an estimated 76 percent—of SAR beneficiaries, did not have titles to their lands (Equipo Nitlapán 1994, 22). During the 1980s, the Sandinista government had often distributed land in a disorganized fashion, without a legal process to regularize beneficiaries' tenure. After 1990, the FSLN negotiated with the Chamorro government (1990–1995) to allow SAR recipients to do so. But the economic situation, along with right-wing resistance throughout the 1990s, made this process impossible. By 2001, 75 percent of producers, most of them smallholders, controlled only 20 percent of the land. An unknown number, calculated at close to 50 percent of the rural population by one researcher, were landless (Pérez 2011, 18).

During his campaign in 2006, Ortega vowed to resolve this issue. Land titling, however, proceeded at a snail's pace (Cáceres 2010, 14–15), and no one can account for the delays. In August 2011, a campesino leader told me that the FSLN had decided to address insecurity in urban property first. Projecting an FSLN victory in the upcoming November 2011 national elections, he stated that rural property would be addressed in Daniel's *next* presidential period. How many hold this sanguine view is anyone's guess. What is clear is that frustration is running high among many: another campesino mentioned that cooperatives in Rivas had recently marched to protest the lack of progress in land titling.

A second campaign promise has fallen far short of expectations: the creation of a state bank geared toward supporting small and medium-sized producers. Ortega's promise was that this bank, to be funded through the Bolivarian Alternative for the Americas (ALBA), would allow campesinos—most of whom had returned to subsistence production over the past 16 years—to once again combine subsistence with production for the market. The bank—Banco Produzcamos—would indeed become a reality, but not until April 2010, over three years into Ortega's term.

The Banco Produzcamos and ALBA-CARUNA (Caja Rural Nacional), a state-owned micro-lending cooperative financed through ALBA that works primarily with cooperatives, are now part of the sector of micro-lending institutions serving small and medium-sized producers as well as cooperatives. While ALBA-CARUNA has a considerable budget, the government offers little information about it. Gauging its impact is thus next to impossible. As for the Banco Produzcamos, its budget is too small to accommodate the demands of Nicaragua's credit-starved campesinos. As a friend working with the bank explained about his loan, "It is a form of support [but] it does not amount to financing." Asked why he did not go to micro-lenders, he replied that their interests were too high and requirements too onerous for someone with as little collateral as himself. In short, the state bank is underfunded and most micro-lending institutions will not loan to campesinos such as my friend—who make up the vast majority of small producers—because they are considered at too high a risk of default. As a result, as of 2010, only about 25 percent of rural producers were receiving credit (Grigsby 2010, 15).

Zero Hunger?

Also negatively impacting campesino livelihoods has been the rise of commodity prices, including basic grains, which occurred as gasoline prices rose over the years, skyrocketing in 2008 and again in 2011. To ameliorate the effects of gas prices on food consumption, in 2007 the government implemented a program funded through ALBA to sell basic grains at 60 percent lower than market prices. However, the program has been inconsistently implemented across time and regions, and has been plagued by favoritism. More successful was the government's intervention, in the face of the 2011 gas price hikes, to control the export of red beans as a means of keeping the price of this product stable. As Perez (2011) argues, however, to address the food crisis and improve rural living standards in a sustained manner, not to mention generate employment among the rural population (roughly 44 percent of the country's total population), it is imperative to move away from palliative measures and instead resolve the structural problems of the agricultural sector. This would require, among other things, increasing land access and credit, and addressing commercial policies that undermine the viability of small and medium scale production. Addressing commercial policies would entail, minimally, demanding more reciprocity from free trade treaties such as the Dominican Republic-Central America-United States Free Trade Agreement (CAFTA-DR; see Lyon, this volume) that pose unfair competition to Nicaraguan products while offering little in return; and dismantling food marketing cartels that monopolistically set food prices that benefit them at the expense of the country's producers.

Rather than address structural issues, Ortega has proposed to resolve the food crisis through initiatives aimed at increasing grain production or access to subsidized food products. The most ambitious of these initiatives is the Zero Hunger program, whereby 80,000 rural women are slated to receive a "productive food bonus," valued at $1,500.00 (U.S.), consisting of a package of seeds and farm animals, along with materials to house the animals. Beneficiaries must pay back 20 percent of the bonus value into a collective fund and organize themselves to administer the fund for loans to members.

The Zero Hunger program could make a difference in food consumption in the countryside and provide a basis for organization. Unfortunately, it has been inconsistently funded and the projected organization has not taken place. Moreover, according to Paul Kester (2010, 32), who evaluated the program in 2009, Zero Hunger is only minimally linked to other components of food security policy, which is itself lacking a coherent strategy that can align national and local actors. More recently, in 2011, the government charged the IDR (*Instituto de Desarrollo Rural* or Rural Development Institute) with inserting 10,000 of these beneficiaries into agroindustrial chains as a way to add value to their production and, ideally, effect structural transformation. Yet how the IDR can help the program live up to its promise is unclear as it and other institutions that support rural sector programs were subject to funding cuts in both 2009 and 2010 (Perez 2011, 22). While these cuts would be understandable given the country's economic crisis, they are less so considering the government's simultaneous diversion of vast amounts of ALBA funds to expand state businesses (some say Ortega's family's and allies' businesses as well) and shore up the party (Equipo Envio 2011).

From Revolution to "Democracy"

On the political front, after 1990 political discourse shifted from languages of revolution to languages of democracy. Unlike in other places that experienced revolutionary movements, especially El Salvador (Moodie 2010), the arrival of this kind of "democracy" after a decade of revolution was greeted not with hope but rather with dread by Sandinistas. This was due partly to FSLN rhetoric, which decried the coming of capitalism with the election of the neoliberal National Opposition Union (UNO). Yet already by then even FSLN discourse was being influenced by the globally circulating liberal democratic discourse. Thus, back in 1990, as it relinquished power after a decade of rule, the FSLN made a point of proclaiming that, in holding free and fair elections and peacefully transferring the government to the UNO, it was bringing democracy to Nicaragua. Other features of conventional definitions of liberal democracy also soon became part of Nicaraguan political discourse, including among some in the political left. For example, reiterating points that had been made for at least a decade, in a 2007 interview Jaime Wheelock pointed to clean elections, increased citizen participation, and a more even distribution of power among social, political, and military sectors as features of democracy that Nicaragua could boast. These achievements, he claimed—rightly, I believe—were a legacy of the Sandinista revolution.

If conventional notions of electoral democracy made their way into Nicaraguan political discourse of all political stripes, in the course of the 1990s the right wing adopted a more radical interpretation of democracy. This interpretation was based on a redefinition of ideas of democracy occurring globally at precisely the moment that the Sandinistas lost to the UNO coalition. In this new understanding, democracy's meaning, at least on "a global, *institutional* level," "had congealed into the powerful synthesis ... of democracy and 'free-' market economics" (Moodie 2010, 140). In the passage from revolution to neoliberalism, then, ideas of social justice, sharing, and popular participation, democratic ideas dear to the heart of Sandinistas in the 1980s, no longer held supremacy in Nicaraguan political imaginaries. Instead, they had to share the field of hegemonic political ideas with notions of democracy that equated it with individual participation in a "free" market.

Still, Nicaragua's revolutionary past has made a difference. Thus, researchers have noted how, in contrast to other Latin American countries where the transition to democratic rule demobilized the population, Nicaragua saw the growth of vibrant social movements, including feminist and lesbian and gay movements (Babb 2001) as well as movements among *maquiladora* (factory) workers (Mendez 2005), indigenous peoples (Field 1999), and campesinos (Edelman 1999). As Babb (2001, 21) writes of the feminist and gay and lesbian movements, so other movements were determined to "do more than rebuild the same society" by "calling upon collective memory" to "reinvent" themselves. Initiatives in citizen participation that began in the 1990s, now standard forms of democracy promotion across the continent (Paley 2001), were also matched by more progressive alternatives.[3] And even conventional programs of democracy promotion, as I explain below, have been subject to more radical interpretations and militant use by people shaped politically during the revolution.

With Ortega's return to power, Nicaraguans were introduced to yet another conception of democracy: "direct democracy," in the form of the Councils for Citizen Power (Consejos del Poder Ciudadano or CPCs). CPCs are government-initiated citizen organizations which, the president claimed upon coming to power, would allow ordinary Nicaraguans to govern through intervention in their communities and in national policy. These councils are organized hierarchically from the village or barrio level, up to the municipal, departmental, and national levels, where they are coordinated by the new Council for Communication and Citizenship, headed by presidential delegate and First Lady Rosario Murillo. From the municipal to the national levels, CPCs are coordinated by Sandinista political secretaries.

The CPC project—which observers dub Ortega's "signature project"—has elicited criticism from both the left and right. Critics charge that CPCs are sectarian and clientelistic organizations aimed at concentrating power in the FSLN and, more specifically—in classic caudillo (and, feminists add, patriarchal) fashion—in the president (or presidential couple). Early in Ortega's tenure, Tuleños and other campesino acquaintances saw the CPCs differently. Harking back to the mobilizations of the 1980s, many believed that Ortega's slogan "El Pueblo Presidente," could be realized through the CPCs. A few years later, however, most campesinos I know acknowledged that CPCs were not providing a space for true citizen participation. (Indeed, it appeared that Costa Ricans' grassroots patriotic committees, organized against CAFTA-DR during this same time, provided a clearer model for citizen participation [Raventós, this volume].) As my friend Rubén has been telling me since at least 2008, the government has failed to train CPC members to work with their communities in researching and formulating their needs. Tellingly, on the other hand, the FSLN has been keen to use the CPCs to build clientelistic relations by charging them with allocating goods (ranging from latrines to sheets of corrugated metal for roofs, to the productive bonus) and requiring that CPCs sign off on all petitions to the government. This use of the CPCs to garner support and maintain control is consistent with the government's refusal to engage with pre-existing departmental, municipal, and community organizations unaffiliated with the FSLN (Prado 2007). Indeed, the government's urge to centralize power has meant that even sectoral organizations such as the FENACOOP (a federation of 620 cooperatives) have often been excluded from participating in formulating policy that affects them directly (Cáceres 2008, 19).

The picture that has emerged from Nicaragua's political establishment under Daniel Ortega seems to combine worrisome trends that began during the revolution and whose results I have documented elsewhere (Montoya 2012) with a return to more classic caudillo politics. I am referring specifically to Sandinismo's tendency toward vanguardist verticalism and a masculinist centralization of power that borders on authoritarianism—made all the worse by an evident tolerance of widespread corruption. At the same time, it is important not to lose sight of the specificities of each situation. Thus, although what was prompting such practices and forms of leadership at the end of the first millennial decade is still a matter of debate, during the 1980s, the war played a determining role in pushing the Sandinistas toward verticalist leadership styles (and probably in allowing a measure of corruption). This was particularly true given the FSLN's background as a (hierarchical) political-military organization. Indeed, most research demonstrates a clear narrowing in Sandinista policy priorities and a shift in leadership style by about the middle of the decade of the 1980s, when the war and economic crisis were consuming most of the country's resources and energies. Yet researchers of the Sandinista revolution have adduced other, less conjunctural factors to explain the tendency to issue top-down directives that probably apply, at least partly, to what was occurring at that moment: Nicaragua's tendency toward authoritarian politics and its entrenched tradition of caudillismo (Vanden and Prevost 1993); the patriarchalism inherent in the state form itself (Rodríguez 1996); and an elitism that is seen as part and parcel of nation-state building and that even revolutionary Nicaragua could not avoid (Field 1999).

While these interpretations may be largely accurate, much is lost in such a monolithic portrayal of the Sandinista leadership and, indeed, the revolutionary project. For one, such portrayals discourage acknowledgement of the immense achievements of the revolution. Thus, as Wheelock observed when I interviewed him in August 2007, unlike the revolutionary movements in El Salvador and Guatemala, in Nicaragua, structural transformation *did* occur and had lasting, if still unresolved, effects—for campesinos, primordially in the form of receipt of land. More specifically, such portrayals have discouraged examination of Sandinista currents that offered alternative visions of revolution and the legacies these left behind.

So, what might be left of the revolution as it applies to Nicaragua's new conjuncture with the FSLN (albeit a very changed FSLN) back in power?

Campesino Activism, Leadership, and the Search for Useful Knowledge

Today in Nicaragua, political actors from different persuasions are attempting to create (at least) two conflicting projects. First, there is Ortega's call for "revolution," *poder ciudadano* or citizen power (a reference to the CPCs), and less commonly these days, "socialism." As I suggested above, this attempt appears to be failing due to the regime's unwillingness to offer spaces for true political participation and inability to do more than offer palliatives to the critical economic situation of the country's poor. To be fair, some of these challenges—especially economic challenges—are exceedingly difficult to overcome in the current global environment. Indeed, the celebrated leftist turn in Latin America has hardly produced the revolutionary results many expected. That some in this movement (former presidents Luiz Inacio "Lula" da Silva of Brazil and Michele Bachelet of Chile, for example) have been accepted by international observers as a "good left" suggests the extent to which their projects have come to accommodate neoliberal principles. And even the so-called "bad" or "populist left"—especially Venezuela's Hugo

Chávez, Bolivia's Evo Morales, and now, Daniel Ortega—have continued to work within largely capitalist programs and faced enormous challenges in either delivering benefits or making the production of these benefits economically sustainable. Still, Ortega's tight alliance with foreign and national big capital, unusual among leftist leaders, is troubling. It is particularly so since, so far at least, he has offered only assistentialist (rather than structural) solutions to the problems of the poor.

Former guerrilla commander Mónica Baltodano (2007; cited in Colussi 2008), now associated with the Alliance Sandinista Renovation Movement (Alianza MRS), a movement that holds anti-capitalist positions and comprises former FSLN militants, faults Ortega for wanting to have it both ways: pleasing the country's investors by providing the necessary assurances for the protection of private property and investment, while using Venezuelan funds to provide relief that will keep the poor at bay and build clientelistic relationships that will bolster his ability to remain in power indefinitely. Yet even this picture now seems optimistic. First, his policies of free education and health care in public hospitals, while positive, are limited given that taking advantage of these measures presumes a level of economic well-being that much of the population lacks (for example, for transportation to schools, or to buy school supplies or medicines, only the most basic of which are free). Second, because his social programs have so far not gone beyond assistentialism, they can only help so much and so many. Still, compared to the neglect experienced by the country's poor over sixteen years of neoliberal rule, Ortega's social programs did bolster his popularity and were likely instrumental in helping him get reelected with 62 percent of the vote in the recent November 2011 presidential election.

Given Ortega's clear intent to remain in power (he had a Sandinista-controlled Supreme Court render a constitutional prohibition against successive reelection inapplicable to his case), a theory of his administration's priorities appears plausible: Could it be that Ortega intends his alliance with big capital to serve to keep the country afloat until the FSLN's own businesses can take over and operate in the interests of the poor? Or is this interpretation too charitable? Even if this theory were correct, his marginalization of subordinate class organizations does not bode well for a democratic future that includes popular participation.

A second attempt at creating a national political project comes from the country's right wing. This sector offers as the solution to Nicaragua's problems the classic capitalist scenario pushed in the country (as elsewhere) over the past sixteen years that argues that individual hard work and entrepreneurship is the way to succeed. As noted, democracy, in this scenario, is equated with freedom to participate in the marketplace. Those who propound this scenario ask people to think of the present as a time beyond history (Fukuyama 1992), in particular in Nicaragua, a time in which revolutionary ideals no longer have a place. Yet my research on the current situation in Nicaragua suggests that the Sandinista revolution remains very much a key reference point for campesinos struggling today.

"Put a Muzzle on the Chainsaw"

Many scholars writing after the revolution have remarked on subordinate classes' capacity and willingness to organize as an important legacy of the Sandinista revolution. Less remarked upon has been the subjective basis that makes such a capacity and will to organize possible. In a larger project on which this article is partly based (Montoya 2012), I argue that change and revolutionary success must be measured not only in terms of large structural transformations, but also in more feminine—and feminist—terms, such as changes in campesino men and women's subjectivities. I claim that campesino (and popular classes') subjectivities indeed changed in empowering ways during the revolution. I support this claim by showing that the revolution produced more than state subjects, whether docile or agentive. Through its emphasis on radical pedagogies in the broader context of popular organization and mass mobilization, the revolution also produced ideas of sociability and sharing beyond one's family and community; a language for articulating a sense of historical agency; and a basis for a deeper understanding of class consciousness and organizing, and of national projects. The revolution also began the process—even if as an unintended consequence—of instilling a critical understanding of gender relations, even as this understanding has been resisted by men. Finally, although revolutionary leaders did not fulfill their promise to use dialogue between state and people to construct a new society, impulses toward dialogical interactions permeated much of revolutionary process. For example, the state's widespread use of popular education methodologies taught many people—as it did Tuleños—how to use a set of critical, democratic methodologies for interrogating their own voice and their conditions of existence as a means to engage in self transformation and transformation of the world. In a September 2000 interview, ten years after neoliberal governments took power, the Tuleño community leader Justino spoke with me about the changes he had undergone during the revolutionary decade. Infused with the language of popular education, his words suggest the subjective basis for the increasingly cosmopolitan figure of Nicaraguan subordinate actors at present:

> You know, you have been in completely developed countries, with advanced technology, and I tell you, Charo, put a muzzle on this chainsaw because I

have to leave, and you will say, what is this muzzle that I have to put on it? ... so you see, [you know] one part of the world, and I know another, then we are equal, [but] we are worth more when we have the capacity to listen to each other and learn, me from you and you from me.

Figure 1.2. Sandinista in Niquinohomo, birthplace of Augusto C. Sandino, pays homage to the national hero.

Justino's words, which resonate widely in El Tule and Nicaragua, are significant in a way that cannot be overstated and is hard to convey to those who have never spent time among campesinos; namely, the appropriation by campesinos of the notion that they have something to offer those with more formal education and power. As he pointed out in that same 2000 interview, before the revolution they literally would have been unable to talk to "someone like you." In a similar vein, Lorraine Bayard de Volo (2001, 213), who worked in Matagalpa with the group Mothers of Heroes and Martyrs notes, "the most common way members expressed empowerment was in terms of voice—learning to communicate, to speak to strangers, and to express themselves." Based on his work with indigenous artisans in Masaya, anthropologist Les Field (1999) also speaks to this effect of the revolution when he argues that Sandinismo created the conditions for the emergence of subordinate and organic intellectuals. These intellectuals are today participating in defining and advancing subordinate demands in the broader political arena, often in ways that challenge Sandinista and elite constructions of national, class, gender, and ethnic identity.

And it is not only activists and political leaders who have been formed by this (state) effect. Listen, for example, to the words of a Tuleño elder in a November 1992 interview. I had asked him what he had liked about the revolution:

> We have met people that we had never met nor heard their conversations, you see, here people have come that we don't understand what we are going to speak about, and they explain what their ideals are, what that one wants, that one speaks, the other [the campesino] is listening and saying he wants such and such, the other *speaks* about such and such a thing, SPEAKS ... as I tell you, other people visit us, they explain how other countries are, how we are, they come here and ask us how we are doing, what results we are having—they not only bring, they [also] take.

Justino's story about learning how to move in urban contexts during the Sandinista period, told to me in September 2000, offers a compelling glimpse into the many facets that are brought into play in this process of subject formation:

> One of the advantages I had, Charo Montoya, is that I stuck behind Alan Bolt [a Sandinista political activist], and my first outings to Managua were with Alan Bolt, to go see soy projects, how one made milk—those processes of the soy bean, that's why he was taking me, so that I would learn. But I was learning even how to open a door, that the doors [in Managua] were not like the doors in El Tule, that you had to pull back a little thing, or push the door frontwards. Because I'm very sure that whoever doesn't go out, whoever doesn't have clashes with other cultures, will never get ahead.

Here Justino makes clear how campesinos need to do more than learn "important" knowledge to succeed in a world increasingly dominated by urban (global) culture. In his view, socializing such apparently insignificant knowledge as learning to open "modern" doors was sufficiently important that when he was elected as mayor of Belén (1996–2000), he changed the old wood latch door in the municipal seat office to glass doors such as those found in Managua offices.

Such impulse toward cosmopolitanism—a legacy of the revolution that has dovetailed with the demands of globalization in the neoliberal era—has led campesino activists to seek knowledge that can be useful in their political struggles, in dialogue with "outsider" others. As Edelman (1998) has noted for Central American campesinos and their organizations, they increasingly depend on crafting alliances with foreign and middle-class professionals (often working in nongovernmental organizations [NGOs]) that can show them how to access information and sources of power not easily found in the "traditional" campesino world. Some NGOs associated with the more progressive efforts in citizen participation have also started helping communities build their capacity to network, negotiate their interests, and self-manage—what is called *autogestión* (self-management)—usually in the context of government and other bureaucracies. Along with an emphasis on taking ownership over one's rights as citizens, the process of autogestión is important in that it contributes to a stance that is radically assertive and centers on concrete proposals for alternative development at a time when protests and violence are seen by many as counterproductive. In challenging themselves to learn how to navigate the complex politics of knowledge of a globalized world, Central American campesinos are "aim[ing] to replace the image of atavistic rustics with that of peasants as politically savvy, dignified, and efficient small producers" (Edelman 1998, 54).

Documenting Disillusionment: *Sálvese Quien Pueda*

Still, as Silber (2010) reminds us in her work among former guerrillas in El Salvador, we must not shy away from documenting the disillusionment and frustration that often accompanies these efforts. First, although obtaining funds for productive projects is of utmost importance to campesinos, the fact remains that they have become dependent on foreign funds for anything beyond bare survival. Second, while the emphasis on networking and autogestión is important, it prepares campesinos to access, but not increase, resources available to their social sector. In short, autogestión has not augmented campesino control over the economic and political parameters that frame their efforts. Thus, the vast majority of campesino men and women are barely getting by.

In evaluating campesino predicaments, it is also important not to engage in either the "ethnographic refusal" (Ortner 1995) or leftist romanticism that encourage us to "sanitize"—in Bourgois's (2001) words—real problems among those (subordinate) actors anthropologists tend to champion. This means, for example, recognizing that a key problem among campesinos (and other social sectors) in the *sálvese quien pueda* (roughly, sink or swim) world of neoliberalism is the question of competition and political fragmentation. These problems were never truly superseded under Sandinismo. With neoliberalism, they came out full blown. Indeed, in El Tule, such problems became apparent as early as 1993. In May of that year, Justino's brother Alberto filed a legal claim against two nephews for cattle theft, breaking the rule among campesinos, one born of their historic distrust of the state, that community problems must be addressed outside government purview. Alberto's action created a split in the family that prompted one sibling to move with her whole family from the village. This event points to underlying tensions within the family that had been caused by disputes over cooperative resources in preceding years and had only been contained by the unifying pressures of the FSLN. As the neoliberal period wore on, such tensions became even more difficult to contain. Today, these same cattle-rustlers continue to operate, causing losses to even their own family members.

In an early draft of this article I asked myself if the new FSLN government would be able to set countervailing tendencies in motion. One policy aimed in that direction: the promotion of *asociatividad* (collective organization). This effort presumably takes the lessons of the 1980s into account in promoting various forms of producer and marketing cooperatives. Significantly, the language used to promote such efforts once again deploys the rhetoric of unity. Yet it does so within a discursive framework that champions competition in the marketplace. Moreover, the political and ethical "aura"—including emotional and psychic tone—that could promote asociatividad as a solidary activity rather than a pragmatic choice in a context that offers few alternatives, does not exist. As Moodie (this volume) argues for El Salvador, so in neoliberal Nicaragua, conjuring up the ideal of a solidary community—a "community of care"—is exceedingly difficult. Indeed, as I found in my recent research, quite the opposite is happening. Thus, tendencies that replicate the dissolution of a revolutionary ethos among FSLN leadership at all levels have made a comeback among campesinos in El Tule and its surrounding region in familiar rural forms: *caciquismo* (boss politics), familialism, and exclusion of women from membership in organizations, leadership positions, and the benefits of resources obtained from either the state or NGOs (Montoya, n.d.). This is not to suggest that they were ever superseded. But it is to point out how in the 1980s, the inspired political-ideological context made unsolidary and undemocratic actions problematic for Tuleños—something they thought about and "worked on"—in a way that I do not see today.

Post-insurgent Individuality among Sandinistas

A political context that can encourage such practices may be elusive, but it is important to take note of real efforts that go against the tide, toward more democratic forms of activism and leadership. As Binford (this volume) has found in Northern Morazán, El Salvador, in Nicaragua, too, former militants who no longer have recourse to collective projects to sustain their revolutionary ideals nonetheless deploy a "post-insurgent individuality" to create projects that articulate aspects of the neoliberal present but continue to reference the class-based project of the recent revolutionary past. My friend Cecilio, for example, to this day espouses and acts (sometimes with a rather naïve trust in the FSLN and its militants) in ways that are consistent with his revolutionary ideals, while adopting aspects of languages and practices of democracy that match these ideals. In doing so, he has often had to confront fellow party members and risk enmities for the sake of principle. In July 2007, for example, he was asked by producers in the region to run for the post of municipal president of an organization that Ortega promised would once again serve to promote producer interests. This was not the first time producers asked Cecilio to take a political post representing campesinos. However, he deferred to party leaders, who consistently dissuaded him from advancing his candidacy. Tired of seeing people take leadership positions only to advance their own interests, this time he decided to run. The result was that he was cheated from the post through a political maneuver by a powerful campesino leader allied with the FSLN's municipal political secretary and other municipal officials.

Despite these rebuffs, and despite receiving very little material or moral rewards for his efforts, he remains committed to the original principles of the revolution—in particular, in his case, to advancing the cause of social justice for campesinos, regardless of political affiliation. As he sees it, this means remaining committed to the FSLN, even as he works to promote changes in the party. In the past years, he has spent countless hours in party-related work. In addition to conventional tasks such as registering potential voters, he has taken the initiative to organize events that help to promote a more solidary ethos—for example, a meeting where local and municipal FSLN leaders spoke to campesino youth about the history and ideals of the revolution. He has also made a point of attending every municipal meeting where the mayor meets with his constituency to decide how municipal monies will be spent. This form of citizen participation, modeled on Porto Alegre's celebrated Participatory Budget (Baiocchi 2005), is a direct outgrowth of citizen participation initiatives of the 1990s. Yet, given the spirit of the initiative, it could just as well be traced to the revolution's efforts toward popular participation. Finally, Cecilio's efforts to transform the FSLN has meant struggling to help to rid the party of self-serving officials. As part of this effort, in 2007 he began attending a course on transparency offered by an NGO that aimed to teach citizens their rights and prepare them to detect and challenge official corruption. Furious upon learning about this, the Sandinista mayor and municipal political secretary demanded that he stop attending. When I asked what he planned to do, he vowed to remain in the course as well as in the Sandinista Front so as to "cleanse it from within." As he stated, "I am loyal to the party, because they gave us the land. But not to the people [that are in it]."

Cecilio is a particularly dedicated leader. Yet day by day during my recent fieldwork on rural transformations under the new FSLN (July 2007–March 2010), I met other leaders who were creatively seeking to address the plight of campesinos. It is not the same with female campesino leaders, however, who are decidedly in the minority. What I have found, instead, is an interest in being organized for economic benefits—but mainly among women who participated actively in revolutionary organizations. Whether the Ortega administration can drum up interest among newer generations of women remains to be seen and depends partly on how large a fund he dedicates to women's projects. In the meantime, we can only hope that seasoned campesino women activists will continue to recuperate insights and lessons from the revolution that can serve all women in their struggle for a better life.

Based on work with Costa Rican and transnational peasant movements, Marc Edelman (1999, ix) argues, "Even when popular organizations 'fail' or fade away, their members' 'social energy' … manifests itself in new forms in future efforts for change." I believe I am seeing this recuperation of energy today, in Cecilio, other campesino leaders, and even in those who are resorting to a politics of caciquismo. What all these people have in common is a commitment to creating political projects of their own making. This commitment, and their belief in their capacity to do so is perhaps the most lasting legacy of the Sandinista revolution.

Notes

1. Although some business ventures of high-level FSLN members are well known (Gutiérrez 2010), there is no systematic study on this topic.
2. For example, to garner votes through the support of the powerful Cardinal Miguel Obando y Bravo, Ortega voted against therapeutic abortion, even in cases of rape or threat of death.
3. For example, the Coordinadora Civil, a coordinating instance for civil society organizations, aims to construct an "active citizenship" and proposes policies for equitable, sustainable development that prioritize society's poorest sectors.

2 The Violence of Cold War Polarities and the Fostering of Hope

The 2009 Elections in Postwar El Salvador

*Ainhoa Montoya**

Many Salvadorans do not vote. Abstention has been high since the late 1980s, with only the 1994 elections surpassing a 50 percent turnout (Artiga-González 2004). After the 1994 elections, popularly known as the "elections of the century" for inaugurating El Salvador's democracy (Cruz 1998), voter turnout fell once again. This decreasing turnout has been interpreted as a symptom of disillusionment with the postwar era and lack of confidence in prospects for peace (Cruz 1998; 2001). The Chapultepec Peace Accords, and the "transition" that followed, focused on political and institutional reforms, neglecting the problems of economic inequality and human rights at the root of the civil war. Postwar privatization of public utilities such as health care and water, increasing unemployment, and rising inflation have only heightened economic insecurity and dependence on migrant remittances. Additionally, homicides and crime, which escalated after the war ended, have stabilized at levels so high that El Salvador ranks among the most violent countries in Latin America (Ramos 2000).

Despite Salvadorans' "democratic disenchantment" (Moodie 2010, 145; and this volume) and skepticism about the potential of elections to effect change, turnout at both the 2004 and 2009 presidential elections virtually doubled from that of previous years (IDHUCA 2004, 23; TSE 2009). Why did Salvadorans vote in the 2009 elections, and participate in campaigns and other related events? This chapter underlines the relevance of wartime rhetoric and symbols to understand Salvadoran voting in 2009. More than other arenas of Salvadoran political life, electoral politics has recreated the divisions of the past, thereby reintroducing unresolved wartime frictions into public discourse.

The 2009 electoral campaign, I argue, allowed Salvadorans to engage—publicly and in a relatively controlled manner—in wartime conflicts with which many of them had not come to terms. Recriminations and hostility between the governing right-wing Nationalist Republican Alliance (ARENA) and the former guerrilla organization Farabundo Martí National Liberation Front (FMLN) have characterized the postwar elections since 1994 (Ramos 1998), but ARENA's mobilization of mass media propaganda to enact a politics of fear in 2004 and 2009 arguably made frictions all the more palpable. The question, then, is what moved so many Salvadorans to vote for the FMLN in the 2009 elections given ARENA's politics of fear? The answer can be found in the campaign of Mauricio Funes, the 2009 FMLN presidential candidate. Funes attempted to transcend a Cold War divide re-enacted by ARENA and FMLN. He addressed pressing social and economic problems, appealing to both the left and the right.

Fieldwork in Santiago Nonualco before, during, and after the presidential elections held on 15 March 2009 provided insights into how Salvadorans perceived and experienced this postwar election. Santiago is a *municipio* (municipality) in the south-central La Paz Department. The population of this rural area practices subsistence agriculture and works in commerce or in the *maquila* factories in the region's offshore El Pedregal zone. Though not considered a former war zone, Santiago nonetheless reflects the nation's historical wartime divisions. During the electoral campaign, I attended meetings and rallies of all political parties, held informal conversations with their leaders and constituents, and participated as an international observer on Election Day. Given the heightened animosities characterizing this election, informal conversations about electoral politics cropped up constantly in mundane situations and among people not formally involved in the campaigns.

To some degree, Santiago can be seen as a microcosm of the polarized conflict that persisted in the country during the 2009 presidential elections. Interestingly, since 2000, Santiago has been governed by the National Conciliation Party (PCN), once the dominant military party but now a minority party that has served chiefly as a supporter of ARENA in the Legislative Assembly.[1] The differences in how people cast their votes in municipal and presidential elections are symptomatic of a disjuncture between the citizenship practices that concern the polity of the municipio and those of the nation (see Stack 2003). In other words, while haunting Cold War imageries and memories may patently impact national citizenship, their influence is more limited during the municipal elections of a place like Santiago, where a third party governs. Although the PCN's presence does yield a difference between municipal and presidential elections, the study of municipal elections is beyond the scope of this chapter.

In the Absence of a Public Discussion

The 1992 Chapultepec Peace Accords that marked the end of El Salvador's twelve-year war included the creation of a Truth Commission to investigate and point to those responsible for wartime human rights violations.[2] Its 1993 report included basic information on certain high-profile cases, such as the

El Mozote massacre and Archbishop Romero's assassination (United Nations 1993). It asserted that in order for Salvadorans to reconcile, further investigations on human rights violations were required—although the report was not explicit about how this should be done. These investigations would in turn provide the grounds for moral reparation and adequate material compensation.

Immediately after the commission's recommendations were put forward, El Salvador's ARENA government, headed by President Alfredo Cristiani, passed the 1993 Amnesty Law that precluded accountability for war crimes. Since then, consistent efforts to bring the past back into the public domain have been rare and limited to the work by El Salvador's human rights organizations (though see Binford, this volume, which discusses efforts to incorporate historical memory of the war into tourism and museums in the northeastern department of Morazán). The country's two major political parties, ARENA and FMLN, which represent the war's opposing sides, have not facilitated a public discussion that might provide a forum for reconciliation. Only during electoral periods have ARENA and FMLN publicly addressed the war's causes. Their explanations, however, have been stereotypical and caricatured.

Not only has the absence of a public discussion about the civil war precluded retributive and restorative justice, but some would argue that it has also allowed the government to avoid tackling the socioeconomic problems at the root of the war. The Peace Accords focused on demilitarization. They only secondarily addressed economic reform. Indeed, as the Peace Accords explicitly assert, "The general philosophy or orientation of the Government's economic policy, which FMLN does not necessarily share, is not covered by this Agreement" (United Nations 1992, 31). In emphasizing the dissolution of military rule, the accords implicitly defined democracy narrowly. In short, the democracy laid out by the Peace Accords was procedural, defined chiefly by civil and political citizenship entitlements. The ARENA governments adopted a neoliberal agenda, along with the rest of Central America at the cusp of the new millennium, as many chapters in this volume demonstrate; these parallel transformations that blended political and economic freedoms yielded a "free-market democracy" (see Moodie 2010, 41–45; Binford, this volume).

My focus in this chapter is on what an election can tell us about aspects of Salvadoran politics that are often invisible in everyday life (much as Raventós's account of the Costa Rican referendum in this volume reveals about that country's politics). In El Salvador, memories and experiences of the war usually delineate basic party constituencies in such a way that postwar elections represent expressions of historical divisions and conflicts that do not manifest in other circumstances (see R. Montoya, this volume, for an account of how symbolic uses of recent history have mobilized Sandinista performance in Nicaragua). Even so, the victory of the FMLN in the 2009 presidential elections has to be explained. Mauricio Funes, the FMLN candidate, was able to temper the wartime divide while addressing long overlooked socioeconomic problems of ordinary people.

Postwar Elections as War

Both FMLN and ARENA have basic constituencies rooted in wartime and maintained through the postwar reproduction of a historical divide. In Santiago, in the 2009 elections, party allegiances in a *cantón* (territory within a municipal unit) were predicated upon war experiences and family ties. The central barrios and northern cantón Las Ánimas, where the population was repressed during the war, massively supported the FMLN. The remaining northern cantones, where people had joined paramilitary groups, clearly supported ARENA. Party allegiance echoed throughout the landscape with murals, flags, and candidate portraits. Housefronts, entrance doors, lampposts, the pavement, and even trees were decorated either in the red of the FMLN or the blue-white-red of ARENA. Just as Salvadorans supported FMLN or ARENA on the basis of their wartime experiences, the parties' leaderships devised electoral strategies that resonated with war tactics. These include a fixation with territorial control; death threats, confrontations and physical aggressions perpetrated on the basis of party allegiances; secrecy and rumor about spies; and a denial of neutrality, ambiguity, and middle positions.

Territory was critical in all parties' strategizing. Both FMLN and ARENA were structured locally around a hierarchical leadership that was decentralized via the establishment of support groups or leaders in barrios and cantones. This structure already existed in areas where the parties enjoyed large basic constituencies but had to be created anew for the 2009 elections in others. While the FMLN sought to found "base committees" in each sector, ARENA identified specific leaders supportive of its party who would manage to attract other residents. In both party's meetings, discussions revolved around the barrios and cantones that each party controlled, where FMLN base committees or ARENA leaders were located, and what strategies should be devised vis-à-vis those in control of the opposing party. The dispute over territory became evident in the competition between parties to cover streets, houses, and roads with their colors; often one party's contingent painted and plastered a street or road during the day, only to have members of the opposing party paint or plaster over their work that night. In previous elections, FMLN and ARENA loyalists had clashed in the same way (*La Prensa Gráfica* 1999).[3]

Figure 2.1. Rally for ARENA Election, 2009, Ainhoa Montoya

Physical aggression was not absent during 2009. Several FMLN members told me that as they were trying to found a base committee for the first time in the northern cantón San Antonio Arriba in September 2007, three hooded men attacked their leader. Other neighbors who showed an interest in the FMLN received death threats. FMLN members were confident that these were ARENA attacks. One explained, "The two San Antonios, Arriba and Abajo, and Santa Cruz Loma are all *areneros* (ARENA loyalists), so it is dangerous for us to set foot there dressed in our red T-shirts. Until 2007, the FMLN leadership had not tried to visit these cantones during the electoral campaigns. It was there that the Comandos Chencho Beltrán (death squads) were active during the war." [4]

During FMLN meetings, rumors constantly circulated about the persecution or assassination of party members. At one such gathering, a police officer who had befriended members of the local FMLN leadership told them that news had arrived at his sub-delegation about cars and taxis that had been seen driving around the department of La Libertad without license plates and whose drivers had been hired to assassinate FMLN members. He provided details of the colors and designs of the reported vehicles so that people could watch out for themselves. In the face of this kind of threat, bolstered by the feelings of insecurity stemming from the homicidal violence that makes the daily news in postwar El Salvador, FMLN members either walked home in groups after meetings or, more often, dropped each other off in pick-up trucks. Several FMLN loyalists confessed to me their fear of participating in political activity during elections.

Secrecy also characterized both the 2009 electoral campaign and wartime. Both ARENA and FMLN leaders were suspicious of people they did not know or trust who attended meetings. They became fixated on the possibility that the opposing party was infiltrating their meetings, or that someone from within their own leadership was disclosing information about electoral strategies. This distrust was not groundless, since all parties gathered intelligence, partly on the basis of rumor but also based on the information provided by the members sent to the meetings of the opposing party. Even with their own relatives, party loyalists tended to remain secretive about electoral strategies; the same occurred during the war, when, as some women told me, their own husbands would not share information concerning political and military activity.

No one conceived of neutrality as a possibility. Santiagueños often knew their neighbors' and relatives' allegiances or thought they could guess them. Even I was sometimes viewed with suspicion. The ARENA leadership assumed that I sided with the FMLN because my host family supported this party. The family's house was decorated with a poster of Funes and an FMLN flag, visible from the street, hung from a tall mango tree in the backyard. Several times I was publicly accused in ARENA meetings of having been sent by the Venezuelan and Cuban governments in order to gather information. Nor was I free from suspicion from the FMLN leadership, given my scrupulous silence about what I had heard at ARENA meetings. I thus had to repeatedly justify why I was interested in the elections. I was as open as possible about my attendance at the public meetings of all parties, and I avoided leadership meetings to which I had been invited so as not to raise suspicions.

On more than one occasion I was chided by friends who supported the FMLN for interacting with a member of an ARENA-affiliated family. This happened when I was returning from an event at the Jesuit Central American University (UCA) in San Salvador in a microbus crammed with university students. I spent the journey chatting with two 20-year-old girls who had seen me in Santiago and were curious about what I was doing there, since that municipio is rarely visited by foreigners. A friend accompanying me, an FMLN loyalist, remained silent during the journey. When we got off in Santiago, he explained the two girls were from ARENA families and admonished me for having told them details about myself.

An examination of political parties' strategizing during the 2009 electoral campaigns shows not only the continuing salience of wartime divisions, but also the extent to which FMLN and ARENA were apparently mirror images of one another. Looking solely at the symbolic and performative elements of electoral competition, one could infer that El Salvador's postwar elections had become a struggle unto themselves, in which both sides mimicked the other while the motivation at the root of conflict had dissipated. During the war, both ARENA and FMLN were arguably the products of a fusion of political and military elements. The FMLN structured itself as an army yet originated in mass political organizations. ARENA publicly presented itself as being protected by its own army (Martín-Baró 1991, 298). In addition, ARENA has been linked to wartime death squads (United Nations 1993, 184-86). Obviously the two parties differed radically in ideology. Tracing the genealogy and ideological underpinnings of the two main political parties in the country's postwar era can thus shed light on the frictions between their basic constituencies.

The FMLN, born in 1980 as a Marxist-Leninist guerrilla organization, united the five main revolutionary political-military groups of the 1970s in an effort to wage a "final offensive" against the Salvadoran state in 1981 that turned out to be merely one of the events precipitating the country's twelve-year civil war. The FMLN converted to a legal political party with the 1992 Peace Accords. Its supporters largely comprise ex-guerrillas as well as members of social movements and popular organizations. Since its transformation, the FMLN has become ARENA's main electoral rival.

ARENA was founded in 1981 and gained the presidency in 1989. A nationalist, anti-communist and pro-capitalist party, ARENA responded to the interests of the fraction of the elite dissatisfied with the reformist Christian Democratic Party (PDC)-led junta erected in 1979, especially its implementation of agrarian reform (Martín-Baró 1991). After the war, it expanded its original agro-financial constituency into rural areas where paramilitary groups had been active or where it successfully developed patron-client relationships. While ARENA has promoted neoliberal economic measures conducive to consolidating accumulation by the country's elite, the FMLN, as stated in its charter, originally aimed to transform the status quo radically via the establishment of a socialist state (see FMLN 2006). In practice, however, internecine divisions between orthodox and reformist wings have dissipated the party's goals.

Given the war re-enactment and attendant emotions that so pervaded the 2009 elections, Salvadorans' party loyalties and electoral participation were chiefly motivated by their war positionality and experience. During 2009, many young people participated in both parties' campaigns in Santiago. In general, they joined the parties to which their elder kin were loyal. They readily embraced the party symbols and outward signs. Still, ideologies were relevant, though reformulated to the present-day conjuncture. FMLN leaders have continued to issue systemic and class-based explanations for Salvadorans' economic predicaments. Yet, in their 2009 program, both local and national FMLN leadership conspicuously avoided addressing questions of socialism, strategically distancing the party from its guerrilla face. By contrast, ARENA leaders disseminated a fierce anti-communism, predicated upon the alleged risk that the FMLN would establish a totalitarian regime like those of Venezuela, Nicaragua, and Cuba.

The Politics of Fear and Memory: The Wartime Divide Updated

A "campaign of fear" orchestrated by ARENA and waged via mass media characterized the 2004 presidential elections (García Dueñas 2006; Wolf 2009, 447–54). This campaign was rooted in two threatening scenarios that ARENA claimed would materialize if the FMLN won: first, the consolidation of a communist regime, and, second, the enactment by the United States government of a policy prohibiting Salvadorans in the United States from sending remittances to El Salvador (García Dueñas 2006). The invoking of a communist threat was hardly new; this strategy had been widely deployed by the Salvadoran governments during the pre-war and war years—when El Salvador became a Cold War battleground—to legitimize counterinsurgency violence that often targeted civilians (see Binford 1996). Recourse to "the communist threat" can be traced all the way back to El Salvador's 1932 peasant rebellion, which the government blamed on the Salvadoran Communist Party (PCS), and the army's ensuing repression of 10,000 peasants (Alvarenga 2006; Anderson 1971; Gould and Lauria-Santiago 2008; López Bernal 2007). In the 2004 elections the communist threat was updated to coincide with ordinary Salvadorans' present-day concerns, such as remittances, while maintaining long-lived imageries. This conflation of calculative and affective elements in a politics of fear also characterized the 2009 presidential elections.

ARENA leaders' use of the term "communism" is vague enough to encompass anyone and anything that threatens the country's status quo and elite interests (Martín-Baró 1991, 296). During the 2004 and 2009 campaigns, ARENA's anti-communist rhetoric insinuated that the FMLN sought to establish a totalitarian and military state in the event of a victory in the presidential elections. The effectiveness of this rhetoric on the rural population was evident in the visits that I paid with FMLN constituents to the cantones in Santiago during the 2009 electoral campaign. Especially where residents had participated in paramilitary groups during the war, people were often quite hostile to visitors from the former guerrilla party. A barefoot woman in her 70s who received the FMLN leaders at the entrance of her adobe house in San Antonio Abajo did not want to hear their explanations about their party's electoral program. She declared emphatically that she knew what the FMLN would do if they won:

> I have heard that we will be given a single dress and a single pair of shoes. And it doesn't matter if they are not our size because we won't be given any more of them. I am poor but I do have a few dresses. I also have my own house, and I know that I will have to share it with another family if they win. I also know what they intend to do with the old people, just because we are no longer able to work like the young people. And the coupons—we will be rationed and given weapons as during the war. What can you expect of the people who destroyed the country during the war?

This woman's statement exemplifies how the symbolic and discursive strategies of ARENA leaders percolated through to ordinary Salvadorans and alienated them from the FMLN.

The hostility against FMLN constituents and manifest fear of communism prevalent in areas of northern Santiago stemmed partly from ARENA's deployment of Cold War rhetoric at public meetings during the campaign. ARENA's public meetings, held Sundays, were attended mainly by men and women in their fifties and sixties, most of them peasants. Men wearing peasant hats and women in aprons predominated, their garb indicative of their humble origins. Every meeting began with ARENA's anthem, which everyone had to sing with his or her right fist raised so as to avoid accusations of being an FMLN spy or showing insufficient enthusiasm. The anthem expresses hostility against FMLN members: *El Salvador será la tumba donde los rojos terminarán* (El Salvador will be the grave where the reds [FMLN] will end). Speeches by ARENA leaders then would describe how FMLN guerrillas had destroyed the country through attacks on pylons, bridges, and other infrastructure.

These speeches also portrayed the FMLN as a present-day and future threat given the party's alleged alignment with Hugo Chávez and Fidel Castro. As a local ARENA leader said at a weekly meeting:

> Why is communism so interested in El Salvador? Because this is a country of development. ARENA supports agriculture, the church, sports … ARENA is the party of peace, freedom and progress. We live in a democracy but let's make good use of this democracy. Let's give our children a free country like the one we have enjoyed. If we do not defend ourselves, we might be in great *danger*. The FMLN will hand over the country to Chávez. We should not make the same mistake as the Nicaraguans, who are now *slaves* of Venezuela and Cuba. These elections have to make history. We need to fight for a fifth ARENA government that allows for a perpetuation of freedom and democracy. You are the soldiers who must defend peace against the *threat* of international communism, which is the origin of the current economic crisis. ARENA promotes freedom, economic development, and

> foreign investment. The FMLN only wants *war*. The change proclaimed by the FMLN is one of *war* and communism. (emphasis added)

ARENA's electoral strategy hinged upon a Manichaean representation of postwar political life in which the FMLN epitomized threat, destruction, totalitarianism, economic collapse, and violence. By contrast, ARENA was depicted as righteous, involved in the reconstruction of postwar El Salvador, and a guarantor of freedom and democracy. Democracy, in the rhetoric of ARENA leaders, is the antithesis of communism; it allows the individual freedom to hold private property and undertake profit-driven economic activity.

In ARENA's depiction, political change was equivalent to an ostensible threat to all postwar achievements: democracy, freedom, and private property. For instance, in February 2009, following the closure of several maquilas in El Pedregal and the consequent loss of thousands of jobs, rumors spread that these changes had occurred in response to the prospect of an FMLN president. Indeed, during the electoral campaign, the threat of disinvestment in the event of an FMLN victory was consistently raised. ARENA leaders reminded Santiagueños that even if they were poor, the fact that they owned anything at all was a result of their own party's governance. According to ARENA rhetoric, their possessions might well be taken away by a communist FMLN government. Violence was thus legitimized and encouraged in the event of an FMLN victory.

This rhetoric cannot be considered a mere strategic ploy. On 26 October 2008, when I met with the fifteen men and one woman of the local ARENA leadership in Santiago to explain my interest in attending their meetings, some seemed genuinely concerned about the prospect of an FMLN victory. After I had described the details of my research and addressed their concerns, a man in his late 30s told me: "Everything you have explained to us seems reasonable to me, but you have to understand that our worries are not unfounded. Our country is under the threat of communism, so we cannot trust anyone right now."

The major mass media, mostly pro-ARENA, have played a fundamental role in drawing attention to the threat allegedly posed by the FMLN to the Salvadoran nation and eliciting fear. In the 2009 campaign, on El Salvador's television channels 2, 4, and 6 (all owned by the same ARENA-linked media mogul, Boris Esersky), daily advertisements asserted both the violent nature of the FMLN and the alliance between FMLN presidential candidate Mauricio Funes and the Venezuelan government—an alliance so strong that the country would be handed over to Hugo Chávez in the event of an FMLN victory. One of these TV ads suggested the following:

> Mauricio Funes is a presidential candidate backed by the FMLN, a communist party and an ally of Hugo Chávez. Chávez is the number one *enemy* of the United States. The United States is an ally of El Salvador. Millions of

> Salvadorans live there, send their remittances and thousands have benefited from the TPS.[5] Therefore, if Funes and the FMLN take office we will be subjected to Chávez. Your remittances and the TPS are in ***danger***. In ***danger*** are your freedom, your job, and prices will truly rise sky high. Risky? It is more than that. Funes and the FMLN are a ***danger*** for your pocketbook and a ***real danger*** for El Salvador. (emphasis added)

These advertisements were either anonymous or signed by the organization Fuerza Solidaria, heretofore unknown in El Salvador, which originated in Venezuela to delegitimize Chávez's government. Associations were made in these ads between the FMLN and the Venezuelan, Cuban, and Nicaraguan governments and even Islamist terrorism.[6]

On 13 December 2008 the newspaper *La Prensa Gráfica* reported that the Salvadoran Ministry of Defense was investigating the existence of armed groups in different parts of the country, mostly FMLN strongholds (2008). Concrete details were offered to lend credibility to the charges: "At the coordinates 13°59'07.7" North and 89°13'34.76" West is an area of military training, northeast of the Cinotepeque mountain, in the jurisdiction of El Paisnal, a zone under territorial and military control by the Popular Liberation Forces (FPL) during the war" (*La Prensa Gráfica* 2008a). This news precipitated a widespread discussion in the country's mass media about the ties between these alleged armed groups and the FMLN. Photos of a commemoration held annually on 12 and 13 December in the municipio El Paisnal, in the San Salvador department, to pay homage to the deceased guerrilla Commander Dimas Rodríguez, were published by the media. In this commemoration ex-guerrillas simulated a military march dressed in uniform and carrying plastic or defunct rifles. The media and ARENA used the presence of FMLN members in the photos of this military march simulacrum as evidence that FMLN was arming and training new guerrilla groups.

"The FBI and Interpol could help us with the technical and scientific investigation." These were the words of the country's attorney general regarding the issue of armed groups. "We need to have scientific verification that the photographs are authentic in order to sustain a potential accusation" (*El Diario de Hoy* 2008). The insistence on the scientific nature of the investigation seemed to aim at depoliticizing the issue in the eyes of the Salvadoran public. According to the right-wing media, the investigation simply sought to verify the existence of organizations receiving paramilitary training with the goal of destabilizing the state. Although the ARENA government suggested that the gravity of the issue was such that it had to be reported to international organizations, after a few days of front-page coverage the issue was dropped (*La Prensa Gráfica* 2008b).

In Santiago, incidents in the municipio were interpreted in the light of this news. A relative of my host family recounted to me a rumor that had spread throughout the cantón San Sebastián Abajo, where she lived. According to the rumor, guerrillas might well have been training in Santiago's mountainous cantones since residents had seen armed men not from the area. The mass media's coverage of the FMLN had thus managed to sow seeds of doubt about the nature of this party's political project.

In 2004 and 2009, ARENA resorted to a politics of fear and memory to counter its eroding hegemony—erosion rooted in the unfulfilled promises of the Peace Accords and aggravated by the impact of neoliberal economic policy. It also aimed to demonstrate the quality of the Salvadoran democracy to an international community less supportive of overt counterinsurgency violence than it had been during the 1980s, when the United States provided financial, military, and moral backing to the Salvadoran government. What is distinctive about the Salvadoran case is the prominence of Cold War rhetoric in the country's postwar electoral politics in an era when such rhetoric has waned from both international and Latin American politics. Although the left/right divide is still widely invoked in Latin America, it has become associated with new ideologies, such as Chávez's "twenty-first century socialism."

Aside from the performative aspects described in the above section, which largely reflect war experiences, ARENA's politics of fear also put emotions to work in specific ways (compare with Ahmed 2004). ARENA's free-floating signifier of "the communist" slid sideways among FMLN guerrillas, the Cuban, Venezuelan, and Nicaraguan regimes, and Islamist terrorists. The country's right-wing media and ARENA leadership also deployed historical and contemporary associations of "threat," "danger," "war," and "terrorism" that increased the affective value of the communist threat. Those signs in circulation during elections became commonplace currency for Salvadorans across the political spectrum. El Salvador's 2009 elections constituted one of the few occasions on which Salvadorans publicly aired wartime frictions; yet discussion was limited by campaign rhetoric and political ideologies. Of course, war memories were not elicited to promote dialogue, but rather to evoke fear, exacerbate hostilities, and gain electoral advantage. During the 2004 and 2009 elections, discussion about the parties' economic agendas was eclipsed by the politics of fear that was at work. The heightened animosities, largely stemming from ARENA's politics of fear, stimulated the vote of many disaffected Salvadorans in both 2004 and 2009.

Building a Middle

If the re-enactment of war and ARENA's politics of fear explain the doubling of voter turnout in 2004 and again in 2009, what was different about the 2009 presidential elections that allowed for the FMLN victory? The 2009 results cannot be fully understood from within the paradigm of a rigid national political divide. During the 2009 campaign, Mauricio Funes, the FMLN presidential candidate, addressed the economic and social concerns of ordinary Salvadorans, minimizing wartime political cleavages and appealing to Salvadorans across the political spectrum. Indeed, Funes had not militated in the FMLN until his candidacy. A charismatic left-wing journalist and human rights advocate, Funes was well known for the Salvadoran TV news programs he hosted for more than twenty years. From the moment his candidacy was announced in 2007 he stressed both symbolically and literally the distinction between him and the party. He tried to maintain a degree of autonomy vis-à-vis the party. Funes never appeared in public dressed in the FMLN's red color or raised his left fist and sang the party anthem at political rallies.

In contrast to the FMLN's ubiquitous identification with the Venezuelan and Cuban governments, Funes repeatedly declared his predilection for Brazilian President Luiz Inácio Lula da Silva's governance style and for Brazilian-style participatory democracy. Like Lula, he sought to continue neoliberal policies while developing a social agenda to lessen the impact of these policies on the poor. In a speech delivered during a visit to Santiago on 10 March 2009, Funes stressed his commitment to stabilizing the prices of basic goods, generating jobs, facilitating access to and improvement of basic utilities such as running water, expanding the pension and health care systems, and providing credit and assistance to those working the land as well as social housing and other subsidies for poor families. All of these were concerns for largely rural municipios like Santiago.

In a further attempt to distance Funes from the FMLN, the association Amigos de Mauricio was founded. This association, which included former right-wing advocates and high-ranking ex-military officials, attempted to build up the virtually nonexistent middle in the Salvadoran political spectrum. In Santiago, a former military official belonging to this association accompanied the FMLN departmental deputy Gerson Martínez on his tour of the La Paz Department municipios. In every stop, the former military official explained to audiences that he had fought with the army during the war but that he was supporting the FMLN in 2009 because ARENA had failed to generate economic prosperity. He denied that the military was unanimously supporting ARENA, even though that party's leaders had tried to demonstrate so by marching with members of El Salvador's Veterans Association "General Manuel José Arce" (ASVEM) on San Salvador streets on 7 September 2008, the day of ASVEM's fifth anniversary.

ARENA maintained that Funes's distinction from FMLN was a rhetorical ploy. Ultimately, ARENA claimed, Funes remained firmly allied with the FMLN and Hugo Chávez. While ARENA simply denied the possibility of a middle position, the FMLN managed it in a contradictory fashion. The public endorsement of Funes by former military officials during the campaign benefited the FMLN insofar as it demonstrated that sectors traditionally opposed to the party now supported it. But the FMLN leadership, dominated by the orthodox wing of the party, consistently sought to minimize the distance that Funes had established between himself and the party. In this sense, both ARENA and the FMLN contributed to the increasingly polarized physiognomy of the Salvadoran political spectrum.

The immutability of the divide in the 2009 elections was thus more an *effect* of ARENA's and FMLN's mimicked reproduction of the divide than an *actual feature* of it. This was evidenced by the FMLN victory in the 2009 elections, which many observers believe reflected among other things Funes's successful building of a middle position, despite both parties' efforts to deny or co-opt this possibility. Indeed, on my visits with FMLN members to the northern rural areas of Santiago, where the population is predominantly right-wing, I encountered middle-aged men and women who declared, "I am giving my vote to Funes but not to the FMLN." Some went on to explain that while they did not trust the FMLN, they would vote for Funes, who seemed like a decent man, owing to the country's dire economic situation. I would thus argue that Funes received massive support from the electorate by transcending the Cold War divide re-enacted by ARENA and FMLN. Instead, he proposed concrete programs to address the pressing social and economic problems that had been sidestepped by the Peace Accords and eclipsed by ARENA's politics of fear. In so doing, he promised to satisfy ordinary Salvadorans' aspirations to an expanded vision of democracy.

Conclusion

El Salvador's 2009 presidential elections foregrounded the persistence of war legacies and conflicts, expressed in anachronistic Cold War imageries and rhetoric. These legacies were mobilized by political elites anxious to maintain their privilege through the promotion of neoliberal policies. Yet these legacies persist in Salvadorans' everyday relationships and lives partly because there has been no public discussion of the war beyond political strategizing or that recognizes the ambiguities of the wartime divide and its attached moralities. The resuscitation of wartime confrontations during the 2009 campaign allowed ARENA to avoid a public discussion of pressing economic issues and counter the erosion of the party's hegemony.

Funes's middle position was crucial in determining the FMLN victory in 2009. His charisma, along with his non-participation in the country's civil war (and the massively funded FMLN campaign), allowed for a revaluation, even by disaffected and disillusioned Salvadorans, of the belligerent image of the FMLN. This revaluation was also made possible by Funes's direct address of the social and economic problems that had been consistently overlooked through the consolidation of El Salvador's "free-market democracy."

Notes

* I thank the editors of this volume, Ellen Moodie and Jennifer Burrell, as well as John Gledhill, Stef Jansen, Petra Kalshoven, and David Pretel for their insightful comments on earlier drafts of this chapter. Research for this chapter was funded by the University of Manchester and Fundación Caja Madrid.

1. The PCN was the military's official party since its founding in 1961. Elections were then observed by El Salvador's military governments as a means to gain legitimacy but were also manipulated when necessary, as in 1972 and 1977 (Stanley 1996). After the 1979 coup d'état, the PCN became a minority party. It was recently disbanded (2011) because it had not garnered enough votes.
2. For a critical view on Truth Commissions, see Laplante and Theidon (2007) and Wilson (2001).
3. The most notable case of inter-party violence occurred during the 2004 presidential elections, when two ARENA members were killed while mounting party propaganda (*La Prensa Gráfica* 2004).
4. Chencho Beltrán was well known in Santiago for having led a local death squad and orchestrated numerous assassinations during the early 1980s, until his group was attacked by guerrillas in 1985.
5. The Temporary Protected Status (TPS) program that grants legal residency in the United States to 260,000 Salvadorans was revived by the U.S. government in March 2001, after the two earthquakes that devastated El Salvador, and has since been successively extended (PNUD 2005). Yet the TPS creates a sort of "legal limbo," given that those benefiting from it cannot leave the United States and live with the uncertainty that stems from not receiving a resolution to their status (PNUD 2005, 432–33). Its temporary nature explains why ARENA has deployed the recission of TPS as a threat during presidential elections.
6. See, for instance, the documentaries "Hugo Chávez: Una amenaza real" and "No entreguemos El Salvador," which are available at http://fuerzasolidaria.org/?p=583 and http://fuerzasolidaria.org/?p=723 (accessed 30 September 2011). These documentaries were shown on Salvadoran TV and at ARENA's political rallies.

3 Daring to Hope in the Midst of Despair

The Agrarian Question within the Anti-Coup Resistance Movement in Honduras

Jefferson C. Boyer and Wilfredo Cardona Peñalva

The military coup d'état that ousted President José Manuel Zelaya on 28 June 2009 has generated an unprecedented process of political discernment, polarization, and realignment among Hondurans. Protests and marches have involved thousands of citizens. Leaders and the members of the anti-coup resistance quickly began looking across occupational, class, and ethnic lines in ways that echoed the heady days of labor and peasant organizing of the era between the 1950s and 1970s. Coup supporters behind the interim government of Roberto Micheletti and the November 2009 election of conservative Porfirio Lobo have been forced to take public positions previously kept private.

Yet, as careful observers have noted, most Hondurans have experienced ambivalence and confusion following the coup (see Levy 2010). The stream of protests, the many curfews, and media censorship have unsettled countless citizens. Police, military, and paramilitary violence have created a climate of uncertainty and fear. Honduras's overall murder rate has skyrocketed. By mid-2011 it hit 67 per 100,000 people, four times Mexico's homicide statistics, and one of the world's highest (Kryt 2011c, 7).[1] Military and paramilitary death squads, in part led by former members of the infamous 1980s Battalion 3-16, have murdered more than 100 people. Dozens of resistance leaders and family members have been "disappeared." Thousands have been illegally detained, tortured, and raped.

This fear recalls U.S.-led Cold War politics and security state repression of the 1980s.[2] Many U.S. State Department actions defy hemispheric and world protest: first, its refusal to declare Zelaya's forced removal a coup, clearing Honduras's return to the Organization of American States; then, the North American request to send more military and police hardware to the country. The Obama administration has cast a blind eye toward thousands of human rights violations and the suspension of democratic freedoms.

In this coup/post-coup era, the original banana republic is fairly convulsed in a struggle to cast aside or to maintain past invisibilities as a subservient client state. The question of what kind of democracy to pursue—participatory and inclusive, or traditional party- and global market-based—may at long last have grabbed global attention for Honduras. This intense, painful interrogation of contemporary individual and collective identities necessarily invokes Honduras's contradictory past: as site of resistant agrarian, indigenous, and labor union activists, or of more orderly modern and urbanizing professionals. The coup itself led to brief exposures of naked power relations, followed by their masking. It produced a general state of socio-economic uncertainty and insecurity, and it set off fear of rising violence "from everywhere" (the state, the private sector, one's neighborhood). The Honduran situation resonates with circumstances in El Salvador and Guatemala (see Binford; Burrell; A. Montoya; and Moodie, this volume). However, the struggle to redefine Honduras's political future—relationships between the state and its citizens, with other nations, and especially with the United States—remains extraordinarily contentious.

Rural organizations form a key site in the struggle for what anti-coup resistance actors often refer to as a "new Honduras"—even as mainstream media have focused on the capital Tegucigalpa. Honduran society remains the most rural in Central America, despite the decline of the rural sector as a percentage of population and its share of economic activity.[3] Now, in the post-coup moment, the country's peasant and small farmer movements, split for more than two decades, have begun talking to each other again. This chapter examines prospects for overcoming this breach among rural movements. It explores implications of these processes for addressing the agrarian question in the new millennium, focusing especially on debates over food security and food sovereignty. It is true that Honduras's urban, industrial, and business elites continue to increase their economic and political dominance, as in much of the Global South.[4] But demands for land, for better food-crop prices, and for more secure livelihoods will remain an important feature of the resistance movement and everyday life for years to come (Boyer 2010; see also Tucker; Lyon; and R. Montoya, this volume).

The Worst of Times

The cascading violence emanating from the north coast Aguán Valley has embodied the despair felt across the countryside before and after the coup. Less than a year before Zelaya's removal, eleven peasants were gunned down in Guadalupe Carney, one of the few agrarian reform cooperatives to survive decades of neglect and assaults by neoliberal governments and the private sector. This atrocity sparked international condemnation and demands for justice, thanks mainly to the media campaign mobilized by the world's largest peasant and small farmer coalition, (La) Vía Campesina (The Peasant Way). It also prompted steps by the Zelaya administration to reactivate the agrarian reform program that neoliberal legislation had blocked in the early 1990s.

Figure 3.1. Aguán Agrarian Movement Poster, Public Domain

By the late 1990s, these Aguán Valley lands had become the site of embittered contestation between the reform sector peasants and new landlords associated with Honduras's wealthiest agro-industrialist, Miguel Facussé, the major investor in the corporation Grupo Dinant.[5] What started as confrontations with Dinant's locally hired guns and police expanded into bloodier conflicts with the company's uniformed security force, comprising men recruited from police and paramilitary units in El Salvador and Colombia. President Lobo's desultory attempts to resolve the standoff have only augmented the rural bloodshed. He first offered the cooperative members lands elsewhere, but then forced their relocation with a large troop presence. The scant investigation by public authorities opened the door for accelerated and ever more brutal killings.[6] Our post-coup count of the dead in Aguán Valley by 5 June 2011 was 45; they included the grisly beheadings of a family. In addition, 120 families of the Los Rigores cooperative (part of the *Movimiento Unificado del Aguán*, or Unified Movement of Aguán, MUCA) were forcibly removed by the Dinant security forces in June 2011, an action that continued a pattern of such displacements since 2008.[7]

Only recently have the agribusiness stakes in this valley and elsewhere become apparent. The World Bank's 2010 $30 million (U.S.) loan to Dinant, for expanded production of African palms (Kryt 2011a, 11), was kept quiet because of the corporation's appalling human rights record. This fact not only indicates *what else* is hidden in Central America; it also points to stealthy appropriation of some of Honduras's best farmlands for biofuels—a twenty-first century shift from the increasingly global corporate food regime to its global energy analogue (McMichael 2008).

Beyond the Aguán Valley, the anti-populist, anti-poor tendencies of the coup administrations was soon evident in their "divide and conquer" strategy vis-à-vis the peasant movement, which targeted the fragile solidarities within and between the peasant unions and popular indigenous organizations. Although the coup initially rekindled some of the original militancy of the national Coordinating Council of Peasant Organizations of Honduras (COCOCH), pro-coup congressional leaders soon succeeded in isolating enough leaders with selective favors and funded projects, as well as targeted threats, to weaken this body's initial commitment to the National Popular Resistance Front (FNRP).

Figure 3.2. MUCA Agrarian Movement Poster, Public Domain

Indigenous activism and a selective multiculturalism within the 1990s neoliberal administrations did lead to legislation designed to protect native lands, forests, and watersheds in the 1990s (see Anderson, this volume, regarding the Janus-faced character of many of these gains). But Micheletti and Lobo have dealt harshly with indigenous dissent. Leaders and activists among the Lenca, Honduras's largest Amerindian population (140,000[8]), were among those harassed and beaten by the military and police when they joined the thousands gathered at the Nicaraguan border during Zelaya's attempted return in July 2009. Twelve leaders of Honduras's Civic Council of Popular and Indigenous Organizations (COPINH) were given asylum in the Guatemalan Embassy. By August, the FNRP felt obliged to send mediators to the enraged Lenca community to dissuade them from outright insurrection. Since 2009, municipal and departmental authorities sympathetic to the resistance have been purged among indigenous communities and throughout the country. Leaders of Honduras's largest ethnic minority, the north coast Garifuna (250,000 in 2004 [Thorne 2004]), who were vocal in their dissent against the coup, found the government canceled their regional hospital construction project suddenly in September 2009.

While certainly not all indigenous Hondurans have supported the resistance, Zelaya's pro-poor policies (increased minimum wage, lowered home loan interest rates, expanded public education and health care) and efforts to resolve land disputes earned their favor. Through the Minister of Culture's Rodolfo Pastor Fasquelle, the Zelaya government made a special inroad to indigenous peoples by appointing historian Dario Euraque to broaden the orientation of the prestigious Institute of Anthropology and History (IHAH) beyond its emphasis on classic Mayan archaeology. Euraque began a culturally and geographically diverse educational program with the country's nine recognized ethnic groups, one that privileged their "lived realities" (Euraque 2010, 32–34). His September 2009 dismissal from IHAH ended this culturally sensitive effort. Whatever sense of self-respect that inclusion into the national experience the IHAH outreach offered, its loss added to rising hunger among indigenous groups (see below) as a shift away from legitimating ethnic minorities.

Early Signs of a New Political Alignment

In August 2009 key leaders and members of Honduras's peasant unions for agrarian reform and of the farmer-to-farmer network for sustainable agriculture (some of these indigenous) began talking with each other—for the first time in many years. As the general protest and resistance against the coup began to coalesce into the FNRP, meetings from the local to national levels started to provide the support to think and act in innovative and unifying ways. Union leader Rafael Alegría echoed this potential fusion of, on one side, peasant union concerns for land redistribution *with,* on the other, the cultural and agroecological qualities of peasant and small farm agriculture. Champion of many land occupations, confrontations with hired guns, local police, and the Honduran army, Alegría is a veteran leader of COCOCH, one of the founders of the transnational Vía Campesina, and now part of the national resistance leadership. In August 2009 he held fast to the cultural content of Vía Campesina's campaign for food sovereignty as well as its structural elements.[9] He affirmed the great need for a more locally controlled, culturally diverse sustainable food production system, including the protection and use of Honduras's peasant seed varieties rather than the genetically modified hybrid maize seeds introduced by Monsanto into Honduras for its large-scale commercial production. Alegría views sustainable agriculture as crucial for a revival of Honduras's moribund agrarian reform program. A study by the Honduran Social Forum for Debt Reduction and Development (COCOCH-FOSDEH 2009, 121–22) argues that a renewed land reform is urgently needed to accommodate the 25 percent of the rural population who, by 2008, were landless, as well as the 18.2 percent with less than 1 hectare of land. Alegría's stance has revived sensitivities for a smaller-scale ecological agriculture that most peasant unions had long abandoned. Despite some early experiments in intermediate technology described below, the labor struggles preferred tactics of mass occupations to obtain land and generally accepted the industrial model of larger-scale agriculture recommended by conventional policy makers.

On the other side of a thirty-year agrarian divide, key sustainable farmer-to-farmer network leaders were disgusted with the anti-democratic nature of the coup. Like union leaders, many experienced first-hand, or saw their peasant trainees experience, Micheletti's repression. Two months after the coup, some of these leaders joined the National Resistance Front's deliberations. Two of these, one close to the Lenca struggle and the other a former director of a major support organization for the country's farmer-to-farmer movement, World Neighbors, began to talk with Alegría and other union members in the National Resistance Front.[10] They admitted that their network of training centers and workshops imparting sustainability techniques to peasant farmers could not possibly reach the landless, and near-landless, without some new form of land reform. By September, more professional trainers were accepting the peasants' (including indigenous trainees') views that accorded with Alegría. Without the bottom-up transformation of the county's political system, as Alegría proclaimed in Tegucigalpa's central park, neither agrarian reform nor the growth of inclusive, participatory democracy could emerge.

But what underlies the decades-old split between these two sets of organizations and actors with generally similar claims in their struggles for more equitable and sustainable agriculture and community life among rural Hondurans? The answer lies not merely in their organizational histories, but in the wider context of development history.

The Agrarian Question Then and Now

Here we briefly trace the evolution of key ideas and major debates surrounding the agrarian question (Akram-Lodhi and Kay 2010a; 2010b). The nineteenth-century framers of the agrarian question—Karl Marx, Karl Kautsky, and Friedrich Engels—first saw agriculture's role in capitalist development as generating (capital) accumulation and surplus value needed to fuel industrial and financial growth. Second, with some exceptions, these three were convinced that peasants (petty commodity producers) were technologically and socially incapable of generating sufficient capital accumulation to aid in this industrial, financial (and urban) expansion (Roseberry 1993, 340–41). An elaboration of Kautsky's definition of the agrarian question includes: "the continued existence in the countryside, in a substantive sense, of obstacles to an unleashing of accumulation in both the countryside itself and more generally—in particular, the accumulation associated with capitalist industrialization."[11] These classical analysts looked to the emerging class of fully proletarian wage laborers, exploited and alienated in the labor process, as the only class capable of realizing their own interests and waging socialist revolution. They also thought that peasants, as a class, would gradually disappear. Even today, Cristóbal Kay (2009) reminds us that some analysts continue to predict the final demise of the world's peasants, and therefore, the end of the agrarian question in Latin America and elsewhere.

From the 1960s into the 1980s, scholars documented the major role that peasants played in major twentieth-century revolutions, and they described particular cases of the transformative agency generated by petty (and/or simple) commodity producers. Then, writing at a moment when neoliberal globalization was in full swing, just before his death, William Roseberry (1993, 243–361) began "asking new questions"; he opened the door for peasants, workers, and "urban" supporters to reframe critical questions about agrarian and urban, local-to-global, realities and praxis.[12]

The Origins of Agrarian Movements: 1960s–1980s

In rural Honduras after World War II, explicit discussions of the agrarian question were initially limited to scholars and development professionals. Most of these people saw a "peaceful modernization of the peasant" that, through economic development projects, would become more commercial, and, with advances in education, would play a role in the economic and social progress of Honduran society. But some thinkers refused this analysis. Further, few Marxists and dependency theorists, who viewed future conflict with U.S.-led capitalism as inevitable, saw any rapid disappearance of the county's regional, peasant hinterlands (see Kay 2009). Nevertheless, some key issues inspired by the agrarian question—especially, who should have access to and control over land as a productive resource—have remained a topic of discussion and debate in Honduras. These issues joined with the discussions of the developmental tropes of food security, and later, food sovereignty. Here we briefly summarize Boyer's (2010) analysis of these developmental tropes, including the division of a single agrarian reform movement into two movements with distinct objectives—each claiming to improve the lives of Honduras's peasants, small farmers, and rural poor.

Food security emerged in the 1970s as a development construct of the U.S. Department of Agriculture. It denotes access for people to have enough food for an active, healthy life.[13] It entered into Honduran discourses about rural development and change in a cultural milieu that had long developed understandings of *seguridad* (glossed as security) tied to their society's historical agrarian economic and social formation. Like most societies with large peasantries, the Honduran notion of security in the postwar era of declining access to land, periodic droughts, floods and insect plagues, gouging interest rates for liens on crops and inputs, and fluctuating prices for food crops all combined to make the notion of seguridad in this insecure world very attractive indeed. The food security concerns were inevitably about the adequacy of this season's *milpa* (corn field). Food security was intimately tied to land security, as, by the early 1960s, cattle ranchers, corporate banana and sugar plantations, and new cotton farmers expanded their holdings by frequently enclosing traditional peasant landholdings on public lands. These actions violated the sensibilities of the traditional moral economy, based especially on cattleman landlord and peasant reciprocities (Boyer 2010, 323, 333), and certainly went against ways of thinking in indigenous communities.

This postwar expansion of export agriculture across Central America spawned social conflict and spirited public debates over the goals of modernization, economic development, and, whether overtly or implicitly, the agrarian question. Did to modernize and "to develop" mean an inevitable transformation of peasants into literate commercial farmers and urban dwellers, ending the dense agrarian kin and communal ties and culture? Is agriculture simply to become an aspect of industry? Or is a more culturally and socially appropriate development possible? Or … does modernization and development of an agrarian society call for social and class conflict and even revolution (Kay 2009)?

As peasants protesting enclosures turned to organizing and pressuring the Honduran government to strengthen its initially weak agrarian reform law and fledgling institute,[14] they brought their own deeply held understandings of seguridad into the 1970s and 1980s discussions of the U.S. food security development trope. One of the Catholic Social Movement's (CSM) contributions to the peasant struggle for the land was its use of *concientización* (raising consciousness) taken from Paulo Freire (1973). This pedagogy emphasized interactive, horizontal dialogue in which the teacher guided the process of developing critical awareness of self-worth and social solidarity, of the dignity of peasants' labor, and of privileging local knowledge and skills. As the U.S. notion of food security was floated in the late 1970s and 1980s, the Freireian notion of keywords as part of core cultural frameworks had incorporated the campesino notion of seguridad. This meant that food security became tightly interwoven with land security in peasant discourses. This certainly was not what the U.S Department of Agriculture or the U.S. Agency for International Development (USAID) intended with a definition of food security that never asks how or on whose land food is produced (Boyer 2010).

In Honduras, Freire's pedagogy was also linked to ideas of liberation theology, inspiring new organizational structures within and beyond the church to support its growth. This combination helped peasants across the countryside attain a heightened sense of their own agency through participation, organization, and solidarity to create Christian-based communities that would embody and multiply social justice. The broader CSM organization included community development and religious networks linked to parish and diocese structures, semi-secular regional peasant training centers, and a secular national peasant union, and by the late 1960s, a Christian Democratic Party decidedly to the left of its European sponsors.

In 1975, Brazilian agrarian scholar Santos de Morais (1975) observed that Honduras was the only Central American country wherein the peasants played the decisive role in bringing about agrarian reform. Their participation in unions and militant land occupations arguably involved more of the country's peasants and small farmers at the base than similar movements in the isthmus, including the Sandinista agrarian reform in Nicaragua several years later. These widespread mobilizations, at times involving almost half of Honduras's poorest peasants, also had logistical assistance from the North Coast banana unions, and, until 1976, the support of a reform-minded military government that promulgated a comprehensive agrarian reform law (Posas 1981a; 1981b). By the end of that decade, 22 percent of the country's rural landless and near landless, 206,000 people, had obtained land in a variety of settlements, cooperatives, and some state farms (Boyer 2010, 323–24; Ruhl 1984, 53).

A lesser-known dimension of the 1970s reform decade is that professional allies of ANACH, the UNC, like director Rigoberto Sandoval, were looking far beyond "land to the tiller" issues. They began to train rural and urban aspirants to become a pioneering generation of local-regional and national economic planners, sending some for further training in Costa Rica and Chile. They hoped to initiate a more supportive infrastructure such as farm-to-market roads, local and regional grain storage facilities, small irrigation systems, and soil, water, and forest conservation measures. They wanted to expand local and regional food markets and strengthen the local and regional health and education facilities.[15] Sadly, other forces intervened to cut short this dream.

Honduran efforts to develop its farmer-to-farmer network to improve cultivation and resource conservation methods began *within* the peasant union movement. In the early 1970s the Catholic Church sponsored two teaching and research farms, one on the North Coast and the other in the southern department of Choluteca. Peasants about to enter the reform sector received from daylong to weeklong workshops in improved hillside and open field techniques as well as basic orientation to the ethics and principles of cooperative management. These agronomists were responding to the problems of low yields, soil erosion, and deforestation from traditional swidden (slash and burn) agriculture. They and consultants from the Land Tenure Center (University of Wisconsin) questioned the prevalent attitude that large-scale, industrial agriculture should replace peasant agriculture (Boyer 2010, 326–27). Unfortunately, these schools vanished by the 1980s as public sector support for agrarian reform declined. The Honduran CSM's national peasant training school Escuela para Dirigentes Roque Ramón Andrade (EDDRA) near Tegucigalpa continued some small-scale agricultural experiments. But by the end of the 1980s, the farmer-to-farmer movement was training peasants and small farmers mostly from *outside* of the reform sector.

Security State and Neoliberalism: Fragmenting Agrarian Movements

If the 1980s were "the lost decade for Latin American development," then Honduras was dealt a double whammy. As the initial Washington-consensus neoliberal policy shifts were getting under way, the U.S. military buildup in Honduras, the Contra war, and other isthmian counter-insurgency efforts had a chilling effect on popular movements. Because of infighting over vanishing resources as well as repression, peasant unions had splintered into fourteen competing groups by the mid-1980s (Ruhl 1985, 75).

At the same time, economic restructuring in the midst of mounting foreign indebtedness foretold currency devaluations, inflation, decline in real wages, and reduced social public sector spending (Hernández 1992). Rural development projects, agricultural extension and research declined significantly. Rural hunger and malnutrition climbed in most regions, especially in the west and the south (Boyer 2008). USAID's land titling program was aimed directly at privatizing reform sector lands. While touted as increasing tenure security and credit-worthiness for all farms, its effect was to encourage the sale of agrarian reform lands to the highest bidder (much as R. Montoya, this volume, documents in neoliberal Nicaragua). By 1994 an estimated 30,000 of the original 56,587 hectares that constituted the reform sector lands in the early 1980s had been sold to domestic and foreign agribusinesses, financial oligopolies (like Dinant), retired military officers, and cattlemen (Boyer 2010, 324).

At the same time, the fortunes of the new farmer-to-farmer movement and their sponsoring nongovernmental organizations (NGOs) were on the rise. Surrounding Elías Sánchez at Loma Linda were the noted Honduran crop researcher Milton Flores and the Christian Democratic Party veteran Alfredo Landaverde, all supported by the faith-based North American NGO World Neighbors, and, later, the Ecumenical Project for International Cooperation (EPIC). By 1989, the Catholic foundation Miserior entered Honduras's sustainable agriculture network by supporting a new center, PROCONDEMA (Program for Environmental Training and Conservation) in Choluteca. By the late 1980s and early 1990s, this network of agronomists, educators, and researchers were sharing technical and pedagogical information with each other as they trained thousands of campesinos in regional hinterlands, mostly beyond the reform sector. They saw themselves as the catalysts of a new agriculture. Kaimowitz (1993, 186) described the thinking of the NGOs that brought this "new agriculture" to Central America:

> Two common characteristics ... are: a focus on the micro community and a holistic view of human development in which technical change is only one element. The emphasis on the micro level is partly a function of the NGOs' limited geographical coverage. In addition their relative isolation from national policy-making circles and the importance they attribute to grass roots involvement has led them to concentrate on micro-level activities.

By the late 1980s and early 1990s, Honduras's agrarian reform was fighting for its life while neoliberalism's strategic funding priorities favored the dispersing (and controllable) rural development activities of small NGOs, a pattern noted throughout Central America. Scholar-activist Rafael Del Cid (1989) had lambasted USAID's land titling program, which opened up the sale of reform sector lands. He pleaded with the peasant unions and National Agrarian Institute (INA) officials to reject the U.S. version of food security and retain the Honduran understandings of seguridad that linked food and land access. Unfortunately union leaders within the new COCOCH were distracted by the "divide-and-conquer" tactics of the administration of President Rafael Leonardo Callejas (1990–1993). They had little power to counter the crown jewel of neoliberal legislation, the 1994 Agricultural Modernization Law. Its goals of reducing the government's role in agriculture while expanding agribusiness and export production included provisions that, with exceptions, voided the 1975 agrarian reform law. Inés Fuentes, veteran leader of the national peasant strike for land redistribution in 1988, said in an interview:

> Modernizing the agro [meant] opening up everything to the globalizing policies for those foreign or national investors who can enter the competition with the non-traditional products and produce "with quality." So ... there is no interest, no policy to carry out agrarian reform, no credit or support for it, and now with the general privatization, it's every man for himself! (Boyer 2010, 326)

Fuentes was looking back at the social disintegration caused by the neoliberal development model since the 1980s. Legally blocked from land occupations, many of his COCOCH union cohorts (including Rafael Alegría) turned to support outside the country. The new thinking from progressive, mostly European, funding institutions was critical of the neoliberal policies that fueled corporate globalization condemned by Fuentes. However, their solutions stressed transnational organizing and actions *over* a simultaneous regrouping at local-to-national levels, which dismayed Fuentes. Throughout the 1990s the Honduran peasant leaders led by Alegría played crucial roles in a Central American peasant association, a Latin American peasant and indigenous network, and finally in Vía Campesina. This latter network currently enjoys ties with 149 organizations in 69 countries worldwide. From 1996 to 2004 COCOCH became Vía Campesina's world headquarters. This is when Vía Campesina began championing a food sovereignty campaign to challenge the food security concept.

Struggles to Reframe the Agrarian Question: 1990s–Present

In 1996, Vía Campesina announced its food sovereignty campaign at the World Food Summit sponsored by the United Nations Food and Agriculture Organization (FAO) in Rome. This new development trope included the right of each nation to maintain and develop its own capacity to produce its basic foods, respecting cultural and productive diversity, and the right to carry this out in one's national (and local) territory. The alternative concept and campaign of food sovereignty emerged, according to sociologist Philip

McMichael (2008), because the idea of food security was viewed as simply too burdened with the political baggage of U.S. and neoliberal designs to feed the world with surpluses generated in the North.

How has the food sovereignty campaign fared? While Alegría explained the construct to a 1996 workshop of a dozen national peasant union leaders, Boyer's long-term reconnaissance in the southern, western, and northern regions shows that the idea has not reached as far as it could have. Even a national leader within the peasant union presumably most supportive of food sovereignty frequently lapsed into the old food security discourse during one interview.

The stacking of multiple meanings of "food sovereignty," and its complexity and potential instability, may impede its ready acceptance among campesinos. One example is that sovereignty may confuse those who, until the coup, have only equated sovereignty with states. Here the state-linked understanding of sovereignty may well limit actor-driven potentials (unlike seguridad) with the personal, the particular local, and communal resonances. Without a concerted educational effort to clarify the new meanings of a people-centered sovereignty, we fear this trope's semantic distance from everyday life will continue to pose problems.

In contrast to the beleaguered peasant unions, the better-supported farmer-to-farmer network had formalized itself into the Training Centers for Sustainable Agriculture (CEAS) by the mid-1990s. Today there are twenty-five centers, six of which can host workshops of thirty or more participants. CEAS counts 266 model farms usually owned and run by farmers who have integrated the multi-cropping regimes, terracing and other CEAS techniques and are demonstrating these to neighboring peasant farmers. CEAS serves at least 10,000 peasant farmers each year.

CEAS directors and educators voice reservations about incorporating Vía Campesina's global food sovereignty campaign into their teaching. One director said that he discussed it in his training sessions but taught it as an idea that adds to the strength of food security. Unsurprisingly, these farmer-to-farmer educators are cognizant of seguridad's resonance among campesinos, doubtless made more salient by the many insecurities from nature, markets, family, and community. These trainers have simply reinforced the campesinos' bridging of food and land security, which has always stressed self- sufficiency. This means that the operating definition of food security in both CEAS groups and many peasant unions had anticipated and, in a way, preempted food sovereignty's concern with "local capacities to produce basic foods."

Since Boyer's (2010) initial analysis of these problems, we have come to a somewhat more optimistic view about the role that the concept of food sovereignty *might* play in the praxis of the anti-coup resistance. It could strengthen a publicly acknowledged relevance for a more actor-driven agrarian question, explained momentarily. As rural and urban Hondurans confront government repression, a renewed horizon of a possible citizen-based sovereignty has come into view. If food sovereignty can attach itself to the emerging hopes of "we the people" in Honduras, then its acceptance through campaigns across rural and urban spaces could accelerate. However, the challenges for organizations at subnational and transnational levels remains. First, the CEAS-trained peasants suffering declining access to land should hear clearly the union calls for legitimate agrarian reform. Further, union leaders should respond to the call for sustainable agriculture. They should not be denied CEAS's relevant agroecological practices because of the competitive atmosphere between the two groups. Second, both CEAS and reform sector peasants must sense their mutual interests with Vía Campesina and engage with and discuss the food sovereignty campaign; otherwise why should those who claim to represent them in Rome or Mexico City, or their campaign, matter to the peasants themselves (Boyer 2010)?

The one union criticism often leveled at CEAS that could be shared on both sides is the charge of paternalism. As Roland Bunch (2010, 211) puts it, "They each fear losing 'their villagers' to the other group." Here we can add the new difficulties of the "divide and conquer" tactics by the pro-coup authorities, which have weakened some of the CEAS as well as union solidarities. Moreover, the global recession and Honduras's many human rights violations have combined to dry up international investment capital. Tight budgets constrain the ability of union and CEAS leaders to travel and meet directly with their bases and foster mutual rapprochement. But since both groups compete for the same international donor dollars, the need for cooperation has never been greater.

It was the post-coup crisis that by August 2009 impelled Alegría and CEAS leaders to admit that they needed each other, and that their separate efforts were failing to reach Honduras's 377,000 landless and near landless. Since those early discussions, some CEAS leaders have considered expanding their focus beyond predominantly hand-scale technologies on hillsides. Working with the peasant unions they could take advantage of the better bottomlands and open fields in some reform sector holdings. This would involve returning to intermediate technologies of the CSM farming schools of the 1970s: some tractors and oxen teams along with prudent soil conservation measures. Such sustainable and productive improvements give impetus for expanded agrarian reform, an idea supported by INA ex-director Rigoberto Sandoval. He argues that nothing could better remove the sting of claims of a mismanaged and environmentally damaging industrial agriculture than a well-coordinated, sustainable and appropriate agriculture for its hillside small farms *and* the larger farms in its valleys and coastal plains. This kind of rapprochement between peasant unions and the farmer-to-farmer educational network would establish what Irán Vasquez calls the "synergy of a single strategic vision" (Bunch 2010, 215).

Engaged scholars can help. We can help educational campaigns by pointing out the historical similarities between the food security (in Honduras) and food sovereignty tropes. This effort should clarify the very limited U.S. definition of food security. Carefully prepared workshops with peasant union and CEAS bases (and their leaders) could unpack the various meanings of food sovereignty and go a long way toward ameliorating the problem of stacked, unstable, and confusing meanings. It would reinforce Annette Desmarais's claim that food sovereignty is not merely a checklist of things but rather participates in integrative goals of a praxis that plays out differently from one setting to the next (Boyer 2010, 334). Second, together with peasants and their trainers, we can utilize the horizontal pedagogical methods of "peasants as teachers and teachers as learners" and focus on what Eric Holt-Giménez (2006) calls "structural literacy" sessions, identifying forces arrayed against peasant interests and the resources that they can use to creatively fight back (Boyer 2010, 344).

This praxis, motivated by the political crisis, would finally focus on more subnational "people sovereignty," part of Vía Campesina's stated goals (Desmarais 2007). It is in this sense that food sovereignty might be seen as shifting the agrarian question's focus away from capital accumulation inevitably being transferred to the global corporate food regime, and toward the social reproduction of peasants, small farmers, indigenous groups, rural women and other marginalized rural groups.

Concluding Thoughts

Ultimately it is less important whether Honduras's rural actors decide to keep their understandings of food security or to embrace food sovereignty. This is their decision. As unions and CEAS members struggle to elaborate their "synergy of a single strategic vision," the need to attend to the local in "the new Honduras," by rebuilding community economies, schools, clinics, and supportive services seems paramount.

Most Hondurans are keenly aware of the social decomposition afoot in rural communities as well as urban neighborhoods. Like similar efforts across northern Central America reported in this volume, rebuilding the "Honduran local" must take into account its large international labor migration (and return of migrants to a devastated economy), the society's role in violent narco-trafficking, its youth gangs and brutal state reaction to them, and the growing police and military repression even before the coup. Finally, even the most politically ambivalent Hondurans recognize that the coup itself is part of a hegemonic assemblage tied overtly and covertly to destructive neoliberal policies, failed and often complicit U.S. anti-drug campaigns, and Washington's willingness to fan the fears of a Chavista-style socialism—and thus to deceptively encourage both the coup and ongoing repression.

In May 2010 a delegation representing the FNRP traveled to Madrid where it was officially recognized at the Summit of European, Latin American and Caribbean Peoples. By September the FNRP had gathered more than 1.3 million signatures of citizens demanding a more socially and economically inclusive constitution (Kryt 2011b, 7). In February 2011, 1,500 peasants, teachers, unionists, and small business people, elected from municipalities across Honduras, gathered in Tegucigalpa to draft a more participatory national charter. On 28 May 2011 Zelaya returned to his country after almost two years in exile. Diplomats around the region (including U.S. officials desperately seeking to legitimate Honduras's return to the OAS) had negotiated with the Lobo government to allow his peaceful return. Unsurprisingly, the repression and state-sponsored violence continue.

Notes

1. Honduras's murder rate jumped after the coup, climbing from 57.9 to 66.8 per 10,000 by the end of 2009 (Pine 2010, 3).
2. Battalion 3-16 was established in the early 1980s. Trained by the Argentine military in "dirty war" tactics in the 1970s, and assisted by the CIA, Battalion 3-16 brutally repressed peasant unions (see Gill 2004).
3. Edelman's (2008) analysis using CEPAL data shows the rural population declining to 49.4 percent.
4. See Euraque's (2006) analysis of the shift in dominant power relations within Honduras's class structure over the last thirty years (Boyer 2010, 339–40).
5. Through Grupo Dinant, Facussé began by expanding control over land, food processing, and convenience food companies.
6. "Lobo signs with Aguán campesinos," *Weekly News Update on the Americas,* 20 April 2010. Nicaragua Solidarity Network of Greater New York. Available from: http://weeklynewsupdate.blogspot.com/2010/04/wnu-1029-honduras-government-settles.html (accessed 28 April 2010); Kryt 2011a, 10–11; Cardona Peñalva's interviews in Aguán Valley, March 2011.
7. We have assembled the following Aguán Valley peasant death count taken from Honduran media, the National Congress Rural Workers (CNTC) and self-reporting from the MCA and MUCA groups in Aguán: eleven in 2008, six in 2009, eighteen in 2010, and ten by 5 June 2011.
8. This official population estimate was accessed July 2011 from the *Diario Oficial Gaceta* (Gaceta Official Newspaper).
9. "Structural" here refers to the focus on peasant and small farmer access to and control over land.
10. We are protecting the identity of these two farmer-to-farmer leaders.
11. See Terence Byres's (1996) elaboration of Kautsky (1988 [1899], 12).
12. See Smith (1984) and Wessman (1981).

13. See USDA, "Food Security: Measuring household security." Online report, http://www.ers.gov/Briefing/Food Security/measurement.htm (accessed 14 May 2009).
14. The National Agrarian Institute (INA) began with the attempt by the Kennedy administration through the Alliance for Progress (1961–1962) to counter the Cuban revolution through moderate reforms (Posas 1981a; 1981b).
15. Interviews with Oscar Ortiz, May 2006; with Manlio Martínez, July 2008; with Rigoberto Sandoval, July 2007.

4 "My Heart Says NO"

Political Experiences of the Struggle against CAFTA-DR in Costa Rica

*Ciska Raventós**

Thirty years ago, during the revolutionary crisis in Central America, Costa Rica managed to remain relatively unaffected by the popular insurgency that toppled the Somoza regime in Nicaragua and threatened the Salvadoran government. This does not mean that it emerged untouched, though the results were very different from its Central American neighbors.

In June 1982, shortly after taking office, Costa Rica's President Luis Alberto Monge traveled to Washington, DC, accompanied by a bipartisan committee, to meet with U.S. President Ronald Reagan and the Congressional Foreign Relations Committee. Motivated by the severity of the debt crisis that had led the country to default on its international payments since 1981,[1] he requested the United States' assistance in proving "that democracy and freedom are possible in a tropical nation."[2] In the polarized political context of the early 1980s, in which the Reagan administration viewed the Nicaraguan government to have recently "fallen" to the "communists," the appeal to democracy pointed to precise ideological markers. For more than three decades, in the wording of the Cold War's binary pairs, the opposite of "communism" had been "democracy." The meaning of Monge's petition was not lost on Reagan, who had a long history of militant anti-communism and who had framed the threat of the Nicaraguan revolution as the danger of a "domino effect" that could topple all the remaining Central American governments.

Monge's maneuver entailed two important political shifts. First, he was telling the U.S. government that unlike his predecessor, Rodrigo Carazo, he did not support the Sandinistas. Second, by heading a committee that included members of his Liberación Nacional (National Liberation) party together with the opposition, he was also signaling a pact of "national unity" in the face of the severe economic crisis.[3] This pact with the opposition opened the way for a bipartisan political system.

In the following years, the U.S. government provided massive aid[4] to Costa Rica's economy through non-reimbursable donations, which had the advantage, for both governments, of not requiring congressional approval and thus avoiding public scrutiny of how the funds were being spent. For the Reagan administration, the rationale for the U.S. rescue of the heavily indebted nation was twofold. On the one hand, it used Costa Rica's territory as a base for the Contra attacks on neighboring Nicaragua. On the other, it was to be a showcase of peace and stability, a counterexample to the region's war and political instability. For Costa Rica, its "Sandinista windfall" allowed it to emerge apparently unaffected by the crisis.

However, upon closer examination, it is clear that the massive aid package set the bases for social and economic reform. Besides the two objectives mentioned above, the United States government, through the United States Agency of International Development (USAID), took advantage of its position as donor to further the World Bank and the International Monetary Fund's agendas by including clauses that conditioned aid on economic reform. The donations were targeted toward the creation of subsidies to promote a new export economy and a private banking system.[5] Parallel to economic reform, solvency gave the government leverage to negotiate with anti-austerity protest movements, contributing to political stability, strong support for the government party, Liberación Nacional, and for the opposition Unidad Social Cristiana (Social Christian Union), collaborators in bringing about reform. In this sense, the ultimate "windfall" was the U.S.-backed promotion of a neo-export economy and a private financial sector in a stable political climate, a change that clearly influenced Costa Rica's development as it headed toward the new millennium.

While the economic effects of the aid package of the 1980s are clear, it is less obvious how much of the change can be interpreted as a boost for democracy, as demanded by Monge. Little more than a decade and three administrations later, the bipartisan order that emerged in the early 1980s became increasingly unpopular. Since the mid 1990s, Costa Rican citizens have been increasingly dissatisfied with both political parties, politicians, elected officials and, in general, with governments. Corruption scandals involved the three presidents that served in the 1990s, two of which were judged in criminal courts on charges of accepting bribes. Citizen malaise has been expressed in the decline in voter turnout since 1998, weakened partisan loyalty, decreased confidence in governmental institutions, and rising citizen participation in social movements, protest and mobilization (Raventós et al. 2005; Raventós 2008; Vargas et al. 2006).

Between 2003 and 2007, a social movement developed in opposition to the approval of the Dominican Republic-Central America-United States Free Trade Agreement (CAFTA-DR), sometimes parallel to and sometimes overlapping with electoral politics. This movement (hereinafter, NO, or the NO Movement) generated the largest and most sustained mass mobilization in more than half a century. The conflict was settled through a traditional institutional channel—by vote—in the first referendum in Costa Rican history (see Dary Fuentes, this volume, for discussion of the May 1999 referendum regarding multiculturalism in Guatemala). The popular vote took place on 7 October 2007. The opposition movement lost by a narrow margin, with the "YES to CAFTA-DR" obtaining 51.7 percent of the votes and the "NO," 48.3 percent. Forty percent of the population did not vote.

The CAFTA-DR resistance movement falls within a larger context of citizen mobilization that started with the millennium, beginning with a national uprising against the privatization of telecommunications in 2000. In March of that year, demonstrations, marches, and street blockades challenged legislation that would authorize the entry of private providers for the delivery of telecommunication services. This process of mobilization was successful: the president withdrew the legislation and committed to drafting a new law with the participation of organized civil society.

In the context of what Paul Almeida and Erica Walker (2007) call the second wave of protests against the neoliberal model, Costa Rica has arguably been the country in Central America with the most intense popular mobilization. This is notable in a region known for strong nationally based traditions of protest, opposition, and dissent.

In this chapter, I use data from a survey and in-depth interviews with activists and leaders of the *comités patrióticos* (patriotic committees)—community groups that assumed the greatest burden of the NO campaign during the CAFTA-DR referendum—to contribute to the understanding of this change in citizens' political involvement. I explore the ways in which members of the CAFTA-DR opposition movement appealed to the defense of the welfare state of the previous decades, viewed as under threat by the agreement, and I attempt to link these positions with the ways in which the state had contributed to shaping their lives.

I also explore the double nature of the intense electoral mobilization that took place during the CAFTA-DR referendum campaign (between June and October 2007) as it was simultaneously new, as well as deeply rooted in Costa Rican political history. It was traditional in the sense that it relied on organizing an electoral process—the most common and most established political practice in Costa Rican political culture. It was novel because the content of the election was different: the disagreements over CAFTA-DR were, for both sides, a fundamental political dispute over the country's future. Unlike conventional political campaigns that revolve around the election of government officials, the NO movement framed the content of the CAFTA-DR referendum debate in more overtly ideological terms, as the opposition between a deepening of neoliberal globalization and the defense of national sovereignty and the survival of the Costa Rican welfare state. It was also new in terms of the level of activist involvement, the repertoires of collective action, and the identification with the NO cause.

Historical Context

The two conflicts—the struggle against the privatization of telecommunications, and the opposition to CAFTA-DR—are part of a longer thirty-year dispute between "elites who favor neoliberal reforms and citizens who, to varying degrees, recognize and remain attached to benefits from welfare-state institutions" (Edelman 2007, 95). The neoliberal reforms in Costa Rica clashed with the previous development model of the three post-WWII decades (Edelman 2007; Raventós 1995), which had been characterized by strong state intervention and defined by "modernized, mesocratic and inclusive development" (Rovira 2004, 313), contributing to important economic and social achievements.[6] The neoliberal economic policies of the last twenty-five years, although successful in terms of growth and diversification of the economy, were regressive in terms of the distribution of wealth. State reform, an integral part of these neoliberal policies, weakened the institutions' capacities to resolve the problems they were created to address.

Since the process of neoliberal reform began in the early 1980s, it has been met with resistance by many sectors inside and outside political institutions. Inside government, legislative approval of the first Structural Adjustment Program created distrust and doubt among congressmen, including many from the ruling party (Raventós 1995). Also, important cycles of protest took place during the first two decades of reform. In 1983, urban dwellers organized a series of mass demonstrations to protest the government's increase in electricity rates required by the International Monetary Fund (Alvarenga 2005), and in 1986, farmers protested the elimination of domestic market production subsidies demanded by the World Bank and agreed to by the government (Edelman 1999; Román 1993). Despite the belligerence of these movements, they were generally brief and served only to "soften" the government's position temporarily, ultimately contributing to the movements' demobilization.[7] In the 1990s, public universities protested budget cuts and teachers resisted the reduction of their pensions (1991 and 1995).

However, the conflicts that took place in the first decade of the new millennium, the struggle against the privatization of telecommunications and against CAFTA-DR, acquired a deeper meaning as they went beyond specific conflicts affecting a particular sector or group. They encompassed a broader debate over the model of development and society, as well as the participation of a wide variety of social movement organizations, including unions, environmental groups, student organizations, church-based associations, indigenous communities, and women's groups. They also led to a shift in political debate, from an intra-elite conflict to a conflict between the political elites and a wide array of civil society organizations.

Organization of the NO Movement for the October 2007 Referendum

Opposition to CAFTA-DR began to take shape during the beginning of the negotiations in 2003, but it was not until late 2005 that it burst into mass mobilizations. Between 2004 and 2005, two parallel processes took place that laid the groundwork for the subsequent mobilization: the development of processes of articulation of a diverse group of civil society organizations opposed to the agreement (labor unions, environmentalists, women's organizations, farmers, cooperatives, and businesses) and a public debate over the agreement, the text of which was not disclosed during the negotiation process. In this debate, public universities and groups of intellectuals took a leading role, organizing conferences, roundtables, radio and television programs, news reports, brochures, and books.[8]

In November 2005, demonstrators took to the streets and the number of marches increased. Between 2003 and late 2006, the mobilizations were organized mainly by labor unions, with the support of environmental and cultural movements. Toward the end of 2006, various sectors promoted the creation of the Frente de Apoyo a la Lucha Contra el TLC[9] (People's Front Against CAFTA-DR), composed of intellectuals and public figures, in order to frame the struggle more broadly as citizens' opposition, rather than that of labor unions and social organizations. On 26 February 2007, Costa Rica had the country's largest demonstration on record. The massive turnout led some political actors from both sides of the dispute to propose a referendum to resolve the conflict. In April, at the request of activists of the NO movement, the Tribunal Supremo de Elecciones (Supreme Electoral Tribunal)[10] called a referendum that would determine the agreement's fate. Between April and October 2007, the opposition movement went from mobilizations in the streets to an electoral campaign to the defeat of the agreement in the polls.

Figure 4.1. CAFTA-NO Poster, Public Domain

The campaign was very unequal, given that the Tribunal Supremo de Elecciones did not allocate any economic resources to the parties in favor of or against CAFTA-DR.[11] The pro-CAFTA-DR groups had ample funding since an overwhelming majority of the business sector supported the treaty. The anti-CAFTA-DR activists turned to voluntary organization and formed community groups called "patriotic committees." These committees organized members from labor unions, political parties, environmental groups, and cultural organizations in their residential areas. The committees were loosely structured so that individual citizens could join and participate. In some areas, the patriotic committee was founded by an existing anti-CAFTA-DR organization. In others, local activists called on neighbors, friends, acquaintances, and even family members to form local committees.

The committees brought together neighbors, some of them union members, from various political parties, and individuals without organizational affiliation. Together they organized the campaign against CAFTA-DR at the local level. The organizational motto was to go "house to house" or "door to door" visiting neighbors during evenings and weekends, distributing pamphlets and "NO" fliers and talking to them about the negative effects CAFTA-DR would have on farmers, social security, the environment, and national sovereignty. A central goal was to explain how CAFTA-DR would influence everyday lives.

Most of the committees met at least once a week at a neighbor's house or at a public place (frequently a public school) in order to take care of organizational tasks (production and distribution of posters, creation and sale of T-shirts, buttons, flags, and banners). Depending on the committee, they also used this time to discuss the current situation and plan electoral logistics. Some committees organized cultural festivals of music and theater. Most

Figure 4.2. CAFTA-NO Protesters, San José, Seminario Universidad, Costa Rica, Katya Alvarado

print advertising was paid for by unions and by private contributions from middle-class community members. In August, an organization called the Red de Control Ciudadano (Citizen's Control Network) organized a national campaign to train "NO" electoral officials. The purpose of this action was to have observers at each polling station to prevent fraud. Among the activists and leaders of the NO, there was a great deal of distrust regarding the impartiality of the Tribunal Supremo de Elecciones, so supervising the tables was considered necessary. The Red de Control Ciudadano trained over 5,000 electoral officials across the country, and on 7 October, the vast majority of polling stations had at least one NO observer present. The electoral official program, known as *pele el ojo* (keep an eye out), addressed distrust for the tribunal with increased citizen vigilance. The movement was truly popular in its scope and breadth. No one knows exactly how many committees were formed. The web page concostarica.com lists the e-mail addresses of some seventy contacts, but other sources within the committees calculate that there were between 150 and 180 committees (Cortés 2008).

Who Were the Participants in the Patriotic Committees?

The participants in the patriotic committees were more active citizens than the national average, as is shown by their membership in other social organizations. Around one-third participated in student organizations. Approximately 15 percent participated in environmental organizations or cooperatives, and one-third of the activists participated regularly in community-based organizations. The contrast between participation in labor unions and that of the general population highlight this point; while about 5 percent of Costa Rican citizens form part of a labor union, 30 percent of the committee activists cited union involvement. However, despite their greater participation in social organizations, they were not more active in political parties, and possibly less so. While most committee members—more than half—did not identify with any political party, national survey data from 2007 placed this figure at 40 percent. As expected, those committee members who did sympathize with a particular party supported one of the parties that had taken a stance against CAFTA-DR.

Motivations for Joining the Struggle against CAFTA-DR

Responding to an open-ended question in the survey, patriotic committee activists said their primary motivations included:

1. Defense of the welfare state and its institutions, especially those seen to be most affected by CAFTA-DR, such as the state-owned electric, telecommunications, and insurance providers, and most importantly, the public health care system. Activists feared that the stringent intellectual property rulings included in CAFTA-DR would drain health care funds through increases in the prices of medicine. There was also anger among the activists that the Costa Rican CAFTA-DR negotiators had included the privatization of telecom and insurance, against the will of the country's president and that of the majority of the population.
2. Defense of sovereignty, preventing "what is ours" from being sold or given away; or, that others come to take charge—defending the little the activists said they had left. In some cases, this sentiment was expressed in anti-imperialist language against United States foreign policy, or against the attempt to impose a way of life on the rest of the Americas.
3. Defense of the environment and opposition to the privatization of water.
4. Acting against the increase in inequality. CAFTA-DR was viewed as only benefiting the rich and foreign business and harming farmers, small and medium businesses, the middle class, and the public sector.
5. Defense of a social and environmentally sustainable development, against neoliberalism and neoliberal globalization.
6. Defense of social solidarity, of a society for everyone.
7. Against the suspicious, secret, underhanded, misinformed, non-transparent, and "fishy" way CAFTA-DR was negotiated.

In general the motivations point to claims for national sovereignty, as well as the defense of the welfare state, both viewed as under threat. These were expressed in the nationalist nature of the main symbols used by the movement, in which a heart ("my heart") beats with/in/through the colors of the flag. The subjects of in-depth interviews elaborated on these motivations, but they were more emotional, expressing a combination of fear and anger; in general, CAFTA-DR was perceived as threatening.

> A feeling of losing everything. It is such a terrible feeling to think that if one loses one's homeland, one loses everything. I thought, I have the opportunity to live here with my daughters and to have all the opportunities that come with being born here. To think that everything is being taken away and nobody is protesting. I thought it was my responsibility to protest, before losing everything. I felt I was losing any chance of freedom for my daughters. The possibility of giving them the opportunities I once had. It was a mother's intuition. It still holds true. That feeling of defending what we have. At first I thought it would be something brief, but then I realized it wasn't going to be like that. I started to accept responsibility.

> (Professional woman, 40 years old, without previous political experience, in a rural area)

A woman from another distant rural area expressed similar views. Her perspective differs in her articulation that what was lost had been appropriated by the powerful and the population was left with nothing. In her case, indignation was stronger than fear.

> For me, it is outrageous to see how the huge falcons, the supporters of Arias, have no qualms about violating every right: environmental rights, civil rights, human rights in all fields, because they are violating our health, our environment, like Crucitas,[12] with the dam that they want to construct, leaving indigenous people without their daily bread—it's not fair. This annoys me so much that I am willing to do everything it takes to defend the future of my children, my grandchildren, because tomorrow what will these poor creatures do, these poor people? I am starting to think that this country is divided into pieces. What is left? What is left of our homeland, what are we left with? (Woman, 47 years old, homemaker, without prior political experience, committee leader)

Both women stress the importance of participation in order to defend their children's future, preserving the opportunities that were once available. This motivation is noticeably stronger with the women interviewed, who spoke of their fear of eroding possibilities, than with the men. Most interviewees—men and women alike—stress the importance of higher education as a mechanism for upward social mobility:

> My father was a construction worker. Afterwards, he became a security guard at the Psychiatric Hospital. We were on a fixed income, but we all went to the University. I think this is why we fought, why we continue fighting, because we always studied with scholarships. In high school, we had scholarships and in university we had scholarships. There were four of us and we were all good students. All of us are professionals. One is an agronomist, one a nurse, one a business administrator. (Professional woman, 40 years old, rural patriotic committee leader).

> I love my career ... that I had the opportunity to study with a scholarship. I owe it to this country that gave so many of us the opportunity to study (Professional woman, 52 years old, rural patriotic committee leader).

> I am the son of a rural family, my mother was a single mother, I know my dad ... but she raised me. She started out as a domestic worker, but later, thanks to the agrarian farming model, my mom had some cows and at a certain time began to make curd, and with those cows she industrialized her milk and curds. Therefore, I now say that I am the son of the "cuajada" (curd). My high school studies and part of my elementary school studies were paid for by the curd sales of my mom. (Man, 44 years old, professional, leftist political experience, regional leader in a rural zone)

What is interesting about these quotes is that the interviewees link personal experiences to a society that provided them with opportunities. These movement leaders highlight the importance of society or the state as the source of the opportunities they had. Although they give credit to their mothers and fathers, there is always the state, through scholarships or through the "agrarian farming model" that allowed them to get a degree, or that permitted a mother to buy cows to be able to make and sell curd. This emphasis on society as a source of opportunity could be a result of the context, to the extent that the struggle in defense of the welfare state may have motivated them to tell their stories highlighting the importance of government programs, such as public education, above individual and family factors.

Experience in the Committees, Formation of Collective Identities, and Social Subjectivities

The interviews and survey took place toward the end of the anti-CAFTA-DR movement and emphasize that these were intense experiences for movement participants. In terms of dedication, most members participated in a wide array of activities (some of these are mentioned above): the weekly committee meetings, another weekly meeting of some sub-committee, door-to-door distribution of flyers in neighborhood houses, meetings with neighbors on nights and weekends, the design of print material, and organization of additional activities were all part of political participation during this time. They were very time consuming and often led to the neglect of household and family obligations and/or taking leave from work, or even cutting back on work hours. Everyday life moved from private life to public activities, something that was entirely new for most participants.

On the day of the referendum, the committees organized the voting logistics: voter mobilization, organization of volunteers and observations of the polls. Overseeing the polls with a massive volunteer effort from the NO movement was also decisive (see above). In contrast to the mobilization of thousands of volunteers on the NO side, the campaign in favor of CAFTA-DR was mainly undertaken by professionals, and the publicity and logistics were organized through paid contracts.

The majority of committee members—70 percent—had joined the fight against CAFTA-DR well before the referendum announcement and had already participated in demonstrations, conferences, and debates. The transition to a referendum and participating in committees led to many changes:

1. The transition from street protests to electoral campaigning. Many activists initially resisted this process due to the distrust produced by deciding on CAFTA-DR through an electoral process, in which the op-

position only had the force of volunteers, while big business and government joined money and government power in favor of the treaty.

2. Bringing together historically separate traditions. For those who got involved, the referendum placed activism in the context of electoral rituals, which brought together political traditions that were historically separate. This was particularly true for activists from the left who had less experience than those coming from traditional parties in electoral mobilizations. For them, this became an opportunity to learn about unknown political practices.
3. Renewed significance of the electoral process. Since the 1980s, there had been a "de-politicization" of presidential elections, due to the loss of ideological differences between candidates, as well as the weakening of party organizations. The content of the decision on CAFTA-DR, on the contrary, was highly political and ideological, which raised the stakes of the election.
4. Working with neighbors. Many anti-CAFTA-DR militants had never participated in politics in their communities. Many hardly knew each other and had never worked together on political activities. This led to the construction of social networks and new political practices among activists who came from different political experiences, primarily from civil society organizations (unions, environmental groups, student organizations, etc.).
5. Working with people who came from different militant traditions. The encounters of militants from social activism with political militants of different partisan traditions created new public spheres in which each learned from the others and came to know other forms of political participation.

Interviews indicate that the networks built by neighbors working together in grassroots political action appears to be the main legacy of committee participation. The creation of public spheres, through the discussions and collaboration of people who had never worked together and who in many cases did not know each other previously, is strongly valued by participants, who said things such as:

> [This political work was different] in its reach, diversity, spontaneity … because it did not have a particular political direction, and it seems to me that is what gave the movement its character. … Having shared a space with colleagues from very different political visions and diverse experiences—for me, that was really nice. Having been able to share with Christians, with people of the PUSC, of the Liberación. (Man, 50 years old, left-wing political experience, rural committee leader)

> [In m]y work experience with university youth … I got to know young people better, I learned to respect them much more. … My experience with women's organizations … that patriarchal history in which the man is brave—this is totally false. The bravest, the most courageous, those who raised their voices with the most strength, were women. That is also part of what I am left with. (Man, 50 years old, intellectual, without previous organizing experience, activist in a committee)

> We have traditionally been accustomed to working with people who think like us. There is a hegemonic position and we go and we put it in practice. In this situation, we had to work with people who had very diverse experiences, who had very diverse ways of doing things, with very different visions, and so you have to figure out how to deal with it and move forward. (Man, 50 years old, left-wing political experience, leader of a committee from the suburbs)

The quotes above show, unequivocally, how important the committee experience was for their members. Meeting across generations and gender, political, and organizational paths and knowledge generated a richness of perspectives and released creative energy, impacting all who shared in the experience. The intensity of the work made many put their daily routines aside, reducing their free time, and forcing them to divert all their energy into winning the referendum.

The combination of personal motivation, experience, beliefs, and practices, acts as a melting pot that created new subjectivities. New, because people are no longer who they were, because they are now positioned differently both politically and socially. The individual and social past is revalued through participation in the struggle, and the image of a particularly Costa Rican "us" resonates within individual identity.

These new collective identities were expressed throughout 2008 and 2009 in requests to the political parties for a united political front for the February 2010 presidential election. However, the political parties that supported the NO movement had different approaches to politics and were unable, and to a large extent unwilling, to find common ground for an electoral coalition. This brought further disenchantment of committee members and leadership with political parties.

Conclusions: The NO Movement in the Context of Costa Rican and Central American Politics

The opposition to CAFTA-DR forms part of a period of increased citizen mobilization that started with the new millennium. Unlike the resistance to neoliberal reform in the 1980s and 1990s, the movements in the first years of the new century were citizen movements that brought together activists from different sectors: union, student, environmental, feminist, and community groups. The calling of a referendum to define the CAFTA-DR decision led to the creation of the patriotic committees, which brought together activists—the majority of whom were middle class—and many professionals from the public sector. The life stories of these individuals, as the quotes from the interviews demonstrate, are intertwined in many ways with the development of the welfare state, with the opportunities for education and jobs that it provided, and with the work they do in the public institutions that employ them.

The principal factor that motivated many participants to fight against CAFTA-DR was the perception of losing important aspects in a society in which they grew up and were raised, aspects they considered desirable: an inclusive society with extensive social safety nets and opportunities for social mobility. It is interesting, however, that the threat against this model of society did not begin with CAFTA-DR; for three decades there had been a gradual erosion of the quality of social programs, of public education, and health care. This begs the question as to why the opposition of these social groups consolidated in the early twenty-first century with the resistance against the privatization of telecommunications and CAFTA-DR and not before. A plausible explanation is that CAFTA-DR was constructed in the collective imagination as "the point of no return," possibly due to the fact that the legislation introduced could not be changed internally within the country, and that it depended on a renegotiation of the terms of the agreement with the United States, other Central American countries, and the Dominican Republic.

A second explanation is that it took time for the professional middle classes to visualize the social changes that neoliberalism was bringing about, in terms of increases in inequality as well as changes in the social structure and the labor market. During the second half of the twentieth century, teachers, doctors, agronomists, social workers, and engineers were trained at public universities and employed by government. The state was the main employer of university graduates at public schools, public hospitals, electricity and telecommunication providers, insurance companies, state banks, and welfare and agricultural programs. Many professionals worked for these institutions during their entire careers, obtaining promotions and retiring with dependable pension funds. They were also loyal supporters of governments and defenders of public policies. With the systematic weakening of the welfare state and underfunding of its programs, these groups became increasingly alienated from government authorities who in turn concentrated on the neoliberal reforms that contributed precisely to that weakening and underfunding. For many, their jobs became increasingly difficult and meaningless, as the institutions they worked for were not able to deliver quality services as they had in the past.

Due to the massive donations of the U.S. government in the 1980s, with which I introduced this chapter, these changes were more gradual in Costa Rica than in many other countries and consequently less visible. It took time for them to appear in a clearer form.

A second theme that runs through this chapter is how the particular forms of political participation that arose during the NO mobilization differ from those utilized in the past. The practices that these activists developed reflect specific ways of doing politics that are strongly rooted in Costa Rican political culture. The enthusiasm with which thousands of citizens joined patriotic committees during the referendum campaign highlights the importance of electoral processes within the political culture (Dabene 1986; Lehoucq and Molina 2002). These had been festive events until the mid 1990s, when the corruption scandals and loss of trust in politicians changed this. The NO campaign for the referendum recovered the festivity, although with new forms. Unlike the regular campaigns, the protagonists were no longer political parties or politicians running for office, but people in communities. The joy of acting together, of identifying with each other, and the creation of music, images, and symbols gave a new twist to an old practice and recreated it in a new form. Despite the fact that the referendum was the first in national history, in the end it was an election that shared common elements with the national elections held every four years. Many activists, especially those with experience participating in traditional parties, knew electoral mobilization strategies well, including how to approach voters and how to incorporate volunteers.

However, a new significance emerged from this common practice: the articulation of a campaign around a political dispute, beyond the election of candidate. It thus introduced new meaning to a traditional practice. For many anti-CAFTA-DR activists, this experience redefined politics and elections. In the presidential elections of the past three decades, political and ideological differences between candidates and parties were blurred, creating electoral processes with very little political content. The referendum, on the contrary, was a highly political decision in that the different positions were rooted in deep ideological differences. This factor aroused the interest and enthusiasm of many activists.

The training of electoral officials and the integration of some 5,000 people to volunteer at the polling stations as a response to the mistrust of the Tribunal Supremo de Elecciones, and its impartiality, indicated new levels of criticism, as it meant questioning the purity of elections that had been culturally considered sacred. However, countering distrust by assuming an active role in the vigilance of the polls points to the legacy of decades of regular elections and to the civic values that are part of these citizens' forms of thinking and acting politically. Other practices can also be associated with the backgrounds of most members of the patriotic committees, in terms of their educational and professional attainment: the door-to-door campaigning and visiting neighbors, for example, point to their disposition to educate their fellow citizens.

Compared to other Central American countries, whose politics are the result of different relationships between elites and subordinate groups, the uniqueness of the Costa Rica situation becomes clearer. Three decades ago, broad sectors of people raised arms in Nicaragua, Guatemala, and El Salvador in the fight for social change. In Costa Rica, at this time, the underlying social contract as well as donations from the United States government jointly contributed to a response to the anti-austerity protest movements of the 1980s and to the maintenance of political stability throughout the first two decades of structural adjustment and neoliberal reform. The erosion of political legitimacy over the past decade has, contrary to this history, striking similarities with the Central American crises three decades ago. The lack of willingness of political and economic elites to negotiate and the imposition of a socially exclusive development model are central to this process (Pérez Brignoli 2001). Despite this similarity, the development of the political crisis is very different, and it points to different political histories. In other countries, weak institutions broke down, producing rebellion and war. In Costa Rica, to date, all actors have, to a large extent, moved within the institutional framework. Moreover, it is primarily the critical and oppositional sectors—like the anti-CAFTA-DR movement activists—that most often defend these institutions and denounce their arbitrary uses by political elites.

An important legacy of the social movements of the first decade of the new millennium is a more active and militant citizenry. This chapter focused on the patriotic committees, which were mainly middle class. However, CAFTA-DR was also opposed by indigenous and agricultural communities. In more recent years, the struggle in defense of water in coastal communities threatened by tourist development, or against mining projects, has again brought together different citizen groups. They point to demands for the deepening of democracy in society and the development of public spaces for doing so. However, it is still uncertain if and how the political system will respond to the challenge.

Notes

* This chapter is a result of the research project "El movimiento del "NO al TLC: resistencia contra la globalización neoliberal y construcción de alternativas políticas en Costa Rica," which the author developed at the Social Sciences Institute at the University of Costa Rica,

with the support of a CLASCO-ASDI grant in 2008–2009. This text was prepared for the workshop "After the Handshakes: Rethinking Democracy and Living Transition in Central America," held at the University of Albany 11–13 September 2008. Thanks to Jennifer Burrell for her close reading, requests for precision, and thought-provoking feedback.

1. As Edelman and Kenen (1989) have written, Costa Rica defaulted on its foreign debt a full year before Mexico's moratorium officially inaugurated the Latin American debt crisis. Costa Rica's currency, the colon, fell from an official exchange of 8.6 to the dollar, to 39 in 1981 and in July 1982 reached a low of 65 to the dollar. Inflation came close to 100 percent in 1982, and unemployment doubled (Edelman and Kenen, 1989, 187–88).
2. Speech to the Foreign Relations Committee, U.S. House of Representatives, 22 June 1982 (quoted in Sojo [1991]).
3. As G. Hernández (1998) has shown, Monge negotiated a pact with the opposition to allow it to become a party. At that moment it was organized as a coalition and was in disarray since it had been in office when the crisis struck and was being politically blamed for it.
4. Marc Edelman and Joanne Kenen (1989, 189) highlight the magnitude of the aid package: "U.S. economic assistance between 1983 and 1985 was equivalent to a staggering 35.7 percent of the Costa Rican government's operating expenditures, one quarter of export earnings, and around 10 percent of the country's GDP."
5. Between 1948 and the mid 1980s, Costa Rica had a state monopoly of banking. The USAID package was premised on the promotion of private banking.
6. Jorge Rovira Mas (2004) defines mesocratic as "the important role played by middle class social sectors." It could be added that they were also, to some extent, the beneficiaries in terms of their expansion in society and their increased participation in the distribution of wealth.
7. Protests against the rates forced the government to temporarily suspend the measure and change it to gradual increments. The farmer protests were mediated through the creation of negotiation opportunities.
8. This debate was important in that it "translated" the agreement and made it accessible and understandable, at least for people with secondary education or higher. At the referendum stage, a second translation of the text into popular language was primarily done by academics.
9. TLC is the Spanish acronym for Tratado de Libre Comercio, the Free Trade Agreement.
10. The Tribunal Supremo de Elecciones is an independent branch of the government that has organized and supervised elections in Costa Rica since 1948.
11. The 1952 Electoral Code includes a provision for the state to finance most of the parties' campaign expenses in national elections. The 2006 Referendum Law omitted this financial provision and the 2007 Referendum Regulation did not include it. As a result, the parties had very unequal economic resources.
12. Crucitas, in the northern region of Costa Rica, is the site of an ongoing environmental conflict over open-pit mining that has been taking place for over two decades.

5 Democracy, Disenchantment, and the Future in El Salvador

*Ellen Moodie**

What happens to desires for democracy when violence and corruption continue after a war ends? By many counts violence increased in El Salvador after the 1992 Peace Accords. Within three years, the country's murder rate placed El Salvador as the most violent in Latin America, globally second only to South Africa (Cruz and González 1997a).[1] The phrase "It's worse than the war" circulated across the capital city of San Salvador throughout the 1990s and into the 2000s.

Just what "it" was was not clear. People's fears overflowed quantifiable entities. They often focused on unseen dangers—on dread in daily navigation through public spaces, on invisible global forces such as those that devastated the coffee prices that had once girded the economy (see Lyon; and Tucker, this volume). In everyday talk and mass media discourse, "it" seemed to index common crime (*delincuencia común*). A year after the Peace Accords a survey of urban Salvadorans found 73 percent believed "crime, thievery, lack of authority, robbery, violations and gangs" were the country's principal problem. Eighty-nine percent believed violence had increased (IUDOP 1993, 471).

Not just crime figures but also discourses on crime surged in the postwar moment. I have elsewhere suggested that the joint production of stories of violence worked with other forces to reshape Salvadoran subjectivities (Moodie 2010). After the war people described danger in terms of increasingly personal, or private, experience. This sense of separateness could supplant orientations toward the collectivities that had cohered around struggles for equality and inclusion—including revolution (see Binford; and R. Montoya, this volume). It could loosen attachments to social movements, as well as bonds to a broader ethic of community obligation. In the years after the Salvadoran civil war, then—during the process labeled democratization—citizenship became increasingly structured around individual responsibility for the management of risk.

The "it" implied in the sentiment "worse than the war" thus could also mean democracy. After all, democracy was deemed the key to transition from war (with former guerrillas, legalized as a political party through the Peace

Accords, on the ballot). Some social scientists have theorized that violence and democracy are deeply intertwined in Latin America, particularly in El Salvador (see Arias and Goldstein 2010; A. Montoya 2011). In my research, I have sought to distill the "taken-for-granted" meanings of democratic governance emergent in everyday conversations and public discourses. Here I explore some of the conceptions of democracy circulating in San Salvador in the 1990s and 2000s. I end by suggesting that visions of a different future—hopes for an alternative democracy—still animate Salvadorans, as events of June 2011 and beyond show.

What Democracy?

The negotiations that led to the end of El Salvador's twelve-year civil war began in earnest in the aftermath of the murders of six prominent priests, their housekeeper, and her daughter by soldiers on 16 November 1989 in their residence at the Jesuit Central American University (UCA) during a guerrilla offensive in the capital.[2] Just a few days earlier, the East German government had opened its borders to the west, an act soon iconized as the fall of the Berlin Wall. Both these spectacular events symbolized the conditions leading to the end of the Salvadoran civil war: in Europe, the collapse of "actually existing" (or nonexistent) socialism pointed to an apparent triumph of global capitalism (Coronil 2011, 236), while in El Salvador, worldwide shock at the murders pushed all parties to recognize that, after the failed but violent rebel siege a decade into the conflict, no one was "winning" the war.

These events in some ways structured Salvadoran yearning, at a time in which multiple global discourses and expectations intersected with complicated domestic desires. Indeed, Fernando Coronil (2011) points to 1989 as key to the current Latin American shift *to the left*—for that was also the year of Augusto Pinochet's electoral defeat in Chile by a coalition opposing neoliberalism (though ultimately, not capitalism). Coronil (2011, 240) argues that the vote signaled "the value attached to democracy as the political form through which to pursue collective welfare as a value in itself."

But *what* democracy? For some on the Salvadoran political left at that time, the term democracy, usually said "without adjectives" (whether participatory, social, liberal, or authoritarian) (Collier and Levitsky 1996), appeared to slip almost effortlessly into the slot formerly instilled with revolutionary fervor—into the space once filled with socialist visions (this process was not so effortless in post-Sandinista Nicaragua [see R. Montoya, this volume]). Differences in interpretations of this moment, of what the lurch toward this democracy meant, would soon lead to the splitting of the Farabundo Martí National Liberation front (FMLN) as it transformed to a legal political party.

Some former guerrillas insisted on a participatory, social democratic vision of equality, while others seemed to seek out the market-oriented so-called "Third Way."

While leftists argued among themselves, El Salvador's government, led by the right-wing Nationalist Republican Alliance (ARENA) party, saw the triumph of capital. By the war's end, ARENA had initiated a privatization process the United Nations Development Programme (UNDP) called "one of the most aggressive of Latin America" (2001). That was how democracy emerged in El Salvador's peace. As Julia Paley (2008, 13) writes, "Democracy is now so deeply embedded in a prolonged moment of economic and philosophical liberalism that democracy (as ideology, as experience, as expectation, as policy) is co-produced with market economics, a phenomenon neatly captured by the phrase 'free market democracies.'" The consequences of this political course would soon become clear. While the conservative Heritage Foundation ranked El Salvador as having among the highest Indexes of Economic Freedom in the world, the country also had some of the highest inequality levels in the world (UNDP 2001).[3]

Despite stark inequality and high crime rates, the United Nations began extolling Salvadoran success immediately after the first postwar elections concluded without bloodshed, in 1994—or, without apparent political bloodshed (that would change; see A. Montoya, this volume). The state and the international observer agencies worked hard to "purify" any postwar violence by classifying most murders as "common," everyday, domestic concerns. I call this "critical criminal code switching" (Moodie 2010). The effort was so successful that by the mid 2000s, some U.S. officials held up El Salvador's experience as an exemplary democratic transition, one for Iraq to emulate (see Brooks 2004).

What did this globally lauded instance of democratization mean to the Salvadorans experiencing it? How did postwar ideas about democracy link to historically located senses of the concept? How did these ideas intersect with global hegemonic meanings of the concept? And what consequences did those meanings have—how did these understandings inflect people's interpretations of political events?

Crime Stories

One way to uncover desires for democracy is to listen to everyday talk. When I first arrived in El Salvador in 1994 to begin fieldwork, and in the years that followed, conversations overflowed with crime stories. I soon realized that in many ways crime stories narrate citizens' relationship with the state. People's ideas about governance, about how to organize human coexistence, emerge in such accounts. In the narratives I recorded and analyzed in the first postwar decade, I found that senses of democracy fall into three interrelated, descriptive categories.

First, *order*, in the sense of rule of law and responsive institutions, but also in terms of justice (social and legal); second, *belonging*, drawing on sociocultural factors that bind people in a feeling of community; and, third, *development*, encompassing ideas that prospects for democracy link to a future imaginary of economic well-being—and indeed hints at promises of equality exceeding the incomplete, no-frills democracy equation of one person, one vote.

Another element showed up in discourses: I call it disenchantment. What too often happens is that citizens, expecting dramatic change, can become disillusioned during transitions (see also Silber 2010). The majority of Salvadorans had lived their lives under corrupt, authoritarian regimes. It was much easier to fall back into habitual distrust of politics as usual than to believe in the possibility of a different future.

Democracy, Order, and Justice

The first icon of 1989 for Salvadorans was the Jesuit massacre. That event happened in the midst of a guerrilla offensive in the capital and forced all sides into peace negotiations. The FMLN was largely stymied from bargaining over economics in those U.N.-brokered talks (Wood 1996, 79); reform of the state security apparatus became the left's priority. Many considered the transformation of military police forces into a civilian body a key achievement. The new human-rights-trained civilian force would protect citizens rather than seek enemies of the state. That crime and insecurity *increased* during the process of democratization was not incidental to views of the postwar transition.

Their stories show how Salvadorans often yearned for something that may sound simple. People wanted rule of law. They wanted "decent people" to be protected. They wanted justice. This desire is not abstract after war. It was galling to many people that in 1993 the Amnesty Law passed, prohibiting prosecution for crimes committed during the war (leading to the early release of the two soldiers convicted in 1991 in the Jesuit case).[4] More concretely, much Salvadoran disillusion centered on the state's failure to respond, that is, the state's failure to protect citizen rights and private property. Of course, for most Salvadorans, history weighed too heavily to believe that the state, especially the police, would change quickly. A 1999 World Bank survey found that only 20 percent of San Salvador crime victims reported the incident to the police (Cruz et al. 1999). In most crime stories I recorded the police never came up. So when, recounting their experiences, Salvadorans *did* mention the police, it was telling. It almost always revealed something about disillusion with the new state—about democratic disenchantment.

Lili was one of the few people I knew who explicitly mentioned the state when she told her story. She had come back to El Salvador after the war for peace—for democracy.[5] In the 1980s she had renounced her middle-class roots and had joined an organization that supported the FMLN. In 1988 she fled the country with her tiny daughter and her husband after he was released from prison (and told to leave or he would be killed). She had lived in Canada for seven years as a political refugee. She returned alone.

"It was in March 1997," she told me (two years later), "in the Colonia La Mascota, on a pretty isolated street, but supposedly there are all these places around with security [guards]. In that area you know there are all those big *portones* [garage door-sized gates] and guards. … It was like six at night, but it wasn't dark yet. I arrived there in my car, at my niece's house. It's an old car, not a car that's going to call attention to itself—I mean nobody would want to steal it." So she did not worry when a "nice-looking" man walked in her direction. Not until he walked right to her car.

She had already opened the car door. He reached in. "He began to push me, he said to me, 'Move over there! Move over there!' … He wanted me on the other seat, but—well—he asked me to give him everything that I had. The truth is, I didn't have much—didn't have anything of value—not even money—just my purse. I was coming from work and was wearing a little necklace—but it wasn't valuable. …

"I gave him my watch, but it was just a cheap watch. … But then at that moment it occurred to me—that maybe he wanted something, *sexual,* and then—I really got scared. I thought, well I don't have anything material to give him—don't have any cash, the car isn't worth stealing, the watch is a piece of junk—and also I saw that this guy was pretty well dressed, and I had felt his shirt against me, it was soft, rayon or silk … so right there that frightened me. Because he wasn't suspicious-looking. So it scared me, him saying, 'Move over there!' … And so I just really quickly opened the door on the other side, the passenger's side, and rang the doorbell and started screaming.

"… And he just took off running, he grabbed my necklace and took off running, insulting me."

"What did he say?"

"Like, 'Cunt, now you're gonna lose your purse, you had to scream,' … but I got so scared, and he was running down the street, so I just started yelling with all my strength. I thought maybe the security guard in the shopping center down the way, like two blocks down, might hear me, so I began to scream, 'He robbed me, get him!'" Then Lili, with a maid who had answered the door, began to chase the man in her car. They lost him, though the shopping-center guard admitted he had seen him. When Lili asked the guard why he hadn't stopped a man running with a purse, he replied, "I'm here to protect the stores."

"I went to the National Civilian Police right away," she said, explicitly naming the new, Peace-Accords-mandated police body (the PNC):

> But there are ... well, the only thing there, the impression I remember is that I went, they didn't really help me very much, in fact they really seemed to me to be totally inefficient, an inefficiency that's—embarrassing. They weren't nasty or anything, but it was, like, when *at last* somebody paid attention to me and I told him what happened, he asked me if there had been personal damage, like a death or an injury or something, and when I said, "No," "Ah, well. Ah, well, what can you do?" Then, so he gave me a form to fill out, because I had had a wallet in my purse, with credit cards, I.D., driver's license, all my papers, everything, so I had to get an official letter from the police to go to get a new license.

"What really struck me," Lili concluded, "was that never, never, did it occur to me before that I would ever do anything like that in my life, to go file a report about something with the police. I mean my attitude then, my attitude after what happened, was to go right to the police. Before, I mean in the war, to go to the police would be to go into a snake pit, it was a terrible thing."

Why did Lili go so quickly to the police about her cheap watch and her almost-empty wallet?

> [I]n some ways [after having lived] in Canada, you, I don't know, try to follow the established system a little. But on the other hand, I was conscious of the changes here. The PNC, for example, is one of the changes. Before ... you never knew if the police would grab you, or the National Guard, or whatever authority, or a person dressed in civilian clothes but armed. ... I tell you I don't remember ever having been worried about crime [back then], you know. You weren't trying to protect yourself from the thieves; you were mainly trying to protect yourself from the police, and not thieves, ... a thief just grabs your watch and that's that.

And that's that. But it wasn't; it was so much more. Lili spoke of a sense of nakedness, of a lack of protection. During the war, she expected nothing (or expected the worst) from the authorities. Indeed, one might say that during the war she was effectively one of the state's excluded. A subversive. Now, after the war, she had imagined a kind of liberal democracy that recognized her, one that formally embraced a plurality of identities as equal. But as she ventured into a purportedly democratized public space, all had failed her: the imagined safety of a prosperous neighborhood, the nice-looking, well-dressed man, the image of security projected by the shopping center—and then the PNC, the Peace-Accords police.

Lili's frustration with the police tells us about something more than a moment of bureaucratic insensitivity. El Salvador was not supposed to be the same repressive, authoritarian state as before. It was supposed to be a democracy. Arriving alone, she had expected in some perhaps not-quite-fully conscious way to be cared for or at least cared about as an equal. That the new police were so inefficient and unconcerned about justice was shameful. She was not just complaining; she was telling a story of the nation and a state. To be embarrassed suggests she had had different expectations. I would add here that this desire for a community of care contrasts with the neoliberal rationality of self-care, in which the individual must manage his or her own risk.

A call for "law and order" can be interpreted as a demand to repress all perceived danger, whether racialized minorities, impoverished majorities, the mentally ill, the politically oppositional. State formation is predicated on exclusions to protect the privileges of the powerful, even as the liberal project imagines itself as embracing all identities. One tension in definitions of political order lies in the fact that strong, reliable institutions help regulate a democratic state and mete out justice. Concerns about policing do not necessarily index nostalgia for the constricted safety of the dictatorship.

Democracy and Belonging

Democracy can thus be imagined as feeling like an inclusive community of care: as having something to do with the practice of equality and the pursuit of social justice. This concept draws on a social imaginary of obligation, of compassion in the sense of concern for the well being of others (Woodward 2004). As Greg Grandin (2004, 14) argues, "Latin American democracy as an ideal and practice was always much more participatory and egalitarian than it was procedural and individualistic." In such a world, democratization might be interpreted as a transition to a more inclusive and just public sphere.

Idealized notions of community have been deconstructed as enforcing normativity, as protecting hierarchies of power. Yearning for belonging and togetherness does not necessarily gibe with definitions of liberal democracy that stress openness to multiple perspectives and even friction among competing ideas. But most people do not reflect on normalizing disciplines of unity—usually entailing a willful ignorance of others' suffering (see Joseph 2002).

José Luis, a middle-class accountant from a family with agro-export business interests, spoke as if democratic expectations have been *reversed* over time.[6] This next fragment of conversation follows his account of an assault in which thieves robbed paychecks he was delivering to his family firm's workers:

> Before, I used to enjoy going to the city center to shop. Now, we're part of that joke, we only shop from [affluent] Escalón and above. We go to ... Galerias [a high-end, enclosed mall], any place where there aren't as many people. ... We go out to eat where there aren't people. It's not that we think we're too good: it's just that we think that wherever there are people, there's going to be a problem with violence. Or where people drink, where people are drinking beer for example—we used to go to the Zona Rosa ... now we don't, because something could happen, we could be hit by a bullet, a fight could break out.

He insisted that the problem was not the fact of large numbers or even of poverty; it was how people interacted. "Look, in my childhood [in the 1960s] I was raised—it was a block from the central market of San Salvador. I mean, I lived in the middle of enormous crowds, and it was a peaceful life. My mother left the door open. The only thing we had was a wooden rail across the door, and people would knock on that when they came by to visit."

His story moves from a childhood memory of an imagined egalitarian world near the large municipal market (inhabited by the masses, and symbolic of an idealized equal exchange, a public sphere) to an escape from the crowds to places like the exclusive, air-conditioned and privatized Galerias (patrolled by security guards like the one who wouldn't help Lili). It is not a narrative of upward mobility. Told in the context of a conversation about postwar insecurity, it delineates a trajectory of separation and division, *away* from any imagined possibility of equality and democracy to a neoliberal market order. It does not redefine democracy; it does not deny the social costs of that alienation.

José Luis dreams of a democracy in which all people are abstract equals, interacting respectfully in the public sphere—in his case, literal marketplaces of the San Salvador city market and air-conditioned malls. His worldview may seem distant from the revolutionary visions that impelled guerrillas and committed campesinos (see Binford, this volume). Yet his narrative echoes their accounts of disenchantment.

Yearnings for a future of egalitarian community, whether shaped by well-honed revolutionary imaginaries or less conscious ideas about moral orders and human equality, thus affected reactions to postwar insecurity. They inevitably formed the postwar narrative of democratic disenchantment. The way people share their stories—what fits into a tellable tale—points to what is important in the moment. The lack of a feeling of community came up again and again in conversations about crime in San Salvador.

Rosario and I met in a dark rowhouse in a rough neighborhood of Soyapango, a dense, gang-ridden city next to San Salvador.[7] In her late twenties, she was a humble woman of campesino origins married to an ex-guerrilla. "But yeah," she told me, "you get scared, look, right over by the university, by the Parque Infantil, I don't know if you've been there, that's where these two men came out and took my watch. I didn't fight, but because I was holding on to my watch, a little piece of it stuck into me and made me start bleeding. I thought they'd cut me, but no, it was the watch that I wanted to hold on to, he got it off me and took it. And that was all. Today what we do is, everything that they want we give them, because today, now, this year, they kill the people first, so they can rob them.

"Because last year," she continued, "over there … there they killed a man, they took his gun and some really thick gold chains and then shot him, here, he died right then, didn't last ten minutes, here in the neighborhood, you know, that's how things go in the neighborhood now."

Rosario's story begins in the midst of the epitome of the modern public sphere, the public park. But danger lurks. Unlike José Luis, she cannot withdraw to the protection of a private world—not even *her* own neighborhood. I asked, "There wasn't as much crime before?"

She interpreted my query as about war. "Thank God, my family, everyone's here, you know, nothing happened to them, they are all here and thank God it was luck that none of us died because most families had a lot, families lost their children, not for getting mixed up in politics, but when you got caught in the middle."

She paused. "I almost died once in the city center. At least the Despensa was open, the one by the cathedral [the Despensa de Don Juan, a grocery store chain]. So when the shooting began, and bombs, they let us in, the Despensa. If they grab me in the street, I die, you see, but inside a business or a house there's less chance of that."

Rosario offers another narrative strand of people taking care of each other—and not. In his own neighborhood (and hers), a man was robbed and murdered. Her repetition of *here,* in the *neighborhood,* is significant. In contrast, while she recalled a generalized violence during the war, she pointed to community solidarity—even far from her neighborhood. In the busy city center, strangers opened their doors to her.

The absence of the police in her story reminds us that people like Rosario do not expect the protection of a patriarchal state that Lili desired. Rosario did hope for other people to help her, as they did in the war. But in this new democracy, it felt like people were pulling away from each other.

Democracy and Development

The third aspect of democracy that emerges in crime stories is an association with progress and development. In El Salvador, democracy has always stood as a symbol of possibility—never-fulfilled possibility, like the project of modernity itself (Alonso 1988). In the immediate postwar years, the lived experience of not only everyday violence but also low wages and limited opportunities quickly undermined hopes.

To put it bluntly: How much poverty and inequality can a democracy bear? In its report *Democracy in Latin America* the UNDP (2004, 39) notes, "For the first time in history an entire developing region with profoundly unequal societies is, in its entirety, organized politically under democratic governments. Thus a new and unprecedented situation has emerged in Latin America: the coexistence of democracy, poverty and inequality."

Some Salvadorans in the first postwar decade saw deeper failures in the postwar government—failures that maintained inequality and poverty in the country and, they believed, contributed to high crime rates. This view echoed across social positions. Amparo, a working-class, middle-aged woman also from Soyapango, who had once been part of an urban, Liberation-Theology-inspired Christian Base Community, explicitly pointed to the nation's political economy:

> Here they say an effect of the war is family disintegration, and it's possible, but what I think is that [the problem of postwar crime] really comes from unemployment. The parents don't have any [other] way to maintain their children. What are they going to do? It might not be good what they're doing, but it's a consequence of the war, and not only that, a consequence of class conflict, of our government's politics, also we have to see all this neoliberalism is influencing the situation. ... Those who haven't studied, how are they going to do well, because here not everyone studies—not because they don't want to but because they can't afford it, you know. I don't know if I'm going to be able to afford to send my two grandsons to the university.

The broken promise of progress and the loss of possibilities, of a future, is palpable in her account.

Future Imperfect

Many stories I heard in the first postwar decade manifest a sense of loss of a future, a loss of desired if never-quite-known objects: a fantasy of order and justice, a dream of belonging, and a vision of a community of care even if that care was sometimes shot through with paternalism or patriarchy. The stories reveal democratic disenchantment. But they also evince acute concerns about individual security and private safety. They disclose risks not only to human life but also to property. They very much tell of having and losing stuff.

Lili chased after the "nice-looking" thief who grabbed her purse. Rosario gripped her watch so tightly she bled when the thieves seized it. José Luis wanted to go shopping. Amparo hoped to educate her grandsons. All had allowed themselves to imagine a form of coexistence in which everyone theoretically had a right to the public sphere; but an orderly one, one of civility and respect in which, it must be said, some individuals might be excluded.

There is something incompatible in the qualities of democracy they articulate. Can equality and liberty cohabitate? Can José Luis have democracy only in the air-conditioned malls? Must Lili listen to the desires of the man who wanted her jewels—and maybe more? Chantal Mouffe (2005, 18), building on Carl Schmitt's controversial but productive views, put it this way: Liberal democracy is

> a specific form of organizing politically human coexistence which results from the articulation between two different traditions: on one side, political liberalism (rule of law, separation of powers, human rights—a kind of abstract universalism) and on the other side, the democratic tradition of popular sovereignty—which incorporates ideas of pluralism and conflict.

Schmitt, seeking political unity, declares these trajectories irreconcilable. Mouffe insists that we accept contradictions as inherent in radical democracy. There is no final certainty.

In El Salvador after the war, many people thought democracy would resolve uncertainty. Few considered the tension between wanting to be safe and wanting everyone's voices to be heard.[8] But the security so many people (and not just Salvadorans) desire inevitably requires exclusion of some. Not everyone has a right to be part of the demos, to be equal, in a security-state democracy. It may be easy to point to the contradictions in the developmentalist "will to improve," in order to critique the ultimate illogic in the simultaneous "promotion of capitalist processes and concern to improve the condition of the dispossessed" (Li 2007, 32). But people's desires, contradictory as they may be, are not just products of assemblages of governmentality. They emerge in tangled histories of transformations in consciousness (see Silber 2010, Burrell this volume).

I have argued in my larger project that narratives of postwar violence, in their emergence and transmission, became technologies of citizen subjectivity in the decade after the Peace Accords were signed. Part of the "worse than the war" sentiment, this political feeling of disenchantment, draws from a longstanding popular understanding of democracy in Latin America. It encompasses a future imaginary imbued with what Arjun Appadurai (2007) calls a politics of hope. As post-Cold War democracy has been redefined in terms of the market, however, hope itself has not been at the core of the concept. Instead, Appadurai (2007, 31) writes, "Insofar as the market is seen as one road to freedom (and thus to some version of equality), it is not especially *reliant* on the politics of hope, substituting for hope such virtues as risk-taking, institution building, enterprise, and calculation, all prime virtues in the early lexicon of industrial capitalism."

People still struggle for rights, yearn to belong, seek ways to prosper—they imagine a better future, as so many chapters in this volume attest. The politics of hope remains at the center of many Salvadorans' ideas of democracy. The future-social-imaginary so many Salvadorans projected in the stories they shared in the first decade after the Peace Accords shows that they expected, against the weight of their own history, some kind of moral order that addressed not only violence in the street but also structural violence, the poverty and misery that so often could be linked to violence in the street. Many of their stories spoke of betrayal after the Peace Accords. People had dared to imagine something else.

Alternative Democracies

People first shared crime stories with me in the mid 1990s, in the midst of the right-wing (ARENA) government's reign (1989–2009). So much of my analysis, I realize now, is structured around the logic that ARENA's neoliberalism had betrayed the people. But was the answer really a change in government?

In 2009, the FMLN took the presidency. Among the thousands of red-garbed supporters in the streets—from a wide range of Salvadoran social and economic worlds—hope was flagrant. As Ainhoa Montoya (this volume) documents, several factors converged to create the conditions for the possibility of victory for former journalist Mauricio Funes as the "candidate for change." Certainly the rise of the left throughout Latin America, reacting in part to the failures of neoliberalism, made a difference.

Further, the early 2000s saw a sea change among social movements in El Salvador. Few large public demonstrations or strikes had taken place in the 1990s. People I knew spoke of postwar fatigue at the time. By 2002, however, threats to privatize the Social Security (medical) system led to enormous protest marches (Almeida 2008). Such activism has intensified throughout Central America, especially in the states considered "invisible" during the turbulent 1980s—Honduras and Costa Rica (see Boyer and Cardona Peñalva; and Raventós, this volume).

Despite initial high approval ratings, Funes (perhaps inevitably) disappointed many people. After a shocking June 2010 incident in which gang members burned a bus—with passengers still in it (seventeen died)—Funes quickly agreed to revive hardline *mano dura* (iron fist) policies against criminalized youth, policies he had criticized as a journalist (see Zilberg 2011). Gang members then protested, almost shutting down public movement (with threats to attack bus drivers) and keeping fearful people off the streets in September 2010 (Lémus 2010). The act galvanized the right-wing media, decrying the FMLN's incapacity to quell crime.

Then the next June (2011), despite ever more alarming news of crime waves, thousands of Salvadorans spilled into the streets. Heeding the call of social networks, they anointed themselves Indignados SV (The Indignant-El Salvador [SV is the Internet suffix for El Salvador]). The name comes Spain's 15-M Movement (Twitter hashtag #Indignados), which had emerged a few weeks earlier, protesting politicians and banks and promoting participative democracy.[9] Salvadorans had a more focused demand than the Europeans: they opposed a law that immobilized the Supreme Court—and choked democratic processes. Decree 743 required the five justices of the Constitutional Chamber to vote unanimously in order to declare any resolution unconstitutional. The court had been divided four to one on many rulings.

Figure 5.1. Man signs a petition opposing Decree 743 in San Salvador June 2011.

Figure 5.2. Protestors from "The Indignant El Salvador" gather in front of the National Palace.

The protests may have been sparked by political machinations and abstract procedural rulings. But I would argue that the activists' public calls for a functioning justice system, and their anger at political deal-making, echo common desires expressed in the everyday crime stories that had been circulating since the war ended. That June 2011, Salvadorans went out into the streets demanding order and justice, in the sense of rule of law and responsive institutions; they insisted on being counted, and found common cause that unexpectedly bonded them into a broad-based community; and, they showed their support for development that linked progress with democratic institutions promised in discourses surrounding the Peace Accords.

The political impetus for Decree 743 had to do with the threat to purge small but powerful political parties (the Christian Democrats and the National Conciliation Party) that had not received enough votes in the most recent elections, as required constitutionally. But behind that immediate motive lurked fears that the court would reverse the 1993 Amnesty Law, as well as declare unconstitutional hallmarks of the neoliberalization of El Salvador: the Dominican Republic-Central America-United States Free Trade Agreement (CAFTA-DR) and dollarization (El Salvador dollarized in 2001). The decree passed in a rushed vote without public debate or discussion. But what shocked many observers was that Funes immediately signed it into law. The question of amnesty was not hypothetical: just four days before Decree 743 passed, on 30 May, a Spanish judge had indicted twenty Salvadoran former military officers for crimes against humanity and state terrorism for their roles in the murders of the six Jesuit priests, their housekeeper, and her daughter (CJA 2011). As a tour guide told a group visiting the site of the massacre at the UCA that same week, "Since we can't get justice here in El Salvador for these murders, we have to get it from Spain."[10]

Reaction to Decree 743 came quickly, from across the political spectrum. The National Private Business Association (ANEP) joined many non-governmental organizations (NGOs) and the emergent Indignados in outrage. In their various voices, they demanded institutional integrity, rule of law, justice—and democracy. Soon after Funes signed the decree, about two hundred youth converged on the Presidential Palace. That weekend more than a thousand demonstrated in front of the iconic Salvador del Mundo statue, all the while posting and reposting on Twitter and Facebook their slogan, "*Le llaman democracia y no lo es*" (They call it democracy and it isn't).[11] ANEP published a full-page newspaper advertisement condemning the decree, asserting in black and gray text: "Functional democracies are sustained with institutional and juridical order" (ANEP 2011). Sigfrido Reyes, the FMLN president of the Legislative Assembly, called it "a democratic tragedy" (Acosta 2011).[12]

The decree was overturned on 28 July. Mass media returned its gaze (or glare) to the latest alarming crime statistics. Postings on the Indignados El Salvador Facebook page slowed some. It may be that in such an agitated present, the imagined future of an idealized democracy—of rule of law and justice, of community, of development (and one in which violence is not intrinsic)—seems spectral (Coronil 2011). But Salvadoran youth activists declared they had "awakened from their lethargy": they are now aware of a certain power, alert to a new sense of community, alive to their own struggle (different from that of their more polarized war-era parents). Participants in more traditional Salvadoran social movements express skepticism about the possibility of finding common political ground. Many leftists assume the Indignados and their ilk are manipulated by the right, especially since it appears most of them are educated, Internet-savvy, middle-class (and upper-middle-class). But the Indignados, perhaps situated precisely in the impure, uncertain, friction-filled space that Mouffe calls democracy, carry on. In May 2012, for example, a group coordinated a *zapatazo limpio*, an act culminating with the hanging of old shoes around the building where members of the Legislative Assembly were discussing giving themselves a raise.[13] The Indignados say they want a democracy that functions—like the one described in the country's constitution. As one activist explained to me, "We are pro-system. By that we mean we support a representative democracy that isn't manipulated by parties. Unconsciously, we didn't realize at first that that was what we were doing, but we're supporting the system. We have a constitution here. It's really nice. But they don't follow it."[14]

In El Salvador, corruption remains rife. Violence continues in countless forms. Injustice and impunity for past crimes persist. But some Salvadorans may be moving beyond disenchantment. Democracy does not have to wait for an ever-not-yet future. As Coronil (2011, 260) writes, "The struggle *for* democracy now entails a struggle *about* democracy. ... [P]olitical battles now pursue not an alternative to democracy but an alternative democracy."

Notes

* Portions of this chapter were adapted from chapter five of Moodie 2010. I thank all the participants of the "After the Handshakes" workshop, especially Marc Edelman for his critique, as well as Jennifer Bickham Mendez, Mark Anderson, Florence Babb, Leigh Binford, and Jennifer Burrell.

1. The Instituto Universitario de Opinión Pública (IUDOP) and the Interamerican Development Bank (IDB) found an average of 131 intentional murders for every 100,000 citizens between 1994 and 1996, compared with an estimated 130 violent deaths per 100,000 during the war (Cruz and González 1997b, 956). It is important to note that political scientist Miguel Cruz (2006, 152), former IUDOP director, today questions the accuracy of the original homicide figures but confirms that rates reached a minimum of 80 per 100,000 between 1994 and 1997, still among the highest in the world.
2. The month-long offensive moved violence from rural to urban sites. It shocked many San Salvador residents, a good number of whom had lived at some remove from battles and bodies.
3. The Index of Economic Freedom is a compound index that includes variables such as tax burden, foreign investment regulatory framework, tariff structure, financial system regulation, monetary policy, and the existence of black markets. The UNDP (2001, chapter 4) states that the index's "limited concept of liberties [make] it inconsistent with the human development paradigm. For instance, a low level of public expenditure improves the IEF since it reflects low state intervention, independently of the redistributive role of fiscal policy. The IEF does not take into account equality of opportunities nor physical deprivations such as hunger, which are essential to the human development paradigm."
4. Fourteen members of the Salvadoran military were tried for the murders in September 1991. Two were found guilty but were released in March 1993 after President Alfredo Cristiani signed the Amnesty Law. As noted below, on 30 May 2011 a Spanish judge indicted twenty Salvadoran former military men for the crime.
5. Interview with author, San Salvador, 18 April 1998. All translations mine; all interviewees' names have been changed.
6. Interview with author, San Salvador, 19 January 1999.
7. Interview with author, Soyapango, 27 November 1998.
8. While recognition of diversity in terms of race and ethnicity girds many definitions of democracy in Latin America today (see Anderson; Dary Fuentes; and Pineda, this volume), many Salvadorans do not articulate this multicultural ideal, or do so in terms of class, despite growing indigenous movements in the country (see Peterson 2006; DeLugan 2012).
9. See YouTube video of anti-Decreto 743 protests, "Indignados con nuestros políticos" (Indignant with our politicians), http://www.youtube.com/watch?v=4dlHN4KUHc0 (accessed 3 September 2011).

10. Field notes, Antiguo Cuscatlán, 3 June 2011. Lawyers for the indicted men claim the Amnesty Law protects Salvadorans from international indictments.
11. See Facebook page "Indignados El Salvador," http://es-es.facebook.com/indignados.sv (accessed 3 September 2011).
12. However, the FMLN reversed its stance and supported the decree, following Funes in suggesting that a dialogue among the branches of government would improve institutional clarity and stability. ARENA also reversed its stance, opposing the decree, after receiving assurances that the Amnesty Law would be safe.
13. *Zapatazo limpio* translates, roughly, as a "clean hard kick with a shoe." See http://www.elsalvador.com/mediacenter/play_video.aspx?idr=7507 and http://armandolopz.wordpress.com/tag/zapatazo-limpio/ (both accessed 9 September 2012).
14. Interview with author, San Salvador, 7 September 2012. This 28-year-old activist, an NGO employee from a working-class background, acknowledges the "impurity" of the movement and the many efforts to manipulate its messages for political gain. He describes the Indignados as seeking space to speak within such a political reality. He credits the election of the FMLN to the presidency as breaking with political expectations and as allowing for an alliance (admittedly unsteady) of people from different positions.

Part II

Indigeneity, Race and Human Rights in the (Post) Multicultural Moment

Cuando Nos Internacionalizamos

Human Rights and Other Universals at the United Nations Permanent Forum on Indigenous Issues

*Baron Pineda**

Since World War II, human rights have emerged as a multi-faceted idiom of politics with particular resonance for indigenous activists and communities in Central America. The United Nations has been the main institutional patron for human rights declarations, treaties, and conventions, the most prominent among them the Universal Declaration of Human Rights adopted by the General Assembly in 1948. In the last thirty years, indigenous peoples in Latin America have become increasingly active in this milieu, casting and recasting their struggles for *reivindicación* (redress of grievances) within human rights discourse. This trend has caught the attention of many scholars (Brysk 2000; de la Cadena 2007; Jackson and Warren 2005; Niezen 2003; Sieder 2002; Van Cott 1994; Yashar 2005). Indigenous leaders have also begun making appeals to the wide variety of institutional spaces of the United Nations dedicated to human rights promotion. In many, but certainly not all, cases, the organizations and groups involved in such politics have become specialists who typically do not have a very high profile in national, regional or indigenous community politics. Many Central American leaders speak of this turn to human rights and indigenous politics as the moment "*cuando nos internacionalizamos*" (when we went international).

What follows are observations about this "internationalization" culled from over nine years of ethnographic research at the Permanent Forum on Indigenous Issues. The forum is a meeting held each year, since 2002, at the United Nations headquarters, during which thousands of internationalized and internationalizing indigenous leaders from around the world come together for two weeks of speeches, negotiating, and networking. Since the landmark 1977 U.N.-sponsored International Nongovernmental Organization Conference on Discrimination Against Indigenous Populations in the Americas, held in Geneva, a wide variety of international stages have provided indigenous leaders with unprecedented opportunities to strategically promote their interests among states and other international actors (Lawlor 2003). In addition to the Permanent Forum (Lawlor 2003), these stages include the Working Group on Indigenous Populations (WGIP) (Muehleback 2001; Stamatopoulou 1994) and the Working Group on the Draft Declaration of

Indigenous Rights (WGIP) (Foster 2001), from which, over the course of two decades, the Declaration on the Rights of Indigenous Peoples was eventually adopted by the United Nations General Assembly in 2007 (Xanthaki 2007). Indigenous peoples have also participated alongside other "non-state actors" on a variety of pertinent U.N. initiatives, treaties and meetings, such as the Convention on the Elimination of Racial Discrimination (CERD), the Commission (cum Council) on Human Rights, the World Summit on Sustainable Development, and the United Nations Conference on Environment and Development (UNCED), also known as the Rio Earth Summit. Institutions such as the World Bank and the United Nations Educational, Scientific and Cultural Organization (UNESCO) have, during this time, generated internal policies on "best practices" with regard to indigenous peoples and they now routinely invite them to a wide variety of meetings and events.

Many of the indigenous people with whom I have interacted at the Permanent Forum and other U.N. meetings have a long career of attendance at such events. As a result, they are conversant in the "management speak" that is routinely used in these and many other global settings (keywords include "best practices," "global partners," "stakeholders," "rights holders," "duty bearers," and "experts," among many others). Although scholars have focused on assessing the successes, failures, hopes, and contradictions of global indigenous activism and the discourses that are associated with this kind of politics, few have offered detailed ethnographic accounts of these meetings as local field sites in their own right (Riles 2006). Indeed conferences and meetings in general receive little scholarly attention in themselves as meaningful social spaces.

Human and Indigenous Rights in Central America

Human rights and indigenous politics have made significant gains in Central America in recent years. Such success emerges from a tragic history; it is linked to the brutal way that the Cold War played out in the region, to the perceived weaknesses of Central American states and to the economically precarious position of the region in the global economy.

Three Central American countries have signed and ratified the International Labor Organization (ILO) Indigenous and Tribal Peoples Convention of 1989 (ILO 169)—Costa Rica, Honduras, and Guatemala. This binding treaty, commonly regarded as the most wide reaching within the U.N. system specifically pertaining to indigenous peoples, has been ratified by nineteen countries globally, fourteen in the Americas. This treaty revised the ILO's Indigenous and Tribal Populations Convention of 1957 (ILO 107), which had also been ratified by Panama and El Salvador. All Central American states signed the 1978 American Convention on Human Rights of the Organization of American States (OAS), along with twenty-five other American countries—the United States of America notably absent. The Inter-American Court of Human Rights was established the next year in San José, Costa Rica, to apply and interpret the convention. In 2001, the court delivered a landmark ruling in *Mayagna (Sumo) Awas Tingni Community v. Nicaragua*, which recognized the right of Mayagna communities to the protection of their lands and resources (Anaya 2004; Finley-Brook 2011).

In Nicaragua, the legal and political salience of indigenous and Afro-Nicaraguan peoples was recognized by the Sandinista Administration in the constitutional reform of 1987. This resulted in the creation of two "autonomous zones," incorporating some degree of indigenous and Afro-Nicaraguan representation in the regional assemblies that managed the governance of the region (Fruhling et al. 2007). Similar constitutional recognition of indigenous peoples has occurred throughout Central America and Latin America (Van Cott 1994). While these government actions are not necessarily examples of human rights politics, they have opened spaces for human rights and indigenous politics that have been eagerly filled by indigenous actors. Central American indigenous activists at the Permanent Forum (and beyond) explicitly ground their struggles for indigenous reivindicación within the discourse of international human rights.

U.N. agencies as well as international aid organizations active in the region have also begun to use human rights and indigenous peoples as operational categories in their functioning. As a result, these institutions have become major patrons for organizations and communities who have turned towards human rights politics. In 1991, for example, the World Bank adopted an "operational policy on indigenous peoples," which, in the hedging language of bankers, "underscores the need for Borrowers and Bank staff to identify indigenous peoples, consult with them, ensure that they participate in and benefit from Bank-funded operations in a culturally appropriate way—and that adverse impacts on them are avoided, or where not feasible, minimized or mitigated" (World Bank 2009). Recognizing the role of "neoliberal" institutions in the promotion of human rights discourse and action, anthropologist Charles Hale acknowledges, albeit with ambivalence, that "key transnational institutions within this neoliberal establishment—most notably the World Bank and the Inter-American Development Bank—have been instrumental in opening up the political space and providing funds in support of land claims by indigenous communities" (Hale 2006a, 100). Hale, who testified in the successful Nicaraguan Awas Tingni case, is concerned about the contradictions between human rights politics and institutional structures like the World Bank. In his opinion, the Bank peddles the "menacing allure of neoliberal multiculturalism" (Gordon and Hale 2003, 100).

Central America provides abundant examples of the ambiguities and contradictions of neoliberalism. In this volume Mark Anderson provides an important reminder of the ways in which recognition, glorification, and commodification of ethnic and indigenous "difference" can simultaneously result in the marginalization and disempowerment of these communities, as has been the case for the coastal Garifuna in Honduras's expansion of ethnically oriented tourism. Walter Little (this volume) writes of the frustration and disenchantment that Mayan artisans experience as the promise of free trade agreements to make ethnically marked artisanal goods more profitable has not materialized. Expanding on this theme of disenchantment and frustration about the elusive rewards of neoliberalism, Claudia Dary Fuentes (this volume) shows how, despite the legal and institutional embrace of multicultural discourse by state institutions, racism is alive and well on a day-to-day basis in Guatemala.

Despite the skepticism about the nexus of multiculturalism and neoliberalism, Hale and his colleagues Edmund Gordon and Galio Gurdian acknowledge that the multicultural shift in policy of the World Bank, for example, represents an "opening" in which "[World] Bank resources went in direct support of a narrative of costeño identity, history, and cultural continuity that the Nicaraguan state has vehemently opposed since its inception at the beginning of the nineteenth century" (Gordon and Hale 2003, 380). They add that the "[World] Bank has explicitly endorsed a policy of cultural pluralism. Indigenous cultures are to be recognized, their way of life preserved" (Gordon and Hale 2003, 379).

Apart from the increasing institutional recognition of indigenous identity and *interculturalidad* (interculturality), on a social level there has been a notable rise in the assertion of ethnic and racial pride among indigenous communities throughout Central America. This reverses a long-standing trend that encouraged the suppression or public disappearance of many kinds of cultural and linguistic displays due to the social stigmatization associated with indigeneity. Alongside this cultural revival, expectations have been raised about how states and non-natives will treat indigenous peoples. As an anthropologist/priest who has worked in the Tzeltal communities of Chiapas for the last thirty years recently told me, "*los ladinos no los gritan tan facilmente como antes*" (the ladinos don't yell at them as easily as before). Regardless of whether all of this has resulted in substantive changes in the well-being of indigenous people, the discourse of interculturalidad or multiculturalism (applied well beyond the indigenous case) has made tremendous ideological gains in the last thirty years in Central America. This is observable even in places like El Salvador, where for decades common knowledge dictated that there were no more indigenous peoples in the country (Peterson 2006).

Is There a Global Indigenous Culture?

Scholars are understandably suspicious about the changes that have accompanied the discursive shift to multiculturalism and the internationalization of indigenous rights. In the case of Guatemala, Charles Hale has argued, as noted above, that a shift to multiculturalism is easily channeled into neoliberal reform strategies, such as passing off state responsibilities to civil society. More radical claims, such as fundamental land reform and calls for addressing unequal resource distribution, are more easily deflected within this dominant approach to multiculturalism (Hale 2002). Jean Jackson and Kay Warren (2005, 567) warn against the creation of clientelism and "human rights dependency" when "international NGOs engaged in humanitarianism, postwar reconstruction, and development move on to new crises, leaving indigenous organizations bereft of support that they have come to depend on." Some "patrons," including the U.S. government, have taken issue with the term "indigenous" itself as an illiberal and arbitrary category. At another extreme, anthropologist Adam Kuper (2003, 395) has argued that the growing recognition of indigenous peoples' rights is anti-democratic and even racist:

> The indigenous-peoples movement has been fostered by the U.N. and the World Bank and by international development agencies and NGOs. ... I am doubtful about the justice or good sense of most of these initiatives. Policies based on false analysis distract attention from real local issues. They are unlikely to promote the common good, and they will certainly create new problems. Wherever special land and hunting rights have been extended to so-called indigenous peoples, local ethnic frictions have been exacerbated. These grants also foster appeals to uncomfortably racist criteria for favoring or excluding individuals or communities. New identities are fabricated and spokespeople identified who are bound to be unrepresentative and may be effectively the creation of political parties and NGOs. These spokespeople demand recognition for alternative ways of understanding the world, but ironically enough they do so in the idiom of Western culture theory.

On the ground in Central America, Kuper's sentiment is reinforced by many, in both elite and popular classes, who believe that indigenous demands are particularly harmful and dangerous for Central America in the new millennium because they introduce "special rights" that will only exacerbate tensions that arise from the pressures of the drug war and postwar demobilization (Warren 2002, 149).

Less polemical analysts have also struggled with the concept of "indigenous" as it is expressed in global politics. Some perceive it as a homogenizing term that glosses over the wide cultural heterogeneity of groups categorized in this way. The pronouncements of indigenous peoples in international contexts with regard to their spiritual nature, harmony with nature and connections with Mother Earth, for example, are sometimes greeted skeptically by those who view this kind of identification as a form of essentialism. Others doubt whether global indigeneity is a useful concept, given the range of colonialism and racial domination in different parts of the world; only some situations fit the iconic case of the places like the Americas and Australia, where European settlers violently imposed themselves on native peoples. Many anthropologists have noted the irony that just when anthropologists are deconstructing their most treasured theoretical contributions such as the culture concept, indigenous peoples are embracing them (Jackson and Warren 2005).

Whether or not claims for cultural recognition fit with the current theoretical paradigms in academia, indigenous peoples of the world are organizing. In the process they are *creating* a global indigenous culture. One of the main sites for this cultural production are international meetings in which indigenous peoples encounter one another in person and forge new relationships. The experience of many participants in these encounters is that they palpably discover their commonalities with other indigenous peoples.

For example, a few years ago I met a Guatemalan indigenous women's organization leader who had formerly lived in refugee camps in southern Mexico where many fled during the civil war. When I met her she was involved in a speaking tour sponsored by a North American solidarity group. In an evening of our conversation she told me about an experience of the kind that I identify here. She had visited Thailand, again as a member of an indigenous women's organization, where she was taken to refugee camps that housed indigenous Burmese refugees displaced by the political turmoil in their homelands. She told me that she was shocked at the similarities she shared with this group of people: their bright textiles, straight, dark hair, small stature and, of course, their common experience of state violence and refugee status. Experiences like these give substance to the abstract and complicated notion of global indigeneity. As a researcher I am interested in documenting and analyzing these feelings and experiences. While doing this, however, I want neither to paternalistically refuse to critically engage with them nor to dismiss them as inauthentic or "fabricated" (Kuper 2003).

The Form of the Permanent Forum

The United Nations Permanent Forum on Indigenous Issues occurs in New York for two weeks each May. The Permanent Forum itself comprises sixteen "experts" (to use the appropriate "U.N.-speak" term), eight of whom are nominated by member governments. The others are nominated by indigenous organizations. In turn, the staff of the Economic and Social Council (ECOSOC), an administrative division of the United Nations, is in charge of overseeing the process through which nominees are appointed to three-year terms (which can be renewed once). The governmental delegates, who generally are not indigenous, are distributed among five standard geographical regions used by the United Nations in its work—Asian states, African states, Eastern European states, Central and South American and Caribbean states, and finally Western Europeans and other states (including the United States). In deference to the particularities of the global geography of indigeneity as apprehended by organizers, and in order to "give broad representation to the world's indigenous peoples," a separate Arctic, Pacific, North American and Central Asian/Siberian region was added (Secretariat 2007, 8). The mandate of the Permanent Forum is to 1) "provide expert advice and recommendations on indigenous issues to the U.N. system through ECOSOC"; 2) "raise awareness and promote the integration and coordination of relevant activities within the U.N. system"; and 3) "prepare and disseminate information on indigenous issues" (Secretariat 2007, 6). The mandate of the forum overlaps with other areas of the United Nations that deal with indigenous issues, including the recently dissolved Working Group on Indigenous Populations that was, in effect, replaced in 2007 by the Expert Group on the Human Rights of Indigenous Peoples of the new Human Rights Council and the Special Rapporteur on the Situation of Human Rights and Fundamental Freedoms of Indigenous Peoples. Among all of these ways in which indigenous peoples interface with the United Nations, the Permanent Forum is the one that has the most popular participation. At this moment, however, it wields little formal legal leverage—less than ILO 169, a legally binding convention (which few countries have ratified), and less than the Declaration on the Rights of Indigenous Peoples, passed by the General Assembly, both indisputably weak forms of international law. The Permanent Forum has been set up, to the consternation of most of the indigenous participants, as a space for "discussion" with no formal "muscle" behind any of the recommendations that are made.

At the yearly meetings about two thousand indigenous participants come to New York—some at their own expense, some at the expense of the NGOs they direct or that support them, some at the expense of governments, and others funded by United Nations agencies or the United Nations Voluntary Fund for Indigenous Populations. They are joined by lower-level representatives of some member governments, and representatives of many of the agencies within the U.N. system. Each meeting has an agenda determined at the close of the preceding year's meeting—previous themes include education, youth, and millennium development goals. The sixteen members of the Permanent Forum hold a hearing in which they gently probe U.N. agencies and member states on their policies vis-à-vis indigenous peoples. U.N. agencies and some states present reports on their efforts with regard to indigenous issues, and these are then commented upon by members of the forum. Daily, the floor is opened up to indigenous representatives invited to deliver prepared statements to the forum varying in length from three to five minutes. In light of the hundreds of representatives who wish to deliver statements, the chairperson of the forum gives priority to joint statements signed by a variety of indigenous organizations and caucuses. The forum is expected to take into account at least some of these statements when it drafts its final recommendation to the member states and U.N. agencies. Over the course of the year the forum ideally tracks their voluntary compliance. Beyond this official process, there are a wide variety of side events that occur in the rooms around the main meetings and in buildings off the main U.N. complex. These side events include workshops sponsored by NGOs, movie presentations, dance performances, art exhibitions, and caucus meetings.

The central "action" of the forum is the hearing led by the sixteen members. For many participants this focus is the gathering's most frustrating, yet most rewarding, feature. Approximately half of the working hours during the two-week session are spent in a general hearing format. The general hearing takes place, not in the much larger General Assembly room with its

Figure 6.1. United Nations Indigenous Forum, United Nations, UN Permanent Forum on Indigenous Issues

instantly recognizable velvety-green background, but rather in what some participants deride as the "basement" of the U.N. headquarters, which contains two (perfectly lovely) amphitheater-like salons with a large dais in front surrounded by concentric semi-circles of chairs and tables with large cards identifying each country or U.N. agency represented. On the back wall, opposite the dais, are sound-proofed cabins where the U.N. staff translates the proceedings into English, Spanish, French, Arabic, Russian, and Chinese. Each seated participant has access to an earpiece (to hear the translations) and microphones from which to speak when called by the chairperson. On the east side of the room is a bank of windows with beautiful views of the East River and Queens; and on the other side is an elevated bank of chairs with headphones but no microphones, for observers.

Re-marginalizing Indigenous Peoples

State representatives sit on the east side of the room behind their respective cards. Because on any given day rarely more than twenty state representatives (of a possible 192) are present, many Permanent Forum participants occupy the empty positions—placing hand-written cards, typically with the name of an NGO but sometimes an indigenous nation, over the plastic cards of states. On the west side of the room are places for members of the U.N. agencies and affiliated institutions (such as World Bank, UNESCO, and UNDP). These seats are also left unoccupied; forum participants also "squat" in these places. Each member of the forum has a seat and card in the inner circle, but none of the other participants are officially recognized in this way. This is not intended as a slight on the part of the organizers (people working for the ECOSOC secretariat assigned to the Permanent Forum), some of whom are indigenous peoples themselves and all of whom clearly are sympathetic and conscientious hosts. Nevertheless some participants feel that this absence of recognition in the form of cards and demarcated space for indigenous peoples (beyond members of the forum) within the conference room is symbolic of the broader problems of non-recognition that typically motivate participants to attend the forum in the first place. In a recursive way, this struggle for recognition in the microdynamics of the conference proceedings is emblematic of the studied absence of Central America from the global imaginary that Jennifer Burrell and Ellen Moodie chronicle in the introduction to this volume.

One response to this sensitivity to being re-marginalized spatially at the conference has been to stake out space within the conference room through the use of signs, cameras, and video equipment, flags (which are banned from the proceedings), and "traditional" dress (defined as dress that is associated with indigenous peoples and is not considered everyday wear) on the part of certain delegations. For example, the Center for Hawaiian Studies, a unit of the University of Hawaii at Manoa, brings large multi-generational groups of native Hawaiians on a yearly basis under the leadership of professor/activists Lilikala Kame'eleihiwa, Jonathan Osorio, and others. Members of the delegation, mostly college-aged Hawaiian students, wear bright red sashes with native Hawaiian motifs. They encourage students to deliver position papers and they often film their own interventions. They have produced documentary films on the events. They see the experience at the Permanent Forum not only as an attempt to advance their native Hawaiian political agenda, but also as part of the formation of the next generation of leaders who must prepare for a career of struggle. Part of their aim is to create solidarity and a sense of common purpose among native youth—solidarity they see as threatened by assimilation and cultural and linguistic loss. Sámi delegations from the European Arctic region also send large delegations that, especially for the first few days of the conference, proudly wear colorful traditional dress and carve out specific spaces within the conference room. By far the largest contingent of participants from any region are the Kichwa Otavaleños of Ecuador, who send delegations, often largely at their own expense, of upwards of thirty people, including many women wearing the distinctive feminine dress of the region—black dresses and shawls over fine white blouses.

Central America sends small contingents of Kuna, Miskito, and Guatemalan natives, as well as, occasionally, Bribri, Garifuna, and Afro-Central American Creoles. A number of Guatemalan women participate in the forum, most prominently Dr. Myrna Cunningham Cain, a Miskito and Creole woman from the Atlantic Coast of Nicaragua who currently is the chairperson of the forum. Otilia Lux de Coti, a pathbreaking K'iche woman who was the Guatemala minister of culture and sports from 2000 to 2004 and later, the permanent representative of Guatemala to the UNESCO Executive Council, served for two terms as a member, from 2002 to 2007. Currently, Guatemalan Alvaro Esteban Pop is also serving his first term, from 2011 to 2013. He is a political analyst and member of Naleb, a Guatemalan indigenous development NGO. Rigoberta Menchú Tum makes regular appearances at the forum and enjoys unmistakable celebrity status in the context of the meetings.

Central American activists, well aware of their more limited resources and experience when compared to those from the South and North, often experience a sense of recursive marginality when surrounded by larger and more outspoken delegations. This parallels the vulnerability of indigenous peoples as a whole within their respective nation-states. Purely in terms of numbers, Central American delegations are small in comparison to large groups like those from Otavalo, Ecuador and typically number twenty to thirty. The Kuna Nation is frequently the largest contingent from the region, with five delegates. In my conversations with Native American delegates from the

Figure 6.2. Central American participants, Otilia Lux de Cojti and colleague, United Nations Indigenous Forum, UN Permanent Forum on Indigenous Issues

United States, I have noted their tendency to speak of their Latin American colleagues as less seasoned at this kind of international advocacy. Latin American delegates, in turn, sometimes express their resentment of the paternalism of their North American Indian colleagues. This sense of reliving an historic marginalization is then experienced at a variety of levels by a wide range of native peoples. For example, in the initial years of the forum, participants noted the irony in the fact that the first chairperson of the Permanent forum was a "white" European—a Sami leader and former president of the Sami parliament, Ole Henrik Magga. It was not that Henrik Magga's leadership was unwelcome or perceived as illegitimate. However, among participants "on the ground," after five hundred years of European dominance over native peoples, the idea that the Permanent Forum would be led by a European was seen by some as a recapitulation of the history that this meeting was meant to counter. It also speaks to the tensions that inevitably arise when a category as new and as broad as global indigeneity is put into practice in a particular setting.

Can the Subaltern Speak in Three Minutes or Less?

Many of the participants in the forum, particularly those less experienced with meetings of this kind, come to New York feeling a tremendous burden at having been chosen to communicate the tragic plight of the peoples with which they identify. The strength with which they feel compelled to accomplish this mission often comes into conflict with the parliamentary and other structures of the forum. Each general hearing session is guided by an agenda that is often quite specific; for example, "the disaggregation of census data pertaining to indigenous peoples." Yet given that one thousand to two thousand participants come to the forum for a chance to be heard, many legitimately fear not being heard at all if they wait to make their intervention on the day that the agenda most closely corresponds to the message that they want to deliver—often an impassioned plea for help and intervention to remedy the plight of their people. In order to be placed on the speaker's list, participants must wait in line at the side of the conference room and submit a written version of their intervention—sometimes drafted communally well in advance of the meetings, in other cases drafted while at the meetings. Even when a participant gets on the speaker's list, the chairperson of the session limits him or her to two or three minutes, regardless of the length of the written statement. In order to accommodate the very difficult work of the translators, speakers are also reminded that they must speak slowly—a rule often violated by those who have come thousands of miles. The chairperson finds herself in a position in which she has to repeatedly intervene during the speech, either to slow down the speaker, or cut him or her off entirely.

Although, again, this structure is not intended to generate ill will, it leaves some participants feeling angry and disillusioned. Frustration, in the minds of some participants, is heightened by the fact that state representatives are given longer time periods to speak and are sometimes taken entirely off the clock. This reconfirms the indigenous experience of marginalization vis-à-vis the state. Of course, members of the forum who note mostly empty state chairs have a well-grounded concern that the meetings are ignored, or boycotted by states. Among the Latin American participants in particular, the most common complaint about the forum has to do with the policies of *la palabra* (having the floor to speak). For this and other reasons, many of the non-indigenous participants that attend the forum as part of their work for U.N. agencies and state governments view it as chaotic and disorderly. In addition, the leveling aspect that potentially places local community activists alongside mid-level (and some high level) officials generates a variety of tensions, as both are unclear about appropriate behavior and norms.

It should be no surprise that many of the unhealthy social dynamics that lead to mistrust and misunderstanding among people in the wider world are replayed at this international level. What happens at the forum can be seen as a kind of political theater, a rehearsing of the universally accepted (if consciously rejected) historical scripts of the "Columbian Exchange" of European colonialism and indigenous marginalization and resistance. Indigenous participants are ready and willing to frame their experience at the forum in the context of these plot lines. At the 2007 forum, for example, an indigenous participant from Latin America delivered an impassioned protest (instead of a three-minute speech) about the humiliation she suffered when she was made to remove her headdress for a photo necessary for the ID that all participants (and U.N. staff and state representatives) must wear. She categorized this experience as another in a long history of insensitive treatment of indigenous peoples by dominant societies that refuse to recognize and respect cultural difference (see Dary Fuentes, this volume). Her protest was received with a rousing (and forbidden) round of applause, providing a welcomed break in the monotony and boredom many participants experience during the exhausting general sessions. Still, many of the participants I have spoken with about the frustrating structure of the forum derive inspiration and resolve from their participation and their role in this drama. They also acquire an embodied appreciation of the common structural positions, if not cultural parallels, that they share with their fellow indigenous protagonists.

Key Moments in the Forum

Not all experiences at the United Nations are frustrating re-enactments of history. Many find it rousing to share conference room space with the representatives of their respective countries. Frustration and skepticism over the format and the overall lack of "muscle" of the forum are sometimes dispelled at key moments in which state delegations express anger at public criticism. At different moments over the years, the governments of Bangladesh, Colombia, Vietnam, the United States, New Zealand, Australia, and others have all protested the criticism of their policies by particular indigenous speakers in the course of the general hearing. Indigenous participants have told me that these moments have, to them, demonstrated the potential efficacy of the forum.

The electoral victory of Evo Morales as president of Bolivia in 2005, and his subsequent participation in the Permanent Forum, has become a source of great pride for the participants. He and his ministers have delivered exuberant speeches to the forum, touting his victory as a watershed moment in global history. These speeches have been received with jubilation (a clear demonstration of Morales's "rock star" status) by participants from across the globe. For example, on 17 May 2006, new Bolivian Vice-minister of Communitarian Justice Valentín Ticona Colque, delivered the following words to an electrified audience at the forum:

> Since December 18th of last month a new era has begun in Bolivia. After 500 years of exclusion, pillage, intolerance and ignorance the native in-

> digenous peoples of Bolivia now govern Bolivia, which was a part of *Kollasuyo*, which had been our home. The *Jachauru* (new dawn) has begun, my brothers, and it has begun in Bolivia with the goal of reconstituting the *Tawantinsuyos* and continuing on from there. From his position in the government, our brother Evo Morales is putting into practice bold measures to restore the dignity of our indigenous peoples. We are part of the earth ("Pacha"), of the natural resources, the plants and animals—and they have taken all of this away from us. ... You must understand, my brothers, that this work will not be easy because the elites will try to do something about the fact that their illegal occupation is ending but we are ready to defend our new changes and we are going to need the help of our indigenous brothers and sisters. That is why we ask that in its final document the forum make a pronouncement supporting the government of our indigenous brother Evo Morales. In addition, we believe that the indigenous peoples of Bolivia are the mirror of all of the indigenous peoples of the world, and we represent their legitimate rights so that we can open new pathways for all of our indigenous brothers.

In this speech Ticona positioned the Morales administration as a global focal point for indigenous power and implicitly recognized the importance of the forum as well as each of the indigenous participants by asking for their support in the global struggle for harmony and justice. On 23 April 2008, Morales himself used the pulpit of the Seventh Session of the Permanent Forum, and the agenda item of climate change, to lay out his programmatic indigeno-socialist statement on saving the world, "The Ten Sins of Capitalism and the Ten Commandments to Save the Planet, Humanity, and Life." The increasing global recognition of and anxiety about global warming has emboldened an emerging universalist project of global redemption through indigenous values that in many ways turns the critique of the human rights universalism on its head. In other words, while anthropology has spent the last sixty years debating whether or not the Universal Declaration of Human Rights is Western values masquerading as universal rights (Engle 2001; Merry 2003), global indigenous movements are developing an alternative universalism (which is sure to be judged by some as being equally Western or perhaps menacingly "neoliberal"), using the human rights mechanisms of the United Nations as an incubator.

While the election of Evo Morales and the signing of the Declaration on the Rights of Indigenous Peoples in 2007 have received global attention, participants have used the forum as a place to affirm and publicly score smaller victories for indigenous peoples and human rights politics more broadly. As I noted before, indigenous participants do not have official placards on the tables in the general meeting room and they, sometimes bitterly, take note of the special treatment that state and U.N. delegations receive. A number of participants who have standing as "indigenous parliamentarians," and other indigenous individuals who hold government jobs, have taken the initiative to solicit permission to participate as representatives of their respective states. So, for example, on 20 May 2007, Carlos José Aleman Cunningham, an indigenous parliamentarian from Nicaragua under the "Autonomous Region" plan first implemented by the Sandinistas in the late 1990s, proudly told the forum that, "[f]or the first time in the history of our country, representatives of our indigenous communities in Nicaragua are participating as the official delegation in this sixth session of the Permanent Forum of Indigenous Peoples." He finished his statement by reminding the members of the forum that the government of Nicaragua was a co-sponsor of the Declaration on the Rights of Indigenous Peoples and wants the General Assembly of the United Nations to pass it. The following year, another Nicaraguan indigenous parliamentarian, Lloyd Bushey Davis, who is Miskito, opened his speech to the forum with the following word

> The delegation of Nicaragua is filled with great pleasure that we are all meeting here at this forum after so many centuries of struggle and resistance. This is an achievement that obliges us to intensify our efforts to defend and reinstitute the values and traditions of our ancestors. That is why we want to recognize the excellent organization and management of the Seventh Session of the Permanent Forum on Indigenous Issues and we warmly greet the rest of the members, the secretariat and our indigenous brothers and sisters that make this meeting possible. Our indigenous peoples have always lived in harmony with nature—as a part of her. In the last two decades of the last century with the Washington Consensus, globalization and neoliberal hegemony all in force, a politics of pillaging and sacking of natural resources has prevailed. Global warming is a consequence of these policies.

Bushey Davis expressed to me the pride that he and his fellow indigenous parliamentarians felt at being able to publicly occupy the "seat" of Nicaragua at the United Nations. This affirmation was particularly heightened by the fact that other indigenous participants (with the exception of Bolivian members of the Morales administration, among a few others) did not have a spatial home of their own within the conference room. Their status as indigenous parliamentarians within this particular U.N. setting contrasted sharply with their experience of marginalization in Nicaragua where the *consejos regionales* (regional councils, as they are known in Nicaragua) find themselves underfunded, subject to the whim of the national government in Managua and lacking legislative or executive muscle.

Clearly the experience of participating in international human rights-related conferences such as the Permanent Forum can and does play a role in the political and ideological formation of the Central American people who participate. They represent, among other things, a kind of political theater in which actors re-enact (in a potentially radicalizing and solidarity-building way) well known historical scripts of indigenous marginality. But they also represent an alternative and highly prestigious world in which these scripts can be inverted. As they engage these dramas, Central American participants forge a sense of commonality and, yes, sisterhood and brotherhood with the indigenous peoples of the world. Although the jury is still out about the liberatory potential of this kind of international politics, it would be impossible to deny that, in the years since the peace agreements have been signed, Central Americans are engaging with human rights discourses and institutions with increasing frequency and depth. In the process they are forging new identities and new political programs that both challenge and accept the universalist pretensions of human rights politics and institutions.

Note

* This chapter draws on ideas that I am developing in a book manuscript that is based on my fieldwork at the United Nations titled "Indigenous Conventions: Human Rights and Cultural Politics at the United Nations."

7 Acknowledging Racism and State Transformation in Postwar Guatemalan Society

Claudia Dary Fuentes

Introduction

During the last ten years several political events have forced Guatemalans to publicly discuss the nature of interethnic relations, discrimination, and racism. Not only has there been a discussion of racism, but also specific state bureaus have been opened to address cases of alleged racism and discrimination.[1] This was absolutely unthinkable ten or fifteen years ago. None of this would have been possible without the political spaces that were opened after signing the Peace Accords in 1996, and without the encouragement and observance of international organizations. Of course, Maya organizations and other civil society initiatives have also played an important role in getting racism out into the open in Guatemala.

In this article I analyze a variety of circumstances that forced the state to acknowledge that discrimination and racism affect social relations in the country. I also reflect on the symbolic and actual implications of having discrimination typified as an offense that can be punished by law. Although not general knowledge, a law has now been passed that penalizes different forms of discrimination, and a commission created the Presidential Commission against Discrimination and Racism (CODISRA) to guide victims and monitor accusations. There is also an indigenous issues bureau in the Prosecutor's Office. However, both racism and prejudice continue to be widespread among Guatemalans. As Edelberto Torres-Rivas (2005, 7) states, "Social discrimination is experienced by all; racism, by Indigenous peoples."

The few public policy makers concerned with highlighting ethnic differences and socioeconomic inequality find reason to worry. When examining the economic costs of discrimination, they conclude that racism affects all Guatemalans as it creates exclusion. This deepens inequality, widens the poverty gap, and ends up dragging the country down in terms of human development. Wilson Romero reports that discrimination costs in 2003 went up to 6,000 million quetzales ($750 million [U.S.]), equivalent to 3.3 percent of the country's gross domestic product. Statistical measurement of racial discrimination is complex. An economic model, known as Blinder-Oaxaca, is used to estimate the differences in salary between the indigenous and non-indigenous population. Salaries are divided into two components: A) one that takes into account economic and personal aspects (such as salary, level of education, place of residence, gender, among others); and B) another that takes discrimination into account. The Blinder-Oaxaca model supposes that if there were no discrimination, the salaries of indigenous and non-indigenous persons who have had the same years of schooling and training and possess the same abilities would be identical. Nonetheless, as this is not the case, the difference in salary is attributed to subjective causes—in this case, discrimination (Romero 2006, 82). As Michael Reich (1971, 320) noted, "Racism is a key mechanism for the stabilization of capitalism and the legitimization of inequality."

What implications does the legal recognition of ethnic discrimination have for Guatemalan society? What does this tell us about the state and existing power relations? Is a law sufficient to alleviate or soften the daily rough edges of human behavior? Does this law, together with government bureaus that deal with cases of racism, indicate that the Guatemalan state is not as assimilationist as it used to be? I argue that the steps taken to acknowledge the existence of ethnic discrimination in Guatemala and its penalization are relevant, but are not good enough of a parameter to measure sociopolitical changes over the last ten years. However, the state offices created to deal with racism and the recent law that penalize it have an important impact symbolically, as well as socially, which may enhance better social relationships in the years to come.

State, Multiculturalism, and Structural Racism

Racism constitutes a system of oppression that creates and maintains privileges (rights and opportunities) for the social group that has a position of advantage. It does this to the detriment of others who occupy openly subordinated positions. The basis of this historically and socially constructed system is the projection on the part of elites of a "naturally" inferior condition of a group, which justifies one group's domination over the other. A particular culture or skin tone has been commonly used as an excuse to justify attitudes of disdain toward the other. Hence, in Guatemala, *criollos* (creoles), *ladinos* (non-indigenous people), and, sometimes *mestizos* (mixed- race people) have been regarded as superior groups, while Indians are seen as inferior. Racism is an ideological construction with a structural base, which means that it is related to practices and not only to ideas. When suggesting that racism must be approached from a structural point of view, I refer to Eduardo Bonilla-Silva's (1996) insistence that it constitutes an organizing principle of social relations.

It is not easy to speak about racism in Guatemala. This is especially true for middle and upper social classes, ladinos, mestizos, and descendants of foreigners. But it is also a difficult issue for indigenous people. The denial of racism is due not only to an explicit intention to maintain current hierarchies and power relations, but also to the very way that the terms "race" and "racism" are popularly conceived. How the issue is lived, thought of, and discussed (or not) at home, in schools, and through images shown in movies and on television play an important role in the conception of racism. Therefore, at the heart of addressing deeply seated racism and prejudice in Guatemala is the dismantling of popular conceptions of race common among Guatemalans. Scholars such as Jorge Solares and Gilberto Morales (2003) have initiated this work by analyzing visual and mental images as well as popular discourses that contribute to ongoing racism. Solares and Morales examine what ladinos understand by an ethnic group (*etnia*), race (*raza*), and indigenous people (*indígenas*). Middle-class non-indigenous people these authors interviewed noted their own vague racial origins. Although they expressed uncertainty about their ethnic and historical roots, they nonetheless felt superior to indigenous people based on their claims to European bloodlines. Among ladinos, social hierarchies are established and maintained according to the "purity" or "pollution" of one's blood. That is to say, many ladino people seem to hold a latent belief in the old colonial idea of "blood purity." By maintaining the idea, they feel superior to others. Developed countries, according to this ideology, are inhabited and ruled by people who do not mix because *mestizaje* has unfortunate economic and social consequences. Non-indigenous people manage a double discourse: on the one hand, they state that racism is wrong ("I'm not racist, but ..."); and, on the other, they will claim Indians are lazy, dirty, foolish, and treacherous. Solares and Morales also point out that non-indigenous people avoid speaking about racism by using subterfuges, such as: "here, we are all equals," "we are all Guatemalans," or "we are all God's children."

The research directed by Solares and Morales considered the views of lower- and middle-class ladinos. Twenty years earlier, Marta Elena Casáus Arzú (2009, 184) carried out a survey on racism that took into account only Guatemala's oligarchy. She writes, "Almost 80 percent of the elite sample in the interview considered themselves to be white or Creole. All of them perceived the difference between indigenous and non-indigenous people in terms of biological-racial aspects." Some interviewees believed that Indians were an inferior race through genetic transmission. One of their solutions to improve the Indians, reports Casáus, was to marry them to Germans who had immigrated to Guatemala. The survey respondents showed a constant desire to differentiate themselves from indigenous people because "they considered them to be uneducated, contemptible and inferior." In sum, the ideas of middle-class ladinos do not differ greatly from those of the elite.

Decades after her survey of the oligarchy, in 2005–2006, Casáus coordinated a research team and published *Diagnosis on Racism in Guatemala* (Vicepresidencia, 2007). Interestingly, this initiative was approved and funded by the vice-presidency of the republic during Oscar Berger's administration. Five volumes on racism and discrimination were published. As a result of this extensive undertaking, a public policy against racism and discrimination was issued in 2007. Unfortunately, neither the books nor the public policy have been widely disseminated among the citizenry.

To place this report in context, it is useful to understand how scholars have analyzed the issue of racism (and then approached it) from the point of view of the state. In the early 1980s, two national institutions existed that were extremely important in understanding prevalent twentieth-century currents of thought: the National Indigenist Institute (Instituto Indigenista Nacional), and the Seminary of Social Integration (Seminario de Integración Social). Both institutions were created between 1945 and 1956, with the idea that indigenous peoples and their cultures presented a "problem" for Guatemalans. To solve the "problem," the indigenous population would have to be integrated into the social, political, and economic life of the country. Their culture would then slowly disintegrate and disappear, and would be replaced with ladino culture. This current of thought, known as *indigenismo* (indigenism) and *integracionismo* (integrationism), is no longer in force, but it must be pointed out that the aforementioned "problem" used the language of culture over ethnicity and race. Nowadays the paradigm of multiculturalism is prevalent. It emphasizes recognition of indigenous peoples' collective rights and cultural expressions. However, some scholars argue that in practice the cultural rights of indigenous people outweigh their economic and political rights; therefore, multiculturalism is becoming a variety of neo-indigenism or neo-folklorism. As Charles Hale (2002, 491) states, "Powerful political and economic actors use neoliberal multiculturalism to affirm cultural difference, while retaining the prerogative to discern between cultural rights consistent with the ideal of liberal, democratic pluralism, and cultural rights inimical to that ideal." Ultimately, this version of multiculturalism, according to Hale, is a defense of neoliberal capitalism.

Social scientists in Guatemala have taken on the issue of racism only recently, although there is ample historical and political source material from colonial times to the present. As anthropology students in the 1980s at the National University's School of History, we used to discuss anthropological concepts like culture, ethnocentrism, cultural relativism, assimilation, social integration, and others. However, neither ethnicity nor ethnic identity, and certainly not racism, were included in the curricula. These issues were usually limited to the history of the American continent, where we learned about the apartheid atrocities in the United States, Martin Luther King's struggle for civil rights, and the latest news on Nelson Mandela's suffering in South African prisons. In the 1980s, the press never used the term "racism" to refer to developments in Guatemala.

Until the 1970s, the huge social distance between the country's different ethnic groups had not been conceived as racist. The abuse suffered by Indians was thought to bear no relation to racism, let alone the attitudes of middle-class students from private schools in the capital. This was because both social sciences and left-wing political discourse, save a few exceptions, were influenced by historical materialism, in which the concepts of class and class struggle take a crucial position as the motor of history. According to this perspective, racism is basically an ideological phenomenon, which, if it does exist, would be eliminated with the structural change achieved through the revolutionary heroic deeds led by the proletariat. Few authors went through the task of articulating the categories of race, ethnicity, and class. (Among those who did were Carlos Guzmán Böckler, Jean Loup Herbert, and later on, Casáus). In the end, the lack of analytical depth contributed to the continued denial of the existence of deeply entrenched racism in Guatemala. Consequently, ignoring the existence of racism is a tendency that prevails to this day. In spite of this resistance, the 1996 Peace Accords brought the term and its discussion to the foreground in contemporary debates.

Liberal social scientists believed, and still do believe, that racism is merely ideology. According to this line of thought, ideology deals with individual attitudes that some people show against African-descendants, Jews, natives, and other ethnically distinguishable groups. This thought was long reinforced in Guatemalan schools by the inclusion of readings such as *Uncle Tom's Cabin* that highlighted specific historical events of racism, like the period of slavery in the southern United States. Nowadays, this book is read with distrust and considered to have racist messages. Images shown in movies reinforced the idea of racism as a thing of the distant past, having no relation to contemporary Guatemalan society and the everyday social relations that take place in public and in corporate offices.

Racism is certainly an ideological construction, but it also has a structural basis, one that is associated with practice (Bonilla-Silva's [1996] "organizing principle of social relations") in addition to ideas. In this sense, it must be approached structurally and materially, as well as ideologically. I focus here on Guatemalan ethnic and racial discrimination existing in a system of oppression that contributes to maintaining privileges and advantages of some social groups over others.

Ideas and prejudices that arose in relation to Indians during the period of Spanish colonization transformed into social practices that were later institutionalized. This does not necessarily imply that they remain written as such, but rather that discrimination is embedded in attitudes, ways of speaking, and ways, for example, of hiring workers. It is when this happens that we can point out the existence of structural racism and state racism.

The liberal nation-state conceives the ideal population as being culturally and ethnically homogeneous and civilized. Santiago Bastos (2005, 3) suggests that the state (at least in theory) has currently ceased assimilationist and universalist policies and instead adopts a multicultural discourse that approves of indigenous peoples' individual and collective rights. In the Accord on the Identity and Rights of Indigenous Peoples (*Acuerdo de Identidad y Derechos de los Pueblos Indígenas* [AIDIPI], March 1995), one of the agreements negotiated within the Peace Accords, cultural rights are mentioned frequently, whereas political and economic rights seldom come up. However, this accord also addresses the issues of indigenous women's rights, Maya consuetudinary law, and the fight against racism and discrimination, which are not essentially only "cultural issues."

It would have never been possible for the Guatemalan state to address or discuss for the first time the topic of racism in the public sphere had it not been for the process that evolved into AIDIPI and then the Peace Accords. Some social actors have played a vital role in implementing the recommendations that these treaties proposed, especially the Mayan movement, but also intellectuals, research centers, and international organizations, particularly the United Nations Verification Mission in Guatemala (MINUGUA). These groups contributed substantially to this project, as did reports from the U.N. Rapporteur of Indigenous People. International groups as well as journalists writing in the mass media have also played an important role. These actors have collectively pressured the last three governments to fight against racism. They have pushed the state to raise public awareness of discrimination.

Reactions to the Possibility of Change

Law is not neutral; it is historically inscribed by a society's ruling classes to legitimize particular ideologies and power relations. In other words, "legal systems can be understood as quarreling points of meanings in which dominant ideas and values provide the framework for making a case" (Sieder and Witchell 2002, 58). I argue here that to penalize ethnic, racial, and gender discrimination, among other types, implies a fundamental reformulation of the nature of the Guatemalan state. For almost six years now, Guatemala has had a law that makes discrimination as a crime (Decree 57-2002). Nevertheless, the five-year period before its approval was full of events that reflected tensions in interethnic relations, prejudices, as well as remorse, particularly when Indians began to take on politically important and visible positions. I discuss several examples below.

When Rigoberta Menchú, a prominent indigenous leader, was nominated for the Nobel Peace Prize in 1992, reaction was swift. Innumerable discriminatory expressions, jokes, cartoons and mocking comments showed wholesale rejection or uncertainty about her worthiness for the award. In analyzing this moment, anthropologist Diane Nelson (1999, 176) shows how jokes reveal Guatemalan society's ambivalence when an indigenous woman manages to cross borders of nationality, ethnicity, and gender previously thought to be impermeable.

Things were stirred up again in November 1996 when Rigoberto Quemé,[2] the Maya-K'iche' candidate for mayor nominated by the Civic Committee Xel-Jú, won his election in Quetzaltenango, the second largest city in Guatemala. For many decades Quetzaltenango had been ruled by ladinos. When Quemé took office, he was the target of racist attacks. In the first months after the elections, ladino people painted the city walls with graffiti: "Go fix the streets Indian!" (*vos indio Quemé Chay arreglá las calles*), and "Out filthy Indians!" *(Indios shucos afuera)* (Verdugo et al. 2007). According to Alberto M. Fernández (1999, 1), the victory of the Xel-jú civic committee, under the leadership of K'iche' public intellectuals Rigoberto Quemé and Ricardo Cajas was crucially important because "it symbolized precisely the metamorphosis of an indigenous civic-cultural organization into a political machine."

Apart from the anti-Quemé graffiti that appeared on city walls, other reactions were even more grotesque. When Quemé's supporters labeled these actions as racist, several newspaper columnists opined that the words racism and discrimination were being abused; people who used such words only wanted to revive ill will and pit various factions against one another. Acts of discrimination against Quemé were not reported to the prosecutor's office. No cases concerning these reactions reached the courts. In these years, racism was not yet decreed a punishable offense.

Undoubtedly, the Peace Accords, and especially AIDIPI, not only opened the door for in-depth debate acknowledging indigenous peoples' culture and rights but also promoted the creation of a law against discrimination in congress. But not everything was rosy. As mandated by the Peace Accords, in May 1999 the Guatemalan population voted in a *consulta popular* (popular referendum) to approve or reject some fifty modifications to the nation's constitution. Voters were required to vote yes or no to four blocks of questions. The first addressed national social rights, including the definition of Guatemala as a multicultural, multilingual, and multiethnic nation. This implied the acknowledgement of Guatemala's rich linguistic and ethnic diversity, which had been largely ignored and/or denied until that point by dominant sectors in Guatemalan society. The referendum results were worrisome: only one out of every five people on voter registration roles voted, and ultimately, the proposals were rejected.

Lucía Verdugo de Lima et al. (2007, 20) analyzed the mass media's racist discourse related to the referendum. They discovered many opinion columns arguing that to vote affirmatively would result in "throwing more wood into the fire" and increasing the flame of resentment, making Indians turn against ladinos, thus reinforcing the perverse "Indian-ladino" dichotomy. Warnings abounded that the country would become a "Guatemalan Kosovo," a version of the Balkan War where Indians would take over, discriminate against criollos and ladinos and invade land. According to these accounts, an affirmative vote was encouraged by the left wing, "opportunistic" former revolutionaries wishing to advocate for political gains. Those against the constitutional modifications claimed the left was supported by an international community interested in intervening in issues of national sovereignty. Voting "Yes" in the referendum could also result in support for pagan religions and witchcraft. As to making Mayan languages official, opponents painted Guatemala as a "Tower of Babel," a country marked by underdevelopment and backwardness as it struggled to incorporate a multiplicity of voices. In the end, these attitudes confirmed "colonial fears of an Indian uprising" and exposed prejudices and social and physical distance between indigenous and non-indigenous people in Guatemala. These mass media's reactions and debates around the referendum illuminated dominant conceptions of racial and ethnic relations in Guatemala on the part of ladinos and capital dwellers and shed light on the way they conceived of the country: Spanish-speaking, culturally homogeneous, with distinct spaces for social and ethnic groups.

Toward the Transformation of the Nation-State Model?

To penalize discrimination—ethnic-racial, gender, or otherwise—means to reformulate the structure of the Guatemalan state, no matter how incipient this change may be. The Myrna Mack Foundation (2006, 49) points out that "to determine an offence is a process that arises from discussions and negotiations between civil society and the State, and from among States themselves." In order to comply with emerging anti-racist law, the Guatemalan state has been forced to include indigenous people in its social policies. Maya-K'iche' lawyer Benito Morales (2006, 27–29) has explained the torturous road and tense relations among members of congress in the debates leading up to the incorporation of an anti-discrimination article in the penal code. The proposal to create the ethnic and racial discrimination offense originated in 1995.[3] It was proposed by Congressman Pablo Duarte, and seconded by indigenous Congresswomen Rosalina Tuyuc and Manuela Alvarado. This proposed law was based on international human rights agreements and treaties that Guatemala had already ratified. However, it was not until October 2002, after reviewing several proposals, that Decree 57-2002 was promulgated, reforming the penal code by adding an article (202 bis) that penalizes discrimination.[4]

By this time, a number of cases had attracted national and international attention regarding racism in Guatemala and may have indirectly contributed to its penalization some months later. Most notable was the public criticism toward an act of discrimination suffered by anthropologist (and then University of Texas, Austin graduate student) Irma Alicia Velásquez Nimatuj, who was banned from entering the Tarro Dorado Bar by security guards in June 2002 because she was wearing her traditional indigenous clothes. This case received much attention from the national press. Velásquez Nimatuj stated in a press interview that "very few are the actions of racism that become formal accusations, for legal structure in Guatemala has limitations, mainly for the Mayan population. It involves a personal, social and cultural expense for those who dare to accuse an offender" (Barrios 2002, 9–10). In September 2002, Rodolfo Stavenhagen visited Guatemala on a fact-finding mission for his report on the situation of indigenous people. In it, he highlighted the indigenous population's situation of extreme poverty–and devoted several pages to institutionalized racism and ethnic discrimination in the country.

Article 202 bis to the penal code, approved by more than two-thirds of the congress members, states, "Discrimination is defined as all differences, exclusions, restrictions or preferences based on reasons of gender, race, ethnicity, language, age, religion, economic situation, sickness, marital status or any other reason that may hinder or interfere with a person, group of people or associations to exercise an established right, including common law, according to the Nation's Political Constitution and International Treaties regarding human rights." Moreover, it establishes that any person responsible for such acts may be convicted with one to three years of imprisonment and a fine ranging from 500.00 quetzales to 3000.00 quetzales ($65.00 to $400.00 [U.S.]). The article also condemns the dissemination of discriminatory ideas and actions. Although the approval of Decree 57-2002 is a step forward for Guatemala, it has been criticized and widely debated. Lawyer Martín Sacalxot, an advocate and defender of indigenous rights, argues that although the law makes a reference to the International Labor Organization Agreement (ILO) Convention 169 on Indigenous and Tribal Peoples, it ignores an important mandate within it regarding historical precedence (Barrios 2002, 9). For Carlos Fredy Ochoa, this mandate can only lead to partial improvement; the lack of due consideration to the historical situation of indigenous peoples in Guatemala renders the normative part of the law too broad (Bastos 2005, 20). Some indigenous organizations and public intellectuals have argued that the decree should have been limited to ethnic and racial discrimination against indigenous peoples. Still others wish to see a broader mandate that also supports wider constituencies, including, for example, women, the disabled, and homosexuals.

Regardless of how we view the law, attacks on indigenous people's dignity, self-esteem and fundamental rights as citizens remain common. By 14 June 2008, the Office of the Human Rights Ombudsman had received more than three hundred accusations of broad-based discrimination. Indians' accusations of ethnic discrimination constitute the vast majority of cases. Between 2003 and 2005 CODISRA received 17 cases reporting access restrictions to public places, 78 accusations of acts of discrimination in 2006, and 64 in 2007, out of a total of 142 accusations in 2 years. Of these, 30 are classified as actions against the free practice of Mayan spirituality. Sixty percent of the accusations were registered in the capital, which could be related to the level of information available to the population in the city and access to offices to file complaints (Pérez 2007).

In the school system, ethnic and racial discrimination is very common, although it is rarely denounced and made public. Angela, a young K'iche' girl from Quetzaltenango with whom I had an informal conversation, told me that she has experienced and witnessed many discriminatory acts, including mockery, scorn, and insults. She has never reported these because the school principal was ladino or mestizo and she suspected that her complaint would not be heard. Deep down, the fear of being expelled held her back. This was not the case for two female students at a business school in Quetzaltenango, Virginia Toj and Claudia Tax. In February 1999, they filed a formal denunciation when they were unable to register for school because they attended classes in *traje* (traditional handwoven clothes). The school principal told the father of one of the girls that "it was his fault [they] were called 'Indians' (in a scornful way) because he allowed them to dress that way." The case was brought to the Office of the Human Rights Ombudsman and judged as "a human rights violation to culture and education by the school principal and teaching staff." (At the time the decree criminalizing racism had not yet been passed.)

To this day, six court cases concerning discrimination charges have been resolved. In these cases the legal tool for handing down the sentences has been Decree 57-2002, as well as the International Convention on the Elimination of All Forms of Racial Discrimination (CERD), and ILO Convention 169. The first case that reached oral debate occurred in 2005. Five Guatemalan Republican Front (FRG) members directed racial slurs to Rigoberta Menchú when she visited the Constitutional Court on 9 October 2003. "Go sell tomatoes in the market" and "traitor" were among the phrases spoken by the offenders. They clearly intended to intimidate the Nobel Peace laureate and to nullify or deny the value of her political participation. The Menchú Foundation supported the victim. One of the difficulties in this case was that the district attorney's office initially "considered a discrimination offence non-applicable in this particular case" (Morales 2007, 34).

Indigenous lawyer Benito Morales explains that Decree 57-2002 is somewhat difficult to apply. The article states that an action may be typified as discrimination if there is a behavior of distinction, exclusion, restriction, or preference. The dilemma is that a particular behavior may be taken out of historical and cultural context. If this is the case, there is not an act of discrimination as such. In Rigoberta Menchú's case, when the expressions "Go and sell tomatoes in the Terminal market!" and "Tomato seller!" (*tomatera*) are taken out of context, they may not be considered racist. What, after all, is objectively wrong with calling a person a "tomato seller?" The problem becomes one of demonstrating to a jury that these expressions are, in fact, racial slurs. In this case, Morales explained, it was necessary to take into account the socio-linguistic and historical context in order to demonstrate that such expressions have been used to undervalue the indigenous population as people whose "place" is distinct from that of ladinos. Ultimately, five people were sentenced to prison for three years and two months, with an option to commute the sentence for 75.00 quetzales ($10.00 [U.S.]) per day. The accused commuted their sentences.

The second case to be heard by judges occurred in 2004, when defendants were sentenced in the case of Víctor Lem, who was denied access to a bar in Quetzaltenango (León 2008). A third case occurred in 2005. A private security guard was charged with denying María Cleofás Tuyuc entrance to a cafe bar in the nightlife district of Guatemala City in 2004. The case was settled before it reached court. The Myrna Mack Foundation and AVANCSO,[5] in their support of this case, commented on the lack of chain of command provisions within Article 202 bis. The law does not provide for the punishment of those who ordered the security guard to prohibit the entrance of Maya people to the club.

The case of discrimination against Cándida González Chipir, a Tz'utujil Maya who was at the time second vice-minister, is the fourth case. It occurred in August 2006, as González visited the regional offices of the Labor Ministry in the small city of Tecún Umán (San Marcos). Three employees, two women and one man, refused to talk to her and instead locked themselves in an office to laugh and mock her. González immediately lodged a formal complaint with the Criminal Court of Coatepeque, Quetzaltenango and the three accused were convicted on 22 September (Bonillo 2009, 4).

On 13 February 2008, in the fifth case, the Criminal Court in San Benito, Petén (northern Guatemala), acquitted a student who verbally attacked José Antonio Cac Cucul (Maya-Q'eqchi'), a 24-year-old rural university student. Two years before, in April 2006, Cac formally accused a classmate of having attacked him with racial slurs that referred to his indigenous origin, among them: "Indian, little Indian; Indian; son of a bitch; you are as ignorant as other Indians in the street ... ; you cannot even talk. I am better than you because I am a ladino." Cac had problems at first but eventually registered his complaint with the prosecutor's office. This case is particularly interesting because the plaintiff, who received support from the Menchú Foundation, was initially unable to garner the necessary cooperation of witnesses to the incident. When interviewed by the press, Cac publicly announced that Guatemala requires more social sensitivity on ethnic discrimination and that this should begin with the justice system. At his hearing, judges determined that to offend a person's dignity "is not a crime." They also determined that there was not a power relationship between the accused and the plaintiff and, therefore, the discrimination charge did not apply in this case.

This sentence indicates the breadth and vagueness of the Penal Code Article 202 and supports some of the critiques it has received. The prosecutor appealed the verdict.[6] Romeo Tiú, presidential commissioner against discrimination and racism at the time, labeled the judicial system "hostile." Indigenous lawyers from CODISRA supported Cac's case and gave him advice in the juridical process. A new trial commenced and finally the accused classmate was sentenced to one year and four months in prison, and to a fine of 700.00 quetzales ($93.33 [U.S.]) and a compensation of 25,000.00 quetzales ($3,340.00 [U.S.]) (*Prensa Libre*, 31 March 2010).

The final case emanates from an incident on 1 October 2010, when Ana María Mejía lodged a formal accusation against a coworker who insulted her in an office in the Department of Justice. "She has told me that I am an Indian that it would be better for me to stay in the market rather than in an office; that my parents are Indians who dressed as such, and so forth" (*Prensa Libre,* 2 October 2010). On the occasions that this happened, the accused physically pushed Mejía and threw her paperwork on the floor. The aggressor was subsequently sentenced to prison. The accused spent fourteen days in Santa Teresa's Women's Prison and paid a fine of 10,000.00 quetzales ($1,350.00 [U.S.]) (*Prensa Libre*, 2 October 2010).

Psychological evaluations of the victims showed that in the majority of discrimination cases, severe emotional trauma was present. For instance, student Cac dropped out of school, although he later matriculated at the law school of another university. In all the cases, judges determined that for the plaintiffs, the right to express cultural and ethnic identity was not upheld when their human dignity and equality of treatment was violated (CODISRA-DEMI-OACNUDH 2010).

The fact that so few accusations go to trial is related to a complex series of factors. As explained above, one of the problems is the difficulty in determining whether an attitude or behavior can be described as a crime of exclusion, difference, restriction, or preference, according to the decree. Investigations involving collection of evidence and legal procedures are long and complicated, and expert linguistic work is required to prove the context in which an expression, phrase, or word was used and therefore whether or not it was discriminatory. Witnesses usually avoid filing formal complaints because of fear of retaliation. Much depends on how far the victim wants to go with his or her accusation: whether he or she wants an apology—usually the case with most accusations—or if he or she wishes to take the case to court, calling for evidence collection, witnesses, and a significant investment of time and money. Another issue is that the plaintiff must appear in the courtroom several times to narrate the crime, and must fill out countless forms. In doing so, he or she relives the offense suffered; the psychological pain can seem endless. Finally, there are a great number of cases still on hold to be judged and resolved in the courts. Due to this delay, people lose hope of obtaining justice, and they withdraw their cases. The whole process is exhausting for the victim-plaintiffs, who oftentimes require unavailable psychological support.

In April 2011, a weeklong celebration, "Solidarity with People Fighting Discrimination in Guatemala" (*Semana de Solidaridad con los Pueblos que Luchan contra la Discriminación en Guatemala*), took place. A key event honored ex-vice minister of labor, Cándida González Pirir, and the university student José Cac Cucul for denouncing discrimination and daring to carry through with their formal complaints until the end of their respective trials. Both received the designation "Ambassadors of Peace" from Secretary of the Peace Eddy Armas, and their exemplary roles in the fight against discrimination and racism were acknowledged. According to statistical reports issued by the Attorney General's office (the Ministerio Público) (Sistema Informático de Control de Gestión de Casos del Ministerio Público, SICOMP) in the period from 1 January 2005 to 13 August 2010, a total of 614 cases of discrimination and racism were submitted (43 in 2005, 67 in 2006, 63 in 2007, 111 in 2008, 122 in 2009, and 208 through 13 August 2010); the number of cases filed in 2009 is nearly three times that of 2005 (CODISRA-DEMI-OACNUDH 2010). This is a historical watermark in the history of the country, one that would have been unthinkable a decade ago. With such growing momentum for the eradication of racism and discrimination, a culture of denouncing crimes of discrimination (typified in Article 202 bis of the penal code) can be fostered.[7]

Final Reflections

The legal criminalization of racism, while a significant step in post-war Guatemala, is insufficient to eliminate discrimination and racism in the country. We have to be realistic: it is very difficult to modify human attitudes and to ensure that peaceful coexistence and tolerance become a reality. However, the fact that discrimination in public spaces against an indigenous person is now a criminal offense is fundamental to reformulating the quality of interethnic relations. The existence of such a law, despite its shortcomings, means that people will have to think twice before openly despising or offending the dignity of another human. It is clear that overt racism will continue to occur in certain spaces, and prejudice will continue to be reproduced unless people are increasingly exposed to interethnic social contact. In order to foment this, we need to carry out greater efforts in citizen education regarding democratic values, so that all Guatemalans understand and comply with respectful, basic rules of coexistence.

Slowly, society is changing and the state has had to respond to the pressure of social movements and recommendations from local and international organizations. Reformulating a multiethnic state based on real equality remains an ongoing project in Guatemala. Even though laws that acknowledge and support indigenous peoples' rights have been issued, implementing them is still a work in progress because up until now, some multicultural formulas have proven largely superficial.

I conclude by revisiting sociologists Douglas Massey and Nancy Denton's (1988) study on why, following the implementation of pro-civil rights legislation in the United States in 1960, there is still significant residential segregation. In some cities, neighborhoods inhabited by "whites" are clearly separated from those inhabited by African-Americans. Is legislation enough to eliminate racism? Did the civil rights movement succeed or did it fail to overcome the inheritance of segregation and racism? The answers to these questions are complex but applicable to the current situation in Guatemala. The lessons of the United States serve as an example for a broader reflection on the relation between law and social practice, about the scope of a state that proclaims itself multicultural, understanding it not as a mere celebration of cultural diversity, but as an acknowledgement of individual and collective rights of its ethnically different inhabitants. In Guatemala, reformulating a state on the basis of real equality is in progress. Although discrimination has been criminalized (and this has had a deep impact on society), a great gap remains between the formal discourse and its application. Important legal and institutional reforms have been accomplished. An intense debate on racism, discrimination, and multiculturalism has begun. But the daily socioeconomic reality, and the quality of inter-group relations lived on a day-to-day basis on public buses, in schools, at bars, restaurants and cafes, have changed very little. The budget to apply multicultural public policies is limited, and indigenous representation in government spaces is restricted. In Guatemala, we must continue to work toward equality.

Notes

1. The Presidential Commission against Racism and Discrimination (CODISRA), Defensoría de la Mujer Indígena (DEMI), and a special section for indigenous peoples at the Attorney General's office.
2. Rigoberto Quemé is the son of a K'iche' artisan and textile business couple. Quemé studied business administration, public administration, and anthropology. He was the only indigenous candidate among ten contenders for Quetzaltenango's mayor in 1995. Irma Alicia Velásquez Nimatuj (2007), a K'iche' anthropologist and journalist, believes that his victory may be due to his abilities as a speaker, the political support of indigenous women, and his good relations with some Creole families.
3. Guatemala had already ratified the International Convention on the Elimination of all Forms of Racial Discrimination in 1984.
4. "Bis" means "second" (double or repeated); it is a Latin word related to the legislation jargon. In this case, it indicates an article with the same number, but different content.
5. Asociación para el Avance de Sciencias Sociales en Guatemala (Association for the Advancement of Social Sciences in Guatemala).
6. Trial Record Number: C98-2008 (Tribunal de Sentencia Penal, Narcoactividad y Delitos contra el Ambiente de San Benito, Petén).
7. The departments with the greatest number of discrimination offenses presented to the Attorney General's office are: Guatemala with 38.70 percent, Alta Verapaz with 12.17 percent, Quetzaltenango with 10.43 percent, and Quiche with 6.52 percent. The rest of the departments report less than 5 percent of cases. The data collection agency of the Attorney General's Office (SICOMP) does not collect information on the type(s) of discrimination that occur in each case. This data should be collected, since the Guatemalan state has specific international commitments, and it should be categorized in terms of gender, ethnicity, culture, age, and disability, among other markers.

8 Ephemeral Rights and Securitized Lives

Migration, *Mareros*, and Power in Millennial Guatemala

*Jennifer L. Burrell**

In early 1998, when the rain ceased and the brisk, cloudless winter sky of the Cuchumatanes mountain range in northwestern Guatemala lit up like a planetarium with its vast spectrum of stars, I was sitting on a rooftop, enchanted by the glorious display. I was living dangerously that night, hanging out with the so-called *marero* (gang member) Alfonso, a nephew of my landlords.[1] He was, at the time, public enemy number one in the town of Todos Santos Cuchumatán, having recently survived a lynching attempt provoked by the mayor. But, like me, he loved the stars on nights like this and he knew a surprising number of constellations. We talked about stars for a long time. Eventually, though, when things were quieter, I couldn't resist. I asked him about his outlaw persona, and of the difficulties of negotiating life in a small town where popular opinion had turned against him. He was, I remember remarking as I watched a shooting star, at the center of much larger processes in the community.

I've revisited our conversation for well over a decade now. I could not have imagined how Alfonso's story would come to influence my thoughts and even the trajectory of my research interests. I lived in Todos Santos, a Mam Maya town of about 25,000, for 36 months in the late 1990s, researching the war to postwar transition. Although it took years for these processes to unfold, I came to realize as I kept up with friends, read newspapers, and continued to visit Todosanteros (natives of Todos Santos) in Guatemala and the United States, that Alfonso's life and (eventual) death were about the making of modern power and politics, and demonstrated how some of Central America's most important millennial keywords—security, democracy, and human rights—came to take on new meanings in relation to shifting politics and societal values (Williams 1976). His story also shows how these ideas imbricate other crucial processes, like migration, that have come to define the present for millions of Central Americans.

On that starlit rooftop, Alfonso candidly discussed some of his dilemmas. He contested the label marero used to categorize him and other young men, especially returning migrants. He clearly saw the problem as an intergenerational conflict over access to local power, albeit with newly violent ramifications. He also expressed his confidence in human rights. It was, in his narrative, a useful set of discourses and practices central to the postwar construction of democracy in Guatemala, and he had come into contact with its potential power as a recent lynching survivor. Amidst the stars, he was hopeful that human rights could protect him from alarming levels of violence animating conflict in this community.

At the time Central America was transitioning from sending large flows of refugees and political asylum seekers to the United States and Europe, to even higher levels of wage labor migrants. More Guatemalans had begun to act on the impatience expressed in the postwar graffiti common at the time, *No hay paz sin trabajo* (there is no peace without work), and were heading north. In Todos Santos, increasing numbers of men and women began to migrate to U.S. satellite communities in Oakland, California; Grand Rapids, Michigan; and Boston, Massachusetts. Alfonso practiced the pattern common in those days—one in which migrants would spend most of the year in the United States, returning for fiestas and other important social occasions, and often, after a few months, contract their *coyotes* (migrant smugglers) to take them over the border again. Although largely undocumented, some held residency papers (green cards), many obtained through the 1986 Immigration Reform and Control Act.[2] (Alfonso acquired a green card through marriage to a U.S. citizen.) By the mid-2000s, these were remembered as the "good old days" in relation to the danger and expense produced by an ever more securitized border between the United States and Mexico, and the deportation regime that has come to define and shape migrant lives and experiences in the north (see Mendez, this volume.)

By the close of the first millennial decade, transnational Todosanteros and their co-nationals comprised the largest group of Central American citizens in the United States: 1.1 million (of a total population of 14 million) in 2009.[3] Remittances rose to $4.13 billion (U.S.) in 2010 (Banco de Guatemala 2011), an amount nearly half the country's exports or one-tenth of the gross national product.[4] The prodigious, overshadowing economic power of remittances and regional anxiety about acute levels of rising crime and violence (see Moodie, this volume) have meant that many grassroots changes produced by transnationalism are understudied in Guatemala.[5] Since the signing of the Peace Accords in 1996, new hybrids of political practice and knowledge have emerged in the country, challenging existing notions of power, democracy, and even civil society.

Political and social intrigue swirled around Alfonso not because he was a migrant, but because he threatened local power hierarchies. Through behavior deemed undesirable in the context of this Mayan community—long hair, piercings, hanging out with a group of young men and drinking in the street late at night, fights with members of a rival group—he came to embody a very specific national anxiety: the marero. This set into motion a process that escalated in unanticipated ways. Alfonso was public enemy number one in Todos Santos because *maras* (gangs) were public enemy number one in Guatemala. Within the postwar political imaginary, urban maras were the worst-case scenario: intolerable, uncontrollable, and extremely threatening, a phenomenon Thomas et al. (2011, 2) refer to as "a new common sense that involves blaming gangs and other unsavory elements of the population for danger and insecurity." Within Guatemala City, historian Deborah Levenson marks their trajectory from groups of young people with communal vision and ideologies of social justice when she first interviewed youth involved in gangs in the 1980s (AVANCSO 1987), to victims of state-sponsored clandestine social cleansing, to killers preoccupied with death, the end product of state necropolitics (Mbembe 2003) and the military's "absolute negation of life as the job of power" (Levenson 2013).[6] In a national context of impunity, where so many get away with murder, whether of one person or tens of thousands, communities were understandably anxious to protect themselves from the specter of escalating violence represented by the marero.

This chapter examines some of the interconnections among security, migration, and human rights, particularly as these coalesced around Alfonso and local efforts to control him and his ilk. In the resulting nexus of relationships and powerful contradictions, many Todosanteros perceive human rights as ephemeral. Part of their chimeric quality, I show, is the ease with which individuals slip in and out of the class of people seen as *having* rights and of being able to access them, especially in relation to community security concerns. Moving between gradations of citizenship (Ong 1999) and entitlement produces a flexible and fluid concept of rights, their meaning and potential uses.

Ephemeral Rights and Justice

Human rights have become a central political idiom and discourse through which groups and individuals make claims, negotiate access and are legitimized (see Pineda, this volume). Knowledge of them allows people to "articulate political claims which make sense in a particular social context," particularly where the state is active in the establishment and expression of political and social orders (Dembour 1996, 33). Human rights (as discourse and practice) constitute a central element of the postwar democratizing project in Guatemala. So many people received human rights training from the late 1990s that those who did not sometimes felt excluded from the state-building project. In 2000, for example, bus attendants in Guatemala City went on strike to protest a lowering of wages and transportation reforms that potentially eliminated their jobs. In an interview with a local news station, their representative made clear that they would end the strike if they were offered human rights training. After all, bus drivers had received it. As Julián López García (2008, 143) explains, "This training is justified as necessary for the attainment of a truly democratic and modern Guatemala that would put an end to the secular state of corruption, the disregard for people's dignity, and to irrational and violent atavisms, of which the most widely known today is lynching." Not offering it to the *ayudantes* (helpers, or fare collectors) signaled their possible exclusion from the full benefits and potentials of postwar citizenship, adding to their already considerable vulnerability as their jobs were threatened.

Radio, television, and billboard campaigns about human rights, as well as newspapers and popular forms such as comic books, were all mobilized in these capacity-building exercises. Children learned about rights in the classroom. Copies of the Peace Accords and rights-related materials were translated into a number of Mayan and other indigenous languages and distributed in communities. Naturally, there were wide degrees of interpolation and highly selective ways in which elements of this knowledge and practice were incorporated, understood, and used to justify specific projects.

In Guatemala, alongside maras, lynchings as a form of violence dominated the political imaginary in the postwar period, especially in indigenous communities. The tendency has been to view both of these as examples of the widespread violence and disintegration that has engulfed Guatemalan society in general and, in the case of lynching, Mayan villages in particular. At the same time, Maya have worked to strengthen forms of indigenous law within the parameters of the postwar multicultural state. This has occurred in conjunction with national processes of ethnic revitalization, generating new types of communal governance and justice that blend with human rights (Sieder 2011), as well as forms of community policing, punishment, and vigilantism that sometimes do not. As Sieder (2011, 174) demonstrates for the case of Santa Cruz del Quiché, Guatemala, the relationship between local justice mechanisms and the state may co-exist uneasily, placing indigenous authorities "in a state of permanent legal in-definition," never sure if their actions will be recognized as legitimate by the state or subject to criminal prosecution.[7]

Maya draw upon community forms of authority and, sometimes, those learned during the war to navigate their way through the postwar period (Godoy 2006). These forms have assumed a particularly generational cast since they involve sets of practices both remembered and put into effect by older members of the community. Migrants, who tend to be young men, often unfamiliar with or scornful of their parents' actions during the war, may be left with few modes of participation in existing community power structures. They point to the lack of leadership roles or employment opportunities that take into account the experiences, like migration, that they have had.

A predicament arises for communities and individuals who are now familiar with if not fluent in the idiom of global human rights: they are often forced to disregard them to address pressing security issues. In postwar Guatemala, an unruly Todosantero testing the limits of community tolerance may invoke rights to protect himself from the ire of an angry mob. The opposite, across transnational borders in the United States, is also true: upright and law-abiding Todosanteros find themselves in peculiarly right-less situations, guilty of the crime (under the current U.S. securitized deportation regime) of wishing for a better life and crossing borders without legal documentation to achieve it. The limits of contexts in which human rights may be accessed are made dramatically clear to transnational migrants, where the stripping of citizenship also entails the disappearance of entitlement.

Another dilemma stems from the incommensurability of rights with Mayan concepts of personhood, society, justice, and collectivity. Human rights discourse encourages individualization and state incursion at the cost of traditional polities such as extended families and indigenous communities. This can contribute to the undermining of local law and order, a tension that Mayan leader Benjamin Son characterizes as the lack of balance between human rights and communal obligations (Ekern 2008).

These slippages contribute to a terrain in which concepts of rights and justice are rendered flexible and constantly evolving, belying the fixity given to them by the international and national mechanisms and postwar mandates: truth and reconciliation committees, peacekeeping forces, civil society organizations. But these rights are evanescent, part of a package of receding hopes for a democratic ideal inclusive of economic and social justice. This is especially true among a growing indigenous transnational population who may be subjected to additional forms of discrimination.

This sense of the transience and selectivity of rights and their inaccessibility for those involved in legitimate livelihood struggles is increasingly expressed by marginalized people throughout the world. In an impoverished urban barrio of Cochabamba, Bolivia, residents decry human rights. Human rights seem to be for delinquents, who get food, clothing, and health care while imprisoned. Poor people engaged in everyday work of on-the-edge subsistence have no access to such resources. Their claims about threats to their survival go unnoticed because they are delivered in economic terms (Goldstein 2007).

In another example, residents of Totonicapán, Guatemala, who were sanctioned for excessive logging in the communally held forest, ignored the request of a communal assembly to desist. As a result, their water supply was blocked. They lodged formal complaints of a human rights violation with MINUGUA (the United Nations Peacekeeping Mission) and other organizations. Rallying the discourse and practice of rights to their cause, the logging families emerged with their water connection restored, and as moral *victors*. A local leader involved in the conflict observed that it was "a typical case of how human rights favor the guilty" (Ekern 2008, 136).

The right to security—in the sense of the ability to protect oneself—often exists in tension with other claims, frequently producing confusion about whose rights will be recognized in particular contexts. As Daniel Goldstein (2010, 489) writes, "An ethnography of rights ... cannot be considered adequate without attention to the 'security crisis' facing the indigenous poor, and such an analysis cannot be adequately undertaken without an understanding of the security/rights conflict as a distinctly neoliberal phenomena."

These various contradictions are evident in Alfonso's story and in the recent history of Todos Santos. Alfonso negotiated the postwar world of human rights with particular skill. By virtue of being poor (although well-off by local standards) and indigenous, he experienced the liminality of transnational border-crossers. As a green card holder, though, his experiences of discrimination and disentitlement were different than those of some of his compatriots. He could wield the discourses and mechanisms of rights violations. But perhaps most importantly, following the attempted lynching, he fashioned himself as the right kind of human rights *victim*.

Meanwhile, his detractors moved ahead in the communal project of defending themselves and their security from a burgeoning "gang problem." They formed security committees based on an older para-statal form, the forced-service civil patrols, paramilitary organizations instituted during the civil war. Alfonso, and the various threats that he represented, served as the impetus for their resurgence.

Human Rights and Wrongs: A Murder and a Lynching

On 30 October 2003, I listened to my voicemail in New York City. No message had been left, but I could hear a conversation in Mam Maya. The call had come from an unfamiliar number in Grand Rapids, Michigan, home of the then fastest-growing community of migrant Todosanteros, and where many people I know live. I called back and learned, from his younger brother and sister, that Alfonso had been shot and killed two days earlier by the Guatemalan National Civil Police (PNC, the force established to keep the peace following the signing of the Accords). A close friend, who had been with them the previous evening, suggested they call me for contacts in the international human rights community. Did I know of anyone who could help them to bring his case to the attention of organizations who might legally address it? They would never get an investigation or justice, they surmised, if they left it up to local or departmental authorities or courts.

I promptly made a series of calls to individuals in New York (where I was living and working in the human rights world)[8] who provided me with contact information for various people and offices, including the Human Rights Ombudsman in the department of Huehuetenango. I also collected names, phone numbers, and e-mail addresses of other people who might be able to assist in the case or potentially provide additional contacts. I called and sent e-mails to Alfonso's family members in Michigan, California, Texas, and Guatemala.

Some of the people I contacted were familiar with Alfonso and his family members, having met or heard about him. Most knew about his near-lynching in 1997: on the Saturday before Christmas, during an unusually crowded market, the mayor had incited a riot by calling Alfonso a thief, berating him for his long hair and the bad influence he had on the town's youth. Some took this as a license to attack, throwing punches at Alfonso and his younger brother who attempted to defend him. As the crowds surged around the altercation, more men joined in and dragged Alfonso out of the central park and on to the streets. There, people threw wooden crates, rotten fruit, and stones at him. Eventually, he broke free and ran forty meters to the weaving cooperative where his father had long served as president. Associates quickly barricaded the doors and windows against the unruly mob. The cooperative was housed in a wooden building along the main street, and for the next hours, talk of burning it circulated through the streets and dirt paths of the town.

Calls to the departmental offices of MINUGUA eventually brought a convoy of vehicles filled with armed police and peacekeeping forces. Amidst a somewhat diminished crowd still calling for his surrender, they removed Alfonso and his father. They took the two to a hospital in Huehuetenango where Alfonso recovered from his injuries. In the days afterwards, Alfonso enjoyed consultations with regional authorities and international specialists regarding his rights, their violation, and his options. Just a year after the signing of the Peace Accords, lynching had emerged as a troublesome indicator of the difficulties of establishing postwar democracy. Few survived these incidents; Alfonso's case represented an opportunity for legal intervention, one that could potentially serve as a potent anti-lynching paradigm. Days later, quietly under the cover of Christmas and New Year celebrations, Alfonso returned to Todos Santos, and that is when we watched the display of stars from a quiet rooftop.

Being a Marero in Todos Santos

Gangs are a preoccupation throughout Central America. This is particularly so in El Salvador, Honduras, and Guatemala, where the rival gangs La Mara

Salvatrucha (MS-13) and Dieciocho (18), born on the streets of Los Angeles, enjoy powerful transnational connections. Young men, sometimes former insurgents or the sons of political refugees, joined these groups after fleeing their countries. In 1992, the U.S. Immigration and Naturalization Service began to deport convicted gang members in an attempt to control their growth. Thousands were returned to Central America, mostly to San Salvador and, to a lesser extent, Guatemala City. However, the majority of gang members are not deportees: postwar struggles and despair, and the poverty of deepening neoliberalism, supply a recruitable base of disaffected youth with little to hope for. With reputations as the most brutal and violent gangs in the world, they have expanded throughout the region (Zilberg 2011).

Until the end of the war in Guatemala, maras were urban-based. In the late 1990s, talk about their infiltration into rural areas gradually suffused the highlands. Soon, many towns reported incipient maras, sometimes "visiting" from nearby cities, or homegrown and often involving young men who had migrated. Before long, they became part of the everyday world of many Maya, their incursion deeply violating cultural norms of intergenerational respect and age-based forms of power.

A prevailing assumption behind this spread is that gangs are everywhere the same, engaging in analogous behavior for comparable reasons, similarly composed in terms of membership, and using markers, such as tattoos, jewelry, or hand signs, that allow them to communicate nonverbally. Yet, evidence from throughout Guatemala suggests that what mara means and what mareros do encompass a broad range of very different kinds of activities, levels of criminality, and modes of participation, from small-scale petty theft to transnational narco- and gun-trafficking. The invocation of the label "gang" for a wide variety of actions, problems, and local conflicts means that anti-gang measures may be applied indiscriminately no matter the action, crime, or particular circumstance of an incident. Widespread consensus that gangs, their violence, and their crime must be eradicated also opens the space for illegal modes of combating them. State anti-gang measures are widely believed to be clandestine forms of social cleansing, and community-based initiatives often remain unsanctioned or continue to operate even after official sanction (Agner 2008; Burrell 2010; WOLA 2006). As Levenson (forthcoming) writes, "Neither rebels nor conformists, orphans of the world, and not only of Guatemala, criminalized by adults and even by the United States Homeland Security for all manner of and every evil, the maras have become a variation of those whom Hannah Arendt once called 'the most symptomatic group,' the left-overs, 'forced to live outside the common world.'"

The behavior of Alfonso and other mareros in Todos Santos—belonging to two groups called the Cholos and the Rockeros—included forming posses of local youth (sometimes young boys would hang out with them), drunk-

Figure 8.1. 'Signing' in Todos Santos Cuchumatán, Image from the film, "Una Vida Mejor" (2011), directed by Olivia L. Carrescia, distributed by Icarus Films, Inc.

Figure 8.2. Mod Hair in Todos Santos Cuchumatán, image from the film, "Una Vida Mejor" (2011), directed by Olivia L. Carrescia, distributed by Icarus Films, Inc.

enness, theft, fighting with other so-called mareros, abusing drunks, and threatening townspeople. Cholo or Rockero graffiti occasionally appeared on the walls of buildings. Alfonso was the de facto head of the Cholos. To my knowledge, he had no associations with other gangs in Guatemala or the United States, nor did he invoke the popularly recognized markers of such groups—guns, drugs, tattoos. Todos Santos mareros were generally sons of the wealthiest families; other young men were usually engaged in family-based subsistence activities where their full-time labor was required. Many of the alleged gang members had long hair, and occasionally, earrings or bandannas, worn with the *traje* (handwoven clothing), distinctive red pants and striped shirts worn by the men of Todos Santos. Only some were migrants, but nearly all had a migrant in the family.

While the backdrop of ongoing structural violence toward young Mayan men is undeniable, the meaning of marero and the social capital it conveys is categorically different in this place. Young Todosanteros negotiate power and gendered roles as they move back and forth between Oakland or Grand Rapids and Todos Santos. With this movement, they become savvy at wielding the transnational baggage of images, consumption, style, and action that surround young people; others hope to emulate them. In Guatemala, means to access local power are often inaccessible to them, as they require slow movement through age grade hierarchies that are impossible for many migrants. In the United States their independence and the bases of their masculinity are undermined by their undocumented status and its corollary: lives lived in fear of deportation and the social suffering this produces. So-called gangs, then, in their local form, grant Todosanteros a means by which to grasp what Roger Lancaster (1992, 195) refers to as "the essence of machismo's ideal of manhood."

Some months after Alfonso's quiet post-lynching return to Todos Santos in 1997, another incident occurred that raised the hackles of villagers. During the much-anticipated carnival outing of schoolchildren and teachers to an alpine meadow in the mountain peaks, a drunken Alfonso and his posse began wrestling with teachers and throwing eggs at students. Terrified children ran and scattered, hiding from the drunken brawlers. In the frenzied aftermath, three children were left behind, only recovered the next day. The posse continued their siege of terror by tossing empty beer bottles into the trucks carrying children back to town. Todosanteros were furious at this senseless attack.

I didn't talk to Alfonso after this incident, and rarely afterward. It's hard to imagine what he was thinking. I have often wondered if his encounter with the then-powerful human rights apparatus encouraged him to think that he was somehow unassailable. After all, he had expressed his hope in these discourses and practices, not only for his own defense, but as a means for all Guatemalans to participate in postwar democracy. Were human rights, in his vision, like a Monopoly "get out of jail free" card?

In response to Alfonso's rampages and his enduring influence on youth, townspeople increasingly began to clamor for resolution to the gang problem. Specific concerns included everyday security matters such as alleged robberies in houses and on the street, harassment and a new lack of respect shown by youth in general in schools and other public places. Teachers, who constitute a strong political block, were confronted with this dismaying shift on a daily basis. It is no accident that the crackdown on mareros escalated when a teacher won the mayoral election.

The Creation and Spread of *Seguridad*

There is no tabula rasa on which to overlay human rights and democratic discourses; on-the-ground histories must be taken into account (Carmack

2005). In this case, the first postwar decade offered cultural and political currents that sometimes mixed cumbersomely. Mayan cultural revitalization, customary forms of law and authority with their emphasis on generation, and the conflicts emerging from migration came together in uneasy tension.

Linking local problems to regional preoccupations with gangs, security, and migration, and employing the marero discourse to do so, now rendered Alfonso a person without rights. "Names become things," as Eric Wolf (1982, 6–7) famously remarked, "and things marked with X can be targets of war." Once it was widely believed that Alfonso was a gang member, it was easier to imagine connections that weren't really there, actions that were never committed, and unlikely future scenarios. Forms of power otherwise questionable in the postwar period of human rights became justifiable, as everyone from representatives of nongovernmental organizations to regional governors to local authorities could not disagree with the desire to control gangs. Security trumped rights.

In early 1999, as mandated by the peace agreements, PNC agents were permanently stationed in Todos Santos and rural communities throughout Guatemala. Villagers were glad to hand the problem of the so-called maras to these forces. But crime did not lessen, youth continued to roam the streets of the town at night, and cantinas paid bribes to the police in order to stay open and serve them. As Ellen Moodie (2010; and this volume) illustrates for San Salvadorans, the democratic hopes invested in policing were also unmet in Todos Santos. In response, over the next several years, curfews were instituted and security committees formed to enforce them and more specifically, to target mareros. Like the civil patrols instituted in Todos Santos by the Army in 1982, adult male service is mandatory. In their early years, *seguridad* (security), as the committees came to be known, was frequently cited for multiple rights violations by the mareros they clandestinely imprisoned, sometimes for up to several days in latrines (*Prensa Libre* 2003a; 2003b; 2003c). The committees issued a death threat to the local justice of the peace when they disagreed with a verdict, requiring him to clear all future decisions with them (*Prensa Libre* 2003a). Repeated attempts by regional authorities to warn the municipality from this course, to indict for human rights violations, to impose penalties, and to otherwise censure illegal acts were met with a steadfast reply: local actions were justified to resolve the pressing gang problem. If the state and/or the police weren't going to step in to resolve these issues, then Todosanteros would handle them on their own.

On 28 October 2003, during the annual fiesta, Alfonso was killed by police officers. Claiming that he was a marero and a dangerous criminal (and that he had antagonized them) the police allegedly broke into his sister's house where he was drinking with his family and fired eight shots into his chest and back. Following his death, the mayor requested that the police leave Todos Santos, citing concerns for their safety during the All Saints Day fiesta, when many people drink to excess and every broken beer bottle becomes a potential weapon.

Alfonso's trajectory from victim to perpetrator and back again reveals some of the mutability and contradictions involved in negotiating the discourses of human rights, security, and migration in postwar Guatemala. As Henrietta Moore (1994, 55) has emphasized, "A single subject can no longer be equated with a single individual." This is certainly true of Alfonso, who simultaneously embraced a number of identities—indigenous, Mam-speaking, traje-wearing, border crossing, green card holding, trouble-making marero and father. At the time of his death, he was in the process of constructing a house on a plot of land he purchased close to family members. According to friends and family, he had been engaged in discussions about the possibility of running for local office. In lamenting the lack of opportunities for young people, he had been thinking about spearheading an oft-mentioned and never-realized plan for a youth center. He had, in other words, been imagining a less confrontational, community-based future.

By 2006, a marked ambivalence characterized conversations about security committees. I reflected on similarities and differences among and between recent conversations I had had with security committees and, years earlier, with civil patrollers. During the war era, Todosanteros reported to those who asked that they had never caught a guerilla insurgent or any other kind of criminal on their patrols, intimating that without army oversight, they would gladly cease these duties.[9] In 2006–2007, men related accounts about patrols that enforced curfews and the 6 p.m. closing of cantinas while they themselves did nothing more than walk the streets. I heard about a patrol that, confronted with a defiant cantina owner, cut her connection to the municipal water supply. "On my patrol," one man remarked, "we could never bring ourselves to do anything that fierce." Reconnecting water, he noted, is difficult and expensive. Another commented, "I know there are problems with it [security] but it works." Leaving aside a minority of fierce and enthusiastic patrollers, many in Todos Santos seemed to share this opinion. Actions that teetered on the brink of legality and potentially violated human rights were considered a fair price to maintain control. When the mayor was asked to respond to concerns that some patrollers carried firearms (rather than authorized machetes and nightsticks) he replied, "It's difficult to tell the people that they can't carry them" (*Prensa Libre* 2007b). Seguridad went on to close cantinas, rendering Todos Santos a "dry" town until cantineros (cantina owners) challenged them in court some years later.

Security committees have spread throughout Guatemala, inspired by claims that they have controlled and even eradicated gangs and local violence, usually at the neighborhood level. As a result, they are actively encouraged by government officials (Sieder 2011), and national and departmental attempts have been made to regulate them through registration processes (Álvarez Castañeda 2007; *Prensa Libre* 2007a). In Todos Santos, this regulation is resisted as it imposes a limit on and sometimes a decrease of committee powers. Abuses continue to be reported; as they have been for at least the past decade, attempts to adjudicate them are ignored.

The human rights sector has by and large recognized that these committees are formed to address "deficiencies of the state" (*Prensa Libre* 2007b). Some human-rights advocates support them as does the Human Rights Ombudsman in Huehuetenango, while others oppose them, like the Presidential Commission on Human Rights (COPREDEH). COPREDEH argues that the duties they fulfill are within the mandate of the police and says it is concerned that many patrollers are armed (*Prensa Libre* 2007b). The contradictory relationship between rights and security is once more manifest in these discussions, as the issue is not *how* citizen security should be achieved, even as rights may be violated through current methods, but the details of how these currently existing processes are to be carried out. After all, they do accomplish the goal of lessening locally based crime and violence. Security once again trumps rights. "Rather than contributing to the seamless reproduction of neoliberal governmentality," Goldstein (2010, 499) contends, "security, like so many other components of transnational political economy and its accompanying discourses, has been adopted and reconfigured in unexpected and challenging ways, serving not necessarily to deepen neoliberal hegemony but to contest the very parameters of governmental responsibility and citizen rights." Alfonso's life and death demonstrate how Todosanteros have been enmeshed in the long-term process of shaping the cluster of relationships and local conflicts that, in Guatemala, have now come to be known as seguridad, the specificity of their history lost to the imperatives of providing citizen safety.

Conclusions

The story of Alfonso, a rural marero and migrant, leads us through a labyrinth of postwar power, of contradictions and channels chiseled by the competing imperatives of human rights and security in this unruly era. I first wrote about his life and his murder in the year after his death. I hadn't planned to do so, but I needed to mark his passage and to figure out what I knew. The narrative that emerged raises a series of global concerns as well as pressing regional and local ones.

As worldwide economic crisis deepens, reorganizing the demographics of Central America and many other places in the world, security, migration, and rights will continue to interconnect and resonate in new ways. Marking how they have already done so is important; it provides a way of tracking the dynamics and relations of power that constitute ever-shifting social terrains. More locally, their interrelationships specify particularities important to the struggle of Mayan communities working to define cultural and political spaces from which to secure futures. Intergenerational dynamics, integral to communities and extended families, and a sensitive issue for Maya throughout modern history, continue to constitute a challenge. These conditions will only intensify as transnational migration continues to manufacture new economic, cultural, gender, and age inequalities that shift security concerns and produce new intersections with human rights discourses.

This volume grapples with how Central America came to disappear from the center of the worldwide geopolitical stage that it occupied in the 1980s at the height of the Cold War. It has been re-visibilized in a variety of respects, but rarely in a sustained way, at the level of local power and agency. Alfonso's life and death demonstrate how individuals and communities negotiate a contemporary political economic landscape, flush with the paradoxes of neoliberalism, democracy, and ongoing political and structural violence, and the idioms like security and human rights, which compose them. This is living through transition, re-imagining the possibilities of democracy and of collective futures.

Notes

* Some material presented in this article was originally published in Burrell (2010). I thank the participants of "After the Handshakes," especially Marc Edelman, Ellen Moodie, Jennifer Bickham Mendez, Mark Anderson, and Florence Babb for their comments.

1. Pseudonym.
2. The Immigration Control and Reform Act of 1986 granted amnesty to an estimated 3 million unauthorized immigrants, many of them from Mexico and Central America (Coutin 2007).
3. "Hispanics of Guatemalan Origin in the United States, 2009," 26 May 2011, http://pewhispanic.org/files/factsheets/76.pdf, accessed 20 June 2011. Seventy-three percent arrived in the United States in 1990 or later, and 68 percent are foreign born (compared with 37 percent of Hispanics and 13 percent of the U.S. population overall). Guatemalans comprised 2.2 percent of the U.S. Hispanic population.
4. Banco de Guatemala, Ingresos de Divisas por Remesas Familiares, Años 2008–2011, http://www.banguat.gob.gt/inc/ver.asp?id=/estaeco/remesas/remfam2011.htm&e=89841, accessed 20 June 2011.
5. Recent discussions include Burrell (2005); Foxen (2007); Moran-Taylor and Taylor (2010); and Taylor et al. (2006).
6. Achille Mbembe (2003) theorizes necropolitics as the subjugation of life to the power of death. The authority to kill is no longer controlled by the state but distributed throughout society.
7. Deborah Poole's (2004) work in Ayacucho refers to this conundrum as "between guarantee and threat," a liminal zone for indigenous authorities.

8. I had been working for several years with the New York office of the Argentine Forensic Anthropology Team. Many Todosanteros were savvy to the players in the human rights world, recognizing that the various forensic teams working in Guatemala were well connected internationally.
9. Both Victor Perera (1993) and Olivia Carrescia (1989) comment that the civil patrol in Todos Santos did not engage in armed combat once during their first seven years of existence, consistent with reports that while Todosanteros fulfilled their patrol duties without protest or rebellion, they were not among the most enthusiastically aggressive or "out of control" participants.

Part III

Dominant, Residual, and Emergent Economic Strategies

9 Honduras's Smallholder Coffee Farmers, the Coffee Crisis, and Neoliberal Policy

Disjunctures in Knowledge and Conundrums for Development

*Catherine Tucker**

When the coffee crisis sent prices plunging in late 1999, José Maldonado[1] was one of thousands of coffee producers in Honduras who had to make tough decisions as his main source of income declined precipitously. José had three children, his wife Eva was pregnant, and he was supporting his widowed mother. They lived in a two-room adobe house with a dirt floor. He had no debts, but no savings. Besides one hectare in coffee, he had a hectare to grow maize and beans for household consumption, and several hectares of forested land. During the coffee crisis, José cut back on fertilizer to save money. He did not hire help to work on his plantation; he was able to keep up with weeding, maintaining, and harvesting his plantation with help from his children and brothers. To compensate for lost income, he cleared a patch of forest to plant more corn and beans. He experimented with a fishpond and joined a group that organized to grow vegetables for local markets. With funds from the sale of a team of oxen, he purchased more land and planted coffee seedlings to expand his plantation. He wanted to be ready when coffee prices rose.

Coffee prices have always been volatile, but the coffee crisis that began in the 1999–2000 harvesting season represented one of the worst market shocks producers had ever experienced. Over a decade later, ripple effects from the crisis continue to shape policies and development programs in coffee-producing regions. During the crisis, global overproduction drove prices to a 100-year low in real terms (Varangis et al. 2003). In Honduras, as in the rest of Central America, falling prices hit smallholder coffee farmers especially hard. They had few sources of income, and many had suffered damages due to Hurricane Mitch, followed by a regional drought (CLACDS 1999). The combination of falling coffee prices and severe weather events coincided with a regional economic downturn. Many people dependent on coffee had barely been meeting their basic needs and slid into poverty. In Nicaragua's coffee sector, poverty rates increased by 2 percent (Lewin et al. 2004). Central America's coffee-producing countries reported dramatic losses of income from coffee, increasing unemployment, elevated malnutrition rates, social tensions, and abandonment of coffee fields (CEPAL 2002). Economists noted that global demand for coffee had stagnated, except for specialty and gourmet coffees. Moreover, transformations in the commodity chain during the 1990s allowed transnational corporations based in coffee-consuming countries to capture an increasing proportion of the profits from coffee (Talbot 2004). Between 1989 and 1996, the approximate profit per cup of coffee paid to producers fell from over ten cents to around two cents (Talbot 1997). Analysts predicted (correctly) that coffee prices might increase slightly as global production fell to match demand (Lewin et al. 2004) in the wake of the crisis, but their warnings have also borne out: coffee producers selling to conventional markets have been unable to claim a greater share of profits.

Assessing the Central American situation, economists and development agencies decided that a competitive transition needed to occur in the coffee sector. Given the structural changes in the commodity chain and the changing composition of global demand, they suggested that Central America emphasize its competitive advantage in producing high-quality arabica coffee grown at higher elevations. The Inter-American Development Bank, U.S. Agency for International Development, and World Bank recommended two major goals:

> 1. Enhancing coffee quality, efficiency, and sustainability in the regions with comparative advantage (specifically, the zones with adequate altitude); developing value added; and pursuing effective promotional marketing; and
> 2. promoting diversification into other agricultural and non-agricultural alternatives, for regions without potential for producing quality coffee. (IDB-USAID-World Bank 2002, i)

Analyses pointed to the potential to expand participation in fair trade and other alternative markets, and the importance of improving transportation and communications infrastructure (CEPAL 2002). In general, economists recommended greater diversification within coffee markets (for example, fair trade certification) or for producers to get out of coffee production (Varangis et al. 2003). The Honduran Coffee Institute (IHCAFE), charged with providing technical services, information, and support to coffee growers, embraced these recommendations and modified its emphasis on coffee expansion to focus on quality improvement. The last thing experts anticipated was that some coffee farmers, including José, would decide to plant more coffee when prices were hitting record lows and prospects for improved profits appeared dismal.

The contradiction between experts' views and José's decision might be viewed as an information gap. Many economists saw the crisis as a manifestation of profound transformations in global coffee markets that severely curtailed coffee producers' share of profits. Few farmers had access to this information and they saw the crisis as part of normal variability in coffee markets (see Lyon, this volume, for a contrasting situation). As the coffee crisis gradually resolved after 2003, however, José's decision appeared to be justified. By 2007, when I returned to visit him, he had doubled the size of his plantation. Profits had been adequate to add a room to his home and lay concrete floors, and he planned to plant more coffee seedlings. In 2008, he joined a newly formed coffee cooperative and continued to expand his plantation in hopes that organic and fair trade certifications would lead to higher prices. Many other coffee producers in his community, where I have been conducting longitudinal research since 1993, had made similar decisions to increase their coffee production. While no one has become wealthy, they believe that they made the right decision. The experience of these coffee farmers suggests that the contradiction between expert predictions and local decisions cannot be explained solely by farmers' inadequate access to market information.

In this chapter, I explore coffee farmers' responses during and after the coffee crisis, and the contexts and rationales underlying them. While José and similar-minded farmers expanded their plantations, others in different circumstances made different choices. The exploration of coffee farmers' decisions provides insight into their lives and helps explain the contrasting perspectives of policy makers who depend on macrolevel information, and producers who make decisions based on their household circumstances and local socioeconomic and environmental contexts. I focus on coffee farmers in two locales in western Honduras, the *municipio* (similar to a county) of La Campa in the Department of Lempira (similar to a state), where José lives, and the municipio of Concepción del Sur in the Department of Santa Bárbara (Figure 9.1). I begin by reviewing the research methods and introducing the study sites. I move on to a historical overview of coffee production in Honduras and discuss the contexts of the coffee crisis. Thereafter, I address the ways in which farmers responded to the crisis and its aftermath, the contexts that shaped their behavior, and the conundrums that challenge coffee producers and the Central American nations that depend on coffee as an economic mainstay.

Data Collection

I drew the data for this study from research in western Honduras that stretches over eighteen years. I first conducted fieldwork in La Campa in 1993 and have returned nearly every year. I started work in Concepción del Sur dur-

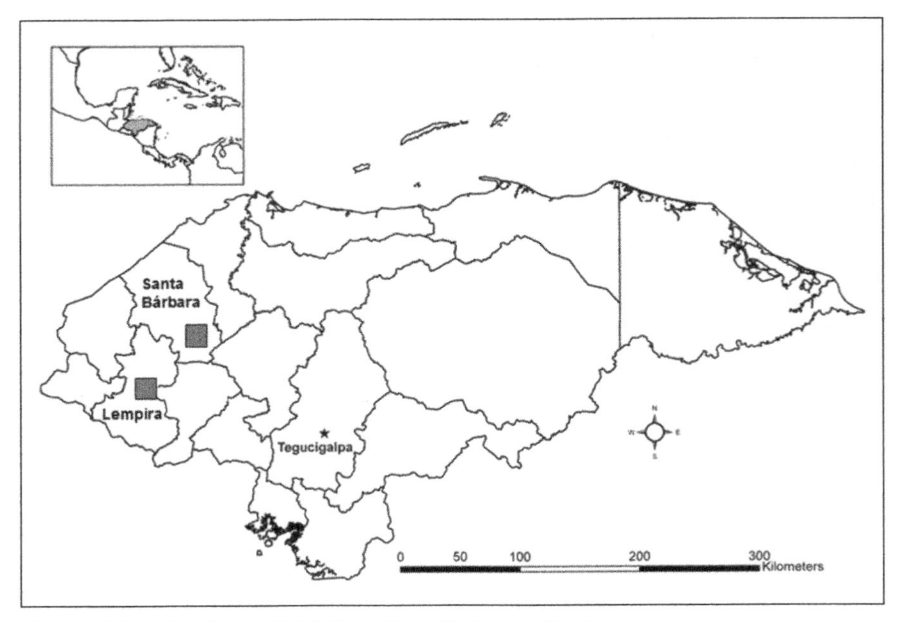

Figure 9.1. Honduran Field Sites Map, Catherine Tucker

ing 2006. My work with coffee producers included household surveys with randomly selected samples, carried out in 2003 and 2007 in La Campa, and in 2007 in Concepción del Sur. Between 2003 and 2010, I interviewed coffee producers, government officials, representatives of development agencies, and others with insights to Honduras's political, economic, and social contexts. Research in municipal and national archives revealed valuable historical details. Participant observation helped me to understand people's daily lives.

Overview of Study Sites La Campa, Lempira and Concepción del Sur, Santa Bárbara

The Department of Lempira (hereafter Lempira), where La Campa is located, ranks as the least developed department in the nation according to the United Nations Human Development Index. It has long been considered a national backwater. The cost of local labor is among the lowest in Honduras. People of indigenous Lenca heritage dominate La Campa's population, which was estimated at 4,461 in 2003 (UNDP 2003). Population density is relatively low at 33.5 people/km^2 (Table 9.1), which translates to approximately 2.9 hectares per person. Based on the household sample, the mean

Table 9.1. Characteristics of the Study Sites

	Concepción del Sur	La Campa
Population	5,916	4,461
Land area	64.4 km2	123.3 km2
Population density	91.8 / km2	33.5 / km2
Range in elevation	400 to 1800 m	800 m to ~1820 m
Elevation range of export coffee plantations	600 to 1800 m	1200 m to ~1750 m
Estimated annual income per capita, US$ (2003)	$2,052.80	$1,543.20
Adult literacy rate (2003)	63.8 percent	73.9 percent

SOURCES: UNDP 2003; Honduras topographic and political maps.

household size was 5.89 members. The median household landholding was 3.9 hectares, often distributed in several parcels, with a median area in coffee of 1.1 hectares (Table 9.2).

La Campa's land is held mainly under village and municipal land titles. Through a national program in the late 1990s, people could purchase private land titles to their individual fields on communal land, but few could afford the fees. Residents have de facto private rights to specific parcels. Similar to other indigenous populations of Honduras, the Lenca people have been experiencing cultural change with increasing exposure to national economic pressures and globalization processes. La Campa's traditional commons have experienced fundamental transformations, and today Campeños regard their fenced land as private property (contrast with Anderson, and Boyer and Cardona Peñalva, this volume). Until recently, people depended on subsistence production of maize and beans as the basis for their livelihoods, and most

Table 9.2. Characteristics of the Coffee Producers

	Concepción del Sur (N=95) Mean (s.d.)	La Campa (N = 66) Mean (s.d.)
Household size	5.25 (2.18)	5.89 (2.54)
Years producing coffee	18 (11.64)	11 (8.98)
Total area owned (ha)	6.8 (10.90) Median: 2.8	8.3 (14.34) Median: 3.9
Total area in coffee (ha)	3.3 (5.66) Median: 1.8	2.6 (5.72) Median: 1.1
Household members who contribute to household income	2.85 (1.74)	3.75 (2.24)

SOURCE: Household Survey 2007.

households continue to produce these staples. Improving transportation networks over the past two decades and agricultural extension programs through the Honduran Coffee Institute (IHCAFE) facilitated the expansion of coffee production and increased linkages to markets. La Campa's main coffee-producing area (1,200–1,800 meters) produces the most highly valued classes of "hard bean" and "strictly hard bean" coffee. Production for household consumption has a long tradition in La Campa, but local experience with export-oriented coffee barely dates back twenty years. Increasing dependence on export coffee has been associated with rising land prices, increasing economic disparities as better-off producers have bought out poorer neighbors, and an emerging class of landless farmers (Tucker 2008; see also Anderson, this volume).

Concepción del Sur is located in the Department of Santa Bárbara (hereafter Santa Bárbara), the fourth poorest in Honduras.[2] In contrast to La Campa, the majority of Concepción del Sur's population is ladino, the nation's dominant ethnic group. As of 2003, it had an estimated population of 5,916 (UNDP 2003) and a population density of 91.8 people/ km^2 (Table 9.1), which translates to approximately one hectare per person. Among respondents to the household survey, the average household size was 5.25 members, and most producers had grown coffee all of their adult lives. The median land area owned by a household was 2.8 hectares, of which a median of 1.8 hectares was planted in coffee. As in La Campa, the median is a better indicator of the middle, because the mean is skewed by a few large landholdings. The majority of the population makes a living by raising coffee for the market and maize for household consumption.

The municipio's elevation ranges from 400 to 1,800 meters, but most of its territory and coffee plantations lie between 600 and 1,200 meters. Below 1,200 meters, its coffee falls into the low quality class of "strictly soft bean," which earns low market prices compared to coffee grown at higher elevations. Nearly all land is privately owned. Although smallholders represent the majority of coffee producers, several absentee landowners own extensive plantations in Concepción del Sur (these did not fall into the random sample). Inequitable distribution of land and wealth has contributed to a history of tensions and violence; large producers carry firearms and travel with bodyguards. To reduce their risks, they usually live in urban areas, visit their plantations intermittently, and require their workers to make the long trip from plantations to a secure urban location to be paid. Santa Bárbara was one of the first departments in Honduras to produce coffee for the market, and coffee has been a mainstay of Concepción del Sur's economy since the late 1800s. Today, Santa Bárbara remains one of the top two coffee-producing departments in Honduras; it has a major IHCAFE office and an experimental station, as well as a team of trained technicians to assist producers.

History of Coffee in Honduras

Coffee arrived in Central America during the late 1700s or early 1800s (IHCAFE 2001). By the mid 1800s, it became apparent that the region's climate and mountainous topography produced high-quality arabica coffee (*Coffea arabica*). Arabica, in contrast to the more bitter robusta coffee (*Coffea robusta*), offers a smooth, mild taste that draws higher prices on the world market. Costa Rica, Guatemala, Nicaragua, and El Salvador instituted liberal policies that facilitated coffee production by titling lands to individuals with resources to establish plantations, and often expropriating communal land from indigenous communities, which simultaneously created a land-poor labor force to work in coffee fields. Honduras did not embrace liberal policies, nor did it undermine communal property (Peckenham and Street 1985; Williams 1994). Instead, successive administrations attempted to promote coffee production through legislation and land grants to communities and individuals. As early as 1849, Decree 5079 declared coffee free of taxes for the first ten years after planting (IHCAFE 2001, 2). By the late 1800s, however, Honduras was the only Central American nation that did not produce coffee as a major export commodity. Historians point to poor infrastructure and a weak state government as the reason; moreover, land suitable for coffee was scattered in small pockets across the mountainous landscape, which complicated the task of building roads to transport coffee (Williams 1994). Unlike its neighbors, Honduras did not develop a coffee elite with sufficient political power to push for investments in roads or railroads, or other beneficial infrastructure. Although coffee became widely adopted, most producers viewed it as a subsistence crop. Farmers grew coffee in orchards and house gardens with fruit trees and other useful plants.

The situation began to change in the late 1940s. Motivated by perceived communist threats in the region, the U.S. government poured thousands of dollars into development programs in Honduras, some of which went to build roads and provide technical assistance to the coffee sector. In succeeding years, the Honduran government instituted policies and programs that proved more effective than prior efforts to expand coffee production. IHCAFE, created in 1970, played a major role in supporting coffee production by promoting modern production methods, including improved coffee varieties and chemical inputs. In 1982, the Coffee Enterprise Protection Law (Decree 78-82) exempted coffee plantations from the Agrarian Reform Law, which encouraged large landholders to expand coffee production because non-coffee holdings could be claimed by landless peasant groups. In 1987, Decree 175-87 gave coffee-producing municipalities subsidies for road building and maintenance in proportion to their production. Poor roads represented an enduring challenge to Honduran farmers, so the subsidies encouraged many growers, including those in Concepción del Sur and La Campa, to expand coffee plantations. National coffee production increased by over 200 percent between 1970 and 1996 (IHCAFE 1997).

The Agricultural Modernization Law of 1992, inspired by neoliberal principles, introduced market-oriented policies intended to jumpstart the national economy and spur economic development. It targeted a long list of goals, such as boosting agricultural production, promoting exports, increasing productive efficiency and technology transfer, augmenting investments in agriculture, and improving infrastructure (República de Honduras 1992; see also Boyer and Cardona Peñalva, this volume). Under this set of policies and generally good prices, coffee became one of Honduras's top three export commodities in the 1990s. Income from coffee overtook that from bananas, the traditional leading export. As of 2007 Honduras was the ninth-largest coffee producer in the world (ICO 2008).

Roots of the Coffee Crisis

Honduras was among many coffee-producing countries that expanded their production significantly during the 1990s. The expansion followed the collapse of the then-current International Coffee Agreement (ICA) in 1989, after the United States opted not to support a renegotiation process. Despite a number of vicissitudes, ICAs had constrained the growth of coffee production during the preceding decades, and its provisions had helped to balance the profit shares of producing and consuming countries. When negotiations failed to renew the ICA, developing countries were freed from quotas on production. At the same time, the transnational companies that dominated coffee sales extended their control over the commodity chain and concentrated value-added processing in the major consuming countries of North America and Europe. New processing technology allowed roasters to reduce their dependence on high-quality arabica beans by mixing robusta and arabica beans in their coffee blends. Processors adopted new inventory-management logistics to reduce inventories and transferred storage costs to suppliers (Lewin et al. 2004). These changes benefitted large, consolidated firms and allowed them to capture a larger proportion of the profits from coffee (Talbot 2004). Although fair trade and a series of alternative marketing strategies (touting bird-friendly, shade-grown, and organic coffees) took off during the 1990s, they represented only a small fraction of coffee contracts globally. Meanwhile, Vietnam began to invest in robusta coffee production and emerged as the second-largest producer in the world after Brazil. In 1999, an unexpectedly large global coffee harvest flooded the market, and prices collapsed (CEPAL 2002).

Honduran Coffee Producers' Responses to the Coffee Crisis and Its Aftermath

As the coffee crisis began, Luís Cortés, a coffee farmer in Concepción del Sur, was still recovering from damage caused by Hurricane Mitch in November 1998. The nine members of his family lived in a three-room adobe house with a cement floor. He had two hectares of land, nearly all of it in coffee. When coffee prices fell, he couldn't afford to buy fertilizer. Even though his plantations produced higher-quality, "hard bean" coffee, the price was too low to pay coffee pickers. He and his family picked some of the coffee, and left the rest to rot. He took on temporary jobs, his wife Matilda found a job at a maquila factory in a nearby town, and their eldest child left school to work in San Pedro Sula. Finally, he made the painful decision to sell a third of his land. In 2007, he reported that things had improved, but he was working longer hours in his plantations to meet quality standards set by the intermediary who purchased his coffee. He had planted corn on rented land to sell locally, but prices had been so low that he had lost money. With a new government program, he had planted forty commercially valuable trees that could be sold as timber in thirty years. His greatest concern was earning enough money to keep his children in school. He wanted them to have an education beyond the third grade that he had completed. He could not imagine a life that did not involve growing coffee, but he wanted better for his children.

Luís's experiences during the coffee crisis represented those of farmers in Concepción del Sur, who in general seemed to be more seriously impacted by the crisis than La Campa's producers. Concepción del Sur had suffered more damage from Hurricane Mitch than La Campa, and many farmers, like Luís, were still recovering when the coffee crisis began. But in both study sites, coffee producers responded in a variety of ways to price volatility and associated economic challenges.

Changes in the Area of Coffee Plantations

Contrary to expectations, many coffee producers had expanded their coffee plantations during the coffee crisis and its aftermath: 30 percent in Concepción del Sur and 86 percent in La Campa (Table 9.3). To make the decision to expand plantations, however, farmers had to feel confident that they would have enough labor to maintain plantations and harvest the coffee. The availability of household support proved to be a key factor in the decision. Farmers who increased their plantations had a mean of 3.83 household members contributing labor and/or income to the household, while farmers who decreased their land in coffee had only 2.5 family members on

Table 9.3. Changes Reported in Quantity of Land Dedicated to Coffee (1997–2007)

	Concepción del Sur (N = 92) percent (N)	**La Campa (N = 66) percent (N)**
Increased plantations	30.4 (28)	86.4 (57)
No change	41.3 (38)	9.1 (6)
Reduced plantations	28.3 (26)	4.5 (3)

average contributing to the household. The difference between these means was highly significant (0.000 level using ANOVA [Analysis of Variance]). The number of years that farmers had been producing coffee also proved significant (0.001 level). Farmers who reduced their land in coffee had produced coffee much longer on average than those who expanded or made no changes in their plantation areas. These older farmers explained that they had given some of their land to grown children or sold it to younger, more energetic farmers. These results coincide with Netting's (1993) observations that smallholder farmers' capacity for intensive agriculture relates to the availability of household labor. Household labor may become more critical as the cost of hired labor climbs and availability of workers falls as people move to urban jobs. In Santa Bárbara in particular, farmers complained about the cost and difficulty of finding skilled labor to pick coffee. For many farmers, the availability of household labor in conjunction with the cost of hired labor appeared to make the difference between decisions to expand or decrease the area in coffee plantations. One farmer in Concepción del Sur noted that he would like to hire an assistant, but could not afford it. He had reduced his area in coffee and increased his own labor to attempt to meet higher quality standards. Thus labor availability appears critical to a farmers' capability to produce higher-quality coffee, as well as influencing decisions to expand or reduce plantation size.

Changes in Agricultural Practices

In addition to making decisions about changing or maintaining the land area in coffee, most farmers made other adjustments in how they managed their plantations and other crops during and after the coffee crisis. A pronounced majority of farmers in Concepción del Sur (70.8 percent) and La Campa (95.5 percent) planted additional trees in coffee plantations. Farmers in both locations noted that they liked to plant trees and did it almost every year, implying that it was a customary practice rather than one brought on by the coffee crisis. They indicated that trees serve multiple purposes, such as providing shade for coffee plants, which reduces the need for agrochemicals, and producing fruit or firewood for household consumption and local markets. Changing the level of agrochemical use was another common decision. In Concepción del Sur, 38.5 percent increased chemical inputs, while 24 percent reduced them. By contrast, 60.6 percent of La Campa's producers had reduced their use of chemical inputs, mainly because they were unable to purchase fertilizer as prices tripled between 1997 and 2007. Farmers reported doing more to manage shade (allowing the canopy to close, or trimming branches). In Concepción del Sur, farmers whose plantations had been damaged during Hurricane Mitch often stated that they had replanted coffee more densely, which had been recommended as a way to increase production and bolster coffee bushes' resilience to wind and rain. A number of farmers had begun to plant valuable timber species in or around plantations as a potential source of income.

La Campa farmers, who reported reducing fertilizer inputs and associated declines in productivity, frequently inquired about how they could gain access to niche markets represented by organic, fair trade, and bird-friendly certifications. By 2008, two coffee cooperatives had formed in La Campa and gained Rainforest Alliance certification, with assistance from IHCAFE. Loans from an external donor helped them to cover the certification fees. Their attention to quality control has helped them to gain better market prices, but they have also had to cover higher labor costs. In contrast to the Guatemalan cooperative members discussed by Lyon (this volume), the La Campa co-ops found the costs of fair trade certification discouraging. As of 2012, only one of the cooperatives still aimed to become fair trade certified.

During and after the coffee crisis, farmers explored a variety of agricultural options beyond coffee production. Unlike their Guatemalan counterparts (Lyon, this volume), the Honduran coffee producers often had fallow land available for new agricultural activities. Nearly half of the Honduran farmers surveyed (48.8 percent) had planted a crop new to their farm, such as tomatoes or onions. Two brothers started a hog farm; it failed when the cost of feed increased more quickly than the price of pork. Campeño women formed a cooperative to raise and sell eggs and chickens; they received a small loan from a development program to get started. One of the members noted that it was hard to make a profit because most households in La Campa raise their own chickens. They hoped to sell to other places as well, but they have been unable to find a way to carry their products to market given the high costs of transportation and occasionally impassable roads. The difficulties faced by Campeños resonate with the situations examined by Little, Boyer and Cardona Peñalva, and Anderson (this volume); we variously note that Central America's agrarian and indigenous populations find it challenging to improve their livelihoods given infrastructural shortcomings, social and economic inequities, and systemic political failings.

Efforts to Diversify Beyond Agriculture and Build Social Capital

During the coffee crisis and subsequent years, many farmers found it necessary or desirable to seek temporary or permanent wage-labor jobs, and some started small businesses. In Concepción del Sur, 64.2 percent reported a new off-farm activity between 1997 and 2007, while 57.6 percent did so in La Campa. Support from several international aid organizations working in La Campa provided seed money for artisanal cooperatives, and groups formed to produce pottery (a long-standing Lenca craft), lumber, wood carvings, and sugar cane. In both sites, farmers joined or maintained membership in local groups (79.2 percent in Concepción del Sur, 89.4 percent in La Campa), including coffee producers' organizations and microcredit cooperatives. Many of these groups supported community development, or served to reinforce social ties (church groups, women's groups, school-related groups). Farmers and their family members were not always sure that the groups provided direct financial or material benefits, but they remained active because participation gave them access to information and included social activities. Most parents of school-aged children took part in efforts to support the schools. While some chafed at the time and labor that school-related activities required, many parents commented that education was important for their children's futures. They hoped that their children would be able to get full-time, wage-labor positions that would provide a stable income, and perhaps help to support the family. Thus farmers saw educating their children as a long-term investment and a form of household diversification.

Access to Credit and Dealing with Debt

A number of farmers have sought loans to maintain their coffee plantations, meet immediate needs, or finance new ventures. During and after the crisis, the Honduran government attempted to alleviate pressure on coffee producers through a series of decrees designed to help them refinance debt, but only a few producers were able to take advantage of it (Republic of Honduras 2003). Most farmers in La Campa did not have any debt, because they had no access to bank loans. Few farmers in La Campa hold private land titles (although this is changing), therefore banks hesitate to grant them credit. By contrast, many farmers in Concepción del Sur entered the crisis with debt. They had greater access to credit as private landowners, and many were accustomed to using loans to purchase fertilizer before the harvest.

In the household survey, 41.7 percent of the respondents reported borrowing money during the previous decade (1997–2007). In Concepción del Sur, 74 percent of these farmers had obtained bank loans. Farmers still in business by 2007 had managed to pay their debts, but many knew of someone who had been forced to sell out due to outstanding debts. In La Campa, only 27 percent of those seeking credit had received bank loans. The rest (73 percent) had taken out small loans as members of local microcredit cooperatives. Although microcredit cooperatives offer small amounts of credit, it is often adequate for farmers to start a small business, buy seeds to try a new crop, or purchase fertilizer for their crops.

Discussion: Conundrums and Challenges

The case studies indicate that farmers have adapted to market volatility through various responses with respect to their household situation, including the cost of labor, which varied by region, the availability of household members to assist in coffee production, and access to land. Thus personal and regional contexts, within the broader pressures of coffee prices and market trends, contribute to farmers' decisions. Disjunctures as well as coincidences have occurred between neoliberal policy recommendations and farmers' experiences. While policy makers and economists realize that farmers face increasing constraints on profitability, their prognostications fall short in recognizing the variability in local contexts that inform farmers' choices. Today, policies and programs favor plantations at higher elevations that produce higher-quality coffee, but these farmers' experiences indicate that ideal land elevation and high quality beans are not sufficient to assure competitiveness or profits. Coffee-picking labor has been "disappearing" from some locations as rural workers seek urban employment, making it difficult to harvest the crop. Climbing costs of fertilizers have cut profits even though coffee prices have risen modestly.

Despite well-publicized promises of economic advantages, the implementation of the Dominican Republic–Central America-United States Free Trade Agreement in 2009 failed to draw the attention of these Honduran coffee farmers, nor do they expect benefits. By contrast, the June 2009 military coup that ousted President Manuel Zelaya ignited intense debates, and some traveled to participate in marches against (or supporting) the coup. Boyer and Cardona Peñalva (this volume) point to the coup as a catalyst that opened doors for agrarian organizations to communicate and collaborate. This trend was less apparent at the local level in La Campa and Concepción del Sur. The farmers, divided by contrasting ideological convictions, could only agree that the coup had worsened their economic prospects as international development assistance evaporated and prices of goods increased. The eventual election of Porfirio Lobo momentarily sparked hope that the nation's numerous problems would be addressed, but as Boyer and Cardona Peñalva note, the nation continues to wrestle with agrarian tensions and many other challenges.

The Conundrum of Labor

The need for low-cost labor presents a particularly difficult conundrum for coffee farmers and national development efforts. Producing high-quality coffee requires attentive pickers with manual dexterity, stamina to work long days, and dedication to picking only ripe coffee beans (Figure 9.2). Yet they often receive wages below the official minimum. If labor costs must remain low to stay competitive, coffee production will depend on an underprivileged labor force, thus perpetuating poverty and social inequity. Producers who are able to train and rely on household labor can reduce labor costs and gain certain advantages. Household production may also reinforce cultural values and provide non-monetary benefits, such as sustainable land-use practices and keeping the family together. However, many households lack the number of members needed to work their plantations.

The Conundrum of Entering Niche Markets

Producing high-quality coffee for niche markets is beyond the resources of most smallholder farmers, and improvements require support. Road improvements are needed to assist timely transport of beans to markets. Coffee qual-

Figure 9.2. Girl Picking Coffee, Catherine Tucker

ity can be improved among the farmers with suitable lands, if they can pick and process beans at the peak of ripeness. To obtain top prices, however, they need to access niche markets, which often requires a certification process. Organic, shade-grown, bird-friendly coffee certifications cost money and involve specialized information and technical assistance. Interest in fair trade coffee has grown, but to obtain fair trade standing, farmers need to obtain a fair trade partner to purchase their beans, and partner businesses require a certain volume of beans to meet their needs. Smallholder farmers typically must join co-operatives to participate in fair trade (see Lyon, this volume). Honduran policies historically have inhibited participation in niche markets because they have not been particularly supportive of co-operatives, non-traditional markets, or quality standards. Thus farmers who wish to produce high-quality beans for a better price in niche markets must overcome the obstacles posed by difficult access, lack of information, shortfalls in technical support and infrastructure, and the need to work with others to pool harvests.

Furthermore, the global volume of certified coffees and fair trade coffee already exceeds the quantity that niche markets can absorb. While these coffees earn higher prices for the coffee farmers, many farmers are not able to sell their entire harvest to a niche buyer. They end up selling some of their coffee to conventional markets at ordinary prices. Farmers face the risk that they may make costly investments that they cannot recuperate. Thus certifications carry unfamiliar risks. Farmers hear that they will get better, more stable prices if they can make the additional investments in time, labor, better equipment, certification, and organizational effort required to produce coffee for niche markets. Once they start competing in these niches, they discover that these markets are becoming saturated and higher prices are not assured (Lewin et al. 2004).

Land and Livelihood Diversification

Most coffee farmers in this study viewed coffee as their best option for improving their livelihoods. While they perceived the problems of coffee markets, they believed that they were better off producing coffee than another crop (Tucker et al. 2010). In both sites, farmers who had expanded their plantations explained that they expected coffee prices to rise, and they wanted to be prepared. Farmers had learned that depressed coffee prices are usually temporary. If farmers had heard the reports that chances of capturing profits had declined in restructured global markets, they evidently trusted their own experience more than the experts' predictions. Yet these farmers did not rely on coffee alone. Most farmers had diversified livelihood strategies and sought more ways to increase their options during the crisis and subsequent years, despite limited financial resources and sparse credit. But while the changes offered more options, they were rarely adequate to improve long-term livelihood security. A number of families had difficulty covering nutritional needs, school costs, and medical care. Compared to Campeños, the farmers of Concepción del Sur revealed more pessimism regarding their future welfare. They expressed concerns for the shrinking rural labor force, the rising costs of labor and basic goods, and agrarian violence that strikes indiscriminately. These producers supported their children's desires to seek better paid, less risky work in urban areas. In La Campa, labor costs remained relatively low, the municipio had comparatively few security concerns, and many young people still hoped to inherit or acquire adequate land to make their living in diversified agricultural pursuits. While farmers in both study sites felt pressure to find alternative livelihood options to help support their families, few expected to completely abandon coffee.

Rationales for Maintaining Coffee in a Context of Risk

The lack of interest in abandoning coffee reflects multiple factors. First, coffee farmers are loath to sell or convert plantations into which they have poured years of labor and care (see also Lyon, this volume). Second, farmers see coffee as having humanlike qualities. They liken the nurturing that coffee plants require to raising a child. One IHCAFE technician used this perception to make a point in a seminar on caring for coffee plants; he noted that coffee seedlings are like children who cannot eat solid food and therefore need to be nourished with fertilizer diluted in water rather than full-strength fertilizer. Third, farmers remain hopeful that prices will increase to levels remembered during the mid 1990s. In the past, recurrent weather calamities in major coffee-producing countries have led to temporarily higher prices that have allowed some coffee growers to make windfall profits. Today, oversupply and large inventories provide a hedge against the likelihood of a major price jump even in the face of climatic variability. Although coffee prices would increase if severe weather decimated Brazil's or Colombia's plantations, the fluctuation would most likely be short-lived.

Fourth, farmers do not know another crop that can provide comparable income. They gladly experiment with alternative crops but are skeptical. They prefer to seek niche markets in hopes of selling their coffee at higher prices. In this aspect, farmers would benefit greatly from technical support, expert advice, and training. IHCAFE has made an effort to meet these demands but is often short-staffed, and regional offices tend to be underfunded. Nonetheless, IHCAFE has made important progress by sponsoring the annual "Cup of Excellence" competition, in which coffee producers around the country compete for recognition from international coffee tasters. The top coffees from this competition are auctioned off to the highest bidder and receive exceptionally high prices. Thus far, however, the contest has not helped the average smallholder, who does not have the resources, quantity, or quality of production to enter. Meanwhile, specialty coffee production in Honduras has been expanding slowly. Successful cooperatives have been supported by international aid organizations, or benefited from a few dedicated organizers. Private coffee producers who sell to niche markets typically come from wealthy coffee-producing families.

Finally, farmers reveal a fondness for coffee that goes beyond its economic value. As mentioned above, growing coffee is a way of life. Several farmers expressed that they have a mutually beneficial relationship with their plantations. Comments during interviews revealed that most farmers cannot imagine doing much else with their lives. Even if they willingly adopt additional activities to get by, they view the travails of coffee markets as part of the risk with which they live (contrast with Lyon, this volume).

Conclusions

The findings from this study suggest that farmers in western Honduras have taken steps to diversify their livelihoods and reduce their dependence on coffee, at least in the short term. The diversification appears to increase their capacity to survive fluctuations in coffee markets and may also serve to reduce their exposure to severe weather events and national economic and political shocks. The competitive transition in the Central American coffee sector urged by neoliberal economists appears to be occurring as more farmers aim to improve quality. Yet the changes do not appear adequate to provide overall well-being for the long term. While neoliberal economists and recent policies have grasped the general implications of changes in the coffee commodity chain for farmers, the realities on the ground are more varied and complex than higher-level policy makers tend to recognize.

Most critically, current policies fail to address the fundamental contradiction of conventional coffee markets: coffee production continues to be viewed as a vehicle for development, but it depends on poorly remunerated manual labor, and implicitly requires part of the population to remain unskilled and uneducated. Thus the business of coffee too often reinforces social inequities, fosters agrarian tensions, and obstructs genuine development. Nevertheless, coffee production is likely to remain an important component of Central American agriculture for the foreseeable future. Perceived economic benefits of coffee appear to be reinforced by non-market factors and cultural dimensions that encourage production despite risks and uncertainties. Similar to other Central American peoples portrayed in this volume, Honduras's smallholder coffee producers struggle to translate their hard work into improved economic well-being and livelihood security.

Notes

* This study received generous funding from the Wenner-Gren Foundation, and the Inter-American Institute for Global Change Research (grant CRN-2060) supported by the U.S. National Science Foundation (grant GEO-0452325). The Center for the Study of Institutions, Population, and Environmental Change at Indiana University provided logistical support. IHCAFE shared invaluable information. Martha Moreno, Jessica Fonseca, Victor Moreno, and Atanacio Perez provided cheerful and expert fieldwork assistance. I am grateful to Jennifer Burrell and Ellen Moodie for inviting me to participate in the "After the Handshakes" workshop, and to all participants for their collegiality.

1. Names used are pseudonyms.
2. Of Honduras's eighteen departments, only Copan, Intibucá, and Lempira are poorer than Santa Bárbara (UNDP 2003).

10 Maya Handicraft Vendors' CAFTA-DR Discourses

"Free Trade Is Not for Everyone in Guatemala"

Walter E. Little

Stephen Gudeman and Alberto Rivera (1990, 1) begin their monograph about peasant household economics stating, "Good conversations have no ending, and often no beginning. They have participants and listeners, but belong to no one, nor to history." They note that they came to realize they had joined an ongoing conversation operating on multiple levels with diverse participants, and that it bridged both verbal and textual domains. In 1994, I joined such an economic conversation—not based in the household but, rather, in the marketplace—that revolved around issues of free trade. It is a conversation in which I continue to participate. At the time, Maya handicraft vendors were interested in international trade initiatives that were being given increasingly more media attention. The internal conflict between guerrillas and the military had lost steam and tourism was increasing, something noted by both Florence Babb and Leigh Binford in their respective contributions on Nicaragua and El Salvador in this volume (also see Little 2004; Stoll 1999). These mutual events—an end to the conflict and more international tourists—coupled with the possibility of more open economic borders, inspired vendors to envision better futures for themselves and their children.

From 1994 through 1998, the conversation occurred in the Compañía de Jésus marketplace, located a block from the Central Plaza of La Antigua Guatemala (hereafter, Antigua). After 1998 it was gradually reconstituted in a new artisan marketplace on the edge of the city, next to the main utilitarian marketplace and bus terminals (see Little 2004). In the original Compañía de Jésus marketplace, there were roughly two hundred vendors, the vast majority Mayas from Kaqchikel-, K'iche'-, and Ixil-speaking areas of Guatemala. In contrast to the majority of my research, which focused on Kaqchikel vendors and was conducted in Kaqchikel Maya, the discussion about free trade crossed linguistic and ethnic boundaries. Spanish was the common language of the discussion. The new artisan marketplace is much larger, representing the consolidation of several fixed marketplaces throughout Antigua that are now closed. The free trade conversation, however, continues among a group of vendors—all originally located in the Compañía de Jésus marketplace.

Free Trade Euphoria: Wide Open Trade Borders

When I joined the vendors' free trade conversations, they were initially in the midst of heated debates about the Zapatistas (EZLN) in Chiapas, Mexico and their rejection of the North American Free Trade Agreement (NAFTA). They were intrigued by the Zapatistas' reaction but not naïve about why persons they identified as peasants and farmers would be suspicious of the agreement. They believed, however, that the Zapatistas' rebellion was preliminary and that, as one vendor ventured, "Those peasants should have waited to see if the free trade agreement was truly bad." Unlike the cases in this volume described by Sarah Lyon, Ciska Raventos, and Catherine Tucker, Maya handicraft vendors greeted news of the free trade agreements with visions of hope and wealth, anticipating increased markets for their products.

Nash (2001, 21) observes that "policies formed at a distance," such as NAFTA, "are now compelling motivations for rebellion of semi-subsistence cultivators" that also have marked the entry of women and indigenous persons into new political arenas. Such participation, she adds, highlights the contradictions between states driven by external capital forces and citizens concerned about their basic needs (see also R. Montoya, this volume). Certainly, Maya handicraft vendors discussing NAFTA that summer of 1994 were well aware of the history of exploitation that they themselves had suffered with the development of export crops and plantation agriculture. At the same time, they were reluctant to dismiss free trade agreements as exploitative.

NAFTA came at an important moment for Maya handicraft vendors—a historical moment, according to Anacleta,[1] a Kaqchikel Maya vendor from San Antonio Aguas Calientes: had the Antigua-based vendors been presented with a free trade treaty, they would have "taken advantage of" (*aprovechar*) it. Indeed, Guatemala in 1994 was in a dramatically different place from Chiapas.[2] The vendors, many internal refugees of the civil conflict that had ravaged the country since 1960, had worked hard to insulate themselves and their children from the political turmoil that still raged on material and ideological fronts (Carmack 1988; Little and Smith 2009; Smith 1990). Antigua was not just a refuge from the conflict, it was a place where many vendors' families were able to make a decent living, put their children in good schools, and also maintain important Mayan cultural practices. The violent reaction of the Zapatistas to NAFTA was contrary to the sentiments of the vendors, who knew family members and friends who had been tortured and killed at the hands of the Guatemalan military. Resorting to violence over a trade agreement seemed absurd to them. Furthermore, from what they could gather from the coverage of NAFTA in the Guatemalan dailies *La Prensa Libre* and *Siglo XXI*, the trade agreement did not seem antithetical to their values.

Manifestations of globalization and neoliberalism like international free trade agreements do not stimulate uniform reactions or political participation across Latin America, or even among different economic, social, and ethnic sectors within individual countries. Handicraft vendors envisioned that free trade agreements would open up international borders and national trade barriers would dissolve. Although they did not frame free trade as providing the potential for "something better" in life, as Edward Fischer and Peter Benson (2006) describe Kaqchikel farmers and workers from Tecpán Guatemala doing, vendors frequently commented that free trade would allow them "to profit from," "to improve economically," and "to take advantage of"—sentiments expressed with the Spanish verb, aprovechar. In fact, they joked, "Even though we don't have free trade, we are taking advantage of the Zapatistas, because tourists will come here and buy our *típica* (handicrafts)." Holding Subcomandante Marcos and Comandante Ramona dolls, they said, "We are making a good profit on these, too." Indeed, Maya vendors have been consistently adept at developing products that fit within tourists' conceptions and the kinds of cultural commodification advanced by the national government and the tourism industry. Such experience with knowing one's consumers, however, is the result of several decades of working in the ethnic tourism industry, something which Mark Anderson (this volume) explores in its more nascent dimensions for Garifuna in Honduras.

By 1997–1998, the newspapers carried news about free trade on an almost daily basis. Then-president Álvaro Enrique Arzú Irigoyen advocated opening Guatemala's borders to foreign investors, privatizing public entities like the post office and telephone company GUATEL, and facilitating a freer flow of goods. Beer and cement from Mexico, apples and other produce from the United States, and tools and toys from China, among many other international products, entered the country. Vendors looked favorably on President Arzú's neoliberal economic policies. They were quite vociferous about the corruption and inefficiency of publicly held companies, and convinced that the Dominican Republic-Central America-United States Free Trade Agreement (CAFTA-DR) would allow them to freely sell their handicrafts throughout Central America, the United States, and Canada. In particular, they believed that the trade agreement would be ethnic-, race-, and gender-neutral, since it was about economics. They reasoned that their products were distinctive and could not easily be found in foreign marketplaces. Handwoven goods, especially, were conceived of as unique and marketable.

One seasoned female vendor from Comalapa said of Guatemalan textiles, "There is nothing comparable in the other Central American countries.[3] There is no weaving. Típica in those countries is made from sewing factory-made cloth, but we weave ours." Another woman from San Antonio Aguas Calientes added, "We even have the advantage over weavers in Chiapas. They, too, weave like us, but they just don't pay attention to the market, what tourists want." Although *tipiqueros* (American and European middlepersons) echoed the latter vendor's comment about the inflexibility of Chiapan weavers, ethnographers in June Nash's (1993) volume, *Crafts in the World Market: The Impact of Global Exchange on Middle American Artisan,* offer examples of Maya handicraft artisans there being equally respondent to market forces. Most vendors had their sights set on Canada or the United States, where they hoped to forge connections with retailers and even establish their own sales outlets. If anything, Arzú's administration inspired vendors to dream, as they anxiously waited for CAFTA-DR's ratification.

Where the handicraft vendors' sentiments converge with the farmers is that CAFTA-DR would allow them to maintain traditional core cultural values and practices. As my research (Little 2004) has illustrated, international tourism to Guatemala has contributed economically to Mayas' livelihoods, allowing vendors and artisans to maintain their languages, household organization, and spiritual practices at the same time as they participate in the global economy. Fischer and Benson (2006) argue that some forms of global capitalism and neoliberalism, such as maquiladoras, serve to alienate workers, while others, such as non-traditional agricultural exports, allow spaces for Mayas to maintain cultural practices. While it is preliminary to generalize this distinction, how specific local communities respond to and are affected by global capital and neoliberal economic and political policies most likely varies widely, as many chapters in this volume show. In fact, Liliana Goldín's (2003, 2009) research in different Maya communities does not show this division between non-traditional agriculture and non-traditional manufacturing. In both sectors, there are winners and losers, and the effects of these non-traditional economic forms appear to differentially affect core Maya cultural values. Handicraft production and sales for the global market, however, may be an economic domain in which indigenous artisans and vendors can have the best of all worlds—material gains and the preservation of what they and their tourist customers conceive of as tradition.[4]

Somewhat suspicious that vendors were merely buying into the neoliberal hype coming from the Guatemalan government and media, I was surprised to hear vendors tell story after story about long distance trade experiences in the past. Kaqchikel vendors from San Antonio Aguas Calientes and Comalapa told stories of selling in Europe, throughout Central America, Mexico, the United States, and even Japan. Before the civil war's violence peaked in the 1980s, Betelina, a Kaqchikel woman from San Antonio, explained that she took over her mother's routes and had clients from Mexico to Panama. As she explained what types of items people in these different places buy, she commented, "Then, you could easily get visas." To this, a female Kaqchikel

Figure 10.1. Maya handicraft vendor, Antigua Guatemala, Walter E. Little

middleperson added, "You could easily get visas even to Europe and the United States."

While there was general agreement that it was easier to get travel documents in the past, especially before the late 1970s, vendors acknowledged that few families actually had visas and traveled internationally for commerce, outside of Mexico and Central America. Nonetheless, vendors explained that international travel for business, especially the promotion and sale of handloomed textiles, is a long-standing tradition that had been ruptured by the violence of the late 1970s and 1980s. One K'iche' man joked, "In the past, I never saw my wife. She was always in different places in Mexico selling her *tapetes* (doillies) and *servilletas* (napkins). With the violence, we had to learn to live and work together." Far more women than men told stories of selling in distant places, and of crossing international borders.[5] Among the older generation of Maya female marketplace vendors and the predominantly Maya female middlepersons who made weekly and, sometimes, bi-weekly trips to Antigua, trips abroad to sell in Mexico and El Salvador were common. Some even made annual trips to Europe and the United States, the result of business relationships forged in Guatemala with foreign buyers and manufacturers. During the civil war, others were invited guests of academics and religious groups. Although vendors acknowledged that these latter arrangements were considered cultural exchanges, one explained, "We took advantage of them to sell our textiles."

While the majority of the Maya vendors selling in Antigua during this time were not internal refugees and were from Kaqchikel towns like San Antonio Aguas Calientes, Santa Catarina Barahona, Santa María de Jesus, San Antonio Palopó, and Santa Catarina Palopó, where there were fewer direct impacts of the guerrilla and military conflict, vendors complained that the violence affected them. It made their ability to conduct business within the nation and across international borders more difficult, if not impossible. Families that had participated as middlepersons and built economic connections abroad found internal travel too dangerous and international travel inaccessible. Even though the media coverage of free trade agreements inspired them to hopeful dreams, it also awakened angry memories about the violence. When I asked a couple of male vendors—Juan, a K'iche' man from Momostenango, and Roberto, a Kaqchikel man from Comalapa—why they did not give tipiqueros a buyers' discount, they laughed. "Why would we do that, since most of these gringos don't do much to help our business?" Juan asked rhetorically. Roberto added that if they could get visas, they could sell for themselves. I replied, "Then do it. Figure out how to get visas and sell," knowing full well that commercial visas and tourist visas were very difficult to obtain in those years. Juan looked at me as if I were foolish, since he knew that I knew this was unfeasible, and said, "The violence, that is why we can't get visas. That is why we have tipiqueros and pastors, and *hermanas* (sisters of faith), and others here reselling our goods." To this Roberto added, "And making good money. I know. I looked on the Internet. I saw the prices."

With the transition to the Alfonso Antonio Portillo Cabrera administration in January 2000, free trade was still years from becoming a reality, though vendors still followed the news coverage as what is now CAFTA-DR took shape. Their speculations about the benefits of free trade turned to preoccupations about violent crime and corruption that made them fear for their merchandise, if not for their lives. Their local economic situation also took a turn for the worse after 11 September 2001. Tourism dropped to such a degree that some tour companies, restaurants, and Spanish-language schools closed. Aside from during Holy Week, there were noticeably fewer tourists on the streets. Tourism did not begin to recover until the summer of 2005. Official Guatemalan statistics (INGUAT, Dirección General de Migración, and the Banco de Guatemala),[6] indicate that there has been a roughly 8 percent annual increase for the past six years. One reason for the modest growth may have to do with the fact that rather than separate those who enter the country into distinctive categories (tourists, businesspersons, etc.), all non-Guatemalans are called "international visitors." The change in categorizing foreign visitors rankled vendors, who called it "just another trick of Portillo" to make the country look economically better off than it was. "It doesn't matter what INGUAT says," opined one vendor during the summer of 2002. "Tourists aren't coming. We are suffering." Portillo's government, however, did work to push CAFTA-DR forward, but vendors in the early 2000s were taking their own measures to economically diversify their households as they worried about crime, instead of fantasizing about the international business they would conduct under free trade.

CAFTA-DR for Whom?: Handicraft Vendor Disappointments

On 1 July 2006, when CAFTA-DR went into effect in Guatemala, Maya handicraft vendors were poised to get commercial visas to sell in the United States and Canada. They saw the passage of the trade agreement a triumph of Óscar Berger Perdomo's presidency. Most had voted for him with the expectation that he would end corruption, reduce discrimination against Mayas, and foster an entrepreneurial climate. Because Berger himself was a member of the wealthy elite and a successful businessman, they had expectations that he would know how to economically guide the country. And because they conceived of themselves as entrepreneurs and independent businesspersons, in addition to being Mayas and artisans, they assumed that his administration's economic policies would ultimately serve their interests.

Of particular interest to vendors was CAFTA-DR Article 3.21: "Duty-Free Treatment for Certain Goods":

> 1. An importing and an exporting Party may identify at any time particular textile or apparel goods of the exporting Party that they mutually agree fall within:
>   (a) hand-loomed fabrics of a cottage industry;
>   (b) hand-made cottage industry goods made of such hand-loomed fabrics; or
>   (c) traditional folklore handicraft goods.
> 2. The importing Party shall grant duty-free treatment to goods so identified, if certified by the competent authority of the exporting Party.

To be clear, most vendors did not read the trade agreement. Media coverage of it tended to focus on agricultural products and industrially produced textiles, but occasionally news directly related to the favored position of handicrafts in the agreement was reported.[7] Vendors also recounted conversations about the agreement with foreign tipiqueros to whom they had been selling merchandise. Some had done Internet searches, and still others learned about the treatment of handicrafts in the agreement through the Viceministerio de la Micro, Pequeña y Mediana Empresa (Vice Ministry of Micro-, Small- and Medium Businesses) online, and by visiting its offices in Guatemala City. In 2007, some vendors participated in a business fair to promote Guatemalan handicrafts sponsored by the Viceministerio and other organizations. Some vendors also participated in other such fairs that were supposed to introduce them to free trade, foment transnational business relations, and in general, promote Guatemala's handicrafts. Through these various sources, vendors learned that they and the network of artisans with whom they work appeared to have a favored position with respect to CAFTA-DR. What they did not know was that CAFTA-DR had little to do with facilitating trade for small merchants like themselves, "but [was] a corporate trade agreement that transforms foreign investment from a privilege to an inalienable right" (Grandia 2005). Such maneuvers are part of neoliberal political-economic policies, as Charles R. Hale (2006b) in the Guatemalan context and David Harvey (2005) and Nash (2007) in global contexts argue. Neoliberal agendas are rarely about what they appear to be about.

It was not long before vendors realized that CAFTA-DR was not really for them. Their attempts to obtain visas for selling in other Central American countries, the United States, and Canada went unrewarded. Consistently, vendors soliciting visas to sell handicrafts were rejected by the United States government. Vendors are very familiar with the regulations for obtaining visas, which cost $96.00 (U.S.) and additional fees to produce documents that prove they meet the following criteria:

1. They have a well-established residence outside the United States.
2. They have a realistic, logical reason to visit the United States.
3. They plan to stay in the United States for a specific, limited time.
4. They have sufficient resources of their own to cover the cost of the trip, regardless of whether or not a relative or friend wants to help to pay for their travel.[8]

Vendors who easily meet all criteria reported their failure to obtain a visa after several attempts costing hundreds of dollars. In general, discussing the process incites vendors to anger. Those who have business connections with ladinos, however, contend that ladino businesspersons do not have these problems. Whether this indicates racism on the part of embassy officials, a concerted joint racist strategy by the Guatemalan and U.S. governments, or random arbitrary decisions by screening officials has been much debated by vendors.[9] As Claudia Dary Fuentes describes in her essay in this volume, racism in Guatemala is a well-entrenched practice that most Guatemalans have difficulty talking about. Free trade rhetoric tends to further mask race/ethnicity/gender differences with neutral language.

Of the very few who have obtained visas, all report having their merchandise seized by U.S. customs agents, losing some or all of it. One Maya colleague, an experienced world traveler who worked for an international human rights organization, had all of her handwoven clothing taken by customs agents upon her arrival in the United States. When she asked what, then, she was to do, the agents told her to buy clothes that she would really use. The experience was emotionally traumatizing and caused her a great deal of shame.[10] As she is the daughter of respected Kaqchikel vendors in Antigua's official handicraft marketplace, her circulating story fueled anger and disgust at continued barriers to participation in the free trade agreement. Vendors started telling me, "Free trade is not fair trade."

Vendors were aware that members of various economic sectors had protested the passage of CAFTA-DR in the years leading up to and following the treaty.[11] Such protests were widely published and broadcast in the Guatemalan mass media. However, the vendors believed that, as with the Zapatistas, some Guatemalans were not willing to give the agreement a chance and figure out ways to take advantage of it (aprovechar). Within a year after CAFTA-DR went into effect and after repeated visa denials, most vendors were disillusioned and began to conceive of alternative ways to sell their products.

Economic Failure and CAFTA-DR

By the end of 2007, few vendors had expectations about participating in CAFTA-DR. In fact, some began to question it, claiming that it negatively impacted their local sales to tourists. Blaming CAFTA-DR was a way for them to explain a complex of factors that contributed to their declining sales. Most vendors agreed that that there were too many of them trying to sell in Antigua. The city government's forced relocation of vendors into one massive handicraft market in 2003, an attempt to stem the flow of vendors into Antigua due to declining opportunities in rural areas and small towns, was perceived as largely unsuccessful.

New vendors and those too poor to have secured places in the new handicraft marketplace resisted city officials' actions to levy fines and expel street vendors. Some creatively sought out new alliances with non-Maya businesspersons who, like the vendors, believed that tourists would want to interact with Mayas when the sales pitch was hidden behind cultural exhibitions of weaving. Others formed associations and took on the city government, eventually gaining permission to sell in front of El Carmen, a church two blocks from the central plaza (Little 2008). Where city officials and the police had difficulties banning vendors from Antigua, the glut of vendors, declining tourists, and declining interest in handicrafts throughout the region (see

Chibnik 2003) created conditions for the exodus of the new, poorer, and more marginalized among them.

Still, vendors claimed this was all due to CAFTA-DR. "The only reason more people from the towns and the countryside came to Antigua was they, too, were not getting anything from CAFTA," claimed one man. A woman in her fifties, who has sold textiles in Antigua since she was a child, said, "These new vendors just didn't have their hearts in it. They are really farmers and maybe they were right to have protested against CAFTA." Others' explanations drew on Mayas' spiritual beliefs that CAFTA-DR was causing people to have unrealistic expectations and to not follow their destiny. As one long-time vendor put it, "Being a vendor is a calling and gift. You can't just decide to be a vendor one day and then be successful."

Not all vendors' failures could be easily explained and as some marketplace stalls began to empty, vendors and ex-vendors scrambled for ways to make a living. Those working in the official artisan marketplace that suffered economic failure followed three different kinds of strategies, sometimes simultaneously engaging in all of them. Those who still had land tried to make it more economically viable, expanding into garden crops that were grown organically and could be sold to restaurants. Those without land or insufficient land looked for work as wage laborers as maids, gardeners, unskilled construction workers, and other positions. Such work was intermittent and wages were low—Q15 to Q30 ($1.87 to $3.75 [U.S.]) a day compared to the Q50 to Q100 ($6.25 to $12.50 [U.S.]) a day a relatively successful vendor made.

Another strategy was to emigrate to the United States or Canada in order to send remittances home.[12] Kaqchikel Maya vendors tend to be urban oriented, especially those working in Antigua. With a long history of labor and strong ties in Antigua and Guatemala City, they have exited the country at a slower pace than those K'iche' Maya and other Mayas from more rural areas. A recent World Bank report (Fazio 2007, 10) indicates the increasing importance of remittances for Maya households with "remittances represent[ing] a higher share of household income in rural areas than in urban areas." Indeed, as Burrell (2005) points out for Mam Mayas in Todos Santos, remittances play a key economic role in the maintenance of cultural traditions and physical growth of the town. I suspect that the Mam Maya vendors in the artisan marketplace who complained about the poor state of business relied on remittances, but they would not discuss it. Kaqchikel vendors themselves were reluctant to emigrate, but they certainly did not discourage extended family members, and even their children who did not "have the gift" of selling, from trying to emigrate. These vendors claimed that the personal risks for them were too great compared to what they would lose, namely, the chance to legitimately sell abroad. Getting caught—always a risk—and deported would give U.S. officials a clear reason to deny them a visa.

The third strategy was to return to the street. This may seem ironic and counter-intuitive for marketplace vendors who had been criticizing those new to tourism sales for glutting the market, but these were vendors who had inventory, and years of experience selling to tourists and working with weavers. While these Maya handicraft vendors had reliable inventory sources, they had insufficient capital to be in the official marketplace, because that required an initial outlay of cash for rent, taxes, and utilities. Even the poorest ex-marketplace vendors who had small, limited inventories tried to sell periodically on the street, hoping for that one large sale to a tourist.

These vendors who lost their places in the marketplace were especially bitter about their economic decline. They complained about having to compete against "farmers, whose hearts and spirits" were not geared toward selling or handicrafts. They railed against the city government and the police for creating intimidating conditions for tourists and vendors. As one asked, "What tourist would want to buy anything from me when they know the police will bother us?" In essence, CAFTA-DR and the regulation it promoted became a convenient way for them to explain away economic failures.

Economic Success Stories: "Not Because of CAFTA"

Successful vendors claimed that their economic gains were "not because of CAFTA." I outline four cases of successful vendors, post-CAFTA-DR ratification. Each has been successful in handicraft sales since the early 1990s. They use distinctive strategies and are examples of vendors who have figured out how to keep their businesses viable through changing economic and political conditions. What they share in common is the general sentiment that CAFTA-DR had nothing to do with their success.

Teresa is a Kaqchikel woman from San Antonio Aguas Calientes. She is a rarity in that she has sold successfully in the marketplace, as an itinerant vendor, and by making alliances with Spanish language instruction schools, hotels, and even bookstores. In the latter businesses, she gave weaving demonstrations and told stories about her town. She is well respected by her peers for her weaving skills.

Teresa's personable attitude and the quality of her weavings helped her to make connections with religious organizations and academics/museums in the United States through men and women to whom she gave demonstrations. When daily sales declined, she looked for new ways to market her goods. She has made several trips to the United States to demonstrate weaving to church congregations and schools. She explained, "You can only make a little money" and "you're not really there for your business." She hoped these prior trips would allow her to obtain a multiple entry visa and import textiles to the United States. Without invitations from her American friends, the U.S. embassy handily turned her down, despite, as she put it, her record of returning and her "favored status as a weaver." Frustrated but determined, she asked an in-law who had married a Honduran man to see if any Maya vendors worked on Honduras's north coast. When he reported back that no such vendors were established, she used extended marriage connections to scout for locations in La Ceiba and then on Roatán Island, a place favored by divers.

For the past two years, Teresa has built a lucrative business importing textiles, staying for weeks during the diving season. When we ran into each other in San Antonio in May 2008, she was home to pick up more merchandise. As she filled me in about her business and gave me updates about her children, I said that I was glad she was having success. "Oh, yes, thanks to God," she said. "God and family, not free trade."

Catarina is a Kaqchikel woman in her mid-20s from Santa Catarina Palopó. She began selling on the streets in Antigua when she was 10 years old, going there with vendors from her town, rather than to school. She is widely recognized by her peers as having unparalleled selling abilities. By the time she was 15 years old, she had made substantial connections with businesspersons from the United States and Europe. Unlike Teresa, she is not a skilled weaver. She excels in her ability to help importers/exporters make connections with reliable weavers, and she knows foreign tastes. She has commented that "free trade agreements never made sense to me" and that she "can always figure out a way to sell, free trade or not." Today, she assists exporters, selling to El Salvador, the United States and Europe, but she travels as a tourist, since it is easier for her to get visas. In effect, she works as a Maya textile expert earning fees for consulting and helping foreigners make connections. Her trips abroad are short and unofficial.

Juan is an Ixil man from Nebaj, who is married to and in partnership with a Kaqchikel female vendor, María, from San Antonio Aguas Calientes. He is just short of a college degree in linguistics. He and his wife draw on artisan networks in Ixil and Kaqchikel communities to diversify their goods and conceive of new products that look distinctively Mayan, but cannot be located a specific place. They developed a strong base of producers who agreed to sell on consignment, reducing the overall capital that Juan and María needed to run their business. He is one of the few vendors who doggedly pursue permission to sell in the United States. On occasion, I tease him about the money he has spent on failed attempts to get a visa. "A small investment, once I start exporting to the United States," he tells me.

As we talked in the marketplace on a rainy day in May 2008, Juan paused from time to time to help his 11-year-old daughter with math homework and to give orders to a teenage girl who worked for him. He explained that he had found a way to expand into additional stalls, even though the rule was that vendors were not allow to sell in more than one. "You know," he said. "I don't make any money here in the market, but I'm doing pretty well." Perplexed, I asked, then why keep the stalls? "That is because I can claim a loss on my taxes," he explained. "Besides, this is my office. I can show my merchandise to exporters and to merchants traveling to other markets. I like being near my children. They learn to manage a business and I make sure they do their homework."

Unlike most other vendors at the time, who had stopped trying to take advantage of CAFTA-DR, Juan was convinced the treaty would work for him. He attended meetings in Guatemala City about the treaty and how to develop an export business. He visited various embassies to explore their regulations. It was on one of these trips that he learned about a competitive contract to sell in Cuba. Armed with samples of merchandise and a vocabulary about trade that he learned from attending various workshops and seminars about CAFTA-DR, he obtained a special contract with the Cuban government. He now travels to Havana several times a year to sell merchandise. He said that he always sells out and at favorable prices. "Cuba," he told me, "is giving my family a nice life. When CAFTA-DR was signed, María and I hoped we could expand to the United States ourselves, but we still rely on tipiqueros and foreigners to sell there. Not Cuba, there I only rely on myself." Pausing to take some money from the girl who works for him, he laughed, "And whatever I take to Cuba sells; it's exotic there."

Tomás is a K'iche' man from Chichicastenango, married to and in a business partnership with a ladina woman. He has obtained an accounting degree and is a thesis away from a law degree. He is exceptionally well read for a Guatemalan—Maya, ladino, or otherwise—and we have spent hours debating everything from Buddhism to classic ethnographies by Sol Tax and Ruth Bunzel. His business is built on a strong extended-family network of artisans working in leather and fabric who are constantly innovating new designs. He is an active market researcher who has expanded business by selling to retail locations throughout Guatemala.

Tomás is not an active exporter, having decided not to bother with CAFTA-DR. "I read about what we Mayas are supposed to get from CAFTA, but I know what we are getting," he said. "Nothing." CAFTA-DR is not for Mayas, he tells me. It is for Americans, it is for ladinos, but it is not for Mayas. When we first met he had just started his accounting studies and relied on the sales he made in the marketplace. Like the other vendors discussed in this section, I knew that Tomás's main sales now came from his role as a middleperson to what are considered official retail outlets in Antigua and Guatemala City. Optimistic but realistic, he closely followed the news about free trade, remaining skeptical about it being of direct benefit to Mayas, especially since the government backed it. Rather than becoming cynical, as he developed an argument that shared much in common with Charles Hale's claims that neoliberal multiculturalism (also taken up by Anderson, Dary Fuentes, and Pineda in this volume) was a strategy to give the appearance of economically helping Mayas rather than actually doing it, Tomás confidently said in May 2008, "You can do well as a merchant right here in Guatemala." He then went on to add, "You don't need free trade, just the Internet to be well informed." By November, he had installed a cable Internet connection in his market locale.

Conclusions

In this chapter, I summarize how Maya handicraft vendors talked about free trade over the past fourteen years. Rather than pass judgment on the positive or negative impacts of free trade agreements, like NAFTA or CAFTA-DR, I focused on the changing attitudes that vendors themselves have had over the years, attending to their self-conceptualizations about how their economic opportunities have lessened or improved in relation to free trade.

Because it is difficult, if not impossible, to draw causal links between the implementation of CAFTA-DR and handicraft vendors' economic successes, I paid attention to how they comprehend their failures and successes in terms of CAFTA-DR. In fact, vendors disagreed among themselves about attributing failures or successes directly to CAFTA-DR, but almost universally they ultimately concluded that "free trade was not for everyone," especially for them. Despite this, some vendors carved out niches in which they were able to expand their marketing enterprises and improve their economic positions. The four successful cases illustrate three common aspects. They were each willing to take risks. They each innovated. And they each built new socioeconomic networks. To varying degrees, however, they studied CAFTA-DR and had once believed that it would benefit them.

Catarina commented to me once, "CAFTA is just an excuse for vendors who don't know how sell." Her sentiment, however, belies the creativity behind being able to take advantage of the situation. It is finding a way to use free trade to one's benefit—an ongoing puzzle some vendors like Juan still attempt to figure out. It is about subverting laws through manipulating immigration officials and forming business alliances with foreigners, as Catarina has done. It is building and drawing on extensive networks of producers, vendors, and retailers, as others described have done. For vendors, CAFTA-DR has been a disappointment, something that inspired economic fantasies, but ultimately it encouraged them to rethink how to be successful in a competitive tourism market that has been strained by changing consumer tastes, transnational political and economic policies, and ongoing internal Guatemalan conflicts.

Notes

1. All names are pseudonyms. The history of local political conflicts with city officials, the police, and some non-Maya foreign expatriate and ladino merchants make using their actual names a dangerous practice. For more on these politics see Little (2004, 2008). All translations from Spanish, Kaqchikel, and K'iche' are by the author.
2. Some of these contrasts are illustrated in Watanabe and Fischer (2004).
3. Clearly, the vendors have a sense of the tourism niche that they and their products fill. See Anderson for an example of how particular tourism niches are being created in Hondurans.
4. In addition to my research (Little 2004), see Colloredo-Mansfeld (1999), Meisch (2002), and Zorn (2004) for examples in the Andes.
5. Many of the essays in this volume address the differential effects that neoliberal political and economic policies have on gender. See, for example, the chapters by Babb and R. Montoya, who document the very different ways in which neoliberalism affects women and men. Dary Fuentes's case study also illustrates the differential treatment of Maya women dressed in *traje* (traditional handwoven clothes) who work in other, non-tourism sectors of the Guatemalan economy that do not prize this form of cultural expression.
6. INGUAT (El Instituto Guatemalteco de Turismo, http://estadisticas.almadelatierra.com/), Dirección General de Migración (http://www.migracion.gob.gt/), Banco de Guatemala (http://www.banguat.gob.gt/).
7. *Prensa Libre,* 27 March 2005; *Prensa Libre,* 14 August 2006.
8. See the United States Embassy in Guatemala web page: http://guatemala.usembassy.gov/non-immigrant_visas.html.
9. See the United States Embassy in Guatemala's "Frequently Asked Questions" page, which contradicts the very criteria that are officially listed and makes it virtually impossible to prove one satisfies the criteria: http://guatemala.usembassy.gov/uploads/images/2oS6l3FyQEdQasEXdW7ENQ/NIVEnglishFAQ.pdf.
10. See Dary Fuentes, this volume, who discusses the case of Irma Alicia Velásquez Nimatuj, a Maya intellectual who was refused service at an elite Guatemala City restaurant because she wore traje.
11. See Yagenova (2005) for an early Guatemalan analysis.
12. The topic of transnational migration and remittances in relation to CAFTA-DR is clearly beyond the scope or focus of this chapter. See Fazio (2007), Materer and Taylor (2003), and, especially, the chapters in this volume by Burrell and Mendez.

11 "Here the Campesino Is Dead"

Can Central America's Smallholders Be Saved?

Sarah Lyon *

Central American farmers are currently struggling for their survival. In the introduction to this volume Jennifer Burrell and Ellen Moodie suggest that Central America as a region has been systematically erased from geopolitical significance as a result of processes associated with neoliberal democratization. Similarly, Central American farmers are being "disappeared" from the agendas of international funders and agricultural support programs in the wake of trade liberalization and capitalist transformations. Emerging in the place of the international commodity agreements and technical and financial assistance, which characterized mid- to late-twentieth century rural development policies, are new market friendly approaches to development, such as fair trade and other certification programs. As this chapter demonstrates, fair trade has brought many benefits to certified small farmers. However, participation is curtailed to producers of agricultural commodities desired by northern consumers. The potential economic and social impact of fair trade is limited by its relatively small market share. It is increasingly clear that fair trade and similar certification regimes which involve production for northern niche markets are not and cannot be the only solutions to the problems faced by smallholders across the region. The movement as it currently exists cannot substitute for the market stability provided by a previous era of international commodity agreements and multi-faceted international and national level support and funding for small farmers. Overcoming the challenges facing the region's smallholders will require creative strategies that move beyond certification regimes.

This chapter explores the extent to which existing market based poverty solutions, such as fair trade, which are based on certification systems and cooperative smallholder production for targeted consumer markets in the north, will be able to mitigate the impact of free trade initiatives, such as the Dominican Republic-Central America-United States Free Trade Agreement (CAFTA-DR). The region's smallholders face several market failures that bring into question the ability of free trade to lift them out of poverty, including lack of market access, imperfect information, lack of access to financial markets, lack of access to credit, inability to switch to other sources of income generation, and weak legal systems and law enforcement (Nicholls and Opal 2005, 19). An ethnographic case study of fair trade coffee producers in Highland Guatemala[1] is employed to illustrate the benefits that fair trade has brought to some rural communities and support the argument that continued reliance on northern niche markets will not provide a sufficient safety net for the region's smallholders who currently face three primary challenges: first, a bias against rural development and a decline in development funding in this sector; second, market liberalization and anticipated price fluctuations; and third, changing market opportunities, including the decline of regional and municipal markets and the growth of supermarkets, which potentially limit coffee farmers' attempts to diversify production. In its current guise, the fair trade movement aims to counterbalance these market failures through the promotion of small-scale producers' products in northern consumer markets. However, research indicates that the traditional divisions between export and domestic markets makes less sense in light of the transnationalization of the contemporary agrifood system and the convergence of international food habits and food standards within a globalizing retail sector. Therefore, the chapter's conclusion explores the possibilities of regional south/south fair trade initiatives that might help smallholders adapt to changing market opportunities while simultaneously reinvigorating the international fair trade movement—which increasingly shies away from critical engagement with international trade policy discussions.

Fair Trade, Free Trade, and Agricultural Development

Agricultural growth, especially growth on small family farms, is "quintessentially pro-poor growth" because agriculture is generally labor intensive and skill extensive. Therefore agricultural growth creates additional employment with low entry barriers (Bezemer and Headey 2008; see Tucker, this volume). Despite this, over the past three decades there has been a systemic bias against agriculture and the rural economy in the allocation of development resources. The real global volume of assistance to agriculture decreased by nearly two-thirds from 1980 ($6.2 billion) to 2002 ($2.3 billion) while agriculture's share of total aid fell from a peak of 17 percent in 1982 to just 3.7 percent in 2002 (Bezemer and Headey 2008). Successful agricultural support programs historically included pricing, taxation, and trade policies as well as support for agricultural research, extension, technological innovation, quality management, information provision, and infrastructural investment. Despite celebratory pronouncements that globalization will flatten the world and minimize inequities, global disparities are maintained and protected in contemporary times through regional and global institutions such as the

World Bank and the World Trade Organization (WTO) which together have successfully structured the global economy around free trade and supposedly pure market relations requiring the reversal of protectionist measures such as tariffs, quotas, and state regulation. The agrifood sector lies at the heart of current efforts to regulate international trade under the auspices of the WTO and other multilateral agencies. Yet, it is simultaneously a central terrain for contesting neoliberalism within alternative globalization initiatives, of which fair trade is a part (Raynolds and Wilkinson 2007).

On 7 October 2007, CAFTA-DR was passed in Costa Rica, the last country to do so, after a narrow margin voted to approve it (see Raventós, this volume). Since few impact assessments of the trade agreement had been conducted, voters were forced to judge the proposal on the basis of the North American Free Trade Agreement's (NAFTA) record of boosting foreign direct investment and some exports while providing little benefit to the rural and urban poor of Mexico. In most of Central America, agriculture remains the largest source of employment. The region as a whole remains dependent on food staples and a few key export crops which are highly vulnerable within volatile world markets. Therefore, it is probable that CAFTA-DR will have a significant (and negative) impact on the small- and medium-scale agricultural enterprises which currently play a critical role in creating rural employment, providing environmental stewardship, and stemming the flow of out migration.

Under neoliberal policies, poverty is increasingly viewed as the result of a lack of effective integration into the market economy. Therefore, at the same time that agricultural support programs are being eliminated, market-friendly approaches to development, such as fair trade, are on the rise as donors initiate programs to harness the forces of globalization to benefit the poor (Dolan 2005, 414). This growing focus on market-based poverty reduction has led some aid organizations to direct their efforts towards more functionally oriented peasant groups, such as commodity-specific producer associations like the fair trade coffee cooperative profiled in this chapter. By facilitating the incorporation of "marginal" populations into market economies, the shifting development focus, of which fair trade is a key component, may indirectly serve neoliberal state goals. In fact, fair trade has experienced a high degree of success recently, in the form of rapid sales expansion and its adoption by institutions such as the World Bank and conventional corporations, due to its neoliberal conception of the market, emphasizing exchange relations over social relations (Fridell 2007, 49). Fair trade shares similar attributes with a variety of certification schemes emerging in response to the failure of interventionist states to meet the demands made of them in globalizing systems (Gereffi et al. 2001), including organic, forest stewardship labels, and the tourism eco-labeling initiatives explored by Luis Vivanco in this volume. While certification initiatives have expanded rapidly in recent years, a pressing political issue remains: if trade is the route for growth and poverty reduction, what rules should govern international trading practices and the formation of international trade agreements and organizations? Many argue that in recent years the international fair trade movement has shied away from this critical issue due to its focus on growing markets and working within the capitalist system.

According to the Fair Trade International, the largest organization responsible for certifying fair trade producer groups, estimated global fair trade retail sales were close to $6.6 billion (U.S.) in 2011, and 1.2 million farmers and workers benefited from access to certified fair trade markets through their membership in one of the more than 991 producer groups in 66 countries registered with the organization (FLO 2012). While these numbers are impressive, there are close to 500 million small-scale and family farmers in the world, and it has been calculated that fair trade sales average only 20 percent of the total sales by registered groups (Wilkinson 2006, 24). In 2007, approximately half (315) of Fair Trade International's certified producer groups were located in Latin America and 84 were located in Central America (FLO 2007). Coffee is the region's largest fair trade commodity with 69 registered producer groups as of August 2008. The increasing popularity of fair trade and the expansion of certified products and producer groups necessitated Fair Trade International's internal split in 2003 into two legal entities: Fair Trade Labeling Organization (FLO) Certification Ltd. is responsible for certification, inspection and trade auditing, while the charitable side of FLO regulates all other activities. Initially, Fair Trade International did not charge producer organizations a certification fee because the organization's operational and marketing expenses were covered by the 5 cents per pound licensing fee paid by roasters. However, in 2003 the board of directors introduced an initial certification fee (for cooperatives with fewer than 500 members, such as the Guatemalan one) of $2,500.00 (U.S.) and an annual renewal fee of $637.00 (U.S.) (base) in order to help the organization "[p]rovide high quality certification and trade auditing services."[2] These fees, which can significantly lower a cooperative's annual profits, are largely invisible to northern consumers, much as the region itself has been "disappeared" from the popular geopolitical imaginary.

There are five widely cited criteria for fair trade coffee certification:

1. small farmers must be organized into democratically run cooperatives;
2. buyers must guarantee a floor price (in 2011, $1.40 plus $0.30 organic differential, plus $0.20 free trade premium equals $1.90 (U.S.) per pound [transfairusa.org]);[3]
3. buyers must offer farmers credit, for up to 60 percent of the value of what they have contracted to buy, to help cover harvest costs;

4. importers and farmer cooperatives must develop long-term trading relationships; and
5. farmers must pursue ecological goals.

Overall, resource transfers within fair trade networks have been significant: transfers from U.S. consumers to southern coffee farmers resulted in an estimated additional producer income of $70 million between 1998 and 2005 (Macdonald 2007, 799). However, despite the recent growth in fair trade markets, the market for fair trade coffee remains insufficient; nearly 30 percent of the world's small-scale coffee producers (over 700,000 [FLO 2007]) now supply the fair trade market and Fair Trade International estimates that the capacity of producers worldwide who could meet certification standards is roughly seven times the current volume exported via fair trade channels (Murray et al. 2006). This translates into stiff competition among producer groups, such as those in Central America, many of whom struggle to secure fair trade prices for their coffee and are often forced to sell a portion of their product to local *coyotes* (middlemen) for a significant discount.

Comparing the experiences of the Honduran small coffee farmers described by Catherine Tucker in this volume and those of the Guatemalan coffee cooperative discussed below illustrates this potential competition and the struggles that groups face in gaining access to these potentially lucrative niche markets. Furthermore, despite the fact that producers have widely disparate production and living costs and that many nations' economies have been ravaged by inflation, between 1988 and 2007 the guaranteed price for fair trade certified coffee was raised only twice. Most recently in 2007, the Fair Trade International board voted to increase the social premium and organic differential with the result that in 2011 certified coffee organizations producing dual certified organic and fair trade coffee were paid $1.51 per pound ($1.21 fair trade minimum plus $0.10 social premium plus $0.20 organic differential). The amount paid to coffee growers might be significantly less depending on an organization's operating expenses. The difficulty in raising the prices for certified fair trade products and the relatively small size of the retail markets combine to limit the long-term potential of the fair trade movement to protect Central America's smallholders from the changing market conditions that further trade liberalization will inevitably bring.

Situating International Trade in Local Spheres

As in many small Maya communities in Guatemala, daybreak in San Juan La Laguna, located on the shores of Lake Atitlan, is punctuated by the staccato sound of diesel-powered corn grinders chugging to life. An early morning walk through the cobblestone streets reveals female Juaneras, young and old, wrapped in secondhand sweaters to ward off the morning chill, slowly making their way to the nearest grinder, where they wait with bowls filled with corn grown by their family members. During the fourteen months I lived in San Juan, I was often awakened by these corn grinders and my early mornings were scented by the fresh tortillas, made of local corn, cooking on the *comales* (griddle) in the houses surrounding my own.

In years past, agricultural production in San Juan involved a regular series of tasks that marked the cyclical planting, tending, and harvesting of locally grown foods, including onions, tomatoes, garbanzos, *milpa* (plots of corn, beans and squash), and coffee. Slowly over time, markets for horticultural products, especially onions and tomatoes, collapsed. Beginning in the 1970s coffee became the agricultural king in San Juan and much of Central America and more land was devoted to its production. However, over the past decade international coffee markets have experienced dramatic booms and busts. *Arabica* coffee prices reached their lowest levels in over a century in 2001 and rebounded a decade later in the spring of 2011 to a thirty-four-year high as a result of market speculation and poor harvests. While smallholders are particularly vulnerable to these commodity cycles, as Tucker points out in her chapter, they are to a certain extent used to these market variations and able to survive them.

Figure 11.1. Farmer with Corn, Sarah Lyon

In order to improve their livelihood prospects, a small number of Juaneros joined together in the late 1970s to form an agricultural cooperative that today boasts over one hundred members and exports high-quality fair trade and organic certified coffee to the United States. Despite their successes in the international fair trade coffee market, cooperative members lament their dependence on this volatile crop and the fact that there are no local markets for other agricultural products. As one cooperative member bitterly explained to me, "Here the campesino is dead. The land of Guatemala produces all the agricultural products but there's no price. We produce quality products but it's not worthwhile because there is no market." While the cooperative provides members with a relatively secure market (the very niche market that Tucker's [this volume] coffee producers struggle to access) through a long-term relationship with its North American coffee buyers, Green Mountain Coffee Roasters, 90 percent of surveyed members expressed a desire to diversify their production and explore additional market opportunities, whether in artisan sales or vegetable production. The 2001 coffee crisis revealed the market's fragility, and some cooperative members doubted the long-term prospects of the crop. At that time 67 percent of surveyed members reported that they planned to plant different crops if the price of coffee continued to drop; however in practice coffee farmers are often reluctant to diversify because of the time and money they have already invested in their trees (see Sick 1997).

The role that globalization and free trade agreements, such as CAFTA-DR, play in lowering market prices for their agricultural products is not lost on Juanero coffee producers. Like the Guatemalan artisans profiled by Walter Little in this volume, they have become stark critics of the limitations free trade places on their future economic prospects. One cooperative member and former mayor explained to me how in 1977 he began a business of growing and buying onions from other community members to bulk together and sell in Guatemala City. Onions earned him a good income, and "the daily wages of the agricultural workers were low and the inputs were inexpensive—one liter of insecticide cost only four quetzales." However that same liter of insecticide today costs over one hundred quetzales and the price of onions is practically the same. With an exasperated air, he told me, "A lot of people say that globalization is good and the markets are free and now everything's good and there's going to be a piece of the market for Guatemala." But he didn't agree with this sentiment, stating, "Globalization will only be good for the countries that subsidize their products. The governments have ruined our [Central American] countries. Now we can't work and we're at the door of something worse because of the numbers." He simply didn't see how people in his community could continue to farm when it cost so much and earned them so little. His comment represents a refusal to accept the erasure and fragmentation of Central America as a regional entity. Burrell and Moodie point out in the introduction to this volume that the very name of the CAFTA-DR trade agreement implies that all participants were equal partners in a deal, a sentiment with which this smallholder clearly disagrees.

Fair Trade's Impact on Cooperative Members and the San Juan Community

Critiques of neoliberal trade policies such as the one above are clearly filtered through cooperative members' long-term experiences within the coffee market and successful production for the relatively lucrative niche market of fair trade, organic, specialty coffee. Participation in fair trade markets has positively impacted the community through access to higher prices, the formation of direct and long-term market relationships, and opportunities for organizational capacity building as detailed below.[4] However, fair trade markets are not able to insulate small coffee producers from the vagaries of a liberalized international coffee market.

Higher Prices

The most direct benefit to individual producers is the guaranteed price they receive for their products, which varies by commodity. In addition to the guaranteed price, producers receive a social premium to be used for community development. The guaranteed price helps to sustain rural communities and households and, when invested in land and education, supports effective local development and is a critical component of fair trade certification, especially for commodities with volatile markets such as coffee. At the height of the coffee crisis, during the 2001–2002 coffee harvest, cooperative members were paid $1.41 (U.S.) per pound ($1.26 guaranteed fair trade price with a $0.15 premium). After taxes and the cooperative's operating costs were deducted, this price was double that paid to non-cooperative members by local middlemen.

The higher income enabled members to continue repaying their debts, maintain their standard of living, retain their landholdings, and pay for their children's education during a period in which many non-members were forced to sell their land and withdraw their children from school. Adequate access to land is a critical component of livelihood subsistence and sustainable rural communities in Central America (see Boyer and Cardona Peñalva, this volume). Therefore, the security of the cooperative members' landholdings is a significant benefit of their higher fair trade incomes. The steady income also enabled cooperative members to continue their subsistence agricultural production. In addition to providing additional cash income and cultural continuity, milpa subsistence farming is a livelihood strategy that helps smallholders cope with uncertain prospects. Finally, the higher prices earned by cooperative members enabled them to educate more of their children for longer periods of time.

Direct, Long-Term Trade Relationships, Stability, and Market Information

In addition to guaranteed prices, fair trade standards require buyers to enter into long-term purchasing agreements with producers. Fair trade's close alliance with northern buyers and retailers and its focus on supporting smallholder access to new markets facilitates a wider distribution of benefits to producers (Taylor 2004). Fair trade buyers and the development agencies that support the market are able to assist specific groups rather than offer blanket aid. The desire to maintain long-term relationships with buyers can provide an incentive for cooperatives to improve their product quality by investing in infrastructural and production improvements. These direct trade relationships allow fair trade producers to bypass the often exploitative local buyers and enable groups to bargain more effectively with large buyers such as Starbucks or Walmart. Furthermore, the market information they obtain through fair trade contracts may make producers more confident in dealing with non-fair trade buyers as well (Ronchi 2002).

The Guatemalan coffee cooperative is visited on an almost monthly basis by representatives from their long-term Vermont-based buyers, Green Mountain Coffee Roasters. Through this steady contact, cooperative members hone their communication skills, enhance their business practices and learn valuable information about quality and certification demands. The fair trade model offers the cooperative a competitive advantage by actively fostering ongoing close contact with their buyers and enabling them to learn international standards for price, quality, and the delivery of export products. Furthermore, through their participation in fair trade markets, many producer associations, including the researched cooperative, have gained access to credit for agricultural improvements and micro-lending programs. Alain De Janvry and Elisabeth Sadoulet (2000, 396) argue that access to credit is minimal among the rural poor in Latin America and this lowers the "income generating capacity of the meager asset endowments that the poor possess." However, participation in fair trade markets can enhance the legitimacy of producer organizations, thereby granting them access to credit institutions and international lenders (Raynolds 2004), a key benefit for smallholders who were often historically excluded from formal lending institutions.

Organizational Capacity Building

Fair trade-certified producers must be organized into independent democratic associations or, in the case of hired labor, must be allowed to join worker unions. This requirement results in one of fair trade's most enduring benefits, organizational capacity building, a process that Ainhoa Montoya's analysis of the Salvadoran electoral process (this volume) demonstrates is particularly fraught with tension across Central America due to the region's tumultuous past. The strength of a producer association's internal organization, members' group identity and leadership skills have been identified as critical components of fair trade success. In turn, the security of fair trade prices and markets enhances a cooperative's general financial and organizational stability (Raynolds 2004) because buyers demand a certain degree of accountability and monitoring. Fair trade consumption in the North is predicated upon consumers' access to information regarding the conditions of production and increasingly the social circumstances and cultural traditions of producers themselves. Therefore, participation in international fair trade markets can lend legitimacy and protection to democratic producer associations, which in turn are able to create safe opportunities for members to work together and reproduce long-term traditions of horizontal cooperation, reciprocity and mutual aid. For example, of the 53 surveyed cooperative members, 77 percent have served on the cooperative's 16-member board of directors at least once over the course of their membership. In regions with a history of targeted rural violence, such as Guatemala, the international nature of fair trade networks buttresses the strength of cooperatives and the secure civic spaces they foster. While many Guatemalans see democratic organizations as essential to confronting poverty and precarious economic circumstances, due to the fact that any social organization not under army control during the war was criminalized, fear remains a significant obstacle to rural organization (REMHI 1999; see Burrell, this volume, for a discussion of recently emerging security committees). However, the democratic and egalitarian ethos of the coffee cooperative serves to mitigate the destabilizing forces that often accompany the production of potentially profitable crops such as coffee.

Indirect Community Benefits

Non-fair trade farmers in small communities such as San Juan benefit from the local multiplier effects of extra income as well as community projects such as roads, health clinics, and schools funded with the fair trade premium (Nicholls and Opal 2005). Furthermore, because fair trade certification requires producers to meet environmental production standards, communities also benefit from locally reduced use of pesticides and reforestation projects, an indirect advantage also potentially realized by the Costa Rican residents studied by Vivanco (this volume) who live in communities with eco-certified tourism projects.

Market Deregulation, Volatility, and Diversification

As noted above, the volatility of the international coffee market has increased since 1989 when the International Coffee Agreement, which set quotas and helped to stabilize prices, was not renewed. Despite some drawbacks, such as the ongoing struggle among producer countries to capture larger quotas and the difficulty new producers faced in entering the market, the ICA system kept coffee prices relatively high and stable. It was these stable prices that led Central American small farmers, such as the Juaneros, to first plant coffee. However, once the ICA system broke down, coffee prices dropped dramatically and except for sharp price spikes in 1995 and 1997 (caused by Brazilian frosts) and the current price highs, coffee earnings remained very low, even below the cost of production. This coffee market volatility is particularly threatening to the millions of small coffee producers around the world who often lack sufficient capital to weather market downturns. Small coffee producers in Central America are especially vulnerable to market fluctuations as they often do not have formal lending institutions or alternative livelihood options, and due to the long-term investment required for coffee production they are reluctant to plant other crops (Sick 1997). Cooperative members in San Juan routinely referred to their coffee as "children" which they had nurtured through many years of production. They were reluctant to replace their trees with new, higher producing varieties, even when their productivity started to decline after decades of growth. Therefore, it is hard to imagine them ripping out their coffee in order to plant another cash crop simply because they face limited options for lucrative diversification.

Additionally, Juaneros historically produced sufficient corn in their milpa fields to feed their families and generate a small amount of profit. However, over the past thirty years, milpa fields were systematically converted to coffee and today many cooperative members use coffee profits to purchase supplemental corn for their families, something that would have been nearly unthinkable in past generations. Corn is central to Maya daily life; milpa is not simply a cornfield but is instead a cultural institution and process (Alcorn and Toledo 1998). In addition to the coffee they produced, all but six of the fifty-three surveyed cooperative members owned milpa and all but five owned at least one cuerda of land devoted to vegetable cultivation.

The continued cultivation of milpa and vegetables is a livelihood strategy that better enables small producers to cope with uncertain prospects; when coffee revenues decline members can rest assured that they can feed their families despite declining cash incomes. This sentiment was expressed in the following statements of cooperative members: "I plant milpa so my family doesn't suffer," and, "It is better [to plant] milpa and beans. Even though we don't have money, we have food." As previous generations of anthropologists have argued, culture plays a very significant role in milpa management and in turn milpa affects culture. However, with the further liberalization of agricultural markets (for example, through CAFTA-DR), it is possible that local markets will be flooded with inexpensive, heavily subsidized U.S. corn, further lowering the price of the preferred local corn and perhaps leading to a decline in production among Juaneros and other smallholders across the region.

Coffee provides an instructive example of the impact that a shift away from international market regulation can have on producers' livelihoods. Under the current model of transnational market deregulation, the nation-state has disappeared from view, replaced by transnational nongovernmental organizations (NGOs) and the buying practices of international consumers (Reichman 2008, 103). The failure of fair trade's proponents to recognize the International Coffee Agreement's significance demonstrates the extent to which political institutions have disappeared from current conceptions of economic and social justice. The difficulties facing small coffee producers in recent years are perhaps indicative of future problems facing smallholders throughout Central America as markets continue to be liberalized according to the dictates of free trade. Due to the corporatization of food markets in Central America, even if small coffee farmers, such as the cooperative members, wanted to diversify into other crops, they would find it increasingly difficult to access local markets. The question posed below is to what extent the fair trade movement can assist rural producers of varied commodities, not just coffee, in the current context of neoliberal markets.

Liberalization and Local Markets

The experience of Central American coffee farmers in the years since the demise of the International Coffee Agreement indicates that without safeguards for small farmers and the agricultural sector, trade liberalization will make Central America's smallholders more vulnerable to downturns in the global economy. The overall outlook for Central America's agricultural exports under CAFTA-DR is poor, as the region's farmers will be forced to compete even more heavily against highly subsidized production in the United States. The United States can now export duty-free products such as cotton, wheat, beef, and processed foods while quotas will be gradually eliminated on exports considered sensitive to Central American trade partners, such as corn. The passage of CAFTA-DR reflects declining support for rural development efforts in the region, as the Guatemalan Ambassador to the United States, Jose Guillermo Astillo, reportedly told journalists when lobbying for CAFTA-DR's passage in the U.S. Congress: "We want to get away from just subsistence farming that keeps so many in poverty" (Campbell 2007).

The potential impact of CAFTA-DR's implementation is foreshadowed by the Mexican experience of NAFTA participation. The National Campesino Federation in Mexico estimates that 200,000 Mexicans a year have fled the countryside for cities or the United States since NAFTA's implementation in 1994 (Koop 2008). Furthermore, according to Mexico's largest bank, BBVA, the country imported 23.6 percent of its corn, 50.2 percent of its wheat, and 75 percent of its rice in 2007, meaning that Mexico is no longer self-sufficient in food, and food prices there are rising at double the rate of wage increases (Rosen 2008). In fact, across Latin America, trade liberalization since the early 1980s made it easier and cheaper to import food and non-food products (Reardon and Berdegue 2002). One consequence of this is that increasing numbers of smallholders are forced to migrate to the United States in search of work (see Burrell; and Mendez, this volume). In short, based on the experience of NAFTA, it is reasonable to assume that without significant support for Central America's small-scale producers, the implementation of CAFTA-DR will contribute to rural out-migration and the growth of precarious urban settlements, increased dependence on foreign food, and increased food prices for already impoverished citizens.

Concurrent with trade liberalization, foreign direct investment in agrifood sectors in the global South has increased markedly in recent years, especially but not exclusively in middle-income countries (Raynolds and Wilkinson 2007). In Latin America this is clearly evident in the rapid growth of supermarkets, which by 2000 represented roughly 50 to 60 percent of the retail sector in the region. In 2002 there were 705 supermarkets in Central America—60 of them in Nicaragua, the poorest country in Latin America, and 128 in Guatemala, the fifth poorest. In Costa Rica about 40 percent of towns with a population of around 25,000 (basically rural towns) had at least one supermarket. In Central American countries, roughly 80 percent of the top 5 supermarket chains are owned by global multinationals (Reardon and Berdegue 2002). As of June 2011, Walmart was the largest supermarket operator in Guatemala with 177 retail outlets across the country, including Despensa Familiar, Hiper Paiz, Supertiendas Paiz, and Maxi Bodega.[5]

The rapid growth of multinational supermarkets in the region has significant implications for small producers of fresh fruits and vegetables (FFV) for local and regional markets. Supermarkets' FFV procurement practices include consolidating purchases in distribution centers and sourcing networks, increasing chain coordination through contracts with wholesalers and growers, and requiring demanding private standards and certification. Furthermore, the supermarkets often engage in commercial practices, such as waiting many days after product delivery to make payment, which favor medium to large growers. Combined, these practices make it difficult for small farmers to compete. As the leading retailer in Guatemala, Walmart recognizes these limitations and claimed to support small farmers in improving their agricultural capacity through a partnership with Mercy Corps and the United States Agency for International Development (USAID), which ended in 2010. The program helped farmers grow "quality, competitively priced produce that is being sold at Walmart stores." The fact that only four hundred families were involved in the three-year program (Walmart 2011) proves it to be a token effort rather than a systematic attempt to effect change. However, the domestic market for FFV in Latin American supermarkets is estimated to be two to three times ($24 billion) the market size of FFV exports ($10.5 billion, including bananas) (Reardon and Berdegue 2002), meaning that with the right tools, this market sector could be potentially lucrative in the future for Central American smallholders.

Conclusion: Supporting Small Farmers through South-South Fair Trade

In 2007 Fair Trade International "took steps to support the development of fair trade sales in developing countries" by instituting an international licensing system that allows companies in countries with no fair trade labeling initiative, such as Fair Trade USA, to sell products bearing the FAIRTRADE mark (FLO 2007). In short, Fair Trade International lent its support for burgeoning efforts to develop south/south fair trade markets in Latin America and other regions that have historically been relegated to the production side of the fair trade equation. In recent years a southern fair trade agenda has emerged (primarily in Latin America) which focuses in part on the development of local, regional, and national fair trade systems.

While the community of Perez Zeledon, Costa Rica, was declared a Fair Trade Town in 2009,[6] Mexico and Brazil have led the way in the development of south/south and national fair trade markets. Although they have enjoyed significant successes, their efforts indicate that the movement faces fundamental challenges in transforming the existing fair trade system into a tool for alternative and sustainable development. Specifically, the initiatives have faced the challenge of developing national labels to differentiate products such as basic foodstuffs, including beans, corn, and manioc, currently not certified with Fair Trade International in addition to creating structures for monitoring and managing production and marketing. Further challenges include increasing consumer awareness, defining market strategies, developing market channels, and involving key private and public actors (Wilkinson and Mascarenhas 2007). Similarly, Comercio Justo Mexico (CJM) was formed in 2001 to create a fair trade market in Mexico when producer organizations realized that the creation of a domestic market was essential to their long-term survival. Currently coffee is sold with its own fair trade label and other products, such as honey, are in process. The ultimate goal of CJM is to place fair trade products in the major supermarkets of Mexico. In 2002 it launched the Café Fertil coffee line targeted at university students and it is now considering launching a chain of tortilla factories using non-GMO (genetically modified) white corn produced by Mexican farm organizations (Renard and Perez-Grovas 2007). While the organization has experienced significant successes, it has also struggled with Fair Trade International over its desire to develop national fair trade standards focused on small producers, rather than plantations (Renard and Perez-Grovas 2007; Wilkinson and Mascarenhas 2007).

The Brazilian and Mexican experiences indicate that south/south fair trade initiatives face distinct challenges in developing their markets, including raising consumer demand, securing state support, and remaining in compliance with international fair trade standards. The Comercio Justo Mexico effort languished in its first years due to insufficient fair trade consumer demand; within Mexico the concept of fair trade has been criticized as being elitist (Renard and Perez-Grovas 2007). In both Mexico and Brazil, the initiatives have struggled to keep fair trade prices attainable for low-income consumers, something that is not a priority within northern fair trade markets. Interestingly, alternative market discussions in Latin America highlight the need to play down the notion of a fair price paid to producers, which is a major selling point for North American and European fair trade consumers. Instead, these initiatives market themselves to consumers on the basis of fair negotiations, the elimination or reduction of intermediaries, and greater market access (Wilkinson and Mascarenhas 2007). Securing state support for policies that deal with deficiencies in technical assistance, credit, and capacity building for small producers is seen as a key component of south/south fair trade initiatives. However, under the current neoliberal international trade agenda, there is a limit to how much support southern governments can provide. As Jaffee (2007, 33) points out, CAFTA-DR contains language that explicitly prohibits national governments from using their tariff-rate quotas to afford import protection to goods from producer groups or nongovernmental organizations. He argues, "This may be an early indication of how the framers of international trade agreements are viewing the potential of the rapidly growing fair trade movement."

The creation of viable south/south fair trade markets may be an opportune venue for reinvigorated support for alternative international trade agendas within the larger fair trade movement. The existing south/south fair trade movements are much more representative of producers' concerns and needs than Fair Trade International itself. As a result, rather than simply hoping for a piece of the existing capitalist market, they express a more radical vision of the necessity for reform of international trade. Strengthening these south/south initiatives would help the larger fair trade movement broaden its appeal, educate consumers, and gain influence within ongoing struggles for an alternative to neoliberal globalization. At the same time, within Central America the emergence of south/south fair trade markets would help to provide small farmers with increased access to changing local markets and help to protect them from continued declines in national and international financial support and the inevitable volatility that will accompany the further liberalization of agricultural commodity markets.

Notes

* This research was generously funded by the University of Kentucky Summer Faculty Research Fellowship, the Wenner-Gren Foundation for Anthropological Research, and Fulbright-Hayes. I would like to thank the anonymous reviewers, the participants of the "After the Handshakes" Wenner-Gren Workshop, and Jennifer Burrell and Ellen Moodie for their comments on this chapter.

1. The chapter employs ethnographic data gathered primarily through participant observation and qualitative interviews during 14 months of research in Guatemala. The larger project also involved 6 months of research in the United States (December 2001–February 2003 and June 2006). The research focused on the 116 members and the administrators of the fair trade coffee cooperative located in a Tz'utujil Maya community of approximately 5,000 people.
2. www.flo-cert.net (accessed 28 August 2008).
3. http//transfairusa.org/press-room/press_release/fairtrade-international-announces-changes-fair-trade-coffee-minimum-price-p (accessed 12 September 2011).
4. For a more detailed exploration of the impacts, both positive and negative, of fair trade market participation on cooperative members, please see Lyon (2011), from which the material in this section draws.
5. http//walmartstores.com/AboutUs/9753.aspx (accessed 14 June 2011).
6. http//www.fairtradetowns.org/about/ (accessed 14 June 2011).

12

Certifying Sustainable Tourism in Costa Rica

Environmental Governance and Accountability in a Transitional Era

Luis A. Vivanco

At a medium-sized ecolodge just outside the village of Puerto Viejo on Costa Rica's Caribbean coast, a typical visitor would spend the day hiking through rain forest, bird watching, wandering the beach, or visiting the nearby Bri Bri indigenous reserve. Visitors can also take a tour of the hotel's environmentally sensitive facilities. But requests for it are unusual.

Nevertheless, along with six others, I recently found myself evaluating the twenty-room ecolodge's laundry facilities. We were conducting a mock sustainability audit, as participants in a workshop at the lodge on sustainable tourism certification and audits. Standards checklists in hand, we appreciated elevated walkways of recycled plastic that connect the guest rooms with the dining hall, and worked our way toward the kitchen to inspect, among other things, how and where the staff disposes of the cooking grease. We paused at the laundry, longer than I thought possible, to evaluate the efficiency rating of the washing machine, consider the biodegradability of the soap, and calculate the quantity of waste water and appraise its potential impact on surrounding flora and fauna. The ecolodge performed well in the audit. It was, after all, already a participant in the Costa Rican government's Sustainable Tourism Certification program, which rewards hotels that minimize ecological and social impacts.

Perhaps we were a peculiar sight, concentrating on banal technical details of hotel operations with almost complete disregard for the exuberant tropical surroundings. Or maybe we were at the cutting edge of environmental activism, if not the vanguard that is transforming the very character of tourism, insisting on and verifying its accountability to global standards of environmental and social sustainability.

This second view is common among advocates of voluntary eco-labeling and audit programs. Although tourism ecolabels are in their infancy—most of the world's 150 or so tourism ecolabels emerged in the 1990s (Honey 2002)—they are often referred to as "tools of the times" and carry an aura of inevitability. Multilateral development institutions with a strong Central American presence, such as the Interamerican Development Bank and the U.S. Agency for International Development, as well as environmental nongovernmental organizations (NGOs) like the Rainforest Alliance, have invested millions of dollars researching the principles of certification, developing technical guidelines, and marketing the programs and hotels that meet standards. In their vision, ecolabels represent not just an aspiration to reform the global tourism industry's negative ecological and social impacts, but also a key mechanism for maintaining ecological balance and growing economies in an era of "sustainable development."

Costa Ricans play a conspicuous role in the transnational sustainable tourism certification movement. The country, a prestigious site of ecotourism since that concept's emergence in the 1970s, is an incubator of certification thought and practice. In addition to its pioneering government program, at least three other tourism ecolabels operate there. The Rainforest Alliance's San José office has played a central role as a coordinating body for determining and promoting baseline criteria for the certification movement throughout the Americas. In other Central American nations—notably Guatemala, Belize, Panama, and Honduras—tourism ministries, environmental organizations, and hotels have developed or are developing another dozen or so ecolabels, mostly modeled on the Costa Rican approach. Thanks to pressure by Costa Ricans, sustainable tourism certification is on the agenda of regional cooperation, including the Mesoamerican Biological Corridor. There has long been a palpable sense that Costa Rica—through small-scale efforts like those taking place in Puerto Viejo—offers a "laboratory" for reconfiguring the tourism industry along lines of socio-environmental sustainability. As this sense has matured, it has lent tourism ecolabels and sustainability audits legitimacy (Cabrera 2003).

Often lost in the celebratory rhetoric and decidedly technical nature of audit practices, however, are questions about the broader cultural and political significance of green certifications for environmental governance. Market-based ecolabels are typically framed as a tool to redress a growing environmental "governance gap" in which states are unwilling or unable to create or enforce vigorous environmental regulations (Cashore, Auld, and Newsom 2004). In response, industries promote voluntary self-regulation through auditing practices that demonstrate accountability to predetermined global standards of efficiency and environmental sustainability. Voluntary certification enables more effective exploitation of resources by promoting resource-efficient technologies that save money and an ability to charge a premium for their product. From a political point of view, the practice staves off potential government regulation by marketing a positive image of self-regulation (Buckley 2001; Font 2002; Honey and Rome 2001; Honey 2002). Certifications emerge squarely out of neoliberal ideology and practice, serving as key mechanisms by which rule-making clout is moving from states to non-state actors. They have important consequences not just for shaping how business will be conducted, but also for defining and legitimating new market-friendly approaches to environmental action.

Costa Ricans' efforts at implementing ecolabels have emerged out of and been shaped during a period of political-economic transition. In contrast with other cases examined in this volume, this transition is not from civil war or military rule, but from an interventionist state with a central role in national political-economic life to a neoliberal regime of significantly reduced latitude, especially in the conduct of the country's commitments to addressing environmental degradation. This transition has had multidimensional impacts on Costa Rican social institutions and lives (see Raventós, this volume) and raises a number of questions I explore in this chapter: Why have issues of environmental governance and accountability in Costa Rica been shifting to market-based mechanisms like sustainable tourism certification? What social and political-economic conditions give rise to these mechanisms? Who participates in certifications, and how are hotels and tourists adjusting to demands for accountability in the environmental and social consequences of their activities? What are the consequences of this shift in accountability for the practice of environmentalism and sustainable development?

Addressing these questions requires attention to the role of the Costa Rican state in the emergence of environmental certification regimes. It has important bearing on this volume's concern with visibility and disappearance in recent Central American cultural and political histories. Contrary to their identity as non-state, market-based mechanisms for environmental governance, the most recognizable ecolabel in Costa Rica—the Certification for Sustainable Tourism (CST)—developed with active state involvement. But because neoliberal ideology and discipline refuse explicit state management, the CST operates in what Michel-Rolph Trouillot (2001) refers to as "the shadows of the state." It is an arena of social action in which state processes and practices intersect with, are shaped by, and in turn shape social action in oblique, ambiguous, and fluid ways. In these shadows, state institutions—once icons of public accountability in Costa Rica—defer pseudo-regulatory functions to private institutions and market-based processes whose public profile is obscured and whose accountability is unclear.

Environmentalism, Tourism, and the State in Transitional Costa Rica

During the past thirty years, Costa Rica has gained international visibility as an iconic "Green Republic" (Evans 1999). It has transformed from a largely agrarian economy to one in which nature conservation, environmentally focused tourism, and sustainability-related initiatives play a prominent role. On a much larger scale than any other country in Central America, the Costa Rican state has vigorously pursued the creation, administration, and expansion of national parks, protected wilderness areas, and a state environmental bureaucracy. It has supported a tourism industry based on protected rain forests, an industry that surpassed coffee and bananas as the primary source of foreign exchange in 1995. The national legislature has passed progressive laws governing forestry, wildlife conservation, and even a constitutional reform guaranteeing all citizens "the right to a healthy and ecologically balanced environment" (Salazar 1993).

However, the state's position on issues of environmental protection and governance has been anything but coherent (Rodriguez 1994). Enforcement of environmental laws has often been weak, inconsistent, and poorly funded. As a result, nobody really expects to achieve constitutionally guaranteed rights to a "healthy and ecologically balanced environment." In addition, throughout the 1980s and 1990s the state aggressively promoted the expansion of ecologically destructive non-traditional agro-exports of ornamental plants and tropical fruits. In the 1980s and 1990s, this "Green Republic" gained the dubious reputation of having the highest rate of deforestation in Central America because of illegal logging and expansion of commercial agriculture (Evans 1999).

No state is monolithic. State institutions and agencies exist at cross-purposes, designing and implementing contradictory policies and enforcing those policies inconsistently. But these contradictions are the product of a particular historical period of transition, in which Costa Rica has undergone a radical transformation from welfare-oriented interventionism to free-market-oriented deregulation and decentralization. These processes (also discussed in Raventós, this volume) have had powerful effects on how issues of environmental governance are framed—as increasingly within the domain of private, market-based initiative with minimal state regulatory control.

The origin of this situation lies in the aftermath of Costa Rica's 1948 civil war. Political leaders eliminated the army and implemented reforms affecting practically all arenas of social development and economic production, from providing price supports and subsidies in rural areas to making substantial investments in universal health care and education (Edelman 1999; Rodriguez 1993). State interventionism and the elimination of the military provided important social stability and legitimacy for the post-war political order, and the government's social compact with the people became, along with "democracy," a key attribute of the country's distinctive identity as a peaceful, prosperous "Switzerland of Central America."

The reality was much more complicated, of course. By the late 1970s, this political-economic model had begun unraveling. Disruptions caused by global recession, declining coffee prices, currency fluctuations, and disruption to overland trade related to the Nicaraguan Revolution exposed fundamental weaknesses in the national economy (Edelman and Kenen 1989). During the period of the 1980s "debt crisis," inflation and unemployment rates soared. The majority of Costa Ricans experienced significant declines in their real wages. Large public sector deficits forced the acceptance of three rounds of IMF structural adjustment measures in the late 1980s and early 1990s. These measures focused on the implementation of free-market policies throughout most of the economy, including dismantling price supports and credits, openness to international markets, and reduction in public services. The reconstruction of a neoliberal state ruptured previous forms of social consensus achieved and maintained through mediating state institutions. The change generated tremendous social unrest and declining confidence in Costa Rica's democratic political processes (Edelman 1999; Trejos 1990; Vivanco 2006). These dynamics continue to the present, symbolized most recently by the country's contentious debate over the Dominican Republic-Central America-United States Free Trade Agreement (CAFTA-DR), which state leaders aggressively promoted in the face of substantial public disagreement and mobilization (see Raventós, this volume).

The construction of environmental policies and bureaucracy took place at the height of the most aggressive pressure for neoliberal reforms. Most analyses of the relationship between neoliberal reforms and the environment focus on the fundamental irreconcilability of the two categories. They point to causal linkages between structural adjustment and environmental degradation, in which the former exerts tremendous pressure on the latter through increases in resource-intensive modes of export-oriented production to address structural indebtedness (Goldman 2001). In Costa Rica, state leaders sought to address these contradictions with the language of "sustainable development," expressed as an approach to economic development that emphasizes the necessity of conserving natural resources, and which addresses local peoples' livelihood concerns by seeking alternatives to resource-intensive productive activities (Wapner 1996, 83). The pursuit of sustainable development has come to define policy debate and public rhetoric, captured best by President José Figueres's regular pronouncements during the 1990s that Costa Rica was a global "laboratory" for the concept. Significantly, the language of "sustainable development" aided state leaders in co-opting the more aggressive and oppositional nature of much environmental activism, which had long been critical of agrarian development patterns that were based on the destruction of natural ecosystems, because it allowed state leaders to express their commitments to nature *and* economic development (see Boyer and Cardona Peñalva, this volume, for an account of approaches to agrarian development in Honduras).

In contrast with the category "environment," sustainable development and neoliberalism share a similar ideological framework. They both commit to capitalist production and markets as the basic model of organizing society. Their ideal, even grounding, assumption, is the priority of perpetual economic expansion through the efficient operation of capitalist markets and sustaining existing consumption patterns. This point has led some critics of sustainable development to call attention to the paradoxical nature of the phrase (Escobar 1995; Mora 1993). Sustainable development may imagine a "nature-friendly" approach, but, these critics assert, it is based on a universalist model promoting a resource-intensive consumer society.

It should also be said that neoliberal reforms and sustainable development both emerge out of suspicion, if not hostility, to state institutions. Neoliberalism assumes that the state prevents efficient allocation of capital and investment; sustainable development recognizes that funds and technical assistance often do not reach communities struggling to develop viable economies because corrupt state institutions divert resources to ineffective initiatives (Goldman 2001). In their most idealistic moments, visionaries of both sustainable development and neoliberalism imagine "rational" and "efficient" communities linking to broader markets without interference from governments (Wapner 1996).

The broader context of neoliberal reforms and their constraints on public budgets have ensured that government initiatives to build environmental regulatory capacity or to undertake other environmental sustainability initiatives have often been weak—or simply shells through which resource exploitation takes place, by, for example, elites who gain special access to permits for logging in protected areas (common in Costa Rica during the 1990s) (Burnett 1997). This situation reflects and has fed into a key tenet of sustainable development: the rhetorical privileging of grassroots initiatives. As Mahjid Rahnema (1990) points out, the language of grassroots community participation, so hopeful in its attention to common people's self-determination and so central to sustainable development's rhetoric, has served as political cover for neoliberalism's commitment to the privatization of control over public goods.

But the convergence between neoliberalism and sustainable development based on ideological kinship is not by itself enough to explain how Costa Ricans built a system of formally protected natural areas and a tourism economy based on a green image. These ideologies were implemented in specific ways under specific political-economic conditions. One of these conditions was the emergence during the 1970s and 1980s of a global movement to "Save the Rainforest," which in its early years invested heavily in Costa Rica. Certain key transnational environmental institutions, including the World Wildlife Fund, The Nature Conservancy, and the International Union for the Conservation of Nature, identified Costa Rica as a politically stable and ecologically important location. With the support of key political figures in Costa Rica, they channeled substantial resources into efforts to create a system of protected areas, a state environmental bureaucracy in the Ministry of Energy and Environment, and a proliferating field of environmental NGOs (Evans 1999). These same organizations also enabled Costa Rica to become an early beneficiary of debt-for-nature swaps, in which a small percentage of foreign debt was cancelled in exchange for investments in protected areas.

Seeking an economic justification for setting aside protected areas in a country with a long history of agrarian conflict, the government rapidly expanded the country's protected area system and linked it to privately controlled tourism development to promote economic growth. With its exceptional biodiversity (five percent of the world's species reside there) and one of the only stable systems of protected areas in the tropical Americas, Costa Rica began drawing North American scientists in the 1960s, laying the groundwork for a nature-based tourism economy (Laarman and Perdue 1989). During the height of the debt crisis, state planning officials seeking new sources of income decided to expand the tourism economy. They implemented plans for infrastructure development, marketing, and regulatory incentives for foreign investment in the tourism sector. President Oscar Arias's receipt of the Nobel Peace Prize in 1987 for his regional peace initiatives further boosted the fledgling tourism industry, offering international visibility of Costa Rica as an island of political tranquility in a conflict-ridden region (Rolbein 1989). The long-term vision of Costa Rican tourism planners has been oriented toward beach resorts (especially in the northwest province of Guanacaste) that could compete with Mexico for middle class North American "sun and sand" tourists—hardly an image of eco-friendliness. But "ecotourism" became a powerful tool used by the state tourism marketing agency that helped attract both international investment and well-educated, higher-income tourists desiring tropical nature.

In channeling those desires, the Costa Rican tourism sector has identified, and indeed helped shape, a lucrative segment of global tourism markets. Under certain conditions of scale and community participation, tourism has indeed become a means of generating nature appreciation among visitors and community members and utilizing natural resources to generate income (Vivanco 2007). But it is typically not as socially and environmentally benign as the prefix "eco" indicates. This contradiction has in the past decade opened the country's eco-efforts to increasing critique by environmental activists, scientists, and tourism monitoring groups (Barkin 1996; McLaren 2003; Mowforth and Munt 2003). An extensive range of activities takes place under labels whose relationship to ideals of environmental sustainability are suspect. Examples range from outright "greenwashing" (empty claims to environmental virtuousness, such as when hotels claim to be ecologically sound by asking visitors to reuse their towels, while obscuring the fact that the hotel spews untreated wastewaters into local gulleys and waterways) to Tarzan swings, bridges through the rainforest canopies, and golf-cart rentals, whose contrast from ecotourism's ideals of contemplation of wildlife and minimal impact on a landscape could not be more apparent (Vivanco 2006). Throughout Costa Rica, tourism development has created tremendous community-level conflict and resentment. Hotel and infrastructure construction has caused ecological destruction; traditional community uses of the landscape have been displaced; poor labor conditions abound and evidence of sexual exploitation has risen; landscapes and cultural traditions have been turned into commodities; communities have felt overrun by outsiders who do not respect local values; and up to eighty percent of what tourists actually spend is "leaked" to foreign-owned providers (McLaren 2003; Vivanco 2007).

Throughout the 1990s, a number of Costa Rica's tourism leaders—in particular, ecolodge owners and government tourism officials—began to face threats to their claims about tourism's credentials for supporting healthy environments and communities. At the same time, a small transnational movement started to emerge among tourism intellectuals and environmental advocates to promote accountability to such claims through audits and certifications. Enter the tourism ecolabel movement, which as Bendell and Font (2004, 152), promoters of sustainable tourism certifications, observe, is "instrumental to improving the long-term viability of this industry."

New Accountabilities: Certifying Sustainable Tourism in Costa Rica

In recent years, the forestry, coffee, and artisanal textile industries have implemented ecolabels to align their productive practices with global regulatory regimes related to the environment (Goldman 2001). But these industries pale in comparison to the size of the global tourism economy, the world's largest economic sector, whose environmental and social impacts have become increasingly acute. So transnational tourism and environmental policy intellectuals turned their attention to ecolabels as a mechanism for supporting reform in the conduct of the tourism industry (Bendell and Font 2004; Font 2002; Honey 2002). Costa Rica's prestige in the global green tourism pantheon, and the specific connections many of these intellectuals already had with the Costa Rican tourism industry and environmental NGOs, made it an apposite location to develop these mechanisms.

The most recognizable tourism ecolabel in Costa Rica is the Certification of Sustainable Tourism (CST), established in 1997. Overseen by the state's

Institute of Tourism (ICT), it is unique among the world's sustainable tourism ecolabels, which are mostly affiliated with private third-party organizations. The CST focuses on hotels. Like many other voluntary market-based certifications, it encourages hotels to achieve standards of ecological, business, and social sustainability "beyond compliance." "Beyond compliance" connotes a standard higher than minimal standards of law and state regulation, based on a presumption of a weak state (Cashore, Auld, and Newsom 2004). It is a space of social action outside of formal laws and regulations, but also not altogether lawless. It exists as a kind of parallel universe in which certain principles and practices assumed universally applicable are meant to be achieved voluntarily.

The commonly accepted rationale among businesses for pursuing the standards is to gain the right to use a label of distinction—in the CST it is anywhere from one to five leaves, depending on the applicant's level of correspondence to the standards. In theory, this label offers an upper hand in competitive marketing as consumers sharing similar values flock to that particular product or service, opening the door to charging a higher premium. It also staves off potentially more stringent "command and control" responses by the state (Cashore, Auld, and Newsom 2004; Honey 2002).

The CST does not claim to address or reform tourist behavior itself, or even claim status as official state policy. Rather, it aims to provide incentives for the national tourism industry to align itself more closely with the country's stated goals of sustainable development without turning to any enforceable regulatory mechanisms. Part of this approach is based in ideology—the neoliberal state should not place barriers to market operations. But it is also practical. Given budgetary limitations, the state would find it nearly impossible to enforce any stringent sustainability-related regulations. Reflecting a broad (and unenforceable) definition of "sustainability," then, the CST audits hotels on dozens of standards, ranging from specific questions about the installation of technologies that might reduce the use of energy and the use of biodegradable cleaning fluids ("infrastructure sustainability") to whether or not the hotel has a customer satisfaction survey and uses standard financial accounting procedures ("business sustainability") to whether it allows patrons to bring sex workers back to their rooms or provides workers with contracts, and how often the hotel contributes funds to events in the outlying community ("social sustainability").

The tendency in sustainable tourism certification schemes is to identify "low hanging fruit"—issues easily addressed. It abridges information about the broader impacts of tourism itself by redirecting attention to technical indicators and the reassurances that a monitoring system is in place (Strathern 2000). The CST is riddled with such contradictions (Blake 2001). For example, the CST audits for high-efficiency light bulbs but does not account for ecological or social disruptions created by hotel construction. Similarly, the CST asks about forms of alternative energy in a hotel but does not inquire if visitors to the hotel used alternative forms of energy to get there. Such reductionism does not just erase the linkages between tourism and environmental degradation, but threatens to gut the very claims to environmental and social "sustainability" inherent in the certification scheme. But perhaps this is asking too much of any certification scheme: as "rituals of verification," they can do little more than ensure that certain minimal standards are met (Power 1997; Strathern 2000).

In a community like Puerto Viejo, where this chapter opened, few local hotels aspire to CST standards. Indeed, only a handful of the several dozen area ecolodges have enrolled in the program, or any sustainability-related certification program. One of the reasons often given by certification advocates is "ignorance" of the program and certification more generally. When I surveyed hotel owners and managers in the area, however, the majority had heard of the program, if not tourism certification regimes more generally, and knew certain key details about the CST. One of those details was that even though the audit is free it would likely require substantial investment in technologies to meet efficiency standards, something out of reach of most local businesses. As one owner of a small, locally owned guesthouse observed, "We just can't pay for [it]! This certification issue seems like it is for the big hotels, the foreign-owned luxury ones, that have thousands of dollars—not *colones* [Costa Rican currency], like we have! We have difficulty sometimes just paying the light and water, especially during the low season. How can we afford those things?" He viewed the issue through a prism of inequality, going on to explain that in Puerto Viejo, local families that opened small guest houses over the years to meet tourist demand for lodging have been increasingly at a disadvantage in relation to larger hotels owned by wealthy foreigners and families from the capital San José, especially when it comes to effective marketing. He was fully aware that enrollment in the CST carried special access to marketing opportunities by the ICT, but that the cost of getting into the CST was too high for the small players like him. Indeed, all three hotels in Puerto Viejo certified when I was conducting this research in the mid-2000s were large upper-end ecolodges (two foreign-owned) that charged $120–$150 (U.S.) per night, a stark contrast with this guest house's $35 per night. He ended on a somewhat bitter note: "Look, we operate on a small scale to begin with, with much smaller impacts than these big hotels. We use fewer resources than they do, and now they get special treatment."

That notion of "special treatment" is an especially awkward issue for the CST, mainly because of its formal affiliation with a state ministry, the Costa Rican Institute of Tourism (ICT). GATS, the General Agreement on Trade and Services, of which Costa Rica is a signatory, prohibits states from putting into place rules that create barriers to trade in services, such as rules that discriminate against actors because it makes their conditions of production too costly or difficult to achieve (Bendell and Font 2004). These rules are intended to prevent countries from giving preferential treatment to domestic economic actors at the expense of foreign investors. The purpose of creating a certification program like the CST is thus not to require businesses to implement certain standards, but rather to support businesses that take steps to mitigate their social and environmental impacts. But even that preferential support—all government-supported certification programs by definition favor businesses that meet certain standards—is susceptible to GATS prohibitions. Right now, sustainable tourism certifications are still small-scale enough not to warrant much attention from GATS and potentially aggrieved foreign investors.

Nevertheless, partially as a result of this broader context of neoliberal trade policy, the state cannot openly manage the program. The CST's operations take place in the shadows. Thus the hyper-transparency expected of applicants to the program—as illustrated in the introduction to this chapter—contrasts sharply with the oblique ways the state "administers" the standards and conducts audits. By executive decree, the National Commission for Accreditation, a hybrid public-private entity institutionally separate from ICT, actually sets the program's standards and conducts audits. The commission's membership includes representation from two state ministries (the ICT and the Ministry of Energy and Environment) and representatives from major educational institutions, the national tourism chamber, and international conservation groups.

On the surface, this hybrid composition establishes the third-party independence and legitimates the standard-setting and auditing processes. But in effect something more dramatic has taken place. *It takes rule-making clout away from a sovereign state.* It moves that capacity to coordinated action among entities, some private and not traditionally involved in high levels of rule-making. The state's role in the accreditation board is as another "interest group" in a process that operates as a kind of parallel state, using material practices and knowledge production closely mimicking state power, with the support of state institutions themselves. But all of this takes place in the shadows of the state where the standard-setting processes themselves are shared between technical experts and not open to public scrutiny.

One result is to replace one kind of accountability—the expectations and claims citizens place on their state institutions—with another in which social institutions with no clear lines of accountability push a citizenry to answer to the standards they implement. One explanation for this situation may be what Michael Herzfeld (1994) calls "bureaucratic indifference"—a phrase that seems to characterize neatly a typical stance of many neoliberal state institutions. But the state's decision to authorize new accreditation regimes shapes social action in subtle ways.. One of these influences, as the guest house owner quoted above clearly understood, was to provide financially well-situated businesses, owned by non-locals, with new marketing access, while locally owned enterprises remain invisible to state marketing mechanisms. Accustomed to living in a politically and economically marginalized region, residents of Puerto Viejo are under no illusions about the state caring about claims about unequal treatment in state tourism marketing programs. (Costa Rica's Caribbean coast has long been peripheral to the national political economy and racial imagination because of its large indigenous and Afro-Caribbean population—see Anderson [this volume] for an account of political-economic positionality in relation to ethnic difference and tourism in Honduras.) But here is where the murkiness of accountability strikes me as most apparent: although this guest house owner did not understand who actually ran the program, when I explained it was an accreditation group composed of two state ministries and mostly private organizations, he responded knowingly, "Ah, yes, environmentalists and the big hotel owners who control the national tourism council." When I asked where he could address his grievances expressed about unequal access, he shrugged, "Why would they listen to me? They don't need to."

It is interesting to contrast this murkiness surrounding the nature of public accountability with the hyper-transparency expected of those who do actually seek certification. For those hotels and lodges, the process begins with a self-audit, which introduces owners and staff to the standards and suggests actions necessary to reach the standards: installing energy-efficient technologies, creating new management policies, implementing training programs for employees, etc. Once those changes are implemented, a team from the National Commission for Accreditation conducts a formal audit, at no charge to the hotel. Depending on what kinds of systems, technologies, and policies are already in place, it can nevertheless be a costly process to prepare the hotel for a formal audit, anywhere from several thousand to tens of thousands of dollars for a medium-sized ecolodge like the one that opens this chapter.

Beyond the financial commitment, the certification process requires cultivating a new awareness in hotel staff—from the management down to the receptionists and laundry and cooking staffs—of how actions each individual takes either meet or diverge from the external standards. At that first ecolodge in Puerto Viejo (not to mention many of the dozen and a half certified hotels I visited), management explained that they strive to develop this awareness through training programs and increased scrutiny of staff activities. Staff did not always completely internalize the expectations, though. Indeed many only vaguely understood the standards, much less their role in an ongoing shift in which their quotidian actions were being conceived as a new form of "environmental governance." But most did recognize that their workplace's enrollment in the program brought higher levels of managerial surveillance. They had to adjust behaviors they had taken for granted before, constantly self-monitoring in the name of efficiency and best practice. Sometimes they were expected to check the standards before doing anything else. For staff at all levels these adjustments take place in the most mundane contexts: managing cooking grease, using cleaning fluids, dealing with trash, repairing broken facilities, monitoring who guests bring into the hotel at night, and so on. These standards also touch on issues of bodily discipline and comportment. As various staff members explained, they had to change well-worn habits and thought patterns in their work lives.

For at least several workers, these processes also increased their awareness about issues of compliance and accountability. As one member of the hotel's kitchen staff commented to me, "Don't get me wrong, I think a lot of these new things we are being asked to do are good. We need to care for nature, and I see that some of the things we do are harmful. But I do ask myself sometimes where these ideas of what we're supposed to do come from, and who is responsible for them." She did recognize that she and her co-workers may not be responsible *for* them, but they are now responsible *to* them. One of the powerful aspects of market-based certifications is that their origins seem authorless. They are typically presented as products of the market itself, and workers are expected to implement the standards universally, across time and space, to ensure compliance and attract consumer attention (Strathern 2000). By locating accountability for environmental sustainability in the relationship between the service provider and the consumer, however, certification regimes place new requirements in particular on service providers—willing or not, as the case may be with hotel workers—to engage in constant self-monitoring.

The trade-off for increased self-monitoring, according to certification's advocates, is that a certified hotel gains specific marketing advantages and the ability to charge higher premiums. Yet one of the puzzles of the CST is that levels of countrywide participation have been quite low—the Puerto Viejo tourism sector is not unique in that regard. Since the program's inception in 1997, the number of participants has fluctuated between approximately 40 and 90 (currently 93), about 8 to 10 percent of the hotel sector nationwide. In addition, every few years, the list of certified hotels changes substantially; some old ones have dropped out of the program, and new ones have taken their place. (Indeed, the same ecolodge that opens this paper is no longer enrolled in the CST.) A major reason for the fluctuation has been that many businesses have not gained the purported benefits of certification because there is little consumer knowledge or demand. Consumers, not workers, have yet to comply with the idea that their travels should adhere to certain standards. In fact, whether that consumer awareness will materialize has emerged as a major concern of certification's advocates and exists as a new front in the movement to promote sustainable tourism ecolabels (Black and Crabtree 2007).

Conclusion

In Costa Rica, environmentalism has rarely risen to the level of a truly "popular" social movement, which is to say, a movement that emerged out of a widespread desire by popular sectors to protect natural resources and pursue more nature-friendly economic development policies. Similar to other Central American countries (Berger 1997), it has been pushed by certain elites—scientists, urban-based intellectuals, a handful of government officials—whose struggles and successes were made possible largely by funding received from international organizations and the rise of a supportive nongovernmental environmentalism sector. All of this took place in the context of a transitional state, whose openness to formal nature protection appeared primarily to support new forms of economic development through tourism. Nevertheless, environmentalism in Costa Rica has been in important respects an oppositional movement. It challenges the destructive effects of uncontrolled logging and elite-controlled export-oriented agriculture, and the absence or venal management of agrarian reform that ended up consolidating productive lands in few (or foreign) hands and pushing landless peasants into marginal lands and fragile ecosystems (Berger 1997; Nygren 2000; Stonich 1993).

Tourism ecolabels are often viewed as a cutting edge of action in support of environmental sustainability. But they hardly seem oppositional. Indeed, they fit very comfortably with neoliberal market processes and discipline, and in fact, emerge squarely out of them. They represent an example of what some scholars have begun calling "neoliberal environmentalism" (Goldman 2001; McCarthy and Prudham 2004), in which green initiatives have been "domesticated"—co-opted and redefined—through the ideological and practical armature of market-friendly "sustainable development." Far from being a neutral tool, neoliberal environmental initiatives dramatically reinforce the role of capitalist markets in guiding the relationship between communities and natural processes. In the process they gut any threats that environmentalism, as an oppositional social movement, might pose toward neoliberal policies (Beder 2001). This is a more complex situation than merely "greenwashing"—the common business practice of referring to green credentials absent in practice. Ecolabels are precisely a form of neoliberal environmentalism, entailing the creation of policies and programs that reflect the priority of extending the market.

Can a market-based mechanism like tourism ecolabels really cover the environmental "governance gap"? It remains to be seen. The fact that these mechanisms tend to address issues such as light bulbs and biodegradable soaps but avoid root problems like the impacts caused by the existence of a hotel in a fragile ecosystem in the first place, raises some doubts. But for Costa Ricans, these mechanisms raise a bigger set of issues about who is responsible for addressing the country's ongoing environmental crises, and which social institutions will take on accountability for those actions. One thing seems certain: under current circumstances, the role of the state is likely to remain largely in the shadows.

13 Central America Comes to the "Cradle of Democracy"

Immigration and Neoliberalization in Williamsburg, Virginia

*Jennifer Bickham Mendez**

It is 7:30 A.M. at the 7-Eleven® convenience store in historic Williamsburg, Virginia. The street is lined with motels, hotels, and chain restaurants that target the estimated four million tourists who visit the area each year. It is still early, but the convenience store has already been a site of bustling activity. Customers dressed in eighteenth century costumes compete with tourists sporting "patriot passes" clipped to their shirts to grab morning coffee before heading to Colonial Williamsburg where they will perform and observe a reenactment of the daily life of European "immigrants" in the colonial capital of Virginia. But others crowd the convenience store, too.

A pickup truck emblazoned with the logo of a local roofing company and driven by a white male in his mid 40s pulls up, and group of young Salvadoran and Guatemalan men rush into the store to buy Cokes, hot dogs, and 7-Eleven®'s newest addition, *taquitos* (rolled tacos), before they head to the job site located in the nearby gated community. On a break from her shift cleaning hotel rooms, a Salvadoran woman in a Country Inn smock enters and selects items from the shelf. As she waits in line for the cashier, she remembers that she needs to take the bus to the local Hispanic foods store to send money to her *cantón* (hamlet) in Santa Ana. School will start soon, and she knows her mother will need extra cash to afford school uniforms for the grandchildren.

Such a scene is increasingly commonplace in Greater Williamsburg,[1] an area perhaps best known as home to the historic sites of Colonial Williamsburg, the capital of the eighteenth century British colony; Jamestown, which was the site of the first European settlement in the United States; and Yorktown with its battlefields dating back to the Revolutionary War. It is also my home, where I have lived, worked, and raised my children for nearly fifteen years. Like the men and women whom I see every day as they walk from their crowded apartments or run-down rentals tucked out of public view to work multiple shifts in tourist-oriented restaurants and hotels, work and family brought me to the place where early immigrants—European settlers and African slaves—first encountered the Powhatan Nation in the 1600s. During the years since I arrived, the area's population has rapidly expanded, as it has transformed into an upscale destination—for tourists who flock to Colonial Williamsburg and theme parks like Busch Gardens and more recently for wealthy, out-of-state retirees attracted to the area's historic appeal, as well as the low taxes, inexpensive real estate prices (relative to the urban centers and suburban areas in states to the north), and high quality of life. But Williamsburg has also become a destination for another group—immigrants from El Salvador, Honduras, Guatemala, Nicaragua, and Mexico who tidy rooms in the area's many hotels, maintain the grounds and golf courses in gated communities, and wash dishes in restaurants where tourists and locals dine (Massey 2008).

In the 1990s my research interests (admittedly shaped by my marriage to a Nicaraguan, immigrant man as well as by coming of age during the solidarity movement of the 1980s) led me to post-revolutionary Nicaragua where I studied the gender dynamics of globalization and women's labor organizing in the growing maquila sector, the neoliberal answer to unemployment and poverty in the region. My research uncovered new gendered dimensions of transnational organizing for labor rights amid the "transition to democracy" after the Sandinistas' defeat at the electoral polls (Mendez 2005). Years later, my continued interest in understanding the ways in which globalization unfurls in local settings led me down a new research path and to the realization that neither my move to this place where colonialism is openly celebrated through daily re-enactments of an antisepticized version of life in eighteenth-century Virginia, nor a painful and traumatic divorce, meant that I had left Central America behind.

Beginning in the late 1990s, like other small towns, cities, rural areas, and suburbs in the South Atlantic seaboard and across the United States, Williamsburg, Virginia began to witness an unprecedented influx of Spanish-speaking newcomers hailing primarily from Mexico and El Salvador (Guzmán and McConnell 2002; Massey 2008). Central Americans, including Hondurans, Guatemalans and Nicaraguans, were drawn to the area by a plethora of entry-level jobs in hotels and restaurants, as well as construction and landscaping. Following devastating natural disasters in El Salvador, Nicaragua, and Honduras, émigrés from these countries received Temporary Protective Status (TPS). Thus, many Central American pioneers were able to secure work permits and valid social security numbers, facilitating their incorporation into the labor and housing markets.

For the growing native-born community the arrival of these newcomers went largely unnoticed at first. The percentage of the local population made up of non-white Hispanics was relatively small in absolute terms (2.6 percent in 2000) (U.S. Census Bureau 2011), and they worked as a largely invisible labor force in the expanding service sector. And like many new immigrant destinations in what has been termed the "Nuevo South" (Mohl 2003), the housing bubble helped spur a boom in population growth and stimulated commercial development, creating a labor demand that brought a steady stream of Latino immigrant workers to the area.[2] Thus, despite the low absolute numbers (though almost certainly undercounted in the 2000 census), an increase in the population of newcomers from Latin America began to signal an unprecedented demographic shift, with the number of Hispanics more than tripling between 2000 and 2010 (from roughly 2,600 to 6,900).[3] As the families of early pioneers began to join them, immigrant women gave birth in local hospitals, and families began to seek health care and other services in the community; brown-skinned, non-English speaking Central Americans and Mexicans became an increasingly visible presence in Williamsburg.

This chapter focuses on the incorporation and exclusion of Central Americans in Greater Williamsburg. I situate this case within a broader, transnational framework in order to shed light on the localized dynamics of global capitalism and the social arrangements that support and sustain them. Of particular interest in this analysis are the spatial dynamics of a neoliberal pattern of development and the ways in which they are implicated in the establishment, enforcement, and maintenance of the parameters of social belonging within the Williamsburg community.

Economic and demographic transitions in "new immigrant destinations" are embedded within a global system of capital accumulation that is sustained by the displacement and regulated mobility of marginalized people. In an era of neoliberal globalization, multifarious processes expropriate small-scale agricultural producers in Central America and incorporate former peasants into newly globally integrated labor markets in restructured economies in the Global North (Harvey 2010). Thus, Williamsburg's transition from a tourist-town in a largely rural setting to a growing upscale destination relies on a transnational labor supply chain and an immigrant workforce attracted to and recruited for seasonal, entry-level service jobs.

The development model that has corresponded with Williamsburg's growth over the last two decades has given rise to a dispersed and de-centralized spatial organization that has inhibited the formation of social connections and networks that contribute to immigrants' social and economic mobility (Deeb-Sossa and Mendez 2008). The isolating effects of the organization of public space in Greater Williamsburg works in tandem with race, gender, and immigration status to construct and maintain a group that is readily incorporated as a temporary and seasonal workforce but whose social participation is constrained as "partial citizens" (Coutin et al. 2002).

In new immigrant-receiving sites across the U.S. South, Central American and Mexican immigrants find themselves in difficult-to-navigate surroundings that lack the comforts and familiarities of the "ethnic enclaves" of gateways like Los Angeles or Chicago (Singer 2004; Smith and Furuseth 2006).

And immigrants' ready incorporation into the labor market is not matched by inclusion as full members of the community (see Lippard and Gallagher 2011). Their access to public space and resources needed for social reproduction are limited, policed through various institutional mechanisms, including the enforcement of immigration policy by local police and restrictions on eligibility for public services and social benefits enforced by various institutional "gatekeepers" (Deeb-Sossa and Mendez 2008). Finally, processes of incorporation and marginalization occur differently for men and women. Central Americans' arrival in Williamsburg demonstrates how gender inequalities both sustain and are exacerbated by neoliberalization.

Williamsburg's development and growth over the last two decades has resembled "rural restructuring" (Gosnell and Abrams 2010), resulting in the transformation of the area from a quaint tourist town in a largely rural setting to a "suburb without a city," with strip malls, big box stores, and a car culture due to limited public transportation. A key source of population growth has been wealthy retirees from Northern Virginia and other states to the north, who sell their homes and purchase multiple times the square footage in picturesque, historic surroundings—perhaps even on a golf course in one of the several gated or retirement communities marketed to this group.[4] The housing and construction boom combined with the influx of this group of "amenity migrants" stimulated commercial development as well as an increased demand for low-wage labor, in turn attracting immigrants from Central America and Mexico (Nelson and Nelson 2011).

Employing a transnational framework to analyze the convergence of local patterns of development sustained by linked migration streams of affluent "transplants" and economically displaced Central Americans with the construction and regulation of social boundaries in greater Williamsburg brings into focus the dual character of neoliberalization. Processes of "accumulation through dispossession" facilitate the establishment of conditions that maximize the free flow of capital, opening local and national markets to global trade (Harvey 2003). Global economic integration has been accompanied by processes that reinforce national borders as well as social (often racial-ethnic) boundaries, delineating and maintaining different forms of social belonging. Newly emerging governing strategies, including intensified immigration control, draw upon and contribute to the construction of both racialized and gendered categories of social membership within nations, with differing rights and privileges accorded to distinct groups (Ong 2006). Thus, the reinforcement of and redrawing of geographic and social "borders" ("rebordering") constitute a central imperative of neoliberalism—the "flip side" of globalization's open markets and free trade (Staudt and Spener 1998).

In Williamsburg economic incorporation and social exclusion draw on social inequalities of gender, race, and even age to render Central Americans both invisible as a labor force and highly visible as racially and culturally distinct group of "others." The erasure of rights and personhood that results from the "legal nonexistence" (Coutin 2000) of undocumented immigrants creates a state of subjugation that results not only in fear and insecurity, but also in confinement to low wage jobs and vulnerabilities as workers, and sometimes even the denial of basic human needs, such as access to housing, education, food, and health care. (Burrell, this volume, traces a similar process.)

This chapter draws on over seven years of ethnographic research with and in the Central American and Mexican immigrant community in Williamsburg. I explore how these dual, countervailing projects of economic inclusion and social and political exclusion (debordering and rebordering) create a set of hardships that impact Central American immigrants as they make lives for themselves in Williamsburg. In the pages that follow I take up these broad questions: What does Central Americans' arrival in the "cradle of democracy" tell us about global politics of social belonging in the context of neoliberalism? And how are social differences of race and gender implicated in them? Specifically, I examine three sets of intersecting structural conditions in Williamsburg and their exclusionary effects on Central American newcomers—social isolation stemming from Williamsburg's suburbanized, spatial organization, criminalization and local immigration enforcement, and gender inequalities in the home and workplace.

This analysis uncovers how the difficult postwar transitions of Central America in the 1990s and early 2000s are embedded within larger processes of neoliberalization that link sites in the global economy through transna-

Figure 13.1. Department of Motor Vehicles—an important "border enforcer" in Williamsburg. A nearby bodega offers international money transfer services for Central Americans to send remittances to their home communitites. Jennifer Bickham Mendez

tional chains of labor supply and demand and separate capital accumulation from social reproduction (see Robinson 2003, chapter 5). From this view we can see local immigration enforcement, the spatial dynamics of suburban/ gentrified development patterns, and gendered and racialized construction of social boundaries as tied to neoliberal reforms in Central American countries and Central America's ever deeper articulation to a growing world economy (Robinson 2003, 253). For former peasants throughout the isthmus who have been displaced from their land and livelihood, migration northward became a logical and singular survival strategy (See Binford; and Burrell, this volume). Thus, Central American economic deportees become the region's latest export destined for a U.S. (labor) market.

Social Isolation and Dependency in a Suburbanized Destination

Recent immigrants from Central America arrive in the Williamsburg area to find themselves in bewildering new surroundings where they face social isolation, a major obstacle affecting their transition to new work and living styles. There are few public spaces where they can gather to socialize, network, and exchange information, a situation exacerbated by limited and isolated low-income housing. The daunting process of accessing medical care in a monolingual environment, applying for a driver's license, or registering children for school imply an added layer of securing transportation and navigating a confusing, suburban landscape. For many, even after a number of years of residence in Williamsburg, trips outside of the journey from home to work consist merely of venturing to the grocery store or Walmart. Social isolation also fosters dependency on family members who arrived earlier or on guides who arrange for immigrants' transit to Williamsburg after crossing the border into the United States, and with whom they reside until they find jobs and housing.

Lorena's[5] experiences are typical of many Central American immigrants in Williamsburg. Hailing from a tenant-farming family, Lorena left her *cantón* (hamlet) to work in San Salvador as a domestic worker after her father abandoned her mother. She returned to her home in the department of Santa Ana when she learned of the opportunity to make the journey northward accompanied by a guide from a neighboring hamlet who had brought her brother to Williamsburg a few years earlier. She made the dangerous journey accompanied by a female friend of the family, crossing most of Guatemala on foot. Upon their arrival in Williamsburg the women shared an apartment with a group of men in a complex tucked behind hotels and restaurants geared for tourists. Few places were accessible on foot, besides a gas station and other

Figure 13.2. A shortage of affordable housing in Williamsburg has resulted from rapid commercial "upscale" development. Williamsburg, VA., Jennifer Bickham Mendez

hotels along the tourist strip. She and her traveling companion soon discovered that her brother and other family members had scattered around the area and had no room for them in their already crowded living arrangements. As a result, they were completely dependent on their host for all their basic needs, for establishing contact with the world around them, and orienting them when they ventured from their secluded location.

Limited low-income housing in the area poses a major hardship, especially in the cases of undocumented immigrant families. The scarce housing market worsened when apartment complexes began to enforce rental requirements more strictly, requiring credit checks, social security numbers, and documentation of income. In addition, a trailer park that housed many Mexican and Central American immigrants was razed to make room for a new hotel, leaving the occupants to seek housing in an increasingly tight market. Some brokered deals with local hotels to live on-site, which increased their isolation and their vulnerability, adding to their dependency on employers. Tired of the sexual advances of the men in the crowded apartment that she shared, Lorena moved in with Leonardo, a young man who hailed from a hamlet not far from her own in El Salvador and whose temporary legal status enabled him to rent an apartment in his name.

Social isolation has a particularly acute effect on women, especially those with young children. The suburbanized organization of public space impacts women's abilities to form social and community ties that help them find less exploitative, better-paying jobs, share childcare, pool resources and develop social capital. Daní admits that "it is easier for the man to work, than for me. Since he [her husband] has a car, he can mobilize to go wherever."

The high cost of childcare and transportation difficulties often gives women no choice but to drop out of the labor market after giving birth. Both Daní and Clara cited their working as positive aspects of their life in Williamsburg, even given their struggles with language differences, mistreatment at the hands of English-speaking co-workers and managers, and transportation issues. However, for both women the birth of their children added joy and meaning, but also hardships to their lives as they struggled to contend with a drop in household income and to care for their babies in relative isolation, far from extended families.

Mothers of small children in an immigrant parent support group spoke tearfully of their loneliness and separation from their families. While they waited for their husbands and partners to return from work, they filled the hours watching Univision or talking on the phone to relatives (a high priority for many recent arrivals was to send remittances so their families could buy a cell phone), rarely leaving their apartments.

Over the years changes slowly began to occur in the community. Local churches offered services in Spanish and became sites for immigrants to gather. A number of money-wiring, Hispanic food groceries, and a few Latino immigrant-owned businesses opened their doors. Nonetheless, the formation of indigenous communal infrastructures and support networks that immigrants have relied on so heavily in other traditional immigrant settlement areas for social capital (Massey 2008; Portes and Zhou 1992) evolved slowly, their progress impeded by the social isolation caused in part by the spatial organization of this recent immigrant destination. In the next section, I examine another facet of the spatialization of immigration: the implications of transportation difficulties in the suburbanized setting of Williamsburg as they relate to immigration enforcement and criminalization.

Local Immigration Enforcement and Policing Public Space

The isolated location of low-cost housing, the infrequency of public transportation and the irregular hours and low wages in entry-level service jobs, which often require Latino/a immigrants to work more than one job, make transportation by private vehicle nearly a necessity. And yet, eligibility requirements for obtaining a license have been dramatically restricted in the wake of 9/11. Indeed, the Commonwealth of Virginia was one of the first to pass and implement a law mandating proof of legal residency in the United States to acquire a driver's license (Rivera 2004).

Operating a vehicle without a legal license puts immigrant drivers at risk for apprehension by local police. Routine traffic violations can even result in deportations when drivers either fail to produce a license or offer an international drivers' license as identification. In Williamsburg in 2006, the U.S. Immigration and Customs Enforcement (ICE), a federal agency empowered to enforce and maintain borders and "bordering," shifted its procedures, and officials began instructing local police to detain immigrants if suspected of illegal status in order to run their information through the immigration database. Previously, immigrants were only apprehended if they were wanted in connection with crimes (Kerr 2006).

Even in cases in which immigration officials do not become involved, driving without a legal license can have a differentially punitive impact on immigrants. In the spring of 2007, the Virginia General Assembly passed the Virginia Remedial Fees, a set of fines for moving violations amounting in up to $3,000.00 (U.S.). This policy was enacted to generate state revenue in order to fund a variety of transportation projects without raising other taxes, with the side benefit of "cracking down" on "abusive drivers"—those guilty of severe traffic offenses such as drunken and reckless driving, but also driving without a valid license (Craig 2007). Because immigrants who lack proper documentation are ineligible for drivers' licenses, routine traffic stops often resulted in charges that incurred these fees—as much as $900.00 for the first violation. And perhaps even more significantly, such offenses required court appearances, a terrifying prospect for immigrants in a context of the new era of strict immigration enforcement.

The enforcement of immigration policy by local law enforcement reflects a recent trend in immigration control in the United States through which "border enforcement" has been "pushed inwards" (Varsanyi 2010). Beginning in the 1990s, a series of immigration reforms have extended the authority to enforce immigration policy beyond the exclusive purview of the federal government, according it to a variety of local, institutional actors. The localization of immigration enforcement has, thus, multiplied the number of interior spaces subject to immigration oversight, expanding the list of those authorized to detain suspected "illegals," alert ICE to individuals' immigration status, or restrict immigrants' access to services and public benefits (Kretsedemas 2008). In this "new era" of immigration enforcement a deep convergence between criminal law and immigration enforcement has also expanded the array of criminal charges—aggravated felonies—that can result in expedited deportation from the United States and narrowed recourses to the courts to prolong or contest removal (Coleman 2007a). The result of sixteen years of law reform has been "the legal transformation of undocumented migrants in the interior into 'permanent criminals'" (Coleman 2007b, 66), increasing vulnerability, uncertainty, and insecurity in immigrants' daily lives (Harrison and Lloyd 2011, 5).

Immigrants' anxiety stemming from deportability extends beyond encounters with law enforcement or fear of ICE to their interactions with other institutional actors and members of the native-born public. Marta called me worried about her teenage son who was scheduled to take his GED test. There was a space on the test to enter the student's social security number. Should he leave it blank? Would omission of the number alert *la migra* (ICE) of her son's immigration status? Lorena was rear-ended on her way to church with her toddler son. When the other driver good-naturedly admitted to being at fault and offered to call the police, Lorena jumped in the car and fled. "Things will just go from bad to worse if the police come," she remembers telling Leonardo. Dolores told me of how she forbade her eleven-year-old son from setting up a lemonade stand in their apartment complex (as several other children had done) for fear of calling attention to their family.

Gendered "Border Patrol" in Williamsburg

The criminalization of "illegals" draws on racially imbued and cultural markers of difference and "illegality." At a recent community forum a crime prevention officer in the Williamsburg area (notably sympathetic to the negative effects of the criminalization of immigrants on crime prevention and community police work) admitted to cases in which patrolling officers were "overzealous" in detaining those who fit the "illegal" profile, generalized to include "anyone with a Hispanic last name and a North Carolina driver's license."[6]

However, the criminalization of immigrants, regulation of their movements and enforcements of the boundaries of social inclusion occur in gender-specific ways, and deportability and the insecurity that it engenders affect men and women differently. For men, racially imbued legality tends to be enforced through the policing of public spaces, as their labor market participation, greater physical mobility, and gendered claims to the street make them more visible targets. Men frequently gather outside hotels or on the sidewalks in front of crowded apartments, making them vulnerable to charges of loitering or drinking in public.

Operating a motorized vehicle is a masculinized activity in the home communities of many immigrants in Williamsburg, and men are more likely than women to arrive knowing how to drive. In many cases men arrived prior to their wives or partners, and were able to obtain a legal drivers' license before the law went into effect. Women must not only learn to drive in unfamiliar surroundings but also run the risk of driving without a legal license if they do so.

In the period following the mass protests of 2006 in which immigrants and their allies mobilized around the country in response to proposed immigration reforms, Williamsburg, like many places, experienced a backlash and a rash of detentions of immigrants suspected of being "illegals" (Kerr 2007). Mothers in the immigrant parent support group that I facilitated shared their anxiety about the various unknowns presented by their undocumented status. One young mother of two remarked, "I'm not worried about myself. I just walk to work and back. But, what do we do when the men don't come home?" Others were terrified by the prospect of being apprehended and not being permitted to contact or arrange for care of their children—or worse being deported and having their children turned over to Child Protective Services.

Indeed, Salvadoran immigrants, for whom "disappearances" of loved ones during their country's civil war was a lived reality and for whom violent crime of the postwar period has brought a different flavor of terror, confronted a new variation of state-sponsored disappearances. Those suspected of illegal presence who are arrested by local law enforcement and turned over to ICE may spend months or even years awaiting court proceedings in detention centers, prisons, or local jails with no way to contact family members (Preston 2011; Coleman 2007a).

Diego was apprehended while smoking with friends outside his apartment and arrested on charges of burglary when identified by a neighbor who located him at the scene of a break-in. Only recently arrived from Mexico, his months-long detainment in a local jail while awaiting court proceedings prevented him from sending remittances to his ex-wife to support their small children, or to make payments on the debt he owed for transport across the border. His situation worsened, however, when he was transferred to a facility two hours away in Virginia Beach, too far for his sister, who communicated with his family, to visit. After months in that facility, he finally pleaded guilty so that he could be released. His troubles were far from over. He faced immigration court as a result of his conviction for an aggravated felony, and was considering requesting a voluntary departure order to avoid deportation proceedings.

Gendered Vulnerabilities at Home and Work

While men's greater likelihood of appearing in public places can make them targets for police detention, women's social responsibilities in the home and their paid work in restaurants and hotels renders them more hidden from public view. And yet, their reproductive activities, such as seeking medical care and social and educational services for themselves and their children, bring them face to face with institutions that regulate their access to social entitlements, restricting their ability to meet the needs of their families (Deeb-Sossa and Mendez 2008). To acquire public services like Medicaid and food stamps, to which their U.S.-born children are entitled, undocumented mothers must step out of the shadows and "enforced clandestinity" occasioned by their immigration status to interact with state agencies, schools, and other institutions (Coutin 2000, 33). This status makes it difficult for them to provide necessary documentation (such as verification of income and birth certificates for their children) to ensure eligibility for services like Medicaid. They fear the scrutiny that they must undergo by social services. In addition, women's domestic sphere responsibilities contribute to their disadvantage in the paid labor force. Employers capitalize on women's gender disadvantage as an ideal temporary workforce who can be laid off in the slow season or fired when they become pregnant. Hotels and restaurants may use contracting agencies to recruit a mostly female, immigrant laborforce as their housekeeping staff.

Women in a local immigrant parent support group that I facilitate complained of the lack of opportunity to learn English. The few English-as-a-Second-Language (ESL) classes often are scheduled in the evenings, a difficult time for mothers with small children. Language acquisition is not likely to occur at the kinds of jobs many hold, because they are confined to backstage areas where they mostly come into contact with other Spanish-speaking workers. Meanwhile, men's better-paid employment in jobs like landscaping, roofing and construction tends to offer more regular contact with members of other groups in Williamsburg, including native English-speakers. Even when they rely on employers or car pools for transportation, driving to different job sites allows men to orient themselves to the spatial geography of Williamsburg, and facilitates their access to information about other opportunities in the area.

Given the high cost of childcare, when women become pregnant they often leave the labor market, reducing household incomes considerably and rendering mothers economically dependent on male partners. Mariana said, "No, no I'm not going to work just to earn enough to pay someone to take care of my daughter!" In cases in which men leave the relationship to take up with other women, their former partners (often pregnant or with small children) can be left with no income, and with little prospect of finding a job that would cover the high cost of rent, childcare, and household expenses.

Clara reflected on the struggles she and her husband have faced since coming to Williamsburg, "Maybe not so much in raising the children [have we faced difficulties], because he's [husband] been working so we have been able to get ahead. But the biggest difficulty for us has been to find someone to take care of the children so that we can both work." In some cases more established immigrants send for younger siblings to take on childcare duties so that both parents can return to work. Irene and María Isabel were high school age when their older brothers paid for their journey to Williamsburg where they moved into small apartments with their brothers and their families. Neither girl attended school, and they both faced a life of isolation and boredom, caring for infants during the day with few opportunities to leave the apartment. Irene eventually returned to Mexico after she complained of her unhappiness to her mother. Much to her brother's outrage, María Isabel escaped her situation by establishing a romantic relationship with a significantly older man and moving in with him.

Social isolation can generate or exacerbate power imbalances within families and other intimate relationships. For women, economic dependency on male partners coupled with reliance on them for transportation and housing can create conditions ripe for domestic abuse. In many cases men maintain a form of spatial control over their female partners. In cases of violence some women find it virtually impossible to exit the relationship. For these women, layered upon the power dynamics of gender and violence—emotional control, fear, and threats—is the insecurity that comes with undocumented immigrant status, making it even less likely that they will seek assistance from domestic violence centers, contact law enforcement, or leave the abusive situation.

Women who are new arrivals from Central America are vulnerable to sexual exploitation and violence at the hands of guides who bring them from their arrival point in the United States to Williamsburg and even sponsoring family members or acquaintances who pay the cost of their transit and with whom they reside until they find their own jobs and housing. After a harrowing journey through Guatemala to cross the border into Mexico and then a terrifying trek through the desert to cross the U.S.-Mexico border, Lorena and Silvia did not find security or safety upon their arrival to Williamsburg. Both felt pressured by males who made sexual overtures in the temporary households that they shared with newly arrived migrants. Lorena eventually escaped this situation by moving in with Leonardo, and as long as their relationship remained stable she enjoyed some degree of security. Marta, a Honduran woman, was not as lucky and was sexually assaulted by a brother-in-law while she, her husband, and their young child were sharing the apartment he rented. They temporarily moved to the hotel where Marta worked, but with a young toddler and pregnant with another child, finding adequate housing at an affordable rate seemed an insurmountable challenge.

Women able to leave violent relationships face the daunting prospect of locating housing in a tight market, made even more difficult to access without proof of stable earnings and acceptable credit. If they lack legal immigration status, they can enter domestic violence shelters, but they are not offered assistance in locating employment. With no transportation of their own and no prospects for finding jobs, immigrant women have nowhere to go at the conclusion of the sixty days of free room and board that clients are given in the shelter.

Conclusions

As we have seen, the lives and experiences of Central Americans in Williamsburg reveal both incorporation (primarily into the job market), but also exclusion and marginalization. Conditions in the realms of the community, workplace, and even intimate relationships and families coalesce to produce a set of hardships that inhibit their participation as full-fledged members of the Williamsburg community. But such local factors and conditions also tell a story about more global processes—the localization of countervailing neoliberal projects that open borders to free trade and markets (including labor markets) and to global forces of supply and demand but also reinforce social boundaries that divide entitled members of the community from groups seen as undeserving, criminal others.

The economic incorporation of Central American immigrants reflective of "de-bordering" processes—the restructuring and global integration of economies and labor markets—is also facilitated through social invisibility, which takes on gendered characteristics. In Williamsburg Central American and Mexicans' labor in the kitchens and hotels of the hospitality industry is hidden from public view, and more masculinized jobs like landscaping and roofing are informalized and organized around sub-contracting chains in such a way that native-born residents may not come into direct contact with this group. Women's invisible labor in the home, often under conditions of extreme social isolation, reproduces this cheap labor source, which has sustained the construction boom and continued touristification and commercial development of Williamsburg.

The dispersed organization of space that emerges from Williamsburg's unique brand of gentrification works in conjunction with other structural conditions to bolster "rebordering." As racially marked "others," Central Americans' appearances as they move through public space are policed through immigration enforcement—facilitated by crowded and isolated housing conditions as well as dependency on private vehicles for transportation. Policing immigrants' physical mobility erases low-income, brown people from public space, preserving the commodified, white-washed image of Williamsburg as "a great place to visit, live and retire." Ironically, Central Americans' public visibility facilitates their criminalization and even their disappearance in immigration detention centers and jails and through deportation.

Central American newcomers to Williamsburg wrestle with the tension between their increased incomes and the social isolation they face in their new host community. For their families left behind they are the ones who have made it. However, insecurity and fear are constants for them, as the threat of state-sponsored disappearances continues to be present in their lives. And though their earnings far exceed any they could hope to generate in the communities of origin, they struggle to afford the costly rent, pay bills in Williamsburg and still have money left over to send back home.

Nonetheless, immigrants in Williamsburg struggle to overcome obstacles to their full inclusion. Daily survival strategies serve as signs of resistance and change. Immigrant mothers have used their participation in social programs for their children as a way to establish ties with each other, building communities. Many have been able to reunite with families by saving money to send for older children, spouses, and siblings, finding fulfillment and hope. Central American and Mexican immigrants have also mobilized resources through their involvement in the Catholic Church and such organizations as Madre Tierra, formed by Central American women in nearby Fredricksburg, Virginia to address specific structural barriers that create hardships for immigrants. One project has organized car pools between home and work. Efforts like these might appear small, but they represent salient grassroots attempts by and for Central Americans to challenge their marginalization. These strategies hold the potential for creating meaningful mechanisms for Central American newcomers to claim space and a voice for themselves in a community that considers itself the birthplace of American democracy.

Notes

* I wish to thank Brent Kaup and Amy Quark for their thoughtful comments on earlier drafts of this chapter. I am extremely grateful to Jennifer Burrell and Ellen Moodie for their patience, encouragement, and dedication to this project. Finally, I am truly indebted to the immigrant men and women who trusted me enough to share their stories with me.

1. Greater Williamsburg is comprised of the City of Williamsburg (est. pop. 14,000) and the larger James City (est. pop. 67,000) and York Counties (est. pop. 65,000) (U.S. Census Bureau 2011).
2. In 2007 James City County was ranked 66th fastest growing county in the nation with a 29.7 percent increase in housing units between 2000 and 2006 (Dawkins et al. 2007, 1). According to the U.S. Census Bureau (2011), population growth over the last ten years in the Williamsburg area was double that of the state as whole. James City County grew 39 percent during 2000–2010, from 48,102 to 67,009—over three times the increase in the state of Virginia. The area as a whole grew by 13 percent—double the rate of growth at the state level—to reach a population of 146,541 people in 2010.
3. There are no reliable data on foreign-born versus U.S.-born Hispanics in Greater Williamsburg. However, a recent study reported that forty percent of Hispanic residents in Virginia were foreign-born (Cai 2008, 2). Ethnographic observation in Williamsburg and data col-

lected by community organizations and schools suggest that a large proportion of Hispanics are immigrants.

4. Between 2000 and 2006 the population of those 65 and older grew by nearly 30 percent in James City County and Williamsburg (U.S. Bureau of Census 2007). A recent study estimated that by 2020, 33 percent of the area's population will be 60 years and older (Vaughan 2010).
5. All names used in this chapter are pseudonyms.
6. North Carolina took longer to implement policies that restrict eligibility for drivers' licenses, and for several years immigrants would travel there to obtain drivers' licenses and register vehicles.

Part IV

A Place on the Map: Surviving on Pasts, Presents, and Futures

14 Migration, Tourism, and Post-Insurgent Individuality in Northern Morazán, El Salvador

Leigh Binford

This chapter analyzes social relations in northern Morazán, El Salvador, twenty years after Peace Accords ended a twelve-year-long civil war between the Salvadoran government (and its international allies) and the Farabundo Martí National Liberation Front (FMLN). I focus on the collective projects that arose during the war, products of an "insurgent individuality," and go on to chronicle their demise in the postwar period of neoliberal political economy that leaves little space for progressive alternatives. Efforts on the part of former insurgents and their civilian supporters to establish agricultural collectives and organize production around local and regional needs collapsed as the region became reintegrated into the capitalist market economy and conservative postwar governments (until the FMLN's 2009 electoral victory) pursued neoliberal policies unfavorable to poor, rural dwellers. Northern Morazán devolved into a major source of migrant labor for U.S. assembly plants and agriculture and service industries. Ironically, though, the (relative) depopulation resulting from the inability of the regional economy to provide the basis for reproduction of growing numbers of people also contributed to environmental recovery and helped attract national and international tourism. In this chapter I discuss several projects directly or indirectly related to tourism and suggest how changing social fields have led to the metamorphosis of former guerrillas' insurgent individuality into a post-insurgent individuality.

The Civil War in Northern Morazán

Along with the department of Chalatenango and the Guazapa area just north of the capital, San Salvador, northern Morazán became the setting for some of the civil war's most prolonged and intense combat and repression. In earlier work I documented more than a dozen army massacres—the largest being the El Mozote massacre of December 1981—and estimated that perhaps a tenth of the region's prewar population of fifty thousand inhabitants died in the conflict (Binford 1996; see Danner 1994; and Tutela Legal 2008). Death squad activity and army massacres declined after most civilians fled and the People's Revolutionary Army (ERP) eliminated National Guard and Treasury Police posts; the rebels gained day-to-day control of northern Morazán in mid 1983. In response, the Salvadoran government erected a military cordon around the zone and bombed, shelled, and periodically invaded northern Morazán with the object of making life impossible for the ERP's civilian support base. However, the advent of electoral democracy in 1984 created a political opening for civilians to demand treatment in accordance with international treaties. Over the next six years, they set up local organizations—coordinated within the Community Development Council of Morazán and San Miguel (PADECOMSM) and established an impressive array of popular grassroots programs in health, education, and production, all with the financial assistance of the Catholic Church and international nongovernmental organizations (NGOs).

The PADECOMSM project was strengthened when 8,400 refugees from a United Nations-sponsored refugee camp in Colomoncagua, Honduras returned overland to Meanguera municipality between November 1989 and March 1990. While in Honduras, Salvadoran refugees had been cut off from the monetary economy and their camp surrounded (and occasionally invaded) by the Honduran military. The refugees survived from donations of food, clothing, equipment, and technical and organizational assistance by the United Nations and international NGOs (Cagan and Cagan 1992). When they returned to northern Morazán, they brought knowledge, machinery, and even the wood from their barracks-style, Honduran dwellings. Perhaps most important, they repatriated with the contacts and relationships forged in exile. Over the next six or eight years, international organizations poured more than $10 million into making Ciudad Segundo Montes, as the inhabitants named it, a model community based on the principles of self-management and participative democracy (Red Europea de Diálogo Social 2004).

The Demise of Collective Projects

As the war wound down and some kind of negotiated solution seemed imminent, FMLN social architects drew up an optimistic plan in which Ciudad Segundo Montes (later renamed Comunidad Segundo Montes) (CSM), would supply pottery, metal goods, clothing, and other industrial products to rural areas of northern Morazán and the neighboring department of San Miguel, whose inhabitants, through PADECOMSM, would reciprocate with food (corn and beans) and raw materials like timber for furniture manufacture and house construction and hemp for rope and hammock fabrication. In rural areas the Christian Base Communities of El Salvador (CEBES) and FMLN-linked civilian organizations such as PADECOMSM, organized ex-combatants and the rebels' civilian supporters into agricultural cooperatives in order to preserve a measure of political clout following the postwar reactivation of municipal administrations and government health and educational institutions. But these projects floundered in the wake of the zone's integration into the postwar neoliberal reality, a shift from international donations to credit-based systems, and intransigent national and foreign (especially United States) government hostility to collective projects. Local and regional organizations, assisted by international NGOs, hatched plans for and invested a great deal of time and money into cooperative farming arrangements, integral rural development projects, nontraditional agro exports and organic coffee production. In time, all succumbed to neoliberal policies, price collapse, limited infrastructure, and/or lack of financing.

I noted above that CSM was formed by Salvadoran refugees who returned from Colomoncagua, Honduras, to El Salvador in 1989–1990, bringing with them machinery, tools, and knowledge acquired during almost ten years in exile. The postwar economic and political climate impeded CSM from transitioning from dependence on NGO handouts to a self-sufficient community in which collective economic "units" would both provide community workers a living wage and supply the regional market with durable basic consumer goods at competitive prices. As one economic unit after another failed, people were forced to fend for themselves. As in the case of Nicaragua's Sandinistas, the sense of solidarity, the *mística* (mystique) that had sustained the refugees through almost a decade of life in concentration camp-like exile, weakened (see R. Montoya, this volume). Those with access to capital established small workshops, restaurants, and stores, often competing with community collectives. By the turn of the millennium, community-related workshops and industries provided work for a mere 7 percent of CSM's economically active population (see Binford 2010; McElhinney 2004; Red Europeo de Diálogo Social 2004).

Eight years later (2008) CEBES, led by Father Rogelio Ponceele and former priest Miguel Ventura, was operating an agricultural loan program for hundreds of non-creditworthy peasant cultivators as well as running a technical training school (artisanal production of paper, soap, and other products, carpentry and haberdashery, among others) in CSM. But however much inhabitants appreciated having access to capital, CEBES's interest rates approached commercial levels. Moreover, the agricultural credit program, training school and other programs were being sustained, in part, by a for-profit bus line, restaurants, and a small hotel owned and operated by the organization. For CEBES strategists, agricultural loans merely underwrite household subsistence production of corn and beans; "true" economic development will depend on raising the regional level of human capital through improved education and technical training programs. That CSM contains one of the region's few *bachilleratos* (high schools)—and in 2012 opened a two-year technical school offering a limited range of specialities—is suggestive of the high priority inhabitants have placed on education since their Honduran exile period. But scarce public and private investment in northern Morazán translates into limited regional job creation and imminent frustration on the part of graduates, who are leaving with less-educated members of their age cohort for other areas of El Salvador or, more frequently, migrating to the United States (see below).[1]

While CEBES remains committed to northern Morazán, PADECOMSM moved its operation to wealthier and more densely populated areas south of the Torola River. Before making the decision to do so, the leadership weathered the collapse of agricultural collectives and the failure of an NGO-supported credit program for small-scale agriculturalists, ranchers and merchants. By 2008 PADECOMSM's president—also elected Perquín mayor in 2009 and again in 2012 under the FMLN banner—stated that the relocated and reconfigured loan program was succeeding, generating sufficient income both to cover overhead in the San Francisco Gotera office and finance outreach programs for sex workers and working children of market vendors in urban San Miguel city. Though formed during the war by civilians residing in a war zone, northern Morazán no longer figures in the organization's plans.

International Migration

Indeed, northern Morazán no longer figures in many plans at all, disappearing much as Central America has faded from global eyes. And it is this lack of figuration that (partly) opens the region to international migration. Temporary labor migration extends well into the pre-war period, when northern Morazán formed part of El Salvador's *tierra olvidada* (forgotten land) (Browning 1971) and served as a seasonal labor reserve for the cotton, sugarcane, and coffee plantations on the South Coast, intermountain valleys, and volcanic cordillera, respectively. Cheap labor was critical to the success of the export-oriented agriculture that formed the backbone of the post-WWII economy (Williams 1986). But as William Robinson (2003, 93) notes, the 1980–1992 civil war disrupted agriculture and became a "key catalyst of change within the elite, damaging landed interests in favor of finance capital, commerce, and export processing."

Low wages and meager formal sector job creation—with the exception of a vibrant maquiladora industry—drive increasing numbers of Salvadorans to the United States, where they generate a reverse flow of remittances that now account for more than 15 percent of the gross domestic product and prop up the neoliberal market model. In 2008 conservative analyst Juan Héctor

Vidal wrote, "As a country we are consuming more than we produce and this gap is financed with family remittances that also have an impact on consumer goods" (cited in Guzmán and Balcáceres 2008, 30–31). Indeed, according to the Central Reserve Bank, remittances grew an average of 13.9 percent annually between 2002 and 2007, reaching $3.7 billion, indicative of a process of generalized impoverishment that leaves no region untouched.[2] However, rugged northern departments like Morazán, many of which were major civil war conflict zones, have been drawn more heavily than others into the process. Morazán ranks third, after the departments of La Unión and Cabañas, in terms of the percentage of households receiving remittances. The percentage rose significantly over the six-year period between 1998 and 2004 from 28 to 34.2 percent (Rosa et al. 2005; Hecht et al. 2005; Kandel 2002).

Yet international migration reached critical mass later in northern areas of the department than those south of the Torola River. In the north former FMLN guerrilla fighters and their civilian supporters survived for several years by gleaning small amounts of food and employment from reconstruction projects financed by foreign governments and nongovernment organizations. But once peace had been restored, democracy of the polyarchic variety consolidated (see Robinson 1995, as well as chapters by A. Montoya and Moodie, this volume), and housing, potable water, and educational infrastructure made available to most, reconstruction funds dried up, and most NGOs moved on—as they usually do—to deal with other crises elsewhere. Also important for the retention of this population was the absence of strong migratory networks, and, for those who might have had them, the liquidity or property guarantees needed to finance the trip, which by July 2012 cost $7,000. On the other hand, many people remained because they were too old and worn out to migrate or, in some cases, because they were committed to the construction of a different kind of society under conditions that, if not those of military victory, were not exactly those of military defeat either.

Even so, by August 2008 most informants opined that every new substantial private construction was being paid for from remittance monies sent to San Francisco Gotera, the departmental capital.[3] International migration had become so normalized that people tended to view it as a "force of nature," immune to human intervention (see Burrell; and Mendez, this volume). Neither tourism nor binational (El Salvador-Honduras) food security programs, World Bank-style targeted poverty alleviation programs (*Redes Solidarias* or Solidary Networks) nor broader access to education were thought capable of stemming the movement northward, much less reversing it.

Reasons are easy to find. The region suffers high levels of un- and underemployment. Wages are extremely low: five to seven dollars daily for agricultural day labor in 2012; ten to twelve for bricklayers and other construction workers—when employment is available. Women working in the kitchen of the Perkín Lenca hotel, mostly single mothers, earned $150.00 (U.S.) monthly in 2012—the same amount as four years earlier—although they also benefited from free meals and enrollment in the state Social Security system. But wages tell only half the story. Prices of basic goods increased shortly after the government replaced the *colón* with the U.S. dollar in 2001, and they have continued to rise. Beans, the regional population's main source of protein, cost as much as $1.25 (U.S.) per pound in July of 2011; at the same time corn prices had more than doubled (over those of a year earlier) to $40.00 (U.S.) per quintal (100 pounds). The official government minimum agricultural wage of $104.97 (U.S.) monthly covered only 37 percent of the basic rural cost of living. People working in commerce and services should receive at least $224.29 (U.S.) monthly but that wage is inadequate to maintain an average household and it is not respected by most rural employers (Equipo Maíz 2011). Most of the fortunate few with jobs in municipal government or working for NGOs as tourism promoters, health aids, school teachers, or in surviving cooperative federations—many of whom have attended many training workshops and possess planning, organizing and/or computer skills—earn slightly above the minimum and, like others, seek to diversify income sources during their "spare time" in order to make ends meet: They raise chickens for eggs, plant corn, produce artisan goods, play musical engagements, haul merchandise, sell newspapers, and so on.

The government displays no interest in anchoring a population that, according to market logic, probably contributes more to the national welfare from the United States than at home in El Salvador, where un- and under employment are synonymous with poverty, crime, and social tension. I refer, of course, to a process of transnational proletarianization in which most of the value generated by Salvadoran migrant workers remains in the United States and a minor portion is remitted to El Salvador, where it props up the service economy, compensates for declining public services, and underwrites the formation of the next generation of migrants (Grammage 2006; Equipo Maíz 2006).

Migrants tend to be young and remain in the United States for extended periods. Most lack defined projects that might draw them back home. The long distance to the United States, the dangers that accompany the journey, high cost, and the illegal status of most migrants rule out regular comings and goings. On the other hand, many formerly displaced persons who migrated during the 1980s regularized their status in the United States through the 1986 Immigration Reform and Control Act. Some who migrated since then secured Temporary Protected Status, which has allowed them to work legally and move about the U.S. labor market. They also produced U.S. citizen children who travel freely and occasionally find northern Morazán a pleasant summer vacation alternative to hot and humid Houston, Texas, or to Brentwood (Long Island), New York.

Remittances produce temporary jobs when invested in house construction, though most of the money is siphoned off into urban areas where construction materials firms, department stores, banks, and other large enterprises are located. Migration also contributes to social differentiation between migrants (or successful migrants) and nonmigrants (or failed ones); and the use of remittances to purchase late-model trucks and pay for expensive *quinceañera* (fifteenth-birthday) parties generates invidious comparison and contributes to the formation of youthful consumerist desires. Finally, nonmigrants relentlessly criticize the negative work ethic of remittance recipients who, according to them, argue that working for a few dollars a day makes little sense when relatives remit several hundred dollars monthly.

The Romance of the Environment

Ironically, postwar development failures in northern Morazán and international migration also contributed to the maintenance and perhaps even reappearance of the "natural" environment that, along with historical sites, draws national and international visitors to the region. Before the civil war El Salvador gained notoriety as one of Latin America's most environmentally degraded countries. High population density, rampant poverty and corruption generated unchecked deforestation and soil erosion that clogged dams, altered rainfall patterns, and contributed to flooding. Northern areas of the departments of Chalatenango and Morazán sheltered most of the nation's scarce remaining forest cover, which was gradually succumbing to pastures and cultivated fields. The civil war might have been expected to interrupt or at least scale back this process—and to a degree it did. But indiscriminate aerial bombing and artillery shelling of civilian towns and suspected guerrilla encampments often set off forest fires. Illegal logging dropped off or ceased during the *cordon sanitaire* period of the early to mid 1980s because there was no way to get the timber out of the zone, but it picked up again after 1986 when civilians first breached the military blockade. It continued unabated into 2012, despite stricter laws and more enforcement personnel.

However, instead of continuing to shrink, forest cover has been expanding. Wartime depopulation was not recompensed by a subsequent postwar repopulation on the same scale. Most of the more than 60 percent of the population that fled the region when fighting intensified in the early 1980s remained in San Salvador, San Miguel, and San Francisco Gotera after the war (or moved northward), discouraged from returning by a lack of housing, transport and basic infrastructure, meager economic prospects, and fear of assaults and property crime, which soared in the mid 1990s. The United Nations Development Program estimated the 2005 regional population at 34,000, two-thirds the number recorded in the last pre-war census, carried out in the 1970s (UNDP 2006, 141). Many northern Morazanians received land through the Land Transfer Program that was part of the Peace Accords (Binford 2010), but high production costs and low product prices brought on (in part) by market liberalization discourage agriculture. Many fields go uncultivated.[4]

These processes have contributed to the expansion of what Hecht et al. (2005, 310) refer to as the "secret forests of El Salvador," by which they mean anthropogenic (as opposed to "wild") forests characterized by "secondary growth and advanced pasture successions." Furthermore, they note that nationally "[a]reas receiving more remittances correlate with the zones of forest recuperation" (312–13). Given high rates of international migration and reverse movement of remittances, that means, especially, Morazán, La Unión, Cabañas, and Chalatenango. Forest recuperation, even of the anthropogenic variety, fosters the survival of fauna and flora and the maintenance of water courses, swimming holes, hiking trails, and scenic mountain vistas crucial to ecotourism projects, the region's sole growth sector. The regional organization Tourism Promoter (PRODETUR) and the Perkín Lenca Hotel are thus able to back up claims about northern Morazán's "fresh air, clean rivers, birds, natural forests, butterflies, waterfalls, tranquility, reflection … and all that has been constructed in its midst."[5] Had the development alternatives proposed by CSM and PADECOMSM succeeded, the bucolic northern Morazanian countryside would surely be more densely populated, more extensively cultivated, less forested and would appeal less to hikers, bird watchers, and nature lovers in general. Ironically, nature lovers, at least the U.S. variety, experience northern Morazán as they do because so much of the native-born population resides outside Morazán in rural and urban areas of the United States from which many of the tourists themselves originate. Neoliberal capitalism, like civil war, refigures landscapes in a stealthy fashion that sometimes passes unnoticed because people fail to ask the right questions.

Postwar Tourism and "Post-Insurgent" Individuality

In the wake of the demise of collective projects and decline of NGO support, tourism came to be seen as a means of bringing money into northern Morazán and generating employment for a population with few postwar alternatives—although the idea of northern Morazán as a zone of attraction for environmentally and historically oriented tourists was first hatched in guerrilla camps before the war ended. Early visitors to northern Morazán consisted of working journalists and others who slipped past army roadblocks and patrols to enter the region in the mid to late 1980s, but CSM—harbinger of what Aquiles Montoya (1993) referred to as the "new popular economy"—served as an important early destination for the progressive political tourism encapsulated in what insiders referred to as the "solidarity delegation."

In 1990 the United Nations rebuilt the Torola River bridge, destroyed by the ERP in the early 1980s, facilitating the movement of goods into and out of the region; within a year struggles by former refugees throughout the country had prospered to the point that the Salvadoran Armed Forces succumbed to national and international pressure and began to issue safe conduct passes that allowed foreign visitors to travel to repopulated and resettled communities in areas under day-to-day FMLN control. In the summer of 1991 officials of the Fourth Military Detachment in San Francisco Gotera stated that my safe conduct pass allowed me to travel no farther north than CSM, which adjoined the Torola River. However, the Salvadoran military maintained no regular, daily presence in northern Morazán. Whereas most visitors slept in wooden barracks in CSM, and spent a good amount of time touring community projects in production, health, education, social communication, day care, and other areas, they invariably took the opportunity to make what I came to think of as the "Grand Tour," which included, besides CSM, the abandoned El Mozote massacre site and the "guerrilla capital" of Perquín, where lucky delegations might obtain an interview with a local FMLN commander. These tours were exciting and particularly before 1992 carried a hint of danger for foreigners, who were, after all, violating a government order (see Babb, this volume). For middle-class North Americans and Europeans, they also held out the promise of a face-to-face encounter with the rebellious Other, and on its turf to boot.

The point that I want to make, though, is that during the civil war, solidarity "tourism," if we can call it that, was used tactically by FMLN rebels and their civilian supporters to increase international pressure on the government and open up space for political organizing. Many solidarity tourists returned home and spread the "truth" of northern Morazán, and El Salvador, by means of public demonstrations, talks before school and church audiences, and campaigns to stop the bombing, cut military aid, and punish the intellectual authors of massacres and other gross human rights violations (Smith 1996). Solidarity tourism continued during the early postwar reconstruction phase, but as the NGOs left, the state abandoned the zone developmentally, collective projects eroded, and international migration exploded, there was less, compared to the past, to be in solidarity with (see Binford 2010). Tourism became more national than international, individualized, and recreationally oriented and thus severed from a political project; the tourism axis expanded to embrace, besides history, nature and the environment.

Post-Insurgent Individuality

In this last section of this chapter, I want to consider the relationship between some tourism and other projects and a hypothesized "post-insurgent individuality" that articulates Morazán's rebellious past with its neoliberal present, resulting in complex subjectivities rent with contradictions but also possibilities. The term draws on Greg Grandin's (2004) conception of "insurgent individuality" and his refusal of a uniform conception of individualism under capitalist modernity. Grandin (2004, 181, see n. 47, 275–76) argues that in Guatemala and elsewhere in Latin America the sense of self that is a hallmark of individuality developed in and through collective action directed toward redressing the worst abuses of capitalism: "Rather than eliminating the boundaries between self and society, collective action distilled for many a more potent understanding of themselves as politically consequent individuals." I argue the same for FMLN guerrillas and their civilian base in northern Morazán and other areas of El Salvador before and during the civil war. Elsewhere I have discussed how training in peasant universities and participation in Christian Base Communities unlocked in peasant catechists a host of abilities and led to a newfound self-confidence that they could make a difference as cogs in a collective movement for social change (Binford 2004). Something similar occurred with the hundreds if not thousands of peasants and workers who acquired previously unimaginable skills in communications, logistics, education, health, and many other areas *por la necesidad* (out of necessity) in FMLN-dominated areas of Morazán, Chalatenango, Guazapa and elsewhere during the civil war. This process has been amply documented in *testimonios* (testimonies), academic works, and solidarity publications released during and after the conflict (for example, Cabarrús 1983; Hammond 1998; Henríquez 1992; López Vigil 1991; Metzi 1988).

I begin by discussing briefly the experience of "Quique" (Antonio Vigil Vásquez), a peasant agriculturalist with a second-grade education who joined the ERP in 1978 and in the 1980s received training as a field health care provider (*brigadista*) and dentist, along with being instructed in combat and the use of firearms. Years after the war, Quique hand-wrote a detailed, 132-page memoir that chronicles many of his experiences, emphasizing his and others' willingness to risk their lives in order to ensure the health and well-being of their comrades in arms. For instance, he provides a detailed narration of a traumatic experience when he injured his leg after stepping on a mine and was carried for hours during a lengthy retreat by "Yonquene" and "Claver"; he also narrates how an ERP patrol spent days combing the forest for a wounded guerrilla hidden in a remote ravine by outmanned rebel soldiers forced to beat a hasty retreat in order to escape encirclement by a superior government force (Vigil Vásquez n.d.). After the war Quique joined an agricultural collective whose members worked without pay (through social labor) in order to restore a small, deteriorated coffee finca obtained in the Land Transfer Program. The project failed, the land was divided up among the members of the collective, and as of 2010 Quique supported his family selling newspapers door-to-door in Perquín, working as a night watchman and practicing a bit of illegal dentistry on demand as he waited upon the results of the cooperative's macadamia nut and bee-keeping projects. In an interview Quique lamented the collapse of collective projects and the growing individualization.

Quique exemplifies a form of "post-insurgent individuality" in which the insurgent individuality developed before and during the civil war has been diminished and eroded under adverse conditions and for lack of a project upon which to focus its subject desires. Post-insurgent individuality stands as a hypothesis, then, posed to account for the surplus meaning of individual and collective projects that adopt neoliberal market forms but that also continue to reference a recent past characterized by a broader, class-based project for social transformation.

I illustrate the possibility of post-insurgent individuality through discussion of northern Morazán's *Promotor de Turismo* (Tourism Promoter or PRODETUR), which was organized with the assistance of a former ERP-linked NGO and registered as a Community Development Association in 2000.

PRODETUR

Although PRODETUR's staff consists of former FMLN combatants and logistical personnel, the organization presents itself publicly as entrepreneurial and apolitical. Yet a brief look beneath the surface reveals details that call for a more complex reading. While PRODETUR strives to be *the* public face of tourism for northern Morazán—organizing package tours, monitoring (and professionalizing) tourism services, and generating publicity for hotels, recreational sites, municipalities, and even restaurants—the organization is also heavily committed to historical memory with a pro-FMLN slant.

Recently PRODETUR finished work on a logo for northern Morazán consistent with its designation as part of La Ruta de la Paz Lenca (Lenca Peace Route), part of a binational project that includes adjoining municipalities in northeastern El Salvador and southern Honduras. The "Lenca Peace" contrasts with the region's bellicose civil war-era image, which persisted for years after the Peace Accords, and warned away return visits by former residents displaced in the 1980s to San Salvador and other cities. But La Ruta de la Paz Lenca is also part of a government Tourism Ministry campaign to mark out a series of appealing *rutas* (routes) for visitors—La Ruta de las Flores, La Ruta de Volcanes—that highlight social, geographical, and/or geological features that distinguish different regions. PRODETUR's logo features an *ocote* pine tree, native to the region, surrounded by birds and butterflies: the foliage represents nature, the trunk Morazán's historic role as a bridge between cultures and geographical areas, and the roots the region's complex and variegated history. A backward look to the precolonial period, when Lenca Indians traded with Copan Maya, and emphasis on the (questionably) peaceful nature of indigenous relations elides the long history of colonial exploitation, military dictatorships, repression, resistance, massacres and bombing and shelling of civilians, as well as celebrated FMLN military successes and early wartime and postwar efforts to restructure regional social, political, and economic relationships.[6]

On the other hand, PRODETUR also avidly promotes historical tourism, which in northern Morazán turns around battle and massacre sites related to the struggle against the Salvadoran state. Most PRODETUR guides were former ERP combatants or support personnel; they have an intimate knowledge of the terrain and can escort visitors overland to abandoned guerrilla camps, bomb shelters, trenches, battle sites, and so on, many of which they experienced very differently a few decades earlier.

PRODETUR participates actively in Perquín's Winter Festival, celebrated each August since 1992, shortly before the last contingent of ERP veterans turned in their weapons to United Nations Peacekeepers and returned to civilian life. The festival features food stalls, competitive games, musical presentations and the display and sale of a variety of artisan goods. Among the many activities two stand out in terms of their real or potential historical significance: the competitive selection and presentation of the Lenca princess and her colorfully clad entourage and a public historical memory forum, organized by PRODETUR since its inception, through which former participants in the war explore a pre-selected annual theme: "The FMLN Leadership" (2006), "The Battle of Moscarón" (2007), "Women in the War" (2008), and "Special Forces and the Military School" (2011).

Organizers state that both the Lenca princess and the Historical Memory Forum have been well received by the public. They envision the former as an effort to recover a lost memory of regional cultural linkages with neighboring areas of Honduras and the latter as a means of remembering the armed struggle, acknowledging the contributions of specific groups involved in it, and providing a forum for popular participation. One PRODETUR worker, who spent much of the war in intelligence activities, characterized the Forum as the materialization of a "developmentalist logic," which he contrasted with a "political logic," pursued both by Perquín's right-wing ARENA (2000–2003, 2007–2009) and left-wing FMLN (1994–1999, 2004–2007, 2009–2012) mayors: "Tourism has no (political or geographical) borders," he said,

Figure 14.1. Contestants for the Lenca Princess participate in the Winter Festival in Perquín, Morazán

"We are just [war] veterans committed to studying and preparing ourselves for our families." This is correct in the sense that those who formed PRODETUR must struggle to make a living in northern Morazán under highly adverse economic conditions; but the Historical Memory Forum has the clear political object of recalling FMLN struggles and victories, such as El Moscarrón, and celebrating the FMLN and its civilian supporters as protagonists whose sacrifice produced the democracy that El Salvador enjoys today. However, these political maneuvers, important in sustaining a certain kind of historical memory, remain in a sort of limbo, and the hypothesized post-insurgent individualities of the ex-rebels who occupy key positions in PRODETUR are *post* precisely because their bearers lack a transformative social project upon which to focus their residual insurgent tendencies. We see something similar in two museum projects initiated by former rebels and ex-members of the civilian base.

Museum Projects

The Museum of the Salvadoran Revolution was created in 1992 on the eve of ERP demobilization, but the combined effects of time, neglect, and theft have contributed to the collection's deterioration.[7] The director insists that renovations financed by a Spanish NGO will increase floor space for the presentation of material currently in storage, improve the lighting and even involve the introduction of interactive computer technology; however, by the summer of 2012, the addition, though completed, had not been integrated into the museum. Many of the guides are ex-FMLN combatants unable to work elsewhere because of debilitating injuries received in combat. They explain to visitors that poverty and oppression were the root causes of the conflict; when queried about their participation, they are usually quick to recount personal experiences. The museum closes its book with the Peace Accords and plaques donated to the FMLN by United Nations observers. Over several interviews one guide focused on free speech, rights of association and political party formation as "gains" won by the FMLN, and said that restructuring the economy, a fundamental wartime objective left out of the negotiation process, remained "*pendiente*," a future task. While the narrative line is clear, the director claims to have sought to avoid overtly politicizing the space—to the consternation of some former guerrillas who accuse him of having sold out to the conservative *Alianza Republicana Nacional* (Republican National Alliance, ARENA) party and of running the operation as a private enterprise. He counters criticism by noting that in 2003 the Minis-

Figure 14.2. Display of photos at the Museum of the Revolution in Perquín, Morazán, illustrating "The Causes that Originated the War."

try of Education removed a longstanding ban on official school visits to the museum, and states that the museum is now educating new generations of Salvadorans about the country's civil war.[8]

In November of 2007, a new community museum named *Shafik Vive* (Shafik Lives) opened in CSM. The museum occupies most of a one-story building that previously housed a communal store. The bulk of the exhibit consists of hundreds of photographs mounted on poster board and grouped by themes referencing key moments in the Colomoncagua refugee camp and later in CSM following the 1989–1990 repatriation: "Health Clinic," "Religion," "Production Workshops," and "International Aid," but also "The Fast against Starvation and Repression," and "The Assassination of Old Man Santo Vigil." Community members contributed about 30 percent of the photos; the remaining 70 percent came from the archives of Mercedes Ventura, the force behind the project. Few photographs have captions, and the portrayal of groups and individuals, posed or involved in daily activities, does little to clarify CSM's complex history. But for CSM residents who lived (and helped make) that history, the photographs and other artifacts may serve to trigger memories of collective struggle.

Also, on every wall of the museum there appear black-and-white photographs or photocopies of *compañeros caidos* (fallen comrades), a reminder of CSM's human contribution to the Salvadoran struggle. But why name it after Shafik Handal, the pre-war head of the Salvadoran Communist Party (PCS), FMLN commander, and rival to commander Joaquín Villalobos and the ERP? The choice becomes understandable in the wake of Villalobos's postwar abandonment of the FMLN and formation of the (now defunct) Democratic Party, a decision that provoked a split in ERP ranks. Many CSM residents—including ex-combatants—remained with the FMLN postwar and eventually supported Handal in his 2004 presidential bid. According to her daughter, Ventura, who died in 2008, admired Handal and unilaterally made the decision to name the museum in his honor.

But as in the case of Perquín's Museum of the Revolution, the *Shafik Vive* museum elides the community's conflictive postwar history, marked by internal political division, social and economic differentiation, and high levels of international migration, especially among youth. Also, it produces a narrative of civilian struggle against repression that erases the key role that the Colomoncagua camp—and CSM after 1989—played in sustaining ERP military capability in northern Morazán. Ventura was herself a *misionera* (one who carried out missions) who risked her life making dangerous, late-night hikes through Honduran military lines in order to deliver food, clothing, and other supplies to ERP camps in northern Morazán.

The founders and administrators of these museums—the first of which attracts many national and international tourists—focus on a past replete with sacrifice and struggle in the service of a project for the reconfiguration of society to the benefit of the poor majority. They carve out space for progressive representations of insurgent actions—useful for countering revisionist histories of Communist "terrorism"—but fail to interrogate the nature of the peace that so many deaths and so much suffering helped bring about. Like PRODETUR the museum projects languish in a kind of historic limbo: they implicitly critique the past but cannot critically evaluate the present in part because they articulate no project for the future. Post-insurgent individualities manifest discontent with the way things are, but the end of armed struggle and the FMLN's formal rejection of socialism leaves them with no alternative but to maneuver within postwar fields of power reconfigured nationally and internationally by neoliberal political economy.

Notes

1. The latest CSM plan focuses around the deepening of the *economía solidaria* (solidarity economy) in which regional inhabitants would substitute locally available raw materials for goods imported from elsewhere, ensuring regional employment growth and currency circulation (interview with a technician of the Segundo Montes Foundation [FSM], July 2011). However, the international economic crisis has led to serious retraction in NGO contributions; a number of regional organizations have scaled back programs. Financial support was provided by the National Science Foundation Grant No. BCS 0962643.
2. Remittances declined by around 10 percent with the 2009 global economic crisis but have since experienced a partial recovery. By the summer of 2011 it appeared that dismal job prospects were combining with anti-immigrant legislation to reduce the number of new, U.S.-bound migrants from northern Morazán.
3. Indicative of the growing importance of remittances is the fact that in July 2011 Western Union opened an office in Perquín.
4. Nationally the UNDP estimated the area devoted to corn declined from 450,000 manzanas (unit of measurement equivalent to approximately 1.72 acres) in 1977–1978 to 350,000 in 2004–2005 (UNDP 2006, 43).
5. However, ecotourism efforts in northern Morazán, as in much of El Salvador, are still nascent and do not play a part in the transnational sustainable tourism certification movement described by Vivanco, this volume.
6. By 2011 the route had been renamed *La Ruta de Paz* (The Peace Route) in order, according to PRODETUR workers, to avoid confusion with La Paz department.
7. For a detailed description and analysis of the museum at its inception, see Binford 1996.
8. The Salvadoran Ministry of Tourism refers to the museum as the *Museo de la Paz* (Peace Museum) in its advertising literature.

15 Intimate Encounters

Sex and Power in Nicaraguan Tourism

*Florence E. Babb**

Central America has suffered historically from both overexposure and underexposure—by those set on influencing its economies and governance and by the global media. Nicaragua is a classic case, as a small nation that loomed large following the 1979 Sandinista revolutionary victory, when U.S. President Ronald Reagan viewed it as a threat in "our backyard." Then the country fell out of international view after the U.S.-backed Contra War contributed to the 1990 Sandinista electoral loss. I first observed this mercurial global gaze in 1978, when as a graduate student I wrote a letter to my city paper decrying the media's portrayal of the resistance. I made my first trip to Nicaragua a decade later when the Sandinista government was struggling against counter-revolutionary forces, and I continued my research there over the course of another two decades. As a feminist anthropologist, I have been eager to understand the gender and class-related implications of the dramatic on-the-ground change and international representations of Nicaragua.

My earlier work in Nicaragua considered the impact, particularly for low-income working women, of the neoliberal turn, when government erasures of hard-won gains and even memories of the Sandinista period gradually led to a falling off of the intense global interest in the revolution. Notwithstanding the evident setbacks to progressive politics in the nation, I examined the new social movements that also claimed a space during the post-revolutionary era (Babb 2001). Later, I was struck by still another turn, this one the refashioning of the nation to accommodate the tourism industry, which became the focus of my four-nation study of tourism in post-conflict and post-revolutionary areas (Babb 2011). In Nicaragua, as elsewhere, desires for robust tourism meant attracting another sort of international attention, the global tourist gaze.

I had just returned from a trip to Nicaragua when the workshop that led to this volume convened in September 2008. Our discussions of the new terms of democratic governance in Central America resonated for me as I mulled over the complex politics and everyday practices since Sandinista Daniel Ortega's 2006 return to the presidency. Most of my research was conducted in the post-1990 period when gains of the revolution were eroded and harsh economic measures meant growing gender and class inequalities, rising unemployment, and reduced state support for social services. My most recent visits, in 2008 and 2010, revealed the increasingly polarized politics in the country since Ortega's return.

Here, I draw on my research in Managua between 2000 and 2010. The transition ushered in with Ortega's comeback has been criticized from right and left as his populist rhetoric is not matched by a demonstrated commitment to shared and just governance (see R. Montoya, this volume). My recent revisits to Nicaragua brought home the disillusionment of many who had earlier participated in and been hopeful about the nation's revolutionary transformation. In what follows, I consider one dimension of the tourism encounter in this Central American nation, the commodified exchange of sex and intimacy. In my conclusions I offer some comparative remarks on Nicaraguan and Cuban tourism drawn from my larger project.[1]

Intimate Encounters in a Transitional Society

On arrival in Managua's airport in summer 2004, I discovered a desk with smiling hosts greeting tourists, answering questions, and offering travel literature. A magazine titled *Between the Waves* boasted a cover photograph of a young woman wearing a bikini perched suggestively on a boat. The magazine's business manager later told me that the advertisers wanted every issue cover to feature a tanned Central American beauty, since "sex sells" (Reinhard Holzinger, personal communication, 24 July 2004). *Between the Waves* is free at the airport and in hotels and restaurants catering to tourists, and advertisers are clearly banking on the cover images enticing potential customers.

In my research in Nicaragua, I have found that the tourism industry mimics those in other tropical destinations in offering "sand and sea" vacations with optional visits to colonial towns. Yet, while Nicaragua has much in common with other nations using "branding" techniques to compete for a share of the global tourism market, it differs from the mainstream in attracting travelers who seek out post-conflict and post-revolutionary locations or who wish to support eco- and communitarian tourism efforts. The tourism I consider here is only indirectly linked to Nicaragua's history, but tourists often choose the country because it has recently been considered off-limits.[2] Travelers expressed to me their desire to visit Nicaragua before it loses this quality and becomes an over-developed tourist site like Costa Rica. (See Vivanco; Anderson; Binford; and Little, this volume, for related discussions of tourism.)

When Nicaragua made a sharp neoliberal turn in 1990, it was among the poorest in Latin America. Tourism emerged as central to the nation's development goals. Since Ortega returned to power sixteen years later, he has not altered this approach to tourism nor its gendered effects. More and more tourists come to enjoy a range of travel opportunities, from backpacker-, eco-, and adventure-tourism to higher-end heritage and leisure tourism. At the same time, other forms of tourism have appeared in the wake of the country's recent economic uncertainties. As in many impoverished places, prostitution, sex work, and "romance" tourism have flourished (Cabezas 2004). Often in what I term the tourist encounter, under conditions that favor the commodification of social relationships, there is no strict line between intimacy that results in a brief exchange of sex for money (sex tourism) and that which leads to longer term involvement in exchange for gifts including cash or, in some cases, love and marriage (romance tourism). I consider the forms the phenomenon takes in this post-revolutionary nation, and how the nation attempts to manage contradictions of official policy and everyday practice.

In Nicaragua, as in other post-revolutionary societies where officials say they seek alternatives to market-driven economies—and call for "wholesome" tourism—the emergence of sex and romance tourism is notable. The revolutionary government of the Sandinista National Liberation Front (FSLN) confronted the sexual exploitation of women in its early years. More recently Tomás Borge, the Sandinista head of the Commission on Tourism, opposed casinos and nightclubs that encourage sexual exploitation (interview, 30 June 2003). Nonetheless, there appears to be ambivalence in efforts to curtail the sex work, doubtless because it provides foreign revenue. I do not mean to suggest that the only gendered effect of tourism is the rise of prostitution and sex tourism; women workers are active in other sectors of the global tourism industry (Bolles 1997; Ghodsee 2005). Even so, my research demonstrates the value of examining the transition from the Nicaraguan revolutionary government's earlier success in reducing the socioeconomic and gender inequalities that promoted sexual exploitation and prostitution, to the present commodification of sex and intimacy accompanying the dependence on tourism to rescue the economy.

Sex tourism generally receives scant official notice in Nicaragua. It is considered too controversial to address publicly, so there is little formal data to draw on. Studies on the subject rely on qualitative more than quantitative research methods. While the narratives and descriptive material of my research may appear impressionistic, I would argue that more detailed ethnographic studies are needed to examine the nuances of socially and historically situated sex and romance tourism. I offer representative illustrations, as well as findings from social research and media reports, to ground my analysis.

Innocence for Sale: The Double-Edged Sword of Tourism in Nicaragua

Before 1979, Nicaragua did not figure significantly as a travel destination. The country saw solidarity travel in the post-revolutionary period (see Binford, this volume, for a comparable case), but only in the past two decades has Nicaragua attempted to fashion itself as a tourism competitor. Known as the second poorest country in the hemisphere and considered unsafe during the 1980s, Nicaragua has had "image problems" to overcome. Yet after the Sandinista electoral loss, by the mid 1990s visitors began coming in growing numbers. A *New York Times* article titled "Nicaragua on the Mend" stated, "Seven years after its brutal civil war, the country is at peace and putting out the welcome mat. ... Nicaragua has changed enormously" (Rohter 1997, 10). Nicaragua's Minister of Tourism, Pedro Joaquín Chamorro, told the reporter, "We are on the brink of an awakening to tourism. ... We want to make tourism the main project of Nicaragua, and we plan to do that by promoting our country as an exotic destination at a reasonable price" (1997, 10).

Even so, personnel in the government tourism office, the Institute of Tourism (INTUR), feared it would be hard to overcome Nicaragua's image as a place of danger. Managers in the departments of Marketing and International Relations told me in 2003 that they were striving to present a "positive impression" (Raúl Calvet and Regina Hurtado, interview, 27 June 2003). Around this time, a new INTUR director, Lucia Salazar, was appointed, and in an interview that appeared in promotional literature for Linblad Expeditions (which had begun operating cruises to Nicaragua) she described her personal motivation for promoting a fresh image for Nicaragua. Her father was killed in conflict with the Sandinistas and her family lived in exile in the United States for fifteen years. Now she views tourism as "one of the only ways that Nicaragua can counter the negative image it was branded with in the 1980s" (Salazar de Robelo 2004, 6). Surprisingly, she worked closely with the Sandinista head of the Tourism Commission in the National Assembly, Tomás Borge, whom she believes is responsible for her father's death (Salazar de Robelo 2004, 7). Borge mentioned their decidedly uncomfortable working relationship in our interview. He emphasized that he looked to Cuba as a model for successful tourism development (Borge, interview, 30 June 2003).

Despite their differences, Salazar and Borge agreed that a "healthy" and "clean" national image would help to develop Nicaraguan tourism. Borge told me, presciently as it turned out, that the Sandinistas would win the next election, and he predicted that they would not only support tourism as the number one industry but would also "make it clean and healthful, free of the sex tourism and casinos that are taking hold in the country" (Babb 2004, 551). Salazar advocated for a safe and clean environment for tourism so that there would be no more talk of "plastic bags being the national flower" (Sánchez Campbell 2004, 9A). Both lauded the second annual convention on tourism, held in the colonial city of Granada in August 2004 (Sánchez Campbell 2004, 9A) with the theme "For a clean and safe Nicaragua" (Zambrana 2004), as helping to establish a secure experience for tourists.[3] Whether or not the tourism industry can project a more clean and wholesome image to mainstream tourists, I found that it presents more mixed messages to prospective travelers.

That same year, I discovered that INTUR had developed five thirty-second television spots to run on CNN's Headline News with the slogan: "Nicaragua: It's hot!" This "brand," or product-marketing device, was identified as a way of selling the country to potential investors and international tourists. One thing that travelers to the country know is that Nicaragua's climate is steamy, relieved only when the rain lets loose in torrents. So, when I had a preview of INTUR's new ads, I had to assume that they were intended to invoke another meaning of the word "hot." Indeed, the spots offered fast-paced and colorful images of the country with captions like "Culture," "History," and "Adventure," implying that Nicaragua is a new and exciting place to visit, and that it is *de moda* (in fashion). But the ads' fleeting images of young women frolicking in bikinis also conveyed a not-so-subtle message that Nicaragua is "sexy" and that visitors would discover tanned beauties eager for the company of foreigners with money to spend. When I commented on the ads' sexual innuendo, I was met by a rather innocent response from the assistant in the marketing department, who had not considered this possible reaction (María Eugenia Sabella, interview, 20 July 2004).[4] This occurred, notably, in a nation where one of the first official acts of the revolutionary government in 1979 had been to ban the use of sexualized images of women in the media.

Since 1990, Sandinista politics had been fraught with compromise and pacts with the political and religious right (which had caused many to part ways and join the Movement for Sandinista Renovation [MRS]). Nonetheless, Ortega's comeback was viewed throughout the region and much of the world as a move leftward, part of the so-called Latin American "pink tide." While Nicaraguan critics have likened his populist refashioning as a sort of New Age caudillo to past dictatorships,[5] the U.S. media link him with Venezuelan president Hugo Chávez. In the current context, tourism has taken a slightly different form, but still ranks as a leading industry along with coffee production.

With the return of Sandinista leadership to the country, visitors passing through the international airport receive lingering impressions of national heroes Augusto César Sandino and Rubén Darío, their huge portraits strategically placed on facing walls. Sandino, in particular, has recovered his place of honor as national icon and is not so closely linked to the controversial 1980s. INTUR announced the prospect of promoting a Sandino tour that would follow a circuit from Sandino's birthplace to the areas where he fought his anti-imperialist campaign in the 1920s and 1930s until his assassination by General Anastasio Somoza García's forces. In addition, there has been an emphasis on sustainable and communitarian tourism in rural sectors, drawing tourists to coffee cooperatives and other sites where they can enjoy the natural environment and contribute to local economies (Cañada, Delgado, and Gil 2006). To some degree, tourism may be moving in the wholesome direction Borge and others talked about in earlier years. Even so, less wholesome strains of tourism are also present and have deeply gendered effects.

Women, Youth, and Tourism

In the capital city of Managua, there has been much talk about the proliferation of casinos and nightclubs. The first casino, Pharaohs, opened on the Masaya highway in 2000. A number of others have since appeared in Managua and other cities. Some Nicaraguans express national pride in this hallmark of modernity. As one writer effused, "[V]isitors will think they have arrived in Las Vegas, in the United States" (Bravo 2004, 4A). Others, like Borge, are concerned that the casinos and nightclubs will attract a growing clientele in search of sexual favors.

I heard that one well-known club, "Lips," owned by a North American, charges over twenty dollars for a drink because it is assumed that men asking for a cocktail wish for a lap dance, too. The club is centrally located across from the Crowne Plaza (formerly, the Intercontinental Hotel) and demands attention with its neon sign displaying large, red lips. My visit at midday during off hours did not dispel the notion that the club offers far more than a bar; a woman employee nodded silently when asked about the practice of charging high prices for drinks, with sexual "extras" provided.

By 2008, the Masaya highway in central Managua had become far more developed commercially, with malls, casinos, hotels, restaurants, and clubs. Several venues, like the Elite and the Diamond Club, are known for their strip shows. The women who perform there may leave with clients who pay the club a fee for their time. More women, and sometimes transvestites or transgendered individuals (*travestis*) who have found a market niche, can be seen along the road later at night, selling sex to both nationals and tourists. Several nongovernmental organizations (NGOs) send out people to carry condoms and encourage the use of clinics for health exams and STD testing. Nicaragua's sexual culture is more evident today than a decade ago and the return of the FSLN has not diminished its presence.

A middle-aged man from the United States who has lived in Managua for some years told me he believes "all Nicas" have their price and will provide sex for money. He mentioned being approached by a teenage boy from his neighborhood who offered sexual favors in exchange for a small sum. This man's perception may be conditioned by stereotyped generalizations regarding sexualized and racialized "others," but it does point to a common view. The practice of exchanging sex for money appeared to be more widespread after the transition from revolutionary to neoliberal government in the 1990s. The transition meant higher unemployment, growing disparities of wealth, and the elimination of the state provision of basic foods and health care.[6] While tourism has contributed to economic development at the national level, it has also introduced new social inequities and new, often unattainable, consumer desires.

Over the years researching in Managua, I lived in one barrio that became a home to me. There, I observed evidence of the sex trade and also of the occasional longer-term relationships between Nicaraguans and foreigners, whether visitors or residents. From the early 1990s, I saw the growing number of women and *travesti* sex workers on the streets near the Intercontinental Hotel and elsewhere in the city. In the working class neighborhood where I stayed, I knew teenaged mothers who dressed up and sought work that would pay better than informal services like taking in laundry or cleaning homes, which they also performed. A 19-year-old with two young children, whom I had known for some years, seemed embarrassed when I saw her one day wearing a faux leather miniskirt and close-fitting laced bodice. I could not bring myself to inquire where she was going. Several young women living with their mother across the street from me made little secret of their livelihood, as clients called for them in luxurious vehicles to go off to motels for amorous and reportedly well-rewarded trysts (Babb 2001, 256–57).[7]

The lives of most sex workers are far from glamorous, however. At Girasoles (Sunflowers), an NGO that provides services to sex workers, I met with "Elvia" in an examination room where we sat and talked. Self-possessed and wearing a long, slim, dark skirt and matching blouse with deep V-neckline, she asked me to guess her age. She revealed that she was fifty-two and had been a sex worker from the time she was twenty-five, when she was abandoned by an abusive husband, the mother of five young children, and recently arrived in the city. She later had five more children, though two of them died. Now, her sister cares for the youngest ones, who do not know what she does to support them. She meets men at a bar and negotiates a price based on the services offered, sometimes providing sex on credit until the men's payday on the fifteenth and thirtieth of the month. She commented that in her barrio it is not uncommon for women to work this way and she does not feel particularly stigmatized, though it is not work that she would choose if she had other options. She prefers to go to the bar with other women, as protection against possible violence. Some sex workers in Nicaragua are starting to organize, but Elvia just counts on the support of sex workers she knows and Girasoles (Interview, 5 June 2008).

The historic city of Granada in Nicaragua has become a primary site of tourism in the country, particularly since foreigners started buying up and renovating properties in the city center. There are language schools, fine restaurants and hotels, and an abundance of tourism offices. Horse-drawn carriages and a quaint look combine with modern comforts at relatively low cost. A number of retirees from the United States have purchased homes in Granada, especially since discovering that the cost of living is substantially lower than in neighboring Costa Rica. Some older men have sought out young Nicaraguan women as their mates and housekeepers, an arrangement that could be viewed as a form of sexual servitude. Several of these men manage real estate and sell properties to other newcomers. Speaking to them in the company of their timid young wives, it was impossible to avoid the impression that these men were exploiting the physical, emotional, and sexual labor of highly vulnerable Nicaraguans. Nonetheless, these women had their own expectations, which often included their husbands' support of their mothers and siblings. In several private conversations the women suggested that they would not put up with abuse over the long term.

Granada's central park, just across from the Hotel Alhambra, has become notorious for attracting tourists seeking young women for a single night or longer. Most perniciously, some seek out children and adolescents, and young people may be seen waiting in the park for potential clients. A long-time resident estimated that about 60 percent of unaccompanied male tourists may come to Granada for sex tourism. On 23 February 2001, a segment of a weekly television program *Esta Semana* (This Week) titled "*Inocencia en venta*" (Innocence for Sale) made the public aware of the situation of adolescents, mainly girls between eleven and thirteen, who are sought out for sex tourism in Granada. With their identities concealed, young girls described being taken to hotels or houses where they were paid for sex, with no questions asked. Until this recent attention, there was little control over such practices, but following national media coverage the city mayor called for legal intervention. In one heavily publicized case in 2003, a pedophile from the United States who recruited children for sex and pornographic photography was arrested and is now serving time in prison.

In recent years, Granada has developed a long corridor with little city traffic, La Calzada, dedicated to expanding tourist options. Besides the hotels, guesthouses, restaurants, and tour offices, the street has also attracted some of the youthful sexual commerce that the city would like to discourage. Women working at an AMNLAE Casa de la Mujer (women's center) on that street expressed concern about the children and adolescents who sell candy to tourists, and who are also known to be sought out for sexual services (Olga María Marenca, interview, 6 June 2008). One of these women told me that she was once surprised to be approached by a man who simply assumed that she would be available to him. A study of the sexual exploitation of children has shown how pervasive the problem is in Granada and elsewhere in the country. The researchers identified several forms of sexual commerce directed at youth, and a commission was organized to educate those in the tourism industry and to call for greater support from the legal system to penalize offenders (Karla Sequeira, interview, 12 June 2008). The feminist NGO Puntos de Encuentro (Points of Encounter) published a booklet directed to young people and their allies to inform them of their rights and to empower them to resist sexual exploitation (La Boletina 2007).

Highly visible cases, often linked to tourism, have prompted action at the national level. INTUR, along with the Nicaraguan Ministry of the Family (MiFamilia) and the National Police, held a forum in the city of Masaya on exploitative sexual commerce of children and adolescents (Linarte 2004, 13B). Experts found connections to family violence and sexual abuse, poverty, and a weak legal system. This kind of sexual exploitation has been increasing in border areas of the country as well as in tourist centers. Officials have called on service providers in the tourism industry to serve as watchdogs so that perpetrators of sexual exploitation of minors may be apprehended. Those service providers either directly or indirectly participating in the sexual commerce of children and youth would be stripped of their licenses under Article 72 of the General Tourism Law.

The Pacific Coast town of San Juan del Sur has become a better-known site for tourism in recent years, attracting those seeking the beach, sea diving, surfing, and other water sports. Cruise ships now stop in the formerly sleepy town, adding only a little revenue since travelers are cautioned against consuming local food and drink. But the travelers have had an impact on the town. Residents are concerned that their youngsters will adopt the ways of "hippie" and other foreign youth, viewed as sloppily dressed and groomed, often with bad manners. Prostitution, although not on the scale found in Granada, is on the rise. In even the best hotels and restaurants, young Nicaraguan women often accompany middle-aged male tourists quite openly. A local woman commented perceptively that tourism is *una espada de doble filo* (a double-edged sword), bringing the good and the bad. As wealthier outsiders, both Nicaraguan and foreign,[8] discover the charms of the coastal town and buy up property, locals like her find it impossible to afford the higher cost of living. She told me that she would like to see a group of women get together to defend the town against the adverse effects of tourism, which could threaten their cultural identity. Despite her misgivings about the impact of tourism, however, she is putting her own daughter through a college program in tourism studies and hopes that her son will pursue the same path once she can send him to college. She remarked ruefully to me that it is no wonder women are entering prostitution, given the cost of living and limited employment opportunities.

I interviewed one young woman, "Margarita," who at twenty-three was widowed with eight-year-old twin daughters in the northern city of Matagalpa. She had come to San Juan del Sur for a few months; she planned to earn enough money to return home and open a small business. Every week she made the lengthy trip back to her family, who thought she was working at a bar, and to take a class to become a beautician. Pretty and smart, Margarita was hedging her bets by preparing for a couple of different employment opportunities. In the meantime she worked in a family-run *putería* (whorehouse) in the seaside town. Margarita came to her workplace through a friend who worked there. She had clients both on-site and elsewhere in the town. The latter commanded much higher rates, but a good part of the payment went to the owner of the putería. She spoke appreciatively of the kind owner and his evangelical wife and their toddler son, but made it clear how important it was to her that she work there only a few months and that her work remain unknown to her family and community.

I had made contact with Margarita through an employee at one of the town's more expensive resorts, where I knew the owners well enough to ask candidly about how guests hook up with sex workers. According to the obliging concierge, or "arranger," he tries never to disappoint a guest. If someone wants "a girl" or drugs, for example, he attempts to manage it in a discrete way that is "safe" for both the resort and the guest (and he always keeps condoms at the front desk). He makes sure that sex workers are escorted to the correct accommodations and that they leave quietly and inconspicuously afterwards. He assured me that every hotel in the area provides such services, often for generous tips. He and other employees at the resort told me that with so many tourists coming to San Juan del Sur, local men sometimes feel that their women are being "stolen away" from them (interviews, 10 June 2008).

Besides those women who choose sex work, others simply prefer to date foreign men, whom they find attractive and often better mannered than local men. I met several young women, frequently with some professional training, who are holding out for an *extranjero* (foreign man) who has better prospects than the Nicaraguan men they know. Some local men are similarly interested in foreign women, often for the advantages that these tourists offer in the form of money to spend, desire for a good time, and so on. Such men may be not only *mujeriego* (womanizers) but *gringa-iego* (specifically seeking women travelers from North America), as one local observer expressed it. This may be a result of the Americanization of youth that has accompanied the growth in tourism from the north. The possibilities for romance, short or long-term, appeal to many. Some direct their attention to language schools and other places that draw tourists. I learned of some young Nicaraguans who had dated a series of foreign students over a period of years, apparently hoping for a long-term commitment or marriage (Aynn Setright, personal communication, 9 June 2008). Although romance tourism is not as well known in Nicaragua as in some areas of the Caribbean (Brennan 2004, Cabezas 2004), it is found in places frequented by foreign travelers, in seaside resorts, retirement communities, and study-abroad programs.

The Hidden Side of Tourism Development

In Managua, video-maker Rossana Lacayo spoke with me about her work, *Verdades Ocultas* (Hidden Truths, 2003), which traces the stories of several sex workers in Nicaragua. The narratives in this award-winning video relate the difficult conditions that propelled the women and one travesti into sex work—inadequate incomes to support their children, histories of violence, and too few choices (common themes for Central America). She described *trata de blanca* or trafficking in people, mainly young girls. Lured away from their families and networks of support, young women from Nicaragua's rural sector are particularly vulnerable to abuse and are sometimes taken to neighboring countries for sex tourism. In other cases, adolescent girls are offered to truck drivers traveling through Nicaragua and along the Pan-American Highway as a form of *comercio sexual* (sexual commerce). She noted that sex tourism is even more hidden than this form of sexual commerce, and so it has received less attention (Lacayo, interview, 28 July 2004).

Several NGOs are documenting this phenomenon and working to offer alternatives to impoverished families that in some instances encourage daughters to perform sexual services for men in order to put food on the table. The feminist director of the NGO Xochiquetzal, an activist organization working in the area of sexuality and human rights,[9] was more passionate on this subject than on any other when I interviewed her. Hazel Fonseca (interview, 23 July 2004) emphasized that her organization works to bring attention to many of the areas of sexual injustice that occur beneath the surface in Nicaragua, calling for an end to these forms of exploitation and discrimination. Thus, the NGO's publication *Fuera del Closet* (Out of the Closet), best known for supporting gay rights, aims to bring all manner of previously hidden sexual exchanges out into public view. Fonseca regards sexual commerce that targets vulnerable youth, whether a result of sex tourism or of sexual predation more generally, as one of the most urgent social problems needing to be confronted—and she advocates for youth empowerment in the process.

Figure 15.1. Outside the Elite Strip Club, Photo by Florence Babb

If we find greater attention to sex work involving young people than adults in Nicaragua, this may be due only in part to the more compelling nature of their situation. It may also be explained in terms of the potential for damaging effects on tourism in Nicaragua's economy. While child prostitution as flagrant criminal activity detracts from the image the country would like to project, adult sex workers and entertainers provide some of the revenue the nation depends on. Writing on Costa Rica, Rivers-Moore (2007) describes the broad and critical attention given to child sex tourism in contrast to the "blind eye" turned to more mature sex workers, even when their rights are violated. She accounts for this by noting the reliance on "gringo" tourism, a part of which seeks out sexual encounters, as well as the vulnerable migrant status of many sex workers—a great number of them Nicaraguans who are undocumented and unprotected, suffering racialized opprobrium they would not experience at home.

Staging Sex and Love in Post-revolutionary Nations

Tourism in post-revolutionary and post-conflict nations reveals the highly ambivalent ways in which gender, sexuality, and race figure in these countries' efforts to develop their economies by refashioning themselves for international visitors.[10] Sex work and romance tourism are just a part of what I have observed in Nicaragua, but they get at some of the most vexing problems that often accompany tourism, particularly in the Global South: the encounters of foreigners who are seeking "exotic" and even intimate experiences with locals, who may in turn desire the financial, and sometimes emotional, support that travelers seem willing to offer. Nicaragua is far from alone in attracting this kind of tourism—we see it in many developing countries. Yet my research on this phenomenon contributes to our understanding of the particular dilemmas faced by post-revolutionary nations as tourism looms large as a principal industry. The ethnographic material presented here sheds needed light on the deeply gendered and sometimes racialized consequences of tourism in societies in transition to more market-driven economies.

There are certain striking similarities between the Nicaraguan case presented here and others I have examined, notably that of Cuba. One such similarity is the desire, or ideological commitment, to offer "wholesome" tourism experiences even as the market pushes these nations toward a tolerance of commodified sex and intimacy. A young Nicaraguan woman I met, a domestic worker studying nights to try to enter tourism administration, told me that her dream was to leave Managua and join forces with another woman to own and operate a guesthouse in the provinces. She was aware of sex tourism in some parts of the country, but, she volunteered, "It's not as bad as in Cuba." This points to the question of whether Nicaragua will follow the direction taken in Cuba, tolerating sex and romance tourism as the tourism industry expands and more pleasure-seekers arrive. While it is true that at present the phenomenon is far more pronounced in Cuba than in Nicaragua, it is also arguable that Cuban sex workers tend to have greater control over these practices than their Nicaraguan counterparts—who are often targeted as highly vulnerable due to their youth, poverty, and lack of social support. When Nicaraguans lost the safety net of social services provided by the revolutionary government prior to 1990, they began relying on NGOs to provide support that was no longer offered by the state. While some access this support, many others do not, leaving them to fend for themselves. Cubans, even if they face social and political restrictions and shortages of needed or desired consumer goods, continue to benefit from state guarantees of education, health care, and other basic rights and resources.

In the last half century, Nicaragua, like Cuba, drew wide international attention as a result of its broad program of social transformation. Although Cuba's revolutionary process has been far more sustained than Nicaragua's, both countries share a legacy of expressed concern for their citizens' social and economic well-being. Without a doubt, their triumphant social revolutions put these nations on the map, in the Latin American region and in the world.

Thus, I was startled when a Managua travel agent told me that with tourism, "Nicaragua is becoming a place on the map" (Careli Tours, interview, 22 July 2004).[11] This at first seemed to me to be a reflection of the nation's historical amnesia. But it could also be a manifestation of the hopes of many Nicaraguans like Cubans, regardless of political orientation, that tourism will do for the future what social revolution accomplished in the past.

However, in an era of neoliberalism and globalization when social inequalities are in great evidence, we should be less sanguine about the distribution of benefits from tourism. We must be chastened by the words of the Nicaraguan woman who described tourism as "a double-edged sword." Could the unofficial "branding" of Cuba as a haven for sex and romance tourism be in Nicaragua's future as well? The political and economic vicissitudes in both countries and the sexualizing of previously "forbidden" lands suggest that this is possible. On the other hand, Nicaragua, like Cuba, has a history of women's active social and political participation, and we could see different currents of change in the future.

The opening up to tourism in Nicaragua paves the way for the sort of "staged authenticity" conceptualized by Dean MacCannell in his classic work *The Tourist* (1999 [1976]) and discussed in relation to sex and romance tourism by Brennan (2004). Men and women perform their desire and "stage intimacy," offering at least the illusion of "authentic experience," insofar as there are mutual benefits in doing so. When the post-revolutionary nation no longer provides the safety net of the past and economic livelihood is no longer a certainty, sex and love appear to be the means by which to grasp opportunities that are otherwise unattainable. Tourists as well as local women and men collaborate in this staged exchange of intimacy and desire with money and other gifts. The trafficking in question is not only in sex, but in hope. The Nicaraguan case I have considered here reveals the profoundly unequal terms of tourism's encounter with gender and power, race and nation, as realities fall short of expectations. More often than not, sex is fleeting and romance remains as elusive as the economic advancement and well-being promised decades ago in this post-revolutionary nation. Yet hope, whether it is for intimacy, democracy, or sustainability, continues to be a significant and at times transformative social vector in Nicaragua and throughout Central America.

Notes

* I wish to thank the organizers of the Wenner-Gren International Workshop, Ellen Moodie and Jennifer Burrell, as well as discussant Jennifer Bickham Méndez and other participants, for their comments. Joseph Feldman and Molly Green assisted in the preparation of this work.

1. Some material presented here appeared in *The Tourism Encounter: Fashioning Latin American Nations and Histories* (2011), with the permission of Stanford University Press.
2. Elsewhere I examine solidarity tourism as a precursor to contemporary tourism in Nicaragua (Babb 2004). See also Hollander (1986).
3. The II Tourism Convention was held in Granada, Nicaragua, and drew participants from throughout Central America.
4. I later spoke with this woman's boss, who said that there was discussion in INTUR regarding the woman in the bikini in the ad. She and other women convinced the advertisers to make the appearance briefer, saying that the ad must appeal to women, who make vacation decisions.
5. In June 2008, the celebrated Dora María Tellez (a commander in the revolution) went on a hunger strike to protest the FSLN attempt to keep the MRS out of upcoming municipal elections. In 2010, I interviewed feminists who were deeply distrustful of the FSLN (Babb and Setright 2010).
6. Many writers have examined this transition. See Babb (2001) for discussion of the neoliberal turn and its gendered consequences in Nicaragua.
7. I am grateful to the late Grant Gallup, whose home I often shared in this barrio, for offering stories of neighbors' lives.
8. I met a Nicaraguan couple from the city of Masaya, a dental surgeon and a lawyer, who were visiting San Juan del Sur and said that tourism is entirely positive as all good things come from outside Nicaragua.
9. The lesbian feminist founders of this NGO have given substantial attention to same-sex sexuality. Their free publication *Fuera del Closet* (Out of the Closet) is distributed widely. See Babb (2003) for discussion of Nicaraguan lesbian and gay culture and politics.
10. Elsewhere I compare highland Peru and Chiapas, Mexico to Nicaragua and Cuba (Babb 2011).
11. See Adrienne Rich's (1986) groundbreaking essay on the politics of location, written after a trip to revolutionary Nicaragua. She famously wrote, "A place on a map is also a place in history" (1986, 212).

16 Notes on Tourism, Ethnicity, and the Politics of Cultural Value in Honduras

Mark Anderson

In 1999, World Bank president James Wolfonson asserted: "There are development dimensions of culture. Physical and expressive culture is an undervalued resource in developing countries. It can earn income, through tourism, crafts, and other cultural enterprises" (Yudice 2003, 13). This effort to promote culture as a source of value raises questions concerning neoliberalism and multiculturalism in contemporary Central America. Why does ethnic difference figure prominently in the marketing of nations as tourist destinations? How does tourism attempt to produce economic value out of culture and ethnicity? How do the bearers of valued "difference"—often indigenous or Afrodescendant peoples—engage the tourist industry?

I explore these questions through an analysis of Garifuna and the Honduran tourist industry. Garifuna communities, located on the Atlantic Coast, are situated in complex, contradictory positions in relation to the tourist industry—as tourist attractions, spaces of cultural difference, coveted property, and ethnic/indigenous/Afrohonduran territories.[1] In this chapter I discuss: 1) efforts to realize the value associated with ethnic difference by state agents and other key actors in the tourist industry; 2) frustrated attempts by Garifuna to realize the value of their own culture; and 3) efforts by Garifuna organizations to critically engage the tourist industry. I argue that the inability of Garifuna to profit from their culture should lead us to examine the cultural and economic appropriation found within tourism, an industry that masks its own forms of cultural exploitation under the guise of cultural promotion and recognition.

This essay is a set of preliminary reflections situated between my previous work on Garifuna and the politics of race and culture in Honduras, and an emerging project on the tourist industry in Honduras. In my earlier work I analyzed the turn towards multiculturalism and the recognition of ethnic rights largely in terms of the politics of race, ethnicity, and indigeneity (Anderson 2007; Anderson 2009). However, a focus on ethnic activism and politics overlooks another dimension to multiculturalism, its perceived marketing potential.

Tourism involves the proactive promotion of ethnic difference that is an important and often neglected feature of contemporary multiculturalism. Charles Hale (2005, 13) analyzes "neoliberal multiculturalism" as an "emergent regime of governance that shapes, delimits, and produces cultural difference rather than suppresses it." He argues:

> Encouraged and supported by multilateral institutions, Latin American elites have moved from being vehement opponents to reluctant arbiters of rights grounded in cultural difference. In so doing, they find that cultural rights, when carefully delimited, not only pose little challenge to the forward march of the neoliberal project but also induce the bearers of those rights to join the march. (2005, 13)

Hale focuses on the governance and management of ethnic activism—efforts to delimit ethnic rights, draw lines between "permitted" and forbidden politics, and define participation. In addition to conceptualizing multiculturalism as a form of governance we should also approach it (critically) as a strategy of capital accumulation. By exploring how value is produced and appropriated out of ethnicity, we can also analyze how multicultural projects induce multiple responses from ethnic subjects enticed to participate by the promises of recognition and inclusion.

In 1997, at the bicentennial celebration of the Garifuna arrival to Central America, Honduran president Carlos Roberto Reina told the audience:

> The new century will be marked by the current technological revolution in which we are living. And if we are not direct protagonists in it, we can take advantage of it all the same because being a people of multiethnic origin we are prepared to develop, from the natural and geographic advantages of our country, an ecotourism industry in which you, above all, can be effective protagonists, taking advantage of the force of your dances, the originality of your foods, the happiness of your character and the natural beauty of these islands and all of the Atlantic littoral of Honduras. (Reina 1997)

President Reina suggests that Honduras's ethnic diversity provides a valuable resource for tourist development. He also suggests that Garifuna will actively participate in the tourist industry, selling their dances and foods, and attracting tourists with their happy character. It is important to critique the kinds of cultural commodification promoted here as representations that fix identities, stereotype peoples, trivialize traditions, and exoticize difference. However, I want to develop a different angle on the marriage of state multiculturalism and tourist development and the role of ethnic/cultural difference in tourism. The tourist industry attempts to profit from culture not simply (or even primarily) by churning out cultural commodities (handicrafts, performances, food, and so on), but also by using images of ethnic difference to bolster the image of Honduras as an attractive destination. The "value" of ethnic culture is more elusive than a focus on commodification allows us to grasp. While images of ethnic difference play a role in efforts to make Honduras a tourist destination, economic rhetoric espoused by powerful actors promises that the tourist industry will benefit marginalized peoples. This logic suggests that a "value-added" process takes place whereby local ethnic groups can participate in tourist markets—beyond the role of workers—to create businesses, sell goods and services, and take advantage of their cultural distinctiveness.

This chapter develops a critical perspective on tourism, ethnicity, and the politics of value by presenting an ethnographic analysis of Garifuna expectations concerning tourism. The chapter is based on fieldwork conducted in the Garifuna community of Sambo Creek between 1994 and 2004, and in the Tela region in 2008 and 2010. I focus on the frustrations Garifuna in Sambo Creek experience with the tourist industry, illustrating how they view their culture as a tourist attraction that primarily profits wealthy mestizos and foreigners. I argue that the tourist industry ultimately reinforces an affirmation of ethnic distinctiveness while reproducing a sense of subjection. I also consider controversies over a large-scale project underway in the Tela region, highlighting divergent positions that Garifuna activists take towards it. One position advocates Garifuna participation and investment in all scales of tourist development, beyond being employees and cultural performers. Another, more critical, position suggests that dominant models of capital-intensive tourist development resemble past enclave economies. This position emphasizes the costs of such development—land displacement, resource deprivation, environmental destruction, and economic dependency. The co-existence of these positions reflects the vexed politics of ethnicity in a multicultural, neoliberal era wherein the marketing of ethnicity produces the promise of inclusion at the potential price of cultural and territorial rights.

The Tourist Industry and Ethnicity in Honduras

In the past two decades the Honduran tourism industry, though smaller than those of Costa Rica (Vivanco, this volume) and Guatemala (Little, this volume), has witnessed substantial growth. Tourism ranks as the country's third leading source of foreign currency, ahead of the agricultural exports characteristic of the twentieth-century "banana republic."

The decline in tourism revenue between 2008 and 2009 resulted from the combined effects of the global financial crisis and the June 2009 coup. The government of Porfirio Lobo continues to promote tourism as a key economic sector with enormous potential.

Table 16.1. Sources of Foreign Currency in Honduras 2008

Economic Sector	Foreign Currency Generated (U.S. $Millions)
Family Remittances	2,807.50
Maquiladora	1,277.21
Tourism	620.40
Coffee	620.20
Bananas	383.80
Palm Oil	205.80
Cultivated Shrimp	99.00
Soap and Detergents	52.40
Wood	29.8

Source: Instituto Hondureño de Turismo (2010, 27).

Table 16.2. Growth of Tourist Industry, 2000–2009

Year	Foreign Currency Generated (U.S. $Millions)
2000	262.8
2001	259.9
2002	304.8
2003	363.4
2004	419.7
2005	465.8
2006	516.0
2007	546.2
2008	620.4
2009	616.0

Source: Secretaría de Turismo (2007, 7–8); Instituto Hondureño de Turismo (2010, 27).

Table 16.3. Growth of Tourist Income in Honduras, 1970–1999 (U.S. $Millions)

1970	1980	1992	1995	1999
4	27	32	80	173

Source: Robinson (2003, 193).

The initial boom in the tourist industry in Honduras began in the early to mid 1990s, stemming from the reduction of Central American conflicts and the introduction of neoliberal reforms that began with the presidency of Rafael Callejas (1990–1994).

In the early 1990s multilateral financial institutions (for example, The World Bank, International Monetary Fund, Inter-American Development Bank) promoted the tourist industry in Central America (Robinson 2003, 193). The Honduran state passed a number of laws to facilitate tourist investment, favoring the interests of transnational capital and national elite (Stonich 2000). The development of tourism as a key sector of the Honduran economy coincided with the official turn towards multiculturalism and the recognition of ethnic rights. Beginning with the presidency of Callejas, the state began to develop initiatives concerning ethnic groups. During the subsequent government of Carlos Roberto Reina (1994–1998), the state consolidated the most important multiethnic reforms to date, including the following: ratification of Convention 169 on Tribal and Indigenous Rights of the International Labor Organization; the institutionalization of bilingual/intercultural education; the creation a new legal office, the Special Prosecutor for Ethnic Groups and Cultural Patrimony; and a program in economic development directed towards ethnic groups called "Our Roots" (funded by the World Bank). The reforms of the early 1990s were spurred, in part, by forms of ethnic activism generated in the 1980s that were connected to the transnational indigenous movement (see Pineda, this volume). As I argue elsewhere (Anderson 2007), in Honduras the key role played by Garifuna activists in ethnic politics contributed to a state multiculturalism in which black (Garifuna and Creoles) and indigenous subjects occupy an equivalent legal position as "ethnic groups" or "peoples."

The official multiculturalism of the 1990s was preceded not just by ethnic organization in the 1980s but also by state efforts to use cultural difference to promote Honduran tourism in the 1970s. For example, in 1972 the national Office of Tourism and the municipal government of La Ceiba sponsored a presentation of Garifuna dances in an effort to transform the city's traditional fair into a Caribbean-style "carnival" (*Tiempo* 1996; *Prensa* 1972). In the mid 1970s, the national government created the office of Secretary of Culture, Tourism and Information, articulating together national cultural patrimony, ethnic difference, and tourist development (Herranz 1996, 232). The secretary sponsored an investigation of Garifuna culture and the dance troupe Ballet Folklórico Garifuna. In the 1970s, newspaper features began to represent Garifuna communities as picturesque attractions, reflected in titles such as "Garifuna Folklore in the Enchanting Landscape of the Caribbean" (*Tiempo* 1979). The promotion of Garifuna culture—compatible with ongoing forms of racism and the normalization of the mestizo subject as representative of the nation—remains key to the making of Honduras and the North Coast as tourist destinations.[2]

The 2000 Honduran census recognizes eight ethnic groups, which include Garifuna, Negro inglés (Creoles), Tolupán, Pech, Misquito, Lenca, Tawahka, and Chortí (Instituto Nacional de Estadística 2001). According to census figures, which are disputed by ethnic organizations as underreporting their populations, these groups constitute 7.2 percent of the Honduran population. The census juxtaposes them against the category of "Other," leaving the majority designation (92.8 percent of the population) racially and ethnically unmarked and unnamed, though the vast majority are known as mestizos or ladinos. You would never guess from state tourist promotions that ethnic groups constitute such a small percentage of the national population. The website for the Honduran Tourism Institute (IHT) provides six categories to attract visitors: nature and adventure; archeology; beaches and reefs; living cultures; colonial cities; and modern cities.[3] The browser allows you to search for places to find those attractions, and tags places with their specific attractions. The Mosquitia, for example, is a site for "Nature and Adventure" and "Living Cultures." Most of the key tourist zones are tied to cultures and ethnicities represented as distinct from the modern mestizo nation. The heritage tourism of the Copan Ruins draws on the glories of the Maya past, though largely bypassing the Chortí Maya who live in the region (Mortensen 2001).[4] The other major tourist destination, the Bay Islands, is primarily a sea, sun, and sand attraction, but evocations of English-speaking blacks add a certain Caribbean appeal and, as on the North Coast, Garifuna appear as living representatives of deep cultural difference. A recent project in Western Honduras, the Ruta Lenca (Lenca Route), modeled on the transnational Ruta Maya project, markets Honduras's largest indigenous population and aims to draw visitors to a highland corridor between Tegucigalpa and the Copan Ruins (Graham 2009; see Binford, this volume). Finally, Garifuna figure prominently in tourist imagery. If you click on "Living Cultures" in the IHT website you find a picture of a smiling Garifuna girl with colorful beads in her braided hair. Above you see a picture of older Garifuna women, garbed in traditional dresses and head wraps, singing as two men hold maracas and a turtle shell. Ethnic representations, especially for tourism, inevitably make disappear any signs of cosmopolitanism, or suffering.

Why does ethnic difference appear so important to tourist promotion? This is a more complex question than it might appear. One convenient explanation lies in a perception of tourist desires: Tourists come to third world destinations to escape their alienated lives, consuming the cultural authenticity otherness signifies (MacCannell 1992). However, to what extent do tourist projects actually strive to provide experiences of cultural difference and authenticity? The function ethnic difference plays in the tourist industry does not reduce to the (direct) commodification of culture and cannot be pinned to commodities and experiences bought and sold in particular places. The marketing of ethnicity by the IHT, guidebooks, and other tourist agents lies in the cumulative effects of juxtaposing multiple attractions, creating an aura of heterogeneous places and peoples that can be enjoyed within a brief time period. Ethnicity adds diversity, distinction, authenticity, and historicity to a nation that could otherwise appear rather bland and, of course, poor. In this regard, its value is immeasurable.

The Elusive Value of Culture

In what ways do ethnic subjects themselves realize the value of culture in the tourist industry, in the dual sense of realize as "to be aware of" and "to profit from"? In order to explore this question I turn to my fieldwork in the Garifuna community of Sambo Creek. During the period between various research trips (1994 to 2004), local opportunities to earn income through culture and tourism were limited. A couple of Garifuna dance groups earned small amounts of money performing at town fairs or other special events. During the Sambo Creek fair, some local families sold "typical" food to visitors. There was one hotel and a couple of inexpensive restaurants that served locals and visitors alike. One restaurant—run by a Garifuna man who had worked as a cruise ship cook—failed within a few years. The most popular destination for visitors was a large restaurant that specialized in fish and some Garifuna foods. It was owned by a well-off mestizo who had a reputation as a scoundrel and who developed real estate in the community. The only hotel owned by Garifuna attracted occasional foreign backpackers; most middle-class travelers stayed at the Canadian-owned hotel across the river. With the exception of a family that made drums, no one produced artifacts for sale in

Figure 16.1. "Women's Cabins": This local tourist project in Sambo Creek is run by a group of single mothers.

the tourist industry. Within the last few years, a cooperative of single mothers, with funding from an international nongovernmental organization (NGO), has erected two tourist cabins on the beach, but they lack the marketing resources and connections to achieve high levels of occupation.

Even in communities with a consistent tourist presence, most Garifuna find few opportunities to cash in on their culture. A study of Punta Gorda, located on the highly traveled island of Roatan, highlights local frustrations (Kirtsoglou and Theodossopoulos 2004). These Garifuna do not mind tourism; in fact they want more of it. But they resent how outsiders make money off of them. For example, members of a local dance company that perform for pre-packaged tours argued that they were never paid enough for their efforts (Kirtsoglou and Theodossopoulos 2004, 147). More generally, Garifuna complained, "They are taking our culture away." When challenged by the foreign social scientists to identify how that process worked, they argued that photos of Garifuna appear in expensive books in fancy hotel gift shops yet no Garifuna receive compensation. I heard similar contentions about a book I owned; the cover photograph depicts an old woman wearing a headscarf. People said she died in poverty and never received money for the photo that helped make the book. These accounts do not merely reflect resentment at the ways outsiders offer little in return for knowledge production about Garifuna or inflated expectations of the monetary rewards such knowledge production entails. They also highlight the gap between the intangible yet potent value of the *image* of Garifuna culture and the devaluation of the producers and performers of Garifuna culture, that is, Garifuna themselves. I will illustrate this argument via a discussion of the position of Garifuna—as labor, culture, and image—in a tourist complex located near Sambo Creek.

The Palma Real Beach Resort and Casino was built in 2001 by wealthy investors from the capital. The tourist complex is designed to attract foreign tourists and Honduran day visitors. It contains a central hotel, bungalows, a swimming pool (with attached bar), snack bar, buffet-style restaurant, nightclub, tennis courts, and waterpark. In 2004, approximately thirty people from Sambo Creek, mostly Garifuna men in their twenties, worked there as porters, bartenders, waiters, cooks, and dishwashers. Several young Garifuna and mestiza women also cleaned rooms. One Garifuna woman worked behind the snack bar and two others earned small amounts of money braiding hair. Employees earned approximately 2,000–2,500 Lempiras a month (between $110.00 and $130.00 (U.S.)), slightly better than the Honduran minimum wage at the time, and porters, waiters, and bartenders (positions given to men) earned additional tip money. Most of the other employees came from La Ceiba or the predominately mestizo town of Jutiapa. The Palma Real strictly regulates entrance and inhibits contact with members of nearby communities who might sell goods and services to tourists. Its "all-inclusive" model has become common in Caribbean tourist enterprises and enforces spatial segregation between tourists and locals (Gregory 2007). Guests at the hotel have little contact with Sambo Creek, and Sambeños interact with guests as low-level hotel employees. The resort also offers snorkeling tours to the nearby cays (the Cayos Cochinos), largely bypassing local fisherman and inhabitants.

If the Palma Real projects a generic Caribbean beach resort experience, some signs of local cultural particularity call forth the image of Garifuna. The bar/disco is called Guifiti, after the Garifuna alcoholic beverage that serves medicinal purposes. A drink at the bar is named "Sambo Creek." Every Wednesday—at least when enough guests are present—the Palma Real offers a "Typical (*Típico*) Garifuna Show" put on by a group of nine men and women from Sambo Creek. Two of my friends, Wilson and Antonio, were musicians in the group. After visiting the Palma Real, I asked several employees how they liked working there. They complained a little about the low wages and labor discipline, but they appreciated the opportunity to interact with foreigners and work close to home. A few days later a different picture emerged when it came to the question of compensation for *cultural* labor.

One evening I hung out with a group of young men, including several resort employees, around a bottle of rum at the house where the musicians

Figure 16.2. Guests check into the Palma Real Beach Resort and Casino.

Antonio and Wilson lived. As often happened on such occasions, the young men discussed their adventures abroad. They compared notes on salaries in different countries and debated which "races" worked the hardest. Elmer, who worked as a porter at the Palma Real, said that he had mestizo friends in San Pedro Sula who would work eighteen hours straight and he didn't know any Garifuna who would do that. Antonio countered that he wouldn't work like that unless "they pay me." Marco, who managed the pool bar at the Palma Real, observed that Antonio and Wilson were not paid enough for their work as musicians at the Palma Real. Everyone, including Elmer, agreed. Wilson asserted: "200 Lempiras [$11.00] for six hours of work. It's not enough! They pay much more in Mexico and Belize." One young man stood up and said, "Look. It's not just anybody that can play music like us, with a rhythm so original, or who can dance like this," briefly demonstrating the famous *punta* to the laughter of everyone. Someone offered more soberly: "They don't know the value of this culture."

The value of culture is elusive. The critique voiced by these young men does not simply suggest that the resort inadequately compensates the skilled labor of musicians; it insists that it undervalues the collective cultural knowledge and inheritance of the Garifuna people. The exploitation of cultural labor thus appears particularly egregious, even to young men who do not directly commodify Garifuna culture. Lying beyond that critique, I argue, is a sense that the Palma Real—and the Honduran tourism industry—appropriates the image of Garifuna to attract customers and differentiate Honduras from other possible destinations.

The rather modest, if crude, evocations of Garifuna culture found at a resort casting itself as a luxurious Caribbean destination take on greater significance when placed in the cumulative symbolic universe of Honduran tourist promotions. An initiative by the Honduran Tourism Institute called SAVE (Scientific-Academic-Volunteer-Educational Tourism) bears the slogan, "Honduras: Nature's Laboratory, Culture's Library," drawing on a still vibrant association between nature and (ethnic/indigenous) culture to perpetuate fantasies of enduring life ways in romantic environments. This program offers travelers the opportunity to explore "authentic natural and cultural landscapes, and at the same time collaborate with local communities to *add value* to these natural and human resources" (emphasis added).[5] The purported benefits for Hondurans include "strengthening of human resources, fostering pride among ethnic communities of their vibrant culture and traditions, more effective conservation of Honduras' rich natural heritage, and the generation of a lasting credibility for Honduras as a destination." The interpretation of value addition here misdirects. The program posits that tourism "adds value" by ignoring how the tourist industry *relies* on (stereotyped) culture and nature as sources of attraction.

What is at stake here is not simply skewed representations of contemporary Garifuna but the use of Garifuna to add value to Honduran tourism. Obvious examples include a tourist agency owned by non-Garifuna that calls itself "Garifuna Tours" and a company with a line of T-shirts depicting figures of Garifuna. However, the problem ultimately goes beyond any single enterprise that might be held accountable for violating intellectual property rights. The image of Garifuna as tourist attraction is produced by a host of actors (the state, the media, tourist guidebooks, travel websites, and so on). Essentially a set of stereotypes, that image circulates liberally in the public domain. It offers the promise of value for those with the means to capitalize on "nature" and "culture" who, by and large, are not Garifuna but more powerful actors in the tourist economy.

Dominant discourses that assume that tourist development inevitably adds value to the producers of culture overstate the benefits of tourism while masking and making disappear—but only partially—the use of their culture and image by the industry. Curious contradictions ensue. The inability of Garifuna to realize market value from their culture and image produces frustration and reinforces their apprehension of racial and cultural discrimination; at the same time, the promotion of Garifuna as a tourist attraction contributes to a sense of ethnic distinction. A leading land activist in Sambo Creek asked me rhetorically:

> Why do international organizations want to invest in Honduras? Why does the World Bank want to invest in Honduras? Because of our culture. Yes. Tourists who come here, do they want to go to Tegucigalpa? They come here and prefer to stay in a house of *manaca* [thatch] and mud because it's cooler. And the government wants to not even give us one percent of our ancestral land? No.

This activist overestimates the desire of tourists to stay in "traditional" houses made of dirt walls and a thatched roof, to have an "authentic" experience of cultural difference; but he calls attention to conflicts over land, resources, and territories deeply implicated in the tourist industry.

Opposition and Participation: Engaging Tourist Development

The most vocal national Garifuna organization critical of dominant tourist paradigms and state treatment of Garifuna communities is the Organización Fraternal Negra de Honduras (Fraternal Organization of Blacks of Honduras, OFRANEH). OFRANEH was initially established in 1977 and is a legally recognized representative of the Garifuna people. In the 1980s, OFRANEH developed a model of political struggle based on an indigenous rights paradigm that promotes Garifuna cultural and territorial rights as reflected in international legal instruments such as ILO Convention 169 (England 2006; Anderson 2007). OFRANEH views the protection of Garifuna territories—a concept that includes the total environment occupied and/or used by communities—as key to the survival and integrity of Garifuna as a people.

As tourist development, and speculation of it, expanded on the North Coast, property values increased dramatically. In Sambo Creek, local Garifuna without good sources of transnational income find it impossible to acquire land to purchase a home, much less a farm, in the community. The local land activist mentioned earlier helped lead a (partially successful) effort to recuperate land in the name of the community from a mestizo family from La Ceiba that acquired several tracts in Sambo Creek in the 1980s (Brondo 2006). Calculations of the potential benefits of tourist development to local communities do not measure the cost of territorial loss resulting from speculative activities and real estate inflation. Indeed, from a purely market calculus these processes would seem to add "value" to local communities; but the individuals best in position to take advantage are those who previously amassed property on the cheap—often through irregular and illegal means—and/or have the capital to invest in real estate. Others find property values rising out of reach.

OFRANEH and other Garifuna organizations such as the Organizacíon de Desarrollo Étnico Comunitario (Organization of Ethnic Community Development, ODECO) have promoted a model of collective land ownership to prevent further property transfer to outsiders. In the 1990s, they pressured the Honduran government to provide collective land titles, coming together in a 1996 demonstration that led to a presidential agreement to provide titles to all Garifuna communities. However, most of the titles eventually produced were limited to residential areas and did not cover community territories (Thorne 2004). In 2004, the Honduran Congress included a chapter in the neoliberal "Property Law" that, despite the objections of OFRANEH, guarantees the rights of third parties on indigenous and Afrohonduran collective lands and creates the option for communities to terminate communal land regimes in favor of private property.

One flash point of conflict is an emergent tourist project located in the Tela Bay area between the Garifuna communities of Miami and Tornabé, known by the company name Desarrollo Turístico Bahia de Tela (Tourist Development of Tela Bay, DTBT) and as Los Micos Beach & Golf Resort.[6] The National Congress authorized the project in 1997, facilitating the transfer of 312 hectares of land from the Jeannette Kawas National Park via the Honduran Tourism Institute to the DTBT. The DTBT is a public-private holding company, with 49 percent of the shares controlled by Honduran Tourism Institute and 51 percent owned by the Fondo Hondureño de Inversión en Turismo (the Honduran Tourism Investment Fund, FHIT), formed by 46 Honduran companies.[7] In 2008, the project's planned first phase involved the creation of a five-star hotel, a four-star hotel, an eighteen-hole golf course, almost 400 privately owned villas, a beach club, a commercial zone, and an equestrian park. The Inter-American Development Bank has provided loans for infrastructural development. The Los Micos project is touted as a centerpiece of Honduran tourist development, designed to A) attract foreign "luxury tourism" and generate employment; B) facilitate foreign capital investment and investor confidence in Honduras; and C) integrate the country's tourist industry, providing a link between the two principal destinations of the Bay Islands and the Copan Ruins. The government claimed that the project would generate more than 12,000 direct and indirect jobs, spur improvements in infrastructure and public services, promote environmental sustainability, and involve local participation.

OFRANEH, Garifuna activists from nearby communities, and others have criticized the Los Micos project on several fronts. They argue that the project exacerbates ongoing processes of land dispossession and that it will compromise access to resources and cause severe environmental damage. In a 2005 communiqué OFRANEH notes:

> It seems as though the dominant elite of Honduras, who are the national associates planning to invest in the tourist project, are not familiar with the basic elements of sustainable tourism or the repercussions that an enclave tourist project will have on the environment, even more so when it is located within a protected area that includes an 18-hole golf course.
>
> But clearly in a country of deaf statisticians, the interests of "minorities" should not be the object of respect. Foreign investment and national capitalists rule; thus, the future development of Honduras depends on foreign capital and the supposed gifts of international organizations, which permanently fatten up the country's external debt.
>
> The "geniuses" managing Honduras are finally carrying out the plundering of Tornabé that has been in the works since the 90s with the complicity of a few "afro-descendant" leaders. They have finally now managed to redefine enclave tourism within a protected area as ecotourism.[8]

The designation of "enclave tourism" represents the current tourist industry as the successor to the banana republic, now run by national elite, foreign investors, and multilateral institutions. However, the critique of complicit "afro-descendant" leaders suggests divisions among Garifuna as to how to approach state multiculturalism, tourist development, and the Los Micos project.

Whereas OFRANEH emphasizes territorial loss and resource degradation associated with large-scale tourist development, other Garifuna organizations seek greater inclusion in capitally intensive tourist development, insisting that Garifuna must be protagonists in the industry. The state encourages this attitude. In order to lend legitimacy to the Los Micos project and mitigate opposition, state representatives have held dialogues with selected Garifuna representatives concerning participation in the Los Micos development. Most notably, during the government of Manuel Zelaya (2006–2009) Garifuna communities in the Tela area were promised a 7 percent share of IHT investments in the DTBT public-private holding company. In connection with the project, the state and Inter-American Bank facilitated microloans for Garifuna to start small-scale businesses such as restaurants. For ORANEH and local leaders opposed to the project, these enticements serve as strategies to divide and marginalize Garifuna opposition, a process already underway via the creation of parallel leadership structures in communities.

The Los Micos Project broke ground during the Zelaya government but the coup that deposed him led to a temporary halt in funding from the Inter-American Development Bank. When I visited the project's main offices in 2010, construction had begun anew, though the manager told me the project design had changed. Due to the impact of the coup and economic crisis on tourism and the inability to attract foreign capital, the Honduran investors in the project had decided to scale back the initial phase to one luxury, "boutique" hotel, which, along with the golf course, would serve as the keystone for future expansion and the selling of private villas. As the manager put it, from a business standpoint, Los Micos is a "real estate project with a hotel." Thus, a state-sponsored but largely privately directed project long justified for its ability to generate employment, built within a national park (claimed by Garifuna as historical patrimony), has become configured as a real estate development for elite vacation homes. In effect, it has become a government-sponsored and subsidized land transfer facilitated by the Inter-American Development Bank.

The future direction of tourism on the North Coast of Honduras remains in question. The long-term effects of the coup and economic crisis on the foreign image of Honduras, and thus tourism, are still unknown while the national resistance movement (see Boyer, this volume), which includes oppositional Garifuna organizations such as OFRANEH, promotes alternatives to neoliberal political economic models driving dominant vision of tourist development. The stakes of contests over "development" and "participation" have never been higher, as witnessed in the assaults and threats on a community radio station in Triunfo de la Cruz that serves as a medium for voicing opposition to the coup, the Lobo government, territorial displacement, and the Los Micos Project. However, if the coup has led to renewed opposition to neoliberalism, we should not underestimate the appeal of the tourist industry and its promises of local participation and benefits. In response to a 2010 newspaper article on tourist development in Tela, a self-identified Garifuna man wrote in online to promote paving the road to his "picturesque" community of San Juan so that all could "realize this dream for the future of Tela" (*Tiempo* 2010). Perhaps tourism can be viewed as a dream because it provides the possibility to stay at home and make a life, in a current situation where that possibility is increasingly precarious. Although we need more research on local Garifuna attitudes towards tourism, my fieldwork in Sambo Creek and the Tela area suggests that many people hope to take advantage of tourism to stay at home to work or become entrepreneurs. They dream of having a small restaurant, hotel, or bar, of selling a locally made product, or of running their own tours. The tourist industry, by its nature dependent on the money and movement of outsiders, also fuels entrepreneurial dreams of independence, a hallmark of our neoliberal world. For this very reason, I find it crucial to highlight the frustrations Garifuna express in their encounters with the tourist industry, and the contradictions generated by the elusive value of culture under forms of capital accumulation that thrive on difference.

Conclusion

In this chapter I have approached the relationship among the state, capitalism, and ethnicity from the standpoint of the production of and struggle over economic value in contemporary tourism. Such an approach can further our analysis of the relationship between multiculturalism and neoliberalism by drawing attention to the proactive efforts to mobilize "culture" and "difference" in projects of accumulation. The state uses ethnicity as one means to differentiate Honduras from other tourist destinations, to make it appear on global maps of attractions. Businesses use the image of Garifuna to add a touch of exotic difference and local authenticity to the places they promote. Harvey (2001, 109) argues that under the competitive pressures of contemporary globalization, capitalists and governments increasingly "seek to trade on values of authenticity, locality, history, culture, collective memories and tradition" in order to differentiate places and create monopoly rents. Harvey (2001, 108) also suggests that such projects open spaces for political opposition because "capital often produces widespread alienation and resentment among cultural producers who experience first-hand the appropriation and exploitation of their creativity for the economic benefit of others, in much the same way that whole populations can resent having their histories and cultures exploited through commodification."

My discussion of Garifuna encounters with the tourist industry certainly reveals examples of such individual and collective resentment, but it also complicates the dialectics of commodification and opposition sketched by Harvey. The dissatisfaction Garifuna express does not simply focus on cultural commodification but on their structural inability to realize significant income from culture. The frustrations that emerge may fuel oppositional politics, efforts to participate in the tourist industry, and a range of possibilities combining the two. Struggles over the value of Garifuna culture cannot simply be reduced to a dichotomy between capitulation and opposition. They involve a complex politics of participation and exclusion.

Under these conditions, the need to hone a critical, conceptual language concerning ethnicity, value, and capitalism is crucial. Although that task must await further work, I end by identifying a few of the issues involved. Marxist language and concepts remain important for critiques of value theory that identify the source of value primarily in the actions of firms and experts that produce "added value," largely occluding the exploitation of labor in the production of profit (Foster 2005). My critique of that discourse in the Honduran case owes much, in spirit, to a Marxist critique of value appropriation. But the use of ethnic difference to create attractive tourist destinations—and thus economic value—in the tourist industry cannot readily be identified with the extraction of surplus value (what type of labor would be involved here?) or even with commodification (in the sense of a direct transformation of something into a good or service for sale). The use of ethnic imagery in tourism involves the consolidation and deployment of culture and authenticity as a kind of collective symbolic capital (Harvey 2001, 103). Insofar as tourism privileges not the direct "producers" of that symbolic capital—the members of the ethnicity themselves—but more powerful economic actors, it appears appropriate to speak in terms of "appropriation" and "exploitation." Certainly when Garifuna say "they don't know the value of our culture" or "they are taking our culture away," they articulate a sense of undervaluation, exploitation, and loss. We must also, however, ask what kind of theft occurs here. What kind of appropriation, and loss, occurs in the use of ethnic images, local cultures, and other collective phenomena to create tourist destinations? Finding adequate responses to such questions is important for developing critical responses towards the use and abuse of multiculturalism in projects of capitalist accumulation.

Notes

1. I consider Garifuna an indigenous people and an Afrohonduran people. I use the term ethnicity as a meta-term to include groups considered indigenous and Afrohonduran.
2. For further discussion of state recognition of ethnic groups in the 1970s, see Euraque (2004, 226–41).
3. Honduran Tourism Institute website, http://www.visitehonduras.com (accessed 14 July 2008).
4. The IHT website lists the Copan Ruins as a site for "living cultures" but fails to mention the Chortí Maya who live in the area. There are current efforts to incorporate local Chortí in tourist development (William Girard, personal communication).

5. This quote is cited from the online report found at http://www.fundacionsave.com/estrate gia_eng.html (accessed 14 July, 2008).
6. I am grateful for the research and analysis Roosbelinda Cardenas has provided on the Los Micos project. In August 2008, I visited the project site and spoke to project and government officials, as well as several Garifuna community leaders. I also visited the Tela area in 2010. For analysis of the project in relation to local Garifuna communities see López García (2006) and Loperena (2010).
7. Honduran investors reportedly include many of the wealthiest families in the country, including prominent figures in both major political parties.
8. The full text of the OFRANEH Public Communique "The Los Micos Tourism Project and So-Called Environmental Protection" is cited in Cuffe (2006).

References

Acosta, Gabriel D. 2011. "A Nation in Uproar: Salvadorans Condemn Funes' Record of Broken Promises." *Council on Hemispheric Affairs* (14 June), online report, http://www.coha.org/a-nation-in-uproar-salvadorans-condemn-funes percentE2 percent80 percent99 record-of-broken-promises/#_ftn1 (accessed 16 June 2011).

Agner, Joy. 2008. "The Silent Violence of Peace in Guatemala." *NACLA Report on the Americas* (May) online report, https://nacla.org/node/4665 (accessed 13 March 2009).

Ahmed, Sara. 2004. "Affective Economies." *Social Text* 22, no. 2: 117–139.

Akram-Lodhi, A. Haroon, and Cristóbal Kay. 2010a. "Surveying the Agrarian Question (Part 1): Unearthing Foundations, Exploring Diversity." *Journal of Peasant Studies* 37, no. 1: 177–202.

———. 2010b. "Surveying the Agrarian Question (Part 2): Current Debates and Beyond." *Journal of Peasant Studies* 37, no. 2: 255–284.

Alcorn, Janis B., and Victor M. Toledo. 1998. "Resilient Resource Management in Mexico's Forest Ecosystems: The Contributions of Property Rights." In *Linking Social and Ecological Systems: Management Practices and Social Mechanisms for Building Resilience*, ed. F. Berkes and C. Folke. Cambridge: Cambridge University Press.

Alegría, Claribel.1988. "The Writer's Commitment." In *Lives on the Line: The Testimony of Contemporary Latin American Authors*, ed. Doris Meyer. Berkeley: University of California Press.

Almeida, Paul. 2008. *Waves of Protest: Popular Struggle in El Salvador, 1925–2005*. Minneapolis: University of Minnesota Press.

Almeida, Paul, and Erica Walker. 2007. "El avance de la globalización neoliberal: una comparación de tres campañas de movimientos populares en Centroamérica." *Revista Centroamericana de Ciencias Sociales* 4, no. 1: 51–76.

Alonso, Carlos J. 1988. *The Burden of Modernity: The Rhetoric of Cultural Discourse in Spanish America*. Oxford: Oxford University Press.

Alvarenga, Patricia. 2005. *De vecinos a ciudadanos*. Costa Rica: Coedición Editorial de la Universidad de Costa Rica and Editorial de la Universidad Nacional.

———. 2006. *Cultura y ética de la violencia: El Salvador 1880–1932*. San Salvador: Concultura.

Álvarez Castañeda, Andrés. 2007. "La construcción social de la seguridad en Guatemala." MA thesis, Facultad Latinoamericana de las Ciencias Sociales Guatemala City.

Anaya, S. James. 2004. *Indigenous Peoples in International Law*. Oxford and New York: Oxford University Press.

Anderson, Mark. 2007. "When Afro Becomes (like) Indigenous: Garifuna and Afro-Indigenous Politics in Honduras." *Journal of Latin American and Caribbean Anthropology* 12, no. 2: 384–413.

———. 2009. *Black and Indigenous: Garifuna Activism and Consumer Culture in Honduras*. Minneapolis: University of Minnesota Press.

Anderson, Thomas P. 1971. *Matanza: El Salvador's Communist Revolt of 1932*. Lincoln and London: University of Nebraska Press.

ANEP (Asociación Nacional de la Empresa Privada). 2011. "Por el respeto de la institucionalidad," full-page advertisement in *El Diario de Hoy*, 22 June: 21.

Appadurai, Arjun. 2007. "Democracy and Hope." *Public Culture* 19, no. 1: 29–34.

Arias, Enrique Desmond, and Daniel Goldstein, eds. 2010. "Violent Pluralism: Understanding the New Democracies of Latin America." In *Violent Democracies in Latin America*. Durham: Duke University Press.

Artiga-González, Álvaro. 2004. *Elitismo competitivo. Dos décadas de elecciones en El Salvador (1982-2003)*. San Salvador: UCA Editores.

AVANCSO. 1987. *Por sí mismos: Un estudio preliminar de las "maras" en la ciudad de Guatemala*. Guatemala: Asociación para el avance de la ciencias sociales en Guatemala.

Babb, Florence E. 2001. *After Revolution: Mapping Gender and Cultural Politics in Neoliberal Nicaragua*. Austin: University of Texas Press.

———. 2003. "Out in Nicaragua: Local and Transnational Desires After the Revolution." *Cultural Anthropology* 18, no. 3: 304–328.

———. 2004. "Recycled Sandinistas: From Revolution to Resorts in the New Nicaragua." *American Anthropologist* 106, no. 3: 541–555.

———. 2011. *The Tourism Encounter: Fashioning Latin American Nations and Histories*. Stanford: Stanford University Press.

Babb, Florence E., and Aynn Setright. 2010. "Gender Justice and Political Inclusion: Sandinistas, Feminists, and the Current Divide." *Enlace Académico Centroamericano*, online report, http://www.enlaceacademico.org/base-documental/biblioteca/documento/gender-justice-and-political-inclusion-sandinistas-feminists-and-the-current-divide.

Baiocchi, Gianpaolo. 2005. *Militants and Citizens: The Politics of Participatory Democracy in Porto Alegre*. Stanford: Stanford University Press.

Baltodano, Monica. 2007. "Debemos desnudar los planes de Daniel Ortega desde la izquierda." *Envio* 309: 13–19.

Barkin, David. 1996. "Ecotourism: A Tool for Sustainable Development," online report, http://www.planeta.com (accessed 20 June 2001).

Barrios, Gabriela. 2002. "En busca de igualdad." *Prensa Libre (Revista Domingo)* 1112, 29 September: 10.

Bastos, Santiago. 2005. "La nación y los pueblos: las propuestas sobre la diferencia étnica en Guatemala." *Cuadernos de Desarrollo Humano*, 2005-3. Guatemala: United Nations Development Programme.

Bayard de Volo, Lorraine. 2001. *Mothers of Heroes and Martyrs: Gender Identity Politics in Nicaragua, 1979-1999*. Baltimore, MD: Johns Hopkins University Press.

Beder, S. 2001. "Neoliberal Think Tanks and Free-Market Environmentalism." *Environmental Politics* 10, no. 2: 128–133.

Bendell, Jem and Xavier Font. 2004. "Which Tourism Rules? Green Standards and GATS." *Annals of Tourism Research* 31, no. 1: 139–156.

Berger, Susan A. 1997. "Environmentalism in Guatemala: When Fish Have Ears." *Latin American Research Review* 32, no. 2: 99–116.

Bezemer, Dirk and Derek Headey. 2008. "Agriculture, Development, and Urban Bias." *World Development* 36, no. 8: 342–1364.

Binford, Leigh. 1996. *The El Mozote Massacre: Anthropology and Human Rights*. Tucson: University of Arizona Press.

———. 2004. "Peasants, Catechists and Revolutionaries: Organic Intellectuals in the Salvadoran Revolution." In *Landscapes of Struggle: Politics, Community, and the Nation-State in Twentieth Century El Salvador*, ed. Aldo Lauria-Santiago and Leigh Binford, 105–25. Pittsburgh, PA: University of Pittsburgh Press.

———. 2010. "A Perfect Storm of Neglect and Failure: Postwar Capitalist Restoration in Northern Morazán, El Salvador." *Journal of Peasant Studies* 37, no. 3: 531–557.

Black, Rosemary, and Alice Crabtree, eds. 2007. *Quality Assurance and Certification in Ecotourism*. Wallingford, UK: CABI International.

Blake, Beatrice. 2001. "Comparing the ICT's Certification of Sustainable Tourism and the New Key to Costa Rica's Sustainable Tourism Rating," online report, http://planeta.com/planeta/01/0104costa.html (accessed 16 February 2004).

Bolles, Lynn. 1997. "Women as a Category of Analysis in Scholarship on Tourism: Jamaican Women and Tourism Employment." In *Tourism and Culture: An Applied Perspective*, ed. Erve Chambers, 77–92. Albany: State University of New York Press.

Bonilla-Silva, Eduardo. 1996. "Rethinking Racism: Toward a Structural Interpretation." *American Sociological Review* 62: 465–480.

Booth, John, Christine J. Wade, and Thomas W. Walker, eds. 2005. *Understanding Central America: Global Forces, Rebellion, and Change*. Boulder, CO: Westview Press.

Bornstein, Erica. 2009. "The Impulse of Philanthropy." *Cultural Anthropology* 24, no. 4:. 622–651.

Bourgois, Phillipe. 2001. "The Power of Violence in War and Peace: Post-Cold War Lessons from El Salvador." *Ethnography* 2, no. 1: 5–34.

Boyer, Jefferson. 2008. "Food Strategies and Sustainable Agriculture in Honduras: Agrarian Structures and Contemporary Neoliberalism." Invited paper, University of North Carolina-Chapel Hill.

———. 2010. "Food Security, Food Sovereignty, and Local Challenges for Transnational Agrarian Movements: The Honduras Case." *Journal of Peasant Studies* 37, no. 2: 319–351.

Bravo, Gerardo. 2004. "Casinos: Una industria en crecimiento." *La Prensa*, 30 June: 4A.

Brennan, Denise. 2004. *What's Love Got to Do with It? Transnational Desires and Sex Tourism in the Dominican Republic*. Durham, NC: Duke University Press.

Brondo, Keri. 2006. *Roots, Rights, and Belonging: Garifuna Indigeneity and Land Rights on Honduras' North Coast*. PhD dissertation, Michigan State University.

Brooks, David. 2004. "Insurgency Busting." *New York Times*, 28 September.

Browning, David. 1971. *El Salvador: Landscape and Society*. Oxford: Clarendon.

Brysk, Alison. 2000. *From Tribal Village to Global Village: Indian Rights and International Relations in Latin America*. Stanford, CA: Stanford University Press.

Buckley, Ralf. 2001. "Tourism Ecolabels." *Annals of Tourism Research* 29, no. 1: 183–208.

Bunch, Roland. 2010. "Can Promoters of Development and Activists of Land Reform Unite? Grassroots Voices." *Journal of Peasant Studies* 37, no. 1: 209–212.

Burgos Debray, Elisabeth. 1984. *I, Rigoberta Menchú: An Indian Woman in Guatemala*. New York: Verso.

Burnett, John. 1997. "Ecotourism." *All Things Considered*. National Public Radio, 3 September.

Burrell, Jennifer L. 2005. "Migration and the Transnationalization of Fiesta Customs in Todos Santos Cuchumatán, Guatemala." *Latin American Perspectives* 32, no. 5: 12–32.

———. 2010. "In and Out of Rights: Security, Migration and Human Rights Talk in Postwar Guatemala." *Journal of Latin American and Caribbean Anthropology* 15, no. 1: 90–115.

———. 2013. Maya *After War: Conflict, Power and Politics Among the Maya*. Austin: University of Texas Press.

Byres, Terence. 1996. *Capitalism from Above and Capitalism from Below: An Essay in Comparative Political Economy*. London: MacMillan Press.

Cabarrús, Carlos Rafael. 1983. *Génesis de una revolución: Análisis del surgimiento y desarrollo de la organización campesina en El Salvador*. Mexico: Ediciones de la Casa Chata.

Cabezas, Amalia Lucía. 2004. "Between Love and Money: Sex, Tourism, and Citizenship in Cuba and the Dominican Republic." *Signs* 29, no. 4: 987–1015.

Cabrera, Jorge. 2003. "Gestión ambiental sostenible: Certificaciones existentes." *Ambientico* 122: 3–5.

Cáceres, Sinforiano. 2008. "Ante la crisis alimentaria, necesitamos más acciones y menos discursos." *Envio* 315.

———. 2010. "Siembran promesas y cosechamos desengaños." *Envio* 338.

Cagan, Steve, and Beth Cagan. 1992. *Promised Land.* New Brunswick, NJ: Rutgers University Press.

Cai, Qian. 2008. "Hispanic Immigrants and Citizens in Virginia." In *Numbers Count,* Demographics and Workforce Section, Charlottesville, VA: Weldon Cooper Center for Public Service, the University of Virginia, online report, http://www.coopercenter.org/demographics/publications/hispanic-immigrants-and-citizens-virginia (accessed 17 March 2008).

Campbell, Monica. 2007. "Guatemala's Poor Infrastructure Puts off Investors and Makes the Country Less Able to Fully Profit from Free-trade Deals." *The Banker,* 1 March.

Cañada, Ernest, Leonor Delgado, and Helena Gil. 2006. *Guía turismo rural comunitario Nicaragua.* Managua: Fundación Luciérnaga.

Carmack Robert, ed. 1988. *Harvest of Violence: The Maya Indians and the Guatemala Crisis.* Tulsa: University of Oklahoma Press.

Carmack, Robert. 2005. "Perspectivas sobre la política de los derechos humanos en Guatemala." In *Los derechos humanos en tierras mayas: Política, representaciones y moralidad,* ed. Pedro Pitarch and Julián López García, 39–54. Madrid: Sociedad Española de Estudios Mayas.

Carrescia, Olivia. 1989. *Todos Santos: The Survivors.* New York: First Run/Icarus Films.

Casáus Arzú, Marta. 1998. *La metamorfosis del racismo en Guatemala.* Guatemala: Editorial Cholsamaj.

———. 2009. "Social Practices and Racist Discourse of the Guatemalan Power Elites." In *Racism and Discourse in Latin America,* ed. Teun A. Van Dijk, trans. Elisa Barkin and Alexandra Hibbett. Lanham: Lexington Books.

Cashore, Benjamin, Graeme Auld, and Deanna Newsom. 2004. *Governing Through Markets: Forest Certification and the Emergence of Non-State Authority.* New Haven, CT: Yale University Press.

CEPAL (Comision Economica para America Latina y el Caribe). 2002. *Centroamerica: El impacto de la caida do los precios del cafe en 2001.* Mexico, DF.

Chibnik, Michael. 2003. *Crafting Traditions: The Making and Marketing of Oaxacan Wood Carvings.* Austin: University of Texas Press.

CJA (Center for Justice and Accountability). 2011. "Spanish Judge Issues Indictments and Arrest Warrants in Jesuits Massacre Case," online report, http://www.cja.org/article.php?id=1004 (accessed 3 September 2011).

CLACDS (Centro Latinoamericano para la Competitividad y el Desarrollo Sostenible). 1999. *La caficultura en Honduras.* Nicaragua and Costa Rica.

COCOCH-FOSDEH. 2009. "Reforma agraria, agricultura y medio rural en Honduras: La agenda pendiente del sector campesino." Unpublished report.

CODISRA-DEMI-OACNUDH. 2010. *Luces y sombras en la lucha contra la discriminación racial, étnica y de género en Guatemala: Informe sobre la situación de la discriminación a partir de casos acompañados por DEMI y CODISRA.* Guatemala.

Coleman, Mathew. 2007a. "A Geopolitics of Engagement: Neoliberalism, the War on Terrorism, and the Reconfiguration of US Immigration Enforcement." *Geopolitics* 12, no. 4: 607–634.

———. 2007b. "Immigration Geopolitics Beyond the Mexico-US Border," *Antipode* 39, no. 1: 54–76.

Collier, David and Steven Levitsky. 1996. "Democracy 'with Adjectives': Conceptual Innovations in Comparative Research." Working Paper 230, Kellogg Institute for International Studies, University of Notre Dame, online document, kellogg.nd.edu/publications/workin gpapers/WPS/230.pdf (accessed 10 November 2009).

Colloredo-Mansfeld, Rudi. 1999. *The Native Leisure Class: Consumption and Cultural Creativity in the Andes.* Chicago: University of Chicago Press.

Colussi, Marcelo. 2008. *Entrevista a la comandante sandinista Mónica Baltodano: "El socialismo real, como lo conocimos, da pistas de lo que no debe ser el nuevo proyecto socialista,"* online report, www.memoriando.com/ noticias/701-800/731.html.

Coronil, Fernando. 2011. "The Future in Question: History and Utopia in Latin America (1989–2010)." In *Business as Usual: The Roots of the Global Financial Meltdown,* ed. Craig Calhoun and Georgi Derluguian, 231–64. New York: New York University Press,.

Coutin, Susan Bibler. 2000. *Legalizing Moves: Salvadoran Immigrants' Struggle for U.S. Residency.* Ann Arbor, Michigan: University of Michigan Press.

———. 2007. *Nation of Emigrants: Shifting Boundaries of Citizenship between El Salvador and the United States.* Ithaca, NY: Cornell University Press.

Coutin, Susan Bibler, Bill Maurer, and Barbara Yngvesson. 2002. "In the Mirror: The Legitimation Work of Globalization." *Law & Social Inquiry* 27, no. 4: 801–843.

Craig, Tim. 2007. "Va. Driver Fees Now Election Weapon: Big Voter Petition Demands Repeal." *Washington Post,* 17 July: A1.

Cruz, José Miguel. 1998. "¿Por qué no votan los salvadoreños?" *Estudios Centroamericanos* (ECA) 595-596: 449–472.

———. 2001. *¿Elecciones para qué? El impacto del ciclo electoral 1999-2000 en la cultura política salvadoreña.* San Salvador: FLACSO.

———. 2006. "Violence, Citizen Insecurity, and Elite Maneuvering in El Salvador." In *Public Security and Police Reform in the Americas,* ed. John Bailey and Lucia Dammert, 148–168. Pittsburgh: University of Pittsburgh Press.

Cruz, José Miguel, Alvaro Trigueros Argüello, and Francisco González.1999. "The Social and Economic Factors Associated with Violent Crime in El Salvador," online report, http://www.wblnoo18.worldbank.org/lac/lacinfoclient.nsf (accessed 1 July 2001).

Cruz, José Miguel, and Luis Armando González. 1997a. "Magnitud de la violencia en El Salvador." *Estudios Centroamericanos* 588: 953–66.

———. 1997b. *Sociedad y violencia: El Salvador en la post-guerra.* San Salvador: UCA Editores.

Cuffe, Sandra. 2006. "Nature Conservation or Territorial Control and Profits?" *Upside Down World,* online report, http://upsidedownworld.org/main/content/view/194/1/ (accessed June 2008).

Dabene, Olivier. 1986. "Las bases sociales y culturales de lo político en Costa Rica." *Revista de Ciencias Sociales* 31: 67–83.

Danner, Mark. 1994. *The Massacre at El Mozote: A Parable of the Cold War.* New York: Vintage.

Dawkins, Casey J. C., Theodore Koebel, Marilyn S. Cavell, and Patricia L. Renneckar. 2007. "Housing Needs Assessment: James City County and Williamsburg," Virginia Center for Housing Research, Blacksburg, VA, online report, http://www.jccegov.com/pdf/bospdfs/bospdfs2007/121107readfile/item3.pdf (accessed 6 January 2008).

Deeb-Sossa, Natalia, and Jennifer Bickham Mendez. 2008. "Enforcing Borders in the *Nuevo* South: Gender and Migration in Williamsburg, VA and the Research Triangle, NC." *Gender and Society* 22, no. 5: 613–638.

DeHart, Monica. 2010. *Ethnic Entrepreneurs: Identity and Development Politics in Latin America.* Stanford, CA: Stanford University Press.

de la Cadena, Marisol, and Orin Starn, eds. 2007. *Indigenous Experience Today.* Oxford: Berg Press.

Del-Cid, Rafael. 1989. "Seguridad y autosuficiencia alimentaria: Delineando un quehacer." *Puntos de Vista* 2, no. 1: 32–36.

DeLugan, Robin. 2012. *Re-imagining National Belonging: Post-Civil War El Salvador in a Global Context.* Tucson: University of Arizona Press.

Dembour, Marie-Bénédicte. 1996. "Human Rights Talk and Anthropological Ambivalence: The Particular Context of Universal Claims." In *Inside and Outside the Law: Anthropological Studies of Authority and Ambiguity*, ed. Olivia Harris, 18–40. London: Routledge.

Desmarais, Annette. 2007. *La Vía Campesina: Globalization and the Power of Peasants.* Halifax and London: Fernwood Publishing and Pluto Press.

Diario de Hoy. 2008. "Fiscalía pide ayuda al FBI y a Interpol," 16 December.

Didion, Joan. 1983. *Salvador.* New York: Vintage Books.

Dirección General de Estadística y Censos. 2007. *Survey of Households, Employment and Unemployment.* San José: Costa Rica.

Dolan, Catherine S. 2005. "Benevolent Intent? The Development Encounter in Kenya's Horticulture Industry." *Journal of Asian and African Studies* 40, no. 6: 411–437.

Dunkerley, James. 1988. *Power in the Isthmus: a Political History of Central America.* London: Verso.

———. 2009. *Dividing the Isthmus: Central American Transnational Histories, Literatures, and Cultures.* Austin: University of Texas Press.

Dye, David R. 2004. *Democracy Adrift: Caudillo Politics in Nicaragua.* Managua: PRODENI.

Edelman, Marc. 1998. "Transnational Peasant Politics in Central America." *Latin American Research Review* 33, no. 3: 49–85.

———. 1999. *Peasants against Globalization: Rural Social Movements in Costa Rica.* Stanford, CA: Stanford University Press.

———. 2007. "Costa Rica: Resilience of a Classic Social Democracy." In *Social Democracy in the Global Periphery: Origins, Challenges, Prospects*, ed. Richard Sandbrook, Marc Edelman, Patrick Heller, and Judith Teichman. Cambridge: Cambridge University Press.

———. 2008. "Transnational Organizing in Agrarian Central America: Histories, Challenges, Prospects." In *Transnational Agrarian Movements Confronting Globalization*, ed. Saturnino M. Borras Jr., Marc Edelman, and Cristóbal Kay, 61–89. Chichester, Oxford: Wiley Blackwell.

Edelman, Marc, and Joanne Kenen, eds. 1989. *The Costa Rica Reader.* New York: Grove Weidenfeld.

Editorial Collective. 2010. "Statement of Editorial Collective." *Humanity*, online report, http://hum.pennpress.org/PennPress/journals/hum/EditorialStatement.pdf (accessed 1 October 2011).

Ekern, Stener. 2008. "Are Human Rights Destroying the Natural Balance of Things?: The Difficult Encounter Between International Law and Community Law in Mayan Guatemala." In *Human Rights in the Maya Region: Global Politics, Cultural Contentions, and Moral Engagements*, ed. Pedro Pitarch, Shannon Speed, and Xochitl Leyva Solano, 123–169. Durham: Duke University Press.

Elyachar, Julia. 2005. *Markets of Dispossession: NGOs, Economic Development and the State in Cairo.* Durham: Duke University Press.

England, Sarah. 2006. *Afro Central Americans in New York City: Garifuna Tales of Transnational Movements in Racialized Space.* Gainesville, FL: University Press of Florida.

Engle, Karen. 2001. "From Skepticism to Embrace: Human Rights and the American Anthropology Association from 1947-1999." *Human Rights Quarterly* 23: 536–559.

Equipo Envío. 2011. "Misterios, tiempos, temores." *Envio* 352.

Equipo Maíz. 2006. *El Salvador: Emigración y remesas.* San Salvador: Asociación Equipo Maíz.

———. 2011. "Salario Mímino, otro atraco contra la clase trabajadora." *La página de Maíz*, 6 May.

Equipo Nitlapán. 1994. "Descolectivización: reforma agraria desde abajo." *Envio* 154.

Escobar, Arturo. 1995. *Encountering Development: The Making and Unmaking of the Third World.* Princeton: Princeton University Press.

Euraque, Darío. 2004. *Conversaciones históricas con el mestizaje y su identidad nacional en Honduras.* San Pedro Sula: Litografía López.

———. 2006. "Estructura social, historia política y la neuva democracia en Honduras." In *Política y desarrollo, 2006–2009: Los escenarios posibles,* ed. Diego Achad and Luis Eduardo Gonzáles, 259–285. Tegucigalpa: PNUD.

———. 2010. "The Honduran Coup and Cultural Policy," *NACLA Report on the Americas* 43, no. 2: 30–34.

Evans, Sterling. 1999. *The Green Republic: A Conservation History of Costa Rica.* Austin: University of Texas Press.

Fadlalla, Amal Hassan. 2008. "The Neoliberalization of Compassion." In *New Landscapes of Inequality: Neoliberalism and the Erosion of Democracy in America,* ed. Jane L. Collins, Micaela di Leonardo, and Brett Williams. Santa Fe, NM: School for Advanced Research Press.

Fazio, Maria Victoria. 2007. *Economic Opportunities for Indigenous Peoples in Latin America in Guatemala.* Washington, DC: The International Bank for Reconstruction and Development/The World Bank.

Fernández, Alberto M. 1999. "Review of Indigenous Movements and their Critics: Pan-Maya Activism in Guatemala by Kay B. Warren." *ReVista: Harvard Review of Latin America,* online document, http://www.drclas.harvard.edu/revista/articles/view/499 (accessed 8 September 2012).

Fiallos, C. 1991. *Los municipios de Honduras.* Tegucigalpa: Editorial Universitaria.

Field, Les W. 1999. *The Grimace of Macho Ratón: Artisans, Identity, and Nation in Late-Twentieth-Century Nicaragua.* Durham, NC: Duke University Press.

Finley-Brook, M. 2011. "'We Are the Owners': Autonomy and Natural Resources in Northeastern Nicaragua." In *National Integration and Contested Autonomy: The Caribbean Coast of Nicaragua,* ed. Luciano Baracco. New York: Algora Publishing.

Fischer, Edward F. 2002. *Cultural Logics and Global Economies: Maya Identity in Thought and Practice.* Austin: University of Texas Press.

Fischer, Edward F., and Carol Hendrickson. 2002. *Tecpán Guatemala: A Modern Maya Town in Global and Local Context.* Boulder, CO.: Westview Press.

Fischer, Edward F., and Peter Benson. 2006. *Broccoli and Desire: Global Connections and Maya Struggles in Postwar Guatemala.* Stanford, CA: Stanford University Press.

FLO (Fair Trade Labeling Organization). 2007. "Generic Fair Trade Standards for Smallholder Organizations," online report, www.fairtrade.net (accessed 30 June 30 2009).

———. 2012. "World's Most Recognized Ethical Label on Solid Ground in Established Markets, Taking Off in New Ones," online report, http://www.fairtrade.net/single_view1.0.html?&tx_ttnews%5Btt_news%5D=312&cHash=66a761f0ab9353f5965eba91d39a2c55 (accessed 16 August 2012).

FMLN (Frente Farabundo Martí para la Liberación Nacional). 2006. *Estatuto del partido politico FMLN.* San Salvador: FMLN.

Font, Xavier. 2002. "Environmental Certification in Tourism and Hospitality: Progress, Process, and Prospects." *Tourism Management* 23, no. 3, 197–205.

Foster, C. E. 2001. "Articulating Self-determination in the Draft Declaration on the Rights of Indigenous Peoples." *European Journal of International Law* 12, no. 1: 141–157.

Foster, Robert. 2005. "Commodity Futures: Labour, Love and Value." *Anthropology Today* 21, no. 4: 8–12.

Foxen, Patricia. 2007. *In Search of Providence: Transnational Mayan Identities.* Nashville: Vanderbilt University Press.

Freire, Paulo. 1973. *Education for Critical Consciousness.* New York: Seabury Press.

Fridell, Gavin. 2007. *Fair Trade Coffee: The Prospects and Pitfalls of Market-Driven Social Justice.* Toronto: University of Toronto Press.

Fruhling, P., Miguel González, and Hans Petter Buvollen, eds. 2007. *Etnicidad y nación: El desarrollo de la autonomia de la costa atlantica de Nicaragua (1987–2007).* Guatemala: F y G Editoriales.

Fukunaga, Cary Joji, dir. 2009. *Sin Nombre*, prod. Amy Kaufman. Universal City, CA.: Universal Studios Home Entertainment, DVD.

Fukuyama, Francis. 1992. *The End of History and the Last Man*. New York: Free Press.

García Dueñas, Lauri. 2006. "La trascendencia de la campaña del 'miedo' en las elecciones de 2004 y la propaganda del 'peligro' en México en 2006." *Realidad* 109: 375–387.

García, María Cristina. 2006. *Seeking Refuge: Central American Migration to Mexico, the United States and Canada*. Berkeley: University of California Press.

Gereffi, Gary. 2001. "Shifting Governance Structures in Global Commodity Chains, with Special Reference to the Internet." *American Behavioral Scientist* 44, no. 10: 1616–1637.

Ghodsee, Kristen. 2005. *The Red Riviera: Gender, Tourism, and Postsocialism on the Black Sea*. Durham, NC: Duke University Press.

Gibson, Brian, dir. 1996. *The Juror*. Culver City, CA: Columbia TriStar Home Video, VHS.

Giddens, Anthony. 2000. "Ethnicidad y raza." In *Sociología*, 2nd ed. Madrid: Alianza Editorial S.A.

Gill, Lesley. 2004. *The School of the Americas: Military Training and Political Violence in the Americas*. Durham, NC: Duke University Press.

Gledhill, John. 2004. "Neoliberalism." In *A Companion to the Anthropology of Politics*, ed. David Nugent and Joan Vincent, 332–48. Malden, MA: Blackwell.

Godoy, Angelina. 2006. *Popular Injustice: Violence, Community and Law in Latin America*. Stanford, CA: Stanford University Press.

Godoy, Emilio. 2008. "Acusan a Guatemala de violar derechos laborales." *La Prensa Libre*, 11 July: 6.

Goldín, Liliana R. 2003. *Procesos globales en el campo de Guatemala: Opciones económicas y tranformaciones ideológicas*. Guatemala: FLACSO.

———. 2009. *Global Maya: Work and Ideology in Rural Guatemala*. Tucson: University of Arizona Press.

Goldman, Michael. 2001. "Constructing an Environmental State: Eco-Governmentality and Other Transnational Practices of a 'Green' World Bank." *Social Problems* 48, no. 4: 499–523.

Goldstein, Daniel M. 2007. "Human Rights as Culprit, Human Rights as Victim: Rights and Security in the State of Exception." In *The Practice of Human Rights: Tracking Law Between the Global and the Local*, ed. Mark Goodale and Sally Engle Merry, 49–77. Cambridge: Cambridge University Press.

———. 2010. "Toward a Critical Anthropology of Security." *Current Anthropology* 51, no. 4: 487–517.

Gordon, E. T., Galio C. Gurdian, and Charles R. Hale. 2003. "Rights, Resources, and the Social Memory of Struggle: Reflections on a Study of Indigenous and Black Community Land Rights on Nicaragua's Atlantic Coast." *Human Organization* 62, no. 4: 369–381.

Gosnell, Hannah and Jesse Abrams. 2011. "Amenity Migration: Diverse Conceptualizations of Drivers, Socioeconomic Dimensions, and Emerging Challenges." *GeoJournal* 76, no. 4: 303–322.

Gould, Jeffrey L., and Aldo A. Lauria-Santiago. 2008. *To Rise in Darkness: Revolution, Repression, and Memory in El Salvador, 1920-1932*. Durham, NC: Duke University Press.

Graham, Daniel. 2009. *Ghosts and Warriors: Cultural-Political Dynamics of Indigenous Resource Struggles in Western Honduras*. Ph.D. dissertation, University of California, Berkeley.

Grammage, Sarah. 2006. "Exporting People and Recruiting Remittances: A Development Strategy for El Salvador?" *Latin American Perspectives* 33, no. 6: 75–100.

Grandia, Liza. 2005. "Hidden in the 2,400 Pages of CAFTA." *San Diego Union Tribune*, 26 July: B7.

———. 2012. *Enclosed: Conservation, Cattle and Commerce among the Q'eqchi' Maya Lowlanders*. Seattle: University of Washington Press.

Grandin, Greg. 2004. *The Last Colonial Massacre: Latin America in the Cold War.* Chicago: University of Chicago Press.
———. 2010. "Introduction: Living in Revolutionary Time." In *A Century of Revolution: Insurgent and Counterinsurgent Violence During Latin America's Long Cold War,* ed. Greg Grandin and Gilbert M. Joseph. Durham: Duke University Press.
Gregory, Stephen. 2007. *The Devil Behind the Mirror: Globalization and Politics in the Dominican Republic.* Berkeley: University of California Press.
Grigsby, Arturo. 2010. "Que pasará en las elecciones con una economia tan incierta y tan austera?" *Envio* 336.
Guardian. 2009. "This is How We Let the Credit Crunch Happen, Ma'am." 25 July.
Gudeman, Stephen, and Alberto Rivera. 1990. *Conversations in Colombia: The Domestic Economy in Life and Text.* Cambridge: Cambridge University Press.
Guilhot, Nicolas. 2005. *The Democracy Makers: Human Rights and the Politics of Global Order.* New York: Columbia University Press.
Gutiérrez, Alejandro. 2010. "The Idealistic Ideological Fog and other Illusions of the 'Danielista' Solidarity Movement," online report, https://nacla.org/news/disconcerting- percentE2 percent80 percent98success percentE2 percent80 percent99-nicaragua percentE2 percent80 percent99s-anti-poverty-programs (accessed 2 October 2011).
Guzmán, B., and Eileen Diaz McConnell. 2002. "The Hispanic Population: 1990–2000 Growth and Change." *Population Research and Policy Review* 21, no. 1-2, 109–128.
Guzmán, Melissa, and Pablo Balcáceres. 2008. "Tamblea el poder adquisitivo." *El Economista,* 24 June: 28–32.
Hale, Charles R. 2002. "Does Multiculturalism Menace? Governance, Cultural Rights and the Politics of Identity in Guatemala." *Journal of Latin American Studies* 34: 485–524.
———. 2005. "Neoliberal Multiculturalism: The Remaking of Cultural Rights and Racial Dominance in Central America." *PoLAR: Political and Legal Anthropology Review* 28, no. 1: 10–28.
———. 2006a. "Activist Research v. Cultural Critique: Indigenous Land Rights and the Contradictions of Politically Engaged Anthropology." *Cultural Anthropology* 21, no. 1: 96–120.
———. 2006b. *Más Que un Indio (More Than an Indian): Racial Ambivalence and Neoliberal Multiculturalism in Guatemala.* Santa Fe: School of American Research Press.
Hammond, John L. 1998. *Fighting to Learn: Popular Education and Guerrilla War in El Salvador.* New Brunswick, NJ: Rutgers University Press.
Hardt, Michael, and Antonio Negri. 2004. *Multitude: War and Democracy in the Age of Empire.* New York: Penguin Press.
Harrison, Jill Lindsey, and Sarah E. Lloyd. 2011. "Illegality at Work: Deportability and the Productive New Era of Immigration Enforcement." *Antipode,* 44, no. 2: 365–85.
Harvey, David. 2001. "The Art of Rent: Globalization, Monopoly and the Commodification of Culture." In *The Socialist Register,* ed. L. Panitch and C. Leys. London: The Merlin Press.
———. 2003. *The New Imperialism.* New York: Oxford University Press.
———. 2005. *A Brief History of Neoliberalism.* New York: Oxford University Press.
———. 2010. *The Enigma of Capital And the Crises of Capitalism.* New York: Oxford University Press.
Hayden, Bridget. 2003. *Salvadorans in Costa Rica: Displaced Lives.* Tucson: University of Arizona Press.
Hecht, Susan B., Susan Kandel, Ileana Gomes, Nelson Cuellar, and Herman Rosa. 2005. "Globalization, Forest Resurgence, and Environmental Politics in El Salvador." *World Development* 34, no. 2: 308–323.
Henríquez Consalvi, Carlos. 1992. *La terquedad del Izote.* Mexico: Diana.
Hernández, Alcides. 1992. *Del reformismo al ajuste estructural.* Tegucigalpa: Guaymuras, S.A.

Hernández, Naranjo, G. 1998. *El sistema de partidos en Costa Rica 1982-1994: Análisis sobre el bipartidismo.* Master's thesis, Universidad de Costa Rica, San José.

Herranz, Atanasio. 1996. *Estado, sociedad y lenguaje: La política lingüística en Honduras.* Tegucigalpa: Editorial Guaymuras.

Herzfeld, Michael. 1994. *The Social Production of Indifference.* Chicago: University of Chicago Press.

Hollander, Paul. 1986. *Political Hospitality and Tourism: Cuba and Nicaragua.* Washington, DC: Cuban American National Foundation.

Holt-Giménez, Eric. 2006. *Campesino a Campesino: Voices from Latin America's Farmer-to-Farmer Movement for Sustainable Agriculture.* Oakland, CA: Food First.

Honey, Martha, and Abigail Rome. 2001. "Protecting Paradise: Certification Programs for Sustainable Tourism and Ecotourism." Washington, DC: Institute for Policy Studies.

Honey, Martha, ed. 2002. *Ecotourism and Certification: Setting Standards in Practice.* Washington, DC: Island Press.

ICO (International Coffee Organization). 2008. *Total Production of Exporting Countries,* online report, http://www.ico.org (accessed 3 June 2009).

IDB-USAID-World Bank (Inter-American Development Bank and United States Agency for International Development and World Bank). 2002. *Discussion Document: The Competitive Transition of the Coffee Sector in Central America.* Antigua, Guatemala.

IDHUCA (Instituto Derechos Humanos de la Universidad Centroamericana "José Simeón Cañas"). 2004. *Observatorio ciudadano de las elecciones presidenciales El Salvador 2004.* San Salvador: IDHUCA.

IHCAFE (Instituto Hondureño del Café). 1997. *Boletín estadístico 1970–1996.* Tegucigalpa.

———. 2001. *Manual de Caficultura.* Tegucigalpa.

Instituto de Investigaciones Sociales and Centro de Opinión Pública de la Escuela de Estadística. 2007. *Post-referendum Survey* (October). San José: Universidad de Costa Rica.

Instituto Hondureño de Turismo. 2010. *Boletín de estadísticas turísticas, 2005–2009.* Tegucigalpa: Instituto Hondureño de Turismo.

Instituto Nacional de Estadística. 2001. *Censo nacional de población y vivienda.* Tegucigalpa: Instituto Nacional de Estadística.

IUDOP (Instituto Universitario de Opinión Pública). 1993. "La delincuencia urbana," *Estudios Centroamericanos* (ECA) 534-545: 471–79.

Jackson, Jean E., and Kay B. Warren. 2005. "Indigenous Movements in Latin America, 1992-2004." *Annual Review of Anthropology* 34: 548–573.

Jaffee, Daniel. 2007. *Brewing Justice: Fair Trade Coffee, Sustainability, and Survival.* Berkeley: University of California Press.

Joseph, Miranda. 2002. *Against the Romance of Community.* Minneapolis: University of Minnesota Press.

Kaimowitz, David. 1993. "NGOs, the State and Agriculture in Central America." In *Non-Governmental Organizations and the State in Latin America: Rethinking Roles in Sustainable Agricultural Development,* ed. Anthony Bebbington and Graham Theile, 178–198. London and New York: Routledge.

Kampwirth, Karen. 2010. "Populism and the Feminist Challenge in Nicaragua: The Return of Daniel Ortega." In *Gender and Populism in Latin America: Passionate Politics,* ed. Karen Kampwirth. University Park: Penn State University Press.

Kandel, Susan. 2002. *Migraciones, medio ambiente y pobreza rural en El Salvador.* San Salvador: PRISMA.

Kautsky, Karl. 1988 [1899]. *The Agrarian Question,* Vol. 1 and 2. London: Zwan Publications.

Kay, Cristóbal. 2009. "Development Strategies and Rural Development: Exploring Synergies, Eradicating Poverty." *Journal of Peasant Studies* 36, no. 1, 103–137.

Kerr, Amanda. 2006. "Immigrant Status Poses a Challenge." *Virginia Gazette,* 12 July.

———. 2007. "Safety Outweighs Status: Immigrants Entitled To Police, Fire Help Regardless Of Legality." *Virginia Gazette,* 3 March.

Kester, Paul. 2010. "Hambre Cero: Desarrollo o gotas de lluvia?" *Envio* 342.

Kirtsoglou, Elisabeth, and Dimitrious Theodossopoulos. 2004. "'They are Taking Our Culture Away': Tourism and Cultural Commodification in the Garifuna Community of Roatan." *Critique of Anthropology* 25, no. 2: 135–157.

Klein, Naomi. 2007. *The Shock Doctrine: The Rise of Disaster Capitalism,* 1st ed. New York: Metropolitan Books.

Koop, David. 2008. "Experts Rethinking Food Supply." *Lexington Herald Leader,* 11 May: A9.

Kretesedemas, Philip. 2008. "What Does an Undocumented Immigrant Look Like? Local Enforcement and the New Immigrant Profiling." In *Keeping Out the Other: A Critical Introduction to Immigration Enforcement Today,* ed. David Brotheron and Philip Kretsedemas, 334–364. New York: Columbia University Press.

Kryt, Jeremy. 2011a. "Campesinos Rising." *In These Times* 35, no. 3: 10–11.

———. 2011b. "Drafting Honduran Democracy." *In These Times* 35, no. 4: 7.

———. 2011c. "Zelaya Returns." *In These Times* 35, no. 7: 7–8.

Kuper, Adam. 2003. "CA Forum on Anthropology in Public: The Return of the Native." *Current Anthropology* 44, no. 3: 389–395.

Laarman, Jan, and Richard Perdue. 1989. "Science Tourism in Costa Rica." *Annals of Tourism Research* 16: 205–215.

La Boletina. 2007. *Cuando te roban la vida: La compra-venta de sexo con adolescentes, niñas y ñinos.* Managua, Nicaragua: Puntos de Encuentro.

Lacayo, Rossana. 2003. *Verdades ocultas* (Hidden Truths), video.

Lancaster, Roger N. 1992. *Life is Hard: Machismo, Danger and the Intimacy of Power in Nicaragua.* Berkeley: University of California Press.

Laplante, Lisa J., and Kimberly Theidon. 2007. "Truth with Consequences: Justice and Reparations in Post-Truth Commission Peru." *Human Rights Quarterly* 29: 228–250.

Lawlor, M. 2003. "Indigenous Internationalism: Native Rights and the UN." *Comparative American Studies: An International Journal* 1: 351–369.

LeFeber, Walter. 1983. *Inevitable Revolutions: The United States in Central America.* New York: W. W. Norton & Company.

Lefebvre, Henri. 1991. *The Production of Space,* trans. Donald Nicholson-Smith. Oxford: Blackwell.

Lehoucq, Fabrice E., and Iván Molina. 2002. *Stuffing the Ballot Box: Fraud, Electoral Reform and Democratization in Costa Rica.* Cambridge: Cambridge University Press.

Lémus, Eric. 2010. "El Salvador semiparalizado por reclamo de pandillas." *BBC Mundo,* 9 September, online document, http://www.bbc.co.uk/mundo/america_latina/2010/09/100906_salvador_funes_maras_n gociacion_pea.shtml (accessed 3 September 2011).

León, César. 2008. "Inútil lucha contra la discriminación." *Prensa Libre,* 30 March.

Levenson, Deborah. 2013. "Guatemala's Maras: From Life to Death." In *Aftermath: War by Other Means in Post-Genocide Guatemala,* ed. Diane M. Nelson and Carlota McAllister, Durham: Duke University Press.

Levy, Jordan. 2010. "Honduran Political Culture and the 2009 Coup: Experiences from San Lorenzo." MA thesis, University of Western Ontario.

Lewin, B., D. Giovannucci, and P. Varangis. 2004. *Coffee Market.* Washington, DC: International Bank for Reconstruction and Development.

Li, Tania Murray. 2007. *The Will to Improve: Governmentality, Development, and the Practice of Politics.* Durham, NC: Duke University Press.

Linarte, Maricely. 2004. "Foro sobre explotación sexual commercial." *El Nuevo Diario,* 5 August: 13B.

Lindo-Fuentes, Héctor, Rafael Lara-Martínez, and Erik Ching. 2007. *Remembering a Massacre: The Insurrection of 1932, Roque Dalton, and the Politics of Historical Memory.* Albuquerque: University of New Mexico Press.

Lippard, Cameron D., and Charles A. Gallagher, eds. 2011. *Being Brown in Dixie: Race, Ethnicity and Latino Immigration in the New South.* Boulder, CO: First Forum Press.

Little, Walter E. 2004. *Mayas in the Marketplace: Tourism, Globalization, and Cultural Identity.* Austin: University of Texas Press.

———. 2008. "Crime, Maya Handicraft Vendors, and the Social Re/Construction of Market Spaces in a Tourism Town." In *Economies and the Transformation of Landscape,* ed. Lisa Cliggett and Christopher A. Pool, 267–290. Lanham, MD: Altamira Press.

Little, Walter E., and Timothy J. Smith, eds. 2009. *Mayas in Postwar Guatemala: Harvest of Violence Revisited.* Tuscaloosa: University of Alabama Press.

Loperena, Christopher. 2010. "Whose Development? IDB Financing, Enclave Tourism, and Garifuna Land Loss in the Bahia de Tela." In *Inter-American Development Bank Megaprojects: Displacement and Forced Migration,* online report, Center for International Policy Americas Program, http://www.cipamericas.org/ (accessed January 2011).

López Bernal, Carlos G. 2007. "Lecturas desde la derecha y la izquierda sobre el levantamiento de 1932: Implicaciones político-culturales." In *Las masas, la matanza y el martinato en El Salvador,* ed. Erik Ching. San Salvador: UCA Editores.

López García, Julian. 2008. "'Here It's Different': The Ch'orti' and Human Rights Training." In *Human Rights in the Maya Region: Global Politics, Cultural Contentions, and Moral Engagements,* ed. Pedro Pitarch, Shannon Speed, and Xochitl Leyva Solano, 145–69. Durham: Duke University Press.

López García, Víctor Virgilio. 2006. *Tornabé ante el proyecto turístico.* Honduras: Impresos Rapido Ariel.

López Vigil, José Ignacio. 1991. *Las mil y una historia de Radio Venceremos.* San Salvador: Universidad Centroamericana José Simeón Cañas.

Lyon, Sarah. 2011. *Coffee and Community: Maya Farmers and Fair Trade Markets.* Boulder, CO: University Press of Colorado.

MacCannell, Dean. 1992. *Empty Meeting Grounds: The Tourist Papers.* New York: Routledge.

———. 1999 [1976]. *The Tourist: A New Theory of the Leisure Class.* Berkeley: University of California Press.

Macdonald, Kate. 2007. "Globalizing Justice Within Coffee Supply Chains? Fair Trade, Starbucks and the Transformation of Supply Chain Governance." *Third World Quarterly* 28, no. 4: 793–812.

Martín-Baró, Ignacio. 1991. "The Appeal of The Far Right." In *Towards a Society That Serves Its People: The Intellectual Contribution of El Salvador's Murdered Jesuits,* ed. John Hassett and Hugh Lacey. Washington, DC: Georgetown University Press.

Massey, Douglas S., and Nancy A. Denton. 1988. "The Dimensions of Residential Segregation." *Social Forces* 67: 281–315.

Massey, Douglas, ed. 2008. *New Faces in New Places: The Changing Geography of American Immigration.* New York: Russell Sage Foundation.

Materer, Susan M., and J. Edward Taylor. 2003. "CAFTA and Migration: Lessons from Micro Economy-wide Models and the New Economics of Labor Migration," paper presented at the American Agricultural Economics Association Annual Meeting, Montreal Canada, 27–30 July 2003.

Mbembe, Achille. 2003. "Necropolitics." *Public Culture* 15, no. 1: 11–40.

McCarthy, James, and Scott Prudham. 2004. "Neoliberal Nature and the Nature of Neoliberalism." *Geoforum* 35: 275–83.

McElhinney, Vincent J. 2004. "Between Clientalism and Radical Democracy: The Case of Segundo Montes." In *Landscapes of Struggle: Community, Politics, and the Nation-State in*

Twentieth-Century El Salvador, ed. Aldo Lauria-Santiago and Leigh Binford, 147–65. Pittsburgh, PA: University of Pittsburgh Press.
McLaren, Deborah. 2003. *Rethinking Tourism and Ecotravel,* 2nd ed. West Hartford, CT: Kumarian Press.
McMichael, Philip. 2008. "Peasants Make History, But Not as They Please ..." In *Transnational Agrarian Movements Confronting Globalization,* ed. Saturnino M. Borras Jr., Marc Edelman, and Cristobal Kay, 37–60. Chichester, UK: Wiley Blackwell.
Meisch, Lynn A. 2002. *Andean Entrepreneurs: Otavalo Merchants and Musicians in the Global Arena.* Austin: University of Texas Press.
Mendez, Jennifer Bickham. 2005. *From the Revolution to the Maquiladoras: Gender, Labor and Globalization in Nicaragua.* Durham, NC: Duke University Press.
Menjívar, Cecilia. 2000. *Fragmented Ties: Salvadoran Immigrant Networks in America.* Berkeley: University of California Press.
———. 2011. *Enduring Violence: Ladina Women's Lives in Guatemala.* Berkeley: University of California Press.
Merry, S. 2003. "Human Rights Law and the Demonization of Culture (and Anthropology along the Way)." *PoLAR: Political and Legal Anthropology Review* 26, no. 1: 55–76.
Metzi, Francisco. 1988. *The People's Remedy: The Struggle for Health Care in El Salvador's War of Liberation.* New York: Monthly Review.
Mohl, Raymond. 2003. "Globalization, Latinization, and the Nuevo New South." *Journal of American Ethnic History* 22, no. 4: 31–66.
Montoya, Ainhoa. 2011. "Neither War nor Peace: Violence and Democracy in Postwar El Salvador." PhD dissertation, University of Manchester.
Montoya, Aquiles. 1993. *La nueva economía popular: Una aproximación teórica.* San Salvador: Universidad Centroamericana.
Montoya, Rosario N.D. "Politics and Ethics Among Sandinista Campesinos Twenty Years after the Revolution." Unpublished manuscript.
———. 2012. *Gendered Scenarios of Revolution: Making New Men and New Women in Nicaragua, 1975–2000.* Tucson: University of Arizona Press.
Moodie, Ellen. 2010. *El Salvador in the Aftermath of Peace: Crime, Uncertainty, and the Transition to Democracy.* Philadelphia: University of Pennsylvania Press.
Moore, Henrietta. 1994. *A Passion for Difference: Essays in Anthropology and Gender.* Cambridge: Polity Press.
Mora Castellanos, Eduardo. 1993. *Claves del discurso ambientalista.* Heredia, Costa Rica: Edtorial UNA.
Morales, Benito. 2007. "El marco jurídico formal contra el racismo y la discriminación desde lo penal." In *Diagnóstico del racismo en Guatemala* 2. Guatemala: Vicepresidencia de la República de Guatemala.
Moran-Taylor Michelle J., and Matthew J. Taylor. 2010. "Land and Leña: Linking Transnational Migration, Natural Resources and the Environment in Guatemala." *Population & Environment* 32, no. 2–3: 198–215.
Moreno, Dario. 1994. *The Struggle for Peace in Central America.* Gainesville: University Press of Florida.
Mortensen, Lena. 2001. "Las dinámicas locales de un patrimonio global: Arqueturismo en Copán, Honduras." *Mesoamérica* 42: 104–134.
Mouffe, Chantal. 2005. *The Democratic Paradox.* New York: Verso.
Mowforth, Martin, and Munt, Ian. 2003. *Tourism and Sustainability: Development and New Tourism in the Third World,* 2nd ed. London: Routledge.
Muehlebach, Andrea. 2001. "'Making Place' at the United Nations: Indigenous Cultural Politics at the United Nations." *Cultural Anthropology* 16, no. 3: 415–448.

Murray, Douglas L., Laura T. Raynolds, and Peter L. Taylor. 2006. "The Future of Fair Trade Coffee: Dilemmas Facing Latin America's Small-Scale Producers." *Development in Practice* 16, no. 2: 179–192.

Myrna Mack Foundation. 2006. *La discriminación: De la inefable realidad a su punibilidad en Guatemala*. Guatemala.

Nash, June C. 1993. *Crafts in the World Market: The Impact of Global Exchange on Middle American Artisan,* ed. June Nash. Albany: SUNY Press.

———. 2001. *Mayan Visions: The Quest for Autonomy in an Age of Globalization*. New York: Routledge Press.

———. 2007. *Practicing Ethnography in a Globalizing World: An Anthropological Odyssey*. Lanham, MD: Altamira Press.

Nava, Gregory, dir. 1983. *El Norte,* prod. Anna Thomas. American Playhouse/Channel Four Films, VHS.

———. 1995. *My Family/Mi Familia*. New Line Home Cinema: Image Entertainment, DVD.

Nelson, Diane M. 1999. *A Finger in the Wound: Body Politics in Quincentennial Guatemala*. Berkeley: University of California Press.

———. 2009. *Reckoning: The Ends of War in Guatemala*. Durham: Duke University Press.

Nelson, Lise, and Peter Nelson. 2011. "The Global Rural: Gentrification and Linked Migration in the Rural USA." *Progress in Human Geography* 35, no. 4: 441–59.

Netting, Robert McC. 1993. *Smallholders, Householders: Farm Families and the Ecology of Intensive, Sustainable Agriculture*. Stanford, CA: Stanford University Press.

Nicholls, Alex, and Charlotte Opal. 2005. *Fair Trade: Market-Driven Ethical Consumption*. Thousand Oaks, CA: Sage Publications.

Niezen, Ronald. 2003. *The Origins of Indigenism: Human Rights and the Politics of Identity*. Berkeley: University of California Press.

Nordstrom, Carolyn. 2007. *Global Outlaws: Crime, Money, and Power in the Contemporary World*. Berkeley: University of California Press.

Nygren, Anja. 2000. "Environmental Narratives on Protection and Production: Nature based Conflicts in Rio San Juan, Nicaragua." *Development and Change* 31, no. 4: 807–30.

Offit, Thomas. 2008. *Conquistadores de la Calle: Child Street Labor in Guatemala City*. Austin: University of Texas Press.

O'Neill, Kevin Lewis. 2009. *City of God: Christian Citizenship in Postwar Guatemala*. Berkeley: University of California Press.

Ong, Aihwa. 1999. *Flexible Citizenship: The Cultural Logics of Transnationality*. Durham: Duke University Press.

———. 2006. *Neoliberalism as Exception: Mutations in Citizenship and Sovereignty*. Durham, NC: Duke University Press.

Ortner, Sherry. 1995. "Resistance and the Problem of Ethnographic Refusal." *Comparative Studies in Society and History* 37, no. 1: 173–93.

Paley, Julia. 2001. *Marketing Democracy: Power and Social Movements in Post-dictatorship Chile*. Durham, NC: Duke University Press.

———. 2008. Introduction to *Democracy: Anthropological Approaches,* Julia Paley, ed. Santa Fe, NM: School for Advanced Research Press.

Peckenham, Nancy, and Anne Street. 1985. *Honduras*. New York: Praeger.

Perera, Victor. 1993. "The Crosses of Todos Santos." In *Unfinished Conquest: The Guatemala Tragedy,* 135–53. Berkeley: University of California Press.

Pérez Brignoli, Héctor and Yolanda Baires. 2001. "Costa Rica en el año 2000: Una crisis política en ciernes." In *La democracia de Costa Rica ante el siglo XXI,* ed. Jorge Rovira Mas. San José: Editorial de la Universidad de Costa Rica.

Pérez, Francisco J. 2011. "Sin cambios estructurales no habrá una reducción sostenible de la pobreza rural." *Envio* 350.

Pérez, Leslie. 2007. "Casos no llegan a debate oral." *Prensa Libre,* 18 December.
Peterson, Brandt G. 2006. "Consuming Histories: The Return of the Indian in Neoliberal El Salvador." *Cultural Dynamics* 18: 163–88.
Pine, Adrienne. 2008. *Working Hard, Drinking Hard: On Violence and Survival in Honduras.* Berkeley: University of California Press.
———. 2010. "Honduras Commemorates Tense Anniversary of Unresolved Military Coup," online report, www.quotha.net (accessed 7 March 2010).
PNUD (Programa de las Naciones Unidas para el Desarrollo). 2005. *Informe sobre desarrollo humano El Salvador 2005: Una mirada al nuevo nosotros. El impacto de las migraciones.* San Salvador: PNUD.
———. 2006 *Indicadores municipales sobre desarrollo humano y objetivos del desarrollo del milenio: El Salvador 2005,* Informe 262. San Salvador: PNUD.
———. 2009 "Abrir espacios a la seguridad ciudadana y el desarollo humano: Informe sobre desarollo humano para América Central IDHAC, 2009-2010," online report, www.idhac-abrirespaciosalaseguridad.org.co (accessed 27 February 2010).
Poole, Deborah. 2004. "Between Threat and Guarantee: Justice and Community in the Margins of the Peruvian State." In *Anthropology in the Margins of the State,* ed. Veena Das and Deborah Poole. 35–65. Santa Fe, NM: School of American Research Press.
Portes, Alejandro, and Min Zhou. 1992. "Gaining the Upper Hand: Economic Mobility among Immigrant and Domestic Minorities." *Ethnic and Racial Studies* 15, no. 4: 491–522.
Posas, Mario. 1981a. *El movimiento campesino hondureño: Una perspectiva general.* Tegucigalpa: Guyamuras.
———. 1981b. *Conflictos agrarios y organización campesina: Sobre los origines de las primeras organizaciones campesinas en Honduras.* Tegucigalpa: Editorial Universitaria.
Power, Michael. 1997. *The Audit Society: Rituals of Verification.* Oxford: Oxford University Press.
Prado, Silvio. 2007. "Se va a poner a prueba de qué está hecha nuestra sociedad civil." *Envio* 298.
Prensa. 1972. "Primer Festival Garifuna Nacional, Punto Clave de Feria Isidra," 15 May.
Prensa Gráfica. 1999. "ARENA denuncia a alcalde viroleño," 3 March.
———. 2004. "Un muerto durante cierre de campaña," 19 March.
———. 2008a. "Defensa indaga existencia de grupos armados," 13 December.
———. 2008b. "Saca llevará a ONU pruebas sobre armas," 17 December.
Prensa Libre. 2003a. "Amenazan a más jueces," 18 February.
———. 2003b. "Amedrentados como el conflict armado," 20 February.
———. 2003c. "Pandillas asuelan en Todos Santos," 4 March.
———. 2007a. "Policía abandonó 9 subestaciones este año," 12 March.
———. 2007b. "Hacen justicia con sus manos: Huehuetenango Abundan Juntas Civiles de Seguridad," 3 December.
Preston, Julia, and Sarah Wheaton. 2011. "Meant to Ease Fears of Deportation Program, Federal Hearings Draw Anger." *New York Times,* 25 August: A13.
Rahnema, Mahjid. 1990. "Participation." In *The Development Dictionary: A Guide to Knowledge and Power,* ed. Wolfgang Sachs. London: Zed Books.
Ramos, Carlos Guillermo. 1998. "El Salvador: Transición y procesos electorales a fines de los noventa." *Nueva Sociedad* 158: 28–39.
———. 2000. "Marginación, exclusión social y violencia." In *Violencia en una sociedad en transición: Ensayos,* ed. Carlos Guillermo Ramos. San Salvador: PNUD.
Raventós Vorst, Ciska. 1995. "The Construction of an Order: Structural Adjustment in Costa Rica (1985–1995)." PhD dissertation, New School for Social Research.
———. 2008. "Lo que fue ya no es y lo nuevo aún no toma forma: Elecciones 2006 en perspectiva histórica." *América Latina Hoy.*

Raventós Vorst, Ciska, ed. 2007. *Survey of Patriotic Committees*. San José, Costa Rica: Unpublished database.
Raventós Vorst, Ciska, et al. 2005. *Abstencionistas en Costa Rica: ¿Quiénes son y por qué no votan?* San José, Costa Rica: Editorial de la Universidad de Costa Rica.
Raynolds, Laura T. 2004. "The Globalization of Organic Agro-Food Networks." *World Development* 32, no. 5: 725–43.
Raynolds, Laura T., and John Wilkinson. 2007. "Fair Trade in the Agriculture and Food Sector: Analytical Dimensions." In *Fair Trade: The Challenges of Transforming Globalization*, ed. Laura T. Raynolds, Douglas Murray, and John Wilkinson, 33–47. New York: Routledge.
Reardon, Thomas, and Julio A. Berdegue. 2002. "The Rapid Rise of Supermarkets in Latin America: Challenges and Opportunities for Development." *Development Policy Review* 20, no. 4: 371–388.
Red Européo de Diálogo Social. 2004. "El Salvador: En el horizonte de un nuevo día." In *El ruido de la milpa: Lucha y organización en Chiapas, El Salvador, Guatemala y Nicaragua*, 64–113. Barcelona: Red Européo de Diálogo Social.
Reich, Michael. 1971. "The Economics of Racism." In *Problems in Political Economy: An Urban Perspective*, ed. David M. Gordon. Lexington, MA: Heath and Company.
Reichman, Daniel. 2008. "Justice at a Price: Regulation and Alienation in the Global Economy." *PoLAR: Political and Legal Anthropology Review* 31, no. 1: 102–117.
———. 2011. *The Broken Village: Coffee, Migration, and Globalization in Honduras*. Ithaca: Cornell University Press.
Reina, Carlos Roberto. 1997. "¡Doscientios años después!" *El Heraldo*, 12 April.
REMHI. 1999. *Guatemala Never Again!* Maryknoll, NY: Orbis Books for the Recovery of Historical Memory Project.
Renard, Marie-Christine, and Victor Perez-Grovas. 2007. "Fair Trade Coffee in Mexico: At the Center of the Debates." In *Fair Trade: The Challenges of Transforming Globalization*, ed. Laura T. Raynolds, Douglas Murray, and John Wilkinson, 138–56. New York: Routledge.
Republic of Honduras. 2003. *Decree No. 152-2003*. Tegucigalpa.
República de Honduras. 1992. "Decreto Número 31-92," *La Gaceta: Diario Oficial de la República de Honduras* 26.713(008569): 1–10.
Rich, Adrienne. 1986. "Notes Toward a Politics of Location." In *Blood, Bread and Poetry: Selected Prose 1979–1985*, 210–31. New York: W.W. Norton.
Riles, Annelise. 2006. "Anthropology, Human Rights, and Legal Knowledge: Culture in the Iron Cage." *American Anthropologist* 108, no. 1, 52–65.
Rivera, Elaine. 2004. "Hardship Cited in Law for Va. License; Some Say Immigrants Are Vulnerable to Scams for Fake ID." *Washington Post*, 12 May: B1.
Rivers-Moore, Megan. 2007. "Untouchable Gringos and 20 or 30 Girls: The State, NGOs and the Costa Rican Sex Trade," paper presented at the Congress of the Latin American Studies Association, Montreal, Canada.
Robinson, William. 1995. *Polyarchy*. Cambridge: Cambridge University Press.
———. 2003. *Transnational Conflicts: Central America, Social Change, and Globalization*. London, England: Verso.
Rocha, José Luis. 2010. "A 31 años de la revolución: La contradictoria herencia de la reforma agraria sandinista." *Envio* 340.
Rodriguez, Ana Patricia. 2009. *Dividing the Isthmus: Central American Transnational Histories, Literatures, and Cultures*. Austin: University of Texas Press.
Rodríguez, Carlos. 1993. *Tierra de labriegos: Los campesinos en Costa Rica desde 1950*. San José, Costa Rica: FLACSO.
Rodríguez, Ileana. 1996. *Women, Guerrillas, and Love: Understanding War in Central America*. Minneapolis: University of Minnesota Press.

Rodriguez, Silvia. 1994. *Conservación, contradicción y erosion de soberanía: El estado costarricense y las areas naturales protegidas (1970–1992)*. PhD dissertation, University of Wisconsin Madison, Spanish translation.

Rodriguez, Silvio. 1980. *Cancion urgente para Nicaragua*. Havana: Estudios Ojalá.

Rohter, Larry. 1997. "Nicaragua on the Mend," *New York Times*, 16 February, sec. 5: 0.

Rolbein, Seth. 1989. *Nobel Costa Rica: A Timely Report on Our Peaceful Pro-Yankee, Central American Neighbor*. New York: St. Martin's Press.

Román, Isabel. 1993. "Estilos de negociación política de las organizaciones campesinas en Costa Rica durante la década de los ochenta." MA thesis, Universidad de Costa Rica.

Romero, Wilson. 2006. "Los costos de la discriminación en Guatemala." In *Diagnóstico del racismo en Guatemala*, Vol. 1, ed. Marta Casáus Arzú and Amílcar Dávila. Guatemala: Vicepresidencia de la República.

Ronchi, L. 2002. "The Impact of Fair Trade Producers and Their Organizations: A Case Study with Coocafe in Costa Rica," Working Paper No. 11, Poverty Research Unit at Sussex (PRUS). Brighton, UK: University of Sussex.

Rosa, Herman, Susan Kandel, and Nelson Cuéllar. 2005. *Dinámica migratoria, medios de vida rurales y manejo de recursos naturales en El Salvador*. San Salvador: PRISMA.

Roseberry, William. 1993. "Beyond the Agrarian Question in Latin America." In *Confronting Historical Paradigms: Peasants, Labor and the Capitalist World System in Africa and Latin America*, ed. Frederick Cooper et al., 316–368. Madison: University of Wisconsin Press.

Rosen, Fred. 2008. "The Basic Food Position: 2008." *NACLA Report on the Americas* 41, no. 4: 4.

Rovira Mas, Jorge. 2004. "El nuevo estilo nacional de desarrollo en Costa Rica entre 1984–2003 y el TLC." In *TLC con Estados Unidos: Contribuciones para el debate. ¿Debe Costa Rica aprobarlo?*, ed. María Florez-Estrada and Gerardo Hernández. San José: Instituto de Investigaciones Sociales, Universidad de Costa Rica.

Ruhl, J. Mark. 1984. "Agrarian Structure and Political Stability in Honduras." *Journal of Interamerican Studies and World Affairs* 26, no. 1: 33–68.

———. 1985. "The Honduran Agrarian Reform under Suazo Cordova, 1982–85: An Assessment." *Journal of Inter-American Economic Affairs*: 63–80.

Rus, Diane and Jan Rus. 2008. "La migración de trabajadores indígenas de Los Altos de Chiapas a Estados Unidos, 2001-2005: El caso de San Juan Chamula." In *Migraciones en el sur de México y Centroamérica*, ed. Daniel Villafuerte Solís and María del Carmen García Aguilar. Mexico: Miguel Angel Porrúa.

Rushdie, Salman. 1987. *The Jaguar Smile: A Nicaraguan Journey*. New York: Viking Press/Penguin Books.

Salazar de Robelo, Lucia. 2004. "A Conversation with Lucia Salazar de Robelo." In *Costa Rica and Nicaragua*, 4–7. New York: Linblad Expeditions.

Salazar, Roxana. 1993. *El derecho a un ambiente sano: Ecología y desarrollo sostenible*. San José, Costa Rica: Asociación Libro Libre.

Saldaña-Portillo, María Josefina. 2003. *The Revolutionary Imagination in the Americas and the Age of Development*. Durham: Duke University Press.

Sánchez Campbell, Gabriel. 2004. "Turismo lanza grito de guerra contra la basura." *La Prensa*, Managua: 9A.

Sanford, Victoria. 2004. *Buried Secrets: Truth and Human Rights in Guatemala*. New York: Palgrave Macmillan.

Santos de Morais, Clodomiro. 1975. "The Role of the Campesino Sector in the Honduran Agrarian Reform." *Land Tenure Newsletter* 47: 16–22.

Schirmer, Jennifer. 1998. *The Guatemalan Military Project: A Violence Called Democracy*. Philadelphia: University of Pennsylvania Press.

Secretaría de Turismo. 2007. *Boletín estadístico: La importancia del turismo en la economía nacional, 2000–2006.* Tegucigalpa: Instituto Hondureño de Turismo.

Secretariat of the United Nations Permanent Forum on Indigenous Issues. 2007. *Handbook for Participants.* New York: United Nations Printing Office.

Sick, Deborah.1997. "Coping with Crisis: Costa Rica Households and the International Coffee Market." *Ethnology* 36, no. 3: 255–75.

Sieder, Rachel. 2002. *Multiculturalism in Latin America: Indigenous Rights, Diversity and Democracy,* ed. Rachel Sieder. New York: Palgrave Macmillan.

———. 2011. "Contested Sovereignties: Indigenous Law, Violence and State Effects in Postwar Guatemala." *Critique of Anthropology* 3, no. 3: 161–84.

Sieder, Rachel, and Jessica Witchell. 2002. "Impulsando las demandas indígenas a través de la ley: Reflexiones sobre el proceso de paz en Guatemala." In *Los derechos humanos en tierras mayas,* ed. Pedro Pitarch and Julián López García. Madrid: Sociedad Española de Estudios Mayas.

Silber, Irina Carlota. 2010. *Everyday Revolutionaries: Gender, Violence, and Disillusionment in Postwar El Salvador.* Piscataway, NJ: Rutgers University Press.

Singer, Audrey. 2004. "The Rise of the New Immigrant Gateways." Washington, DC: The Brookings Institution, online report, www.brookings.edu/reports/2004/02demographics_singer.aspx (accessed 3 September 2011)

Smith, Carol A. 1984. "Local History in Global Contest: Social and Economic Transitions in Western Guatemala." *Comparative Studies in Society and History* 26, no. 3: 193–228.

———. 1990. *Guatemalan Indians and the State: 1540 to 1988.* Austin: University of Texas Press.

Smith, Christian. 1996. *Resisting Reagan: The U.S. Central America Peace Movement.* Chicago: University of Chicago Press.

Smith, Heather A., and Owen J. Furuseth, eds. 2006. *Latinos in the New South: Transformations of Place.* Aldershot, UK: Ashgate Publishers.

Smith, Timothy, and Abigail Adams. 2011. *After the Coup: An Ethnographic Reframing of Guatemala 1954.* Urbana: University of Illinois Press.

Smith-Nonini, Sandy. 2010. *Healing the Body Politic: El Salvador's Popular Struggle for Health Rights from Civil War to Neoliberal Peace.* Piscataway, NJ: Rutgers University Press.

Sojo, Carlos.1991. *La utopia del estado mínimo: Influencia de AID en Costa Rica en los años ochenta.* Managua: CRIES.

Solares, Jorge, and Gilberto Morales. 2003. "Yo no soy racista, pero … : Relaciones interétnicas y racismo fragmentario en Guatemala." In *Discriminación y racismo.* Guatemala: COPREDEH.

Solís Avendaño, Manuel. 2006. *La institucionalidad ajena: Los años cuarenta y el fin de siglo.* San José, Costa Rica: Editorial UCR.

Stack, Trevor. 2003. "Citizens of Towns, Citizens of Nations: The Knowing of History in Mexico." *Critique of Anthropology* 23, no. 2: 193–208.

Stamatopoulou, Elsa. 1994. "Indigenous Peoples and the United Nations: Human Rights as a Development Dynamic." *Human Rights Quarterly* 16, no. 1: 58–81.

Stanley, William D. 1996. *The Protection Racket State: Elite Politics, Military Extortion, and Civil War in El Salvador.* Philadelphia: Temple University Press.

Staudt, Kathleen, and David Spener. 1998. "A View from the Frontier: Theoretical Perspectives Undisciplined." In *The U.S.–Mexico Border: Transcending Divisions, Contesting Identities,* 3–34. Boulder, CO: Lynne Rienner.

Stavenhagen, Rodolfo. 2004. "Indigenous Peoples in Comparative Perspective: Problems and Policies," Occasional Paper/Background Paper for HDR 2004. New York: Human Development Report Office of the United Nations Development Programme.

Stoll, David. 1999. *Rigoberta Menchú and the Story of All Poor Guatemalans.* Boulder, CO: Westview Press.

———. 2010. "From Wage Migration to Debt Migration? Easy Credit, Failure in El Norte, and Foreclosure in a Bubble Economy of the Western Guatemalan Highlands." *Latin American Perspectives* 37, no. 1: 123–42.

Stone, Oliver, dir. 2001 [1986]. *Salvador*, prod. Gerald Green and Oliver Stone. Hemdale Film Coorporation. Santa Monica, CA: MGM Home Entertainment, DVD.

Stonich, Susan. 1993. *I Am Destroying the Land: The Political Ecology of Poverty and Environmental Destruction in Honduras*. Boulder, CO: Westview Press.

———. 2000. *The Other Side of Paradise: Tourism, Conservation and Development in the Bay Islands*. New York: Cognizant Communication Corporation.

Strathern, Marilyn. 2000. "Introduction: New Accountabilities." In *Audit Cultures: Anthropological Studies in Accountability, Ethics, and the Academy*, ed. Marilyn Strathern. London: Routledge.

Talbot, John M. 1997. "Where Does Your Coffee Dollar Go?" *Studies in Comparative International Development* 32, no. 1: 56–91.

———. 2004. *Grounds for Agreement*. Lanham, MD: Rowman & Littlefield.

Taylor, Matthew, Michelle Moran-Taylor, and Debra R. Ruiz. 2006. "Land, Ethnic, and Gender Change: Transnational Migration and Its Effects on Guatemalan Lives and Landscapes." *Geoforum* 37, no. 1, pp. 41–61.

Taylor, Peter L. 2004. "In the Market but Not of It: Fair Trade Coffee and Forest Stewardship: Council Certification as Market-Based Social Change." *World Development* 33, no. 1: 129–47.

The Clash. 1980. *Sandinista!* Epic Records, compact disc.

Thomas, Kedron, Kevin O'Neill, and Thomas Offit. 2011. *Securing the City: Neoliberalism, Space, and Insecurity in Postwar Guatemala*. Durham: Duke University Press.

Thorne, Eva. 2004. "Land Rights and Garífuna Identity." *NACLA Report on the Americas* 38, no. 21–5.

Tiempo. 1979. "Folklore Garifuna en el Encantador Paisaje del Caribe." *Suplemento Turístico*, 15 July.

———. 1996. "Festival Caribe de Danzas Folklóricas Garifunas," 23 May.

———. 2010. "Le Piden a Ministra de Turismo que Saque a Tela del Abandono" (12 August), online document, http://www.tiempo.hn/ (accessed October 2010).

Todd, Molly. 2011. *Beyond Displacement: Campesinos, Refugees, and Collective Action in the Salvadoran Civil War*. Madison: University of Wisconsin Press.

Torres-Rivas, Edelberto, ed. 1981. "Ocho claves para entender la crisis centroamericana." In *Centroamérica: Entre revoluciones y democracia*. Bogotá: Siglo del Hombre Editores.

———. 1993. *History and Society in Central America*, trans. Douglass Sullivan-González. Austin: University of Texas Press.

———. 2005. *La nación multicultural y el racismo*. Guatemala: Cuadernos del Programa de las Naciones Unidas para el Desarrollo.

Trejos, María Eugenia. 1990. "Nuevas fórmulas de consenso social: El ajuste estructural en Costa Rica." In *Mitos y realidades de la democracia en Costa Rica*, ed. Yadira Calvo et al. San José, Costa Rica: DEI.

Trouillot, Michel-Rolph. 1991. "Anthropology and the Savage Slot: The Poetics and Politics of Otherness." In *Recapturing Anthropology: Working in the Present*, ed. Richard G. Fox. Santa Fe, NM: School of American Research Press.

———. 2001. "The Anthropology of the State in the Age of Globalization: Close Encounters of the Deceptive Kind." *Current Anthropology* 42, no. 1: 125–38.

TSE. 2009. *Elecciones 2009: Resultados electorales*, online report, http://www.tse.gob.sv/page.php?51 (accessed 8 May 2010).

Tucker, Catherine M. 2008. *Changing Forests: Collective Action, Common Property, and Coffee in Honduras*. Berlin: Springer.

Tucker, Catherine M., Hallie Eakin, and Edwin Castellanos. 2010. "Perceptions of Risk and Adaptation: Coffee Producers, Market Shocks, and Extreme Weather in Central America and Mexico." *Global Environmental Change* 20: 23–32.

Tutela Legal. 2008. *El Mozote: Lucha por la verdad y la justicia: Masacre de la inocencia*. San Salvador: Tutela Legal del Arzobispado.

UNDP (United Nations Development Programme). 2001. *Report on Human Development in El Salvador 2001,* online report, http://www.desarrollohumano.org.sv (accessed 1 October 2001).

———. 2003. *Informe sobre desarrollo humano, Honduras 2003*. San José, Costa Rica: Editorama, SA.

———. 2004. *Democracy in Latin America: Towards a Citizens' Democracy*. New York: UNDP.

United Nations. 1992. *Peace Agreement,* online document, https://peaceaccords.nd.edu/site_media/media/accords/Chapultepec_Peace_Agreement_16_January_1992.pdf (accessed 8 January 2011).

———. 1993. *Informe de la Comisión de la Verdad para El Salvador: De la locura a la esperanza: La guerra de 12 años en El Salvador*. San Salvador: Arcoiris.

US Census Bureau. 2007. "Annual Estimates of the Population for Counties of Virginia: April 1, 2000 to July 1, 2007," online report, http://www.census.gov/popest/counties/CO-EST2007-01.html (accessed 5 January 2009).

US Census Bureau. 2011. "Virginia—County Race and Hispanic or Latino," Census 2010 Summary File, online report, http://factfinder.census.gov/ (accessed 1 September 2011).

Van Cott, Donna Lee. 1994. *Indigenous Peoples and Democracy in Latin America*. New York: St. Martin's Press in association with the Inter-American Dialogue.

Vanden, Harry and Gary Prevost. 1993. *Democracy and Socialism in Sandinista Nicaragua*. Boulder, CO: Lynne Rienner.

Varangis, Panos, Paul Siegel, Daniele Giovannucci, and Bryan Lewin. 2003. *Dealing with the Coffee Crisis in Central America,* Policy Research Working Paper 2993. Washington, DC: World Bank.

Vargas Cullell, Jorge, Luis Rosero-Bixby, and Mitchell Seligson. 2006. *La cultura política de la democracia en Costa Rica: 2006*. San José, Costa Rica: Centro Centroamericano de Población.

Varsanyi, Monica W., ed. 2010. *Taking Local Control: Immigration Policy and Activism in U.S. Cities and States*. Stanford, CA: Stanford University Press.

Vaughan, Steve. 2010. "Area is Graying Faster than Nation." *Virginia Gazette,* 13 January.

Velásquez Nimatuj, Irma Alicia. 2007. *La pequeña burguesía indígena comercial de Guatemala*. Guatemala: AVANCSO.

———. 2010/11. "Flight 795: A Tale of Structural Racism." *ReVista: Harvard Review of Latin America,* online document, http://www.drclas.harvard.edu/publications/revistaonline/fall-2010-winter-2011/flight-795 (accessed 27 August 2011).

Verdugo de Lima, Lucía, Nicolás Pacheco, Ruth Piedrasanta, and Francisco Tavico. 2007. "Análisis crítico del discurso periodístico racista." In Di*agnóstico del racismo,* V. Guatemala: Vicepresidencia de la República.

Viceministereo de la Micro, Pequeña y Mediana Empresa; Coordinación de Comerzialización y Artesanías; Ministerio de Economía. 2007. "Feria MIPYME, Mazatenango, del 3 al 5 de mayo de 2007," online document, www.mineco.gob.gt/mineco/mipyme/feriamipyme/2007/FeriaMazatenango2007.pdf (accessed 25 August 2008).

Vicepresidencia de la República. 2007. "Informe General y costos de la discriminación." In *Diagnóstico del Racismo en Guatemala* 1, ed. Marta Casáus Arzú and Amílcar Dávila. Guatemala: Vicepresidencia de la República.

Vigil Vásquez, Antonio ["Quique"] N.D. Untitled. Unpublished manuscript.

Vivanco, Luis. 2006. *Green Encounters: Shaping and Contesting Environmentalism in Rural Costa Rica.* New York: Berghahn Books.

———. 2007. "The Prospects and Dilemmas of Certifying Indigenous Tourism." In *Quality Control and Ecotourism Certification,* ed. R. Black and A. Crabtree, 218–40. Wallingford, UK: CAB International.

Wacquant, Loic. 2009. *Punishing the Poor: The Neoliberal Government of Social Insecurity.* Durham: Duke University Press.

Walmart. 2011. "Guatemala Fact Sheet," online report, www.walmartstores.com (accessed 14 June 2011).

Wapner, Paul.1996. *Environmental Activism and World Civic Politics.* Albany: SUNY Press.

Warren, Kay B. 1998. *Indigenous Movements and Their Critics: Pan-Mayan Activism in Guatemala.* Princeton, NJ: Princeton University Press.

———. 2002. "Voting against Indigenous Rights in Guatemala: Lessons from the 1999 Referendum." In *Indigenous Movements, Self-Representation, and the State in Latin America,* ed. Kay Warren and Jean Jackson. Austin: University of Texas Press.

Watanabe, John M. and Edward F. Fischer, eds. 2004. *Pluralizing Ethnography: Comparison and Representation in Maya Cultures, Histories, and Identities.* Santa Fe: School for Advanced Research Press.

Wessman, James. 1981. *Anthropology and Marxism.* Cambridge, Mass.: Schenkman.

Wilkinson, John. 2006. "Fair Trade Moves Centre Stage." Rio de Janeiro: The Edelstein Center for Social Research.

Wilkinson, John, and Gilberto Mascarenhas. 2007. "Southern Social Movements and Fair Trade." In *Fair Trade: The Challenges of Transforming Globalization,* ed. Laura T. Raynolds, Douglas Murray, and John Wilkinson, 125–137. New York: Routledge.

Williams, Raymond.1976. *Keywords: A Vocabulary of Culture and Society.* New York: Oxford University Press.

Williams, Robert Gregory. 1986. *Export Agriculture and the Crisis in Central America.* Chapel Hill: University of North Carolina Press.

———. 1994. *States and Social Evolution: Coffee and the Rise of National Governments in Central America.* Chapel Hill: University of North Carolina Press.

Wilson, Richard. 2001. *The Politics of Truth and Reconciliation in South Africa: Legitimizing the Post-Apartheid State.* Cambridge: Cambridge University Press.

WOLA (Washington Office on Latin America). 2006. "Youth Gangs in Central America: Issues in Human Rights, Effective Policing, and Prevention," online report, http://www.wola.org/publications/youth_gangs_in_central_america (accessed 2 October 2011).

Wolf, Eric R. 1983. *Europe and the People without History.* Berkeley: University of California Press.

———. 1999 [1969]. *Peasant Wars of the Twentieth Century.* Norman: University of Oklahoma Press.

Wolf, Sonja. 2009. "Subverting Democracy: Elite Rule and the Limits to Political Participation in Post-War El Salvador." *Journal of Latin American Studies* 41: 429–65.

Wolseth, Jon. 2011. *Jesus and the Gang: Youth Violence and Christianity in Urban Honduras.* Tucson: University of Arizona Press.

Wood, Elisabeth Jean. 1996. "The Peace Accords and Reconstruction." In *Economic Policy for Building Peace: The Lessons of El Salvador,* ed. James K. Boyce, 73–105. Boulder, CO: Lynne Rienner.

———. 2000. *Forging Democracy from Below: Insurgent Transitions in South Africa and El Salvador.* Cambridge: Cambridge University Press.

Woodward, Kathleen. 2004. "Calculating Compassion." In *Compassion: The Culture and Politics of an Emotion,* ed. Lauren Berlant, 59–86. New York: Routledge.

World Bank. 2009. "Indigenous Peoples Policy," online report, http://go.worldbank.org/F8M G5M86V0 (accessed 2 October 2011).

———. 2011. "Crime and Violence in Central America: A Development Challenge," Sustainable Development Department and Poverty Reduction and Economic Management Unit Latin America and the Caribbean Region, online report, http://siteresources.worldbank .org/INTLAC/Resources/FINAL_VOLUME_I_ENGLISH_CrimeAndViolence.pdf (accessed 30 September 2011).

Xanthaki, A. 2007. *Indigenous Rights and United Nations Standards: Self-Determination, Culture and Land.* Cambridge: Cambridge University Press.

Yagenova, Simona Violetta, ed. 2005. *Guatemala: Una aproximación a los movimientos y las luchas sociales del año 2005: Observando de movimientos, demandas, y acción colectiva.* Guatemala: FLACSO, Editorial de Ciencias Sociales.

Yashar, Deborah J. 2005. *Contesting Citizenship in Latin America: The Rise of Indigenous Movements and the Postliberal Challenge.* Cambridge: Cambridge University Press.

Yudice, George. 2003. *The Expediency of Culture: Uses of Culture in the Global Era.* Durham: Duke University Press.

Zambrana, Emilio. 2004. "Arranca convención de turísmo." *La Prensa,* 11 August: 7B.

Zilberg, Elana. 2011. *Space of Detention: The Making of a Transnational Gang Crisis between Los Angeles and San Salvador.* Durham, NC: Duke University Press.

Zorn, Elayne. 2004. *Weaving a Future: Tourism, Cloth, and Culture on an Andean Island.* Iowa City: University of Iowa Press.

Zúniga, Joaquin, dir. 2006. *Turismo Rural Comunitario.* Managua: Fundación Luciérnaga, DVD.

Zurita, Félix, dir. 2005. *Turismos.* Managua: Fundación Luciérnaga, DVD.

Contributors

Mark Anderson is Associate Professor of Anthropology at the University of California, Santa Cruz. He is the author of *Black and Indigenous: Garifuna Activism and Consumer Culture in Honduras* (University of Minnesota Press, 2009). His research interests include the African diaspora in the Americas, indigenous and Afrodescendant social movements, tourism, and the history of anthropological thought on race and racism.

Florence E. Babb is the Vada Allen Yeomans Professor of Women's Studies in the Center for Women's Studies and Gender Research at the University of Florida. Her work includes *Between Field and Cooking Pot: The Political Economy of Marketwomen in Peru* (University of Texas Press, 1989, revised edition 1998); *After Revolution: Mapping Gender and Cultural Politics in Neoliberal Nicaragua* (University of Texas Press, 2001), and *The Tourism Encounter: Fashioning Latin American Nations and Histories* (Stanford University Press, 2011), which focuses on the cultural politics of tourism in postconflict and postrevolutionary areas. She is now reexamining gender and indigenous identity in the Andean region.

Since September 2010, **Leigh Binford** has been Chair of the Department of Sociology, Anthropology and Social Work of the College of Staten Island, City University of New York. He is also an affiliate of the CUNY Graduate Center's Department of Anthropology. Previously he worked at the University of Connecticut (1985–1997) and the Social Science and Humanities Research Institute of the Autonomous University of Puebla in Puebla, Mexico (1997–2010).

Jefferson C. Boyer is Professor of Anthropology and founder of the Sustainable Development Program at Appalachian State University, Boone, North Carolina. He writes on Central American and Appalachian agrarian movements, rural development, and sustainability issues. Boyer is currently working on a book titled "Once Upon an Agrarian Nation: Modernity and

Globalization Struggles in Postwar Honduras." He was one of the founders of Witness for Peace in 1983.

Jennifer L. Burrell is a cultural anthropologist who teaches at the University at Albany, SUNY. Her book *Maya After War: Conflict, Power and Politics in Guatemala* (University of Texas Press, 2013) details Mam Maya experiences of the post-conflict transition in Guatemala. More recently she has researched transnational migration and issues of security, generation, rights and health care access in Guatemala, Mexico, and the United States. Burrell worked with and continues to consult with the Argentine Forensic Anthropology Team.

Wilfredo Cardona Peñalva is a Honduran agricultural economist with an MS from the Colegio Postgraduados Montecillos, Mexico, who has also studied rural development and education at the Montpellier Agronomic Institute in France. He was the head of research for rural sustainable development in the Honduran Ministry of Agriculture and Cattle Ranching in the early period (2006–2007) of President Manuel Zelaya's government. He is co-founder of the Foundation for Lenca Sustainable Development (FUNDESOL) and is a national leader within Honduras's farmer-to-farmer educational network for sustainable agriculture.

Claudia Dary Fuentes received her MS from the University of Pittsburgh and her PhD in cultural anthropology from the University at Albany, SUNY. She is a researcher in the Institute of Interethnic Studies at the University of San Carlos of Guatemala and the Latin American Faculty of Social Sciences (FLACSO). Her works include *Unidos por nuestro territorio: Identidad y organización social in Santa María Xalapán* (Editorial Universitaria, 2011) and the edited volume *La construcción de la nación y la representación ciudadana en México, Guatemala, Perú, Ecuador y Bolivia* (FLACSO, 1998). Her research interests include labor, gender and indigenous intellectuals, and Maya bureaucracy and the state.

Walter E. Little is Associate Professor in the Department of Anthropology at the University at Albany, SUNY, and Director of the Institute for Mesoamerican Studies. His works include *Mayas in the Marketplace: Tourism, Globalization, and Cultural Identity* (University of Texas Press, 2004), *La ütz awäch? Introduction to the Kaqchikel Maya Language* (University of Texas Press, 2006), and the edited volumes *Mayas in Postwar Guatemala: Harvest of Violence Revisited* (University of Alabama Press, 2009) and *Textile Economies: Power and Value from the Local to the Transnational* (AltaMira, 2011). He currently researches urban street economies and the politics of urban public space in Antigua, Guatemala.

Sarah Lyon is Associate Professor of Anthropology at the University of Kentucky. She is the author of *Coffee and Community: Maya Farmers and Fair Trade Markets* (University Press of Colorado, 2011) and the co-editor of *Fair Trade and Social Justice: Global Ethnographies* (New York University Press, 2010). She has conducted research on globalization, fair trade, and tourism in Guatemala, Mexico, and the United States.

Jennifer Bickham Mendez is Associate Professor of Sociology and Director of Latin American Studies at The College of William and Mary. Her areas of interest include Latino/a migration, gender and globalization, and social movements. Her published work has appeared in academic journals such as *Social Problems, Mobilization, Gender and Society,* and the *Journal of Labor Studies.* She is the author of *From the Revolution to the Maquiladoras: Gender and Labor in Nicaragua* (Duke University Press, 2005). She is currently working on a book tentatively titled "Newcomers in the Cradle of a Nation: Latino/a Immigration to Williamsburg, VA."

Ainhoa Montoya is a social anthropologist with a PhD from the University of Manchester and an MPhil from the University of Cambridge. She has conducted fieldwork in El Salvador examining the relationship between violence and democracy, with a focus on wartime legacies and neoliberalism. Her research interests include the anthropology of violence, democratization studies, the ethnography of the state, political economy, memory studies, and human rights.

Rosario Montoya is an anthropologist and historian who has worked in Nicaragua since 1989. She has published on gender relations and sexuality; gender, political subjectivity, and revolution; and state formation in Nicaragua. Her book, *Gendered Scenarios of Revolution: Making New Men and New Women in Nicaragua, 1975–2000* (University of Arizona Press, 2012) is a historical ethnography of Sandinista state formation from the perspective of a "model" Sandinista community. Montoya received her PhD at the Interdepartmental Program in Anthropology and History at the University of Michigan and is a faculty affiliate at the University of Colorado at Boulder.

Ellen Moodie is Associate Professor in the Department of Anthropology at the University of Illinois. Her research has centered on the transformations of public meanings during political transitions in Central America. In her book *El Salvador in the Aftermath of Peace: Crime, Uncertainty and the Transition to Democracy* (University of Pennsylvania Press, 2010), she explores quotidian experiences of violence and insecurity in a site once saturated by war.

Baron Pineda is a cultural anthropologist specializing in human rights, indigenous peoples and Central America. He is the author of *Shipwrecked Identities: Navigating Race on Nicaragua's Mosquito Coast* (Rutgers University Press, 2006) as well as articles in scholarly journals. He has a bachelor's degree in rhetoric and anthropology from the University of California, Berkeley, and an MA and PhD from the University of Chicago. Since 2002 he has been conducting research on global indigenous politics at the United Nations Permanent Forum on Indigenous Issues. He is currently Associate Professor and Chair of the Department of Anthropology at Oberlin College.

Ciska Raventós is a political sociologist at the Instituto de Investigaciones Sociales and the Sociology Department at the Universidad de Costa Rica. She received her MA in sociology from the University of Costa Rica and her PhD from the New School for Social Research. She has focused on the study of Costa Rican politics, in the form of institutional processes through the analysis of legislative dynamics, as well as elections. More recently, she has turned to the study of protests and contentious collective action in relation to the opposition movement to CAFTA-DR in Costa Rica.

Catherine Tucker is an Associate Professor of Anthropology at Indiana University, Bloomington. Her work integrates perspectives from ecological and economic anthropology with transdisciplinary approaches to explore marginalized populations' experiences and adaptations in contexts of environmental, social, and political economic change. She has been conducting longitudinal research in western Honduras since 1993 and has also worked in Guatemala, Mexico, Costa Rica, and Peru. Her books include *Changing Forests: Common Property, Collective Action and Coffee in Honduras* (Springer Academic Press, 2008), and *Coffee Culture: Local Experiences, Global Connections* (Routledge, 2010).

Luis A. Vivanco is Associate Professor of Anthropology and Director of the Global and Regional Studies Program at the University of Vermont. His scholarship and teaching have focused on the culture and politics of environmentalism in Costa Rica and Oaxaca, Mexico. His books include *Green Encounters: Shaping and Contesting Environmentalism in Rural Costa Rica* (Berghahn, 2006), and (as co-editor with Rob Gordon) *Tarzan was an Ecotourist … And Other Tales in the Anthropology of Adventure* (Berghahn, 2006). He has a strong interest in environmental media and nature films and is undertaking a new project on the culture of urban bicycle mobility.

Index

CPSIA information can be obtained at www.ICGtesting.com
Printed in the USA
LVOW04*2244061014

407568LV00009B/97/P